Wenceslao J. Gonzalez (Ed.)
Philosophy of Psychology: Causality and Psychological Subject

Epistemic Studies

Philosophy of Science, Cognition and Mind

Edited by
Michael Esfeld, Stephan Hartmann, Albert Newen

Volume 38

Philosophy of Psychology: Causality and Psychological Subject

New Reflections on James Woodward's Contribution

Edited by Wenceslao J. Gonzalez

DE GRUYTER

ISBN 978-3-11-057408-1
e-ISBN (PDF) 978-3-11-057605-4
e-ISBN (EPUB) 978-3-11-057398-5
ISSN 2512-5168

Library of Congress Control Number: 2018942830

Bibliographic information published by the Deutsche Nationalbibliothek
The Deutsche Nationalbibliothek lists this publication in the Deutsche Nationalbibliografie;
detailed bibliographic data are available on the Internet at http://dnb.dnb.de.

© 2020 Walter de Gruyter GmbH, Berlin/Boston
This volume is text- and page-identical with the hardback published in 2018.
Printing and binding: CPI books GmbH, Leck

www.degruyter.com

Table of Contents

Wenceslao J. Gonzalez
New Contributions to Psychology as a Special Science: Causality and Psychological Subject —— 1

Part I: Causal Reasoning in the Context of Normative and Descriptive Psychology

Wenceslao J. Gonzalez
Configuration of Causality and Philosophy of Psychology: An Analysis of Causality as Intervention and Its Repercussion for Psychology —— 21

James Woodward
Normative Theory and Descriptive Psychology in Understanding Causal Reasoning: The Role of Interventions and Invariance —— 71

Part II: Causal Cognition and Psychological Explanations: Structural and Dynamic Aspects

James Woodward
Causal Cognition: Physical Connections, Proportionality, and the Role of Normative Theory —— 105

José María Martínez Selva
Psychobiological Explanations in Decision-making and Neuroeconomics —— 139

Michał Wierzchoń
Dynamic Level Interaction Hypothesis – A New Perspective on Consciousness —— 159

Part III: Scientific Status of Psychology and the Psychological Subject

Manuel Antonio García Sedeño
Naturalization of Psychology and Its Future as a Science —— 181

Francisco Rodriguez Valls
The Emotional Subject in Philosophy of Psychology: The Cases of Anxiety and Angst —— 203

Part IV: From Psychology to Psychiatry: Limits of Computational Psychology and the Role of Causes as Interventions in Psychiatry

Pedro Chacón
The Limits of Computational Psychology in J. Fodor —— 221

Raffaella Campaner
The Interventionist Theory and Mental Disorders —— 243

Index of Names —— 269

Subject Index —— 277

List of Abbreviations

ACC	anterior cingulate cortex
AD	Alzheimer's disease
ADHD	attention deficit hyperactivity disorder
AI	Artificial Intelligence
ALDH	aldehyde dehydrogenase
CAT	computerized axial tomography
CRTM	computational and representational theory of mind
CTM	computational theory of mind
DLPFC	dorsolateral prefrontal cortex
DN	deductive-nomological (model)
EEG	electroencephalography
fMRI	functional magnetic resonance imaging
FSIT	functional states identity theory
IGT	Iowa gambling task
IS	inductive-statistical (model)
OCD	obsessive compulsive disorder
OFC	orbitofrontal cortex
PET	positron emission tomography
RCT	randomized controlled trials
RTM	representational theory of mind
TMS	transcranial magnetic stimulation
TNGS	theory of neuronal group selection
VMPFC	ventromedial prefrontal cortex

Wenceslao J. Gonzalez
New Contributions to Psychology as a Special Science: Causality and Psychological Subject

1 A Philosophico-methodological Approach to Psychology Focused on Two Central Issues

Contemporary philosophy of science analyzes psychology as a science with special features, because this discipline includes some specific philosophical problems – descriptive and normative, structural and dynamic – of importance. Some of these are particularly relevant both theoretically (causal explanation) and practically (the configuration of the psychological subject and its relations with psychiatry). Thus, the philosophical analysis developed in this volume seeks to shed new light on philosophy of psychology taking into account descriptive traits and revisionary aspects, which include structural and dynamic features.[1]

Two central aspects in this book are the role of causality, especially conceived as intervention or manipulation, and the characterization of the psychological subject. This requires a clarification of scientific explanations in terms of causality in psychology, because the characterizations of causality are quite different in epistemological and ontological terms. One of the most influential views is James Woodward's approach to causality as intervention, which entails an analysis of its characteristics, new elements and limits. This means taking into account the structural and dynamic aspects included in causal cognition and psychological explanations.

Psychology seen as special science also requires us to consider the scientific status of psychology and the psychological subject,[2] which leads to limits of naturalism in psychology. This is particularly relevant when we move from psychology to psychiatry. Thus, a broad approach to psychology means analyzing other influential views on psychology, such as Jerry Fodor's, which leads to the anal-

---

[1] This book offers a complementary approach to books such as Thagard (2007) or Roessler, Eilen, and Lerman (2011), due to its philosophico-methodological analysis of causality and the psychological subject within the framework of psychology as a special science.
[2] Regarding the characterization of the psychological subject, one relevant aspect is the distinction between human intelligence and Artificial Intelligence. See Gonzalez (2017).

ysis of the limits of computational psychology. In addition, the characterization of the psychological subject has repercussions when dealing with mental disorder, which is also considered in this volume.

Because the approach here is philosophico-methodological, the main themes and objectives are of interest to psychologists and philosophers. Therefore, the book takes into account both scientific areas in terms of interrelation. In this regard, the vision is twofold: (i) psychologists can deal with how subjects learn and reason about causal relationships, and (ii) philosophers can contribute to how people ought to develop reasoning and evaluation about causal relationships (Woodward 2012, p. 961).

Hence, the book considers the descriptive side of the characteristics of psychology as a special science (mainly, the epistemological, methodological, and ontological components) as well as the normative role of philosophy, which is applied in how the psychological explanations – especially causal explanations – and the psychological subject should be characterized. In addition, the volume has an innovative approach, in that it takes into account the viewpoint of causality as intervention and the characterization of the psychological subject from various angles (cognitive, emotional, and computational).

When the philosophical analysis in this book seeks to shed new lights on those key topics, considering descriptive traits and revisionary aspects, Woodward's conception receives more attention than other approaches. But the present volume offers a broader focus than the influential views of the former president of the American Philosophy of Science Association. Consequently, there are also other viewpoints, both on causality and on the role of the subject in psychology as special science. In addition, some of the analyses of Woodward's points are rather critical.

This broader focus of the book can be seen in the structure of the volume, which starts with the consideration of his views and continues with other perspectives. It is structured in four parts: I) Causal Reasoning in the Context of Normative and Descriptive Psychology; II) Causal Cognition and Psychological Explanations: Structural and Dynamic Aspects; III) Scientific Status of Psychology and the Psychological Subject; and IV) From Psychology to Psychiatry: Limits of Computational Psychology and the Role of Causes as Interventions in Psychiatry. It comprises nine chapters, conceived from different angles. They include two original contributions by Woodward, where he gives new important details concerning his characterization of some of these topics.

2 Causal Reasoning in the Context of Normative and Descriptive Psychology

Regarding causation, Woodward is a central figure in the contemporary analysis, due to his original interventionist approach to causation and causal relationships. In addition, he has his own line of research on philosophy of psychology as special science, which is in his perspective dual. On the one hand, it includes a "descriptive" constituent on what there is, based on *empirical grounds* (observations and experiments); and, on the other, it highlights the "normative" component of *theoretical reflections*, which is a component focused on getting what ought to be thought.

Through two chapters, part I of this book presents the central features of Woodward's viewpoint on causal explanation and philosophy of psychology. His elements of naturalism are remarkable, especially in epistemological and methodological considerations. The diversity of these naturalist features in his conception – and the presence of pragmatist elements – are made explicit in chapter 1: "Configuration of Causality and Philosophy of Psychology: An Analysis of Causality as Intervention and its Repercussion for Psychology," by Wenceslao J. Gonzalez. He also points out that in Woodward's approach they are accompanied by a modest realism, as ontological support.

Gonzalez addresses in this initial paper the clear preference in Woodward for causal explanations as well as his interest in psychological cases, inasmuch as they can be connected to philosophical issues, such as causation. He usually defends a neat naturalism (semantic, logical, epistemological, methodological, ontological, axiological, and ethical), but his vision of causal explanations emphasizes hypothetical explanations and ideal interventions. This involves, *de facto*, a sort of methodological anti-naturalism as a factor related to his revisionary program (Gonzalez 2018). Woodward's motley naturalism, embedded with components of pragmatism, tries to combine the descriptive option and the *revisionary* alternative. Undoubtedly, scientific explanations go beyond mere description,[3] but Woodward also looks for a revisionary attitude, which he envisages in the sphere of "normative" grounds (the realm of *ought to be*).

Among the types of scientific explanation that have been more influential so far (deductive-nomological, inductive-probabilistic, functional or teleological,

---

[3] On the characteristics of scientific explanation and its types, see Gonzalez (2002). See also Gonzalez (2015, pp. vi, 15, 31–36, 47–55, 60–62, 68, 77, 84, 87, 96, 104–118, 128n, 130–139, 151–152, 158–162, 167, 180, 195, 205, 217, 231, and 327).

and genetic or historic), Woodward's preference for functional explanations in science seems to be indubitable. He conceives this type of explanation as connected to an "epistemic engineering," where causal cognition is seen as a kind of epistemic technology (i.e., as a tool) that should be judged in terms of how well it serves our goals and purposes (cf. Woodward 2014, pp. 693–694). This view makes it more difficult to address the social events – as well as artificial novelties due to human creativity – that are characterized by historicity, especially those that lead to revolutionary changes.

But Woodward conceives his manipulative or interventionist approach to causality as disconnected from any anthropomorphic component. His focus is mainly on basic science (scientific explanations) and, to some extent, he considers the applications of science (the contextual use of scientific knowledge), but he pays little attention to applied science,[4] where causality has a relation to prediction and prescription. Following these issues on historicity, the different realms on causality in science (basic, applied, and application), and the links between causation and prediction,[5] Gonzalez gives reasons for more pluralism.

Concerning philosophy of psychology as special science, Woodward makes a substantial contribution regarding his conception to this philosophical area in chapter 2 of this volume. Thus, in "Normative Theory and Descriptive Psychology in Understanding Causal Reasoning: The Role of Interventions and Invariance" (Woodward 2018a), he makes explicit new aspects of his characterization of interventions and invariance, which are two key elements of his perspective on causality as well as of his vision of psychological events.

First, Woodward wants to make clear how he understands the distinction between "descriptive" and "normative" regarding causal explanations: it is a difference between how people *de facto* reason causally and how they *ought to* reason. However, he maintains that the descriptive task and the normative endeavor "are in many ways closely related and each can be fruitfully influenced by the other" (Woodward 2018a, p. 75). A central interest is in the significance of invariance, and he focuses

---

[4] On the differences between basic science, applied science, and application of science, see Gonzalez (2013, pp. 17–19). In this regard, Niiniluoto (1993) is also of interest.

[5] These links are related to a number of issues on the connection between causation and prediction. Among them, some are particularly relevant: how the future may sometimes have a causal character (e.g., the knowledge of a hurricane), and how the causal relationship can make the reliability of scientific prediction possible or can increase its level of precision and accuracy. On causality and scientific prediction, see Gonzalez (2015, pp. 17n, 50, 62n, 64, 125, 128, 133, 135–138, 143–144, 276, 302, and 309).

on cases in which a physical connection between cause and effect is present, on examples illustrating the importance of proportionality as a condition on causal claims, and on what happens when, contrary to the strategy I recommend, descriptive investigations are not guided by normative theory (Woodward 2018a, p. 78).

Second, Woodward develops his interventionist account of causal explanation present in his well-known book *Making Things Happen* (2003/2005). His conception includes relationships that are exploitable in principle for manipulation and control. Now his goal in the paper is "to illustrate how the normative components of the theory might be related to various sorts of descriptive investigations" (Woodward 2018a, p. 79). Thus, he looks into the relations between invariance (which can play a role somehow similar to that of laws in other philosophical approaches), proportionality, and specificity.

Third, in his original presentation of the interventionist interpretation of causation, which follows normative and descriptive considerations, Woodward works on a principle of causation (M) based on an intervention as "an idealized unconfounded manipulation."[6] He accepts that such principle of causation is *normative*. Therefore, it is not *eo ipso* connected to empirical psychology. But his aim is just to explore its possible descriptive content: how a subject's behavior and cognition can make up such principle (M).

Fourth, regarding invariance (stability, robustness, and insensitivity) and causal judgments, Woodward develops new normative and descriptive considerations. Thus, he deals with the invariance of the cause-effect relationship that has to do with the extent to which the dependence of the effect on the cause continues to hold as background conditions change from those in the actual situation (Woodward 2018a, pp. 88–90). Finally, he addresses a set of empirical issues raised by the role of invariance in causal judgments. The question is whether we can use this notion of *invariance* to explain specific patterns in the causal judgments that people make (Woodward 2018a, p. 97).

---

6 "(**M**) C causes E if and only if it is possible to intervene to change the value of C, in such a way that if that intervention were to occur, the value of E or the probability distribution of E would change," Woodward (2018a, p. 79).

3 Causal Cognition and Psychological Explanations: Structural and Dynamic Aspects

Closely connected to his previous paper, Woodward develops a conception of "Causal Cognition: Physical Connections, Proportionality, and the Role of Normative Theory" in part II of this book (Woodward 2018b). This chapter 3 is generally structural in the focus on cognition and complements in many ways his text on normative theory and descriptive psychology in order to understand causal reasoning. He considers that the *normative* theorizing (either philosophical or theoretical) about causation and causal reasoning and the *empirical* psychological investigations into causal cognition can be mutually illuminating.

What this paper adds to the previous chapter from Woodward is a discussion on some important issues in this realm, such as the contrast (and relationship) between "actual cause" and "type-level" causal judgments or the ways that the presence of a "physical connection" can be involved in causal judgment (Woodward 2018b, p. 105). Thus, he offers some background on these topics before focusing on a variety of topics: a) the role of information about the presence of a "physical connection" between cause and effect in causal judgment; b) the role of a consideration called "proportionality" in choosing the appropriate "level" of explanation;[7] and c) the role of mechanism information in causal judgment.[8]

As regards the first topic, which Woodward analyzes in three sections (2–4), he pays attention to the distinction between "type" and "token" regarding actual *causal judgments*. His perspective follows the interventionist account on causal explanation, which includes counterfactuals, "specifying the response of the candidate effect variable if interventions on the cause variable were to occur" (Woodward 2018b, p. 106). He also addresses questions connecting processes and causal judgments as well as discussing features linking processes and stability.

On the second topic of the paper, Woodward deals with the idea of *proportionality* and the issue of finding the right level of causal explanation, where he insists on the importance of the notion of invariance and, therefore, stability (see Woodward 2018b, pp. 120–121). He emphasizes that, "as an empirical matter, people exhibit preferences for levels of causal description satisfying a proportionality requirement" (2018b, p. 129). In addition, he suggests taking seriously

---

7 On this topic, see Yablo (1992).
8 Woodward analyzes Ahn, Kalish, Medin, and Gelman (1995).

the possibility that these subjects are behaving reasonably and seeking whether there is some normative basis for this preference.

Meanwhile, on the role of *mechanism information* in causal judgment, Woodward revises an influential experimental paper that illustrates what can happen when empirical investigation is *not* guided by any defensible normative theory. He thinks it is relatively unsuccessful insofar as "it does not make use of any defensible normative framework concerning causal reasoning and judgment" (Woodward 2018b, p. 130). Thus, in this chapter as in the previous one, Woodward's philosophical project is *dual:* on the one hand, to investigate empirically to what extent subjects of various sorts conform to the requirements of the normative theories; and, on the other, to treat subject's reasoning and judgment as possible sources of normative ideas (2018b, p. 131).

This philosophical conception of psychological events is followed by an approach developed by a psychologist, José María Martínez Selva, who also stresses the structural aspects of cognition. He presents a set of results, based on empirical research, on the biological factors that influence behavior in *decision-making*. In particular, he is interested in empirical data that allow us to state that a certain brain structure is intervening in decision-making processes. Thus, chapter 4 deals with "Psychobiological Explanations in Decision-Making and Neuroeconomics," which is an interdisciplinary field where psychology, neuroscience, and economics share common ground.

Certainly, decision-making has been studied by psychologists and economists, such as Herbert Simon.[9] But in recent years there is a new angle of interest: neuroscience, which leads to neuroeconomics.[10] In this regard, what Martínez Selva does is to search for data to offer biological explanations for behavior. This can contribute to knowing more about it and, consequently, to having more empirical knowledge to predict it (cf. Martínez Selva, 2018, p. 139). It is in this search for which biological factors influence decision-making where psychobiology meets cognitive neuroscience. The interest is in neuronal systems that are activated when taking economic decisions. The aim is to contribute to "explaining" the decisions that are taken by the economic actors by evaluating the weight of the variables involved.

Here the type of explanation that can be obtained is functional, according to goals and processes. The empirical knowledge is obtained through

---

[9] Simon has a large number of publications on decision-making from both angles: psychological and economic (see, for example, Simon 1959, 1965, 1979, 1993, 1997). More references to his work in this regard can be found in Gonzalez (2003, pp. 7–63; especially, pp. 40–41 and 59–60).
[10] See, for example, McCabe (2008). This article belongs to a monographic issue on neuroeconomics of the journal *Economics and Philosophy.*

functional magnetic resonance imaging (fMRI), which reveals which areas of the brain participate in a specific behaviour or in a mental process, in this case decision-making. It is usual for many connected regions to be activated, thus leading us to refer to the whole as networks or neuronal systems. Nevertheless, the functions of each region may be different and can be studied separately through specific experiments (Martínez Selva, 2018, p. 140. See also Martínez Selva 2011).

In this search for biological components of behavior related to decision-making in economics, the recognition of the complexity of the processes involved requires us to distinguish what is *causal* from what is merely *correlational*. Thus, Martínez Selva discusses causal and correlational methods for locating mental functions in the brain. He pays special attention to the ventromedial prefrontal cortex in decision-making, which includes considering data obtained from patients with lesions in the ventromedial prefrontal cortex. This leads to his conclusions on the functions of the ventromedial prefrontal cortex in decision-making.

Another contribution made from a psychological perspective is chapter 5: "Dynamic Level Interaction Hypothesis – A New Perspective on Consciousness," where Michał Wierzchoń offers his analysis to identify the neurobiological and cognitive mechanisms of *consciousness*. Certainly, it is a difficult task, which he sees as having two sides: (i) to describe the mechanisms of *access* to the content of consciousness, which involves the differences between conscious and unconscious information processing; and (ii) to establish what *causes* the subjective nature of the experience of this content and, therefore, to know why each person experiences the same world differently.

These issues have a dynamic dimension and are tackled by Wierzchoń in a very direct way. He points out that philosophers have proposed theoretical frameworks for consciousness discussing both sides in context, addressing problems in terms of mind-body, binding or *qualia*. Meanwhile, there are influential scientific models of consciousness focused on investigations of the threshold of awareness and its correlates. But he thinks that they do not really deal with the problem of the subjective character of conscious experience. In addition, there are other, more limited, psychological views, insofar as they research mechanisms of conscious experience related to only one modality (namely, visual perceptual awareness).

Wierzchoń insists on the need to investigate a broad spectrum of different types of content, which, among others, includes perceptual aspects (e. g., awareness of tactile information, interoceptive awareness, etc.) and stored in memory (e. g., awareness of learning and memory representation). But the experimental studies of consciousness and the large amount of data already available is not enough, because "there is still no widely accepted theory simultaneously describing mechanisms underlying conscious access to different types of content and addressing the problem of subjective characteristics of this content" (Wierzchoń 2018, p. 160).

Consequently, Wierzchoń seeks a theoretical model that combines the philosophical and neurobiological approaches, trying to address both issues. He thinks that this could be done by integrating achievements and methods from neurobiological and cognitive studies on awareness. He proposes the *dynamic level interaction hypothesis* to tackle this challenge. He does this in several steps: 1) the relations between conscious access and subjective experience, 2) the search for the interdisciplinary perspective on consciousness, 3) the presentation of the dynamic level interaction hypothesis, and 4) how to test dynamic level interaction hypothesis.

4 Scientific Status of Psychology and the Psychological Subject

Underneath the themes discussed in the previous parts of the book there are two key issues regarding philosophy of psychology: first, what is – and ought to be – the scientific status of psychology, and, second, how can, or should, the psychological subject be characterized. These themes are the focus of part III of this volume. It includes chapter 6, centered on "Naturalization of Psychology and Its Future as a Science," by Manuel Antonio García Sedeño, and chapter 7, concentrated on "The Emotional Subject in Philosophy of Psychology: The Cases of Anxiety and Angst," by Francisco Rodriguez Valls.

García Sedeño raises a very important philosophico-metodological issue regarding psychology: what is – and ought to be – its scientific status? His main concern is in a kind of *naturalization* – mainly ontological – that he calls "physicalization" of psychology (see García Sedeño 2018, p. 181),[11] insofar as it dilutes *de facto* the field of psychology through erasing all the references to mental components. But, *prima facie*, this viewpoint can have different philosophico-methodological versions: from a strong eliminativist position (the mental events are mere neural processes) to other possibilities where psychological events (such as mental acts related to cognition, volition or affection) do not longer have a specific status in this sphere of scientific research.

Among the possibilities regarding the *scientific status* of psychology, there are at least three main options that I think might be compatible with some

---

[11] The term "physicalization" seems to be an echo of the Carnapian approach (see Carnap 1932).

kinds of naturalist approaches. a) To dissolve *de facto* its scientific status into neuroscience, insofar as the key for psychological processes is usually neurological, which is a position commonly supported by ontological naturalists. b) To maintain that psychology is above all a social science, insofar as human beings are mainly social entities – agents in a social milieu – and their characteristics (such as personality, the kind of decision-making, the social interaction, etc.) are quite different from other beings. This option can be accepted by epistemological naturalists (such as those that stress the role of social construction for science), especially those that insist on psychological traits as being socially acquired (for example, gender and social roles). c) To defend that psychology is actually a dual science, which uses methods of natural sciences (e.g., in psychobiology) as well as methods of social sciences (e.g., in social psychology). This perspective is in line with some conceptions of methodological naturalism (especially when naturalism is understood as the acceptance of the methodological practices of the scientists in the field considered).

What García Sedeño aims to do in his paper is summarized in two goals (section 1). First, to show how psychology is being absorbed by neurology in a way that it is becoming endangered due to its excessive physicalization. Second, to display the existence of a scientific psychology that is independent of neurology. This "real psychological science" comes from approaches with a bigger predictive and explanatory capacity, mainly those that appeared after the 60s (cf. García Sedeño 2018, p. 183). Thus, he offers some historical keys of the physicalization of psychology (section 2) and the repercussion in scientific psychology of the philosophico-methodological approaches available after the "historical turn" (section 3).[12] Finally, on the naturalization of psychology (section 4), García Sedeño defends

> the existence of a psychological science with its own identity, independent from neurology and other similar sciences, whose object goal is the explanation of creation and development of human consciousness as a product coming from its own experience. Psychology is a human, social and natural science, in which experience becomes the key for its understanding (García Sedeño 2018, p. 197).

From a different angle, Francisco Rodriguez Valls also looks deeply into the *singularity of psychology*. His paper on the psychological subjects offers an interesting analysis of the emotional subject in philosophy of psychology through the cases of anxiety and angst. This window to the specificity of psychology as sci-

---

[12] His analysis includes R. Giere, Ph. Kitcher, L. Laudan, etc. See, in this regard, Gonzalez (2006).

entific realm with subjects that bear proprieties that, in many ways, are to be found only in them is opened through the abandonment of behaviorism and the subsequent rise of cognitivism. As a consequence, the studies on emotions have experienced exponential growth. Certainly, human emotions are derived from a kind of knowledge, but they commonly have relations to volitions, and their intensity can be observed through human activity.

Rodriguez Valls focuses his analysis on two important *emotions:* anxiety and angst. He maintains that anxiety is a common emotion in both animals and human beings. Its object is connected to a well-defined context and comes as a response before indeterminate dangers. Meanwhile, angst is properly an emotion of human beings resulting from the consciousness of freedom. In this regard, the analysis follows several steps: (i) the scrutiny of the two main options in contemporary theory of emotion (i.e., bodily impulses and cognitive actions); (ii) the consideration of fear and anxiety as natural emotions; (iii) the philosophical treatment of angst, where he includes the metaphysical experience of emotion; (iv) the search for similarities and differences between anxiety and angst; (v) the clarification on the question whether angst is a type of anxiety; and (vi) the conclusion on the irreducibility between angst and anxiety.

Following Rodriguez Valls's analysis, the *psychological subject*, when seen from the viewpoint of emotions, involves different layers in a complex entity.[13] Philosophically, he holds that "the classics consider passions as common to animals and men. That is essentially correct in most cases, as long as we realize that the specifics of what is human (e.g., the self-conscious exercise of the will) can lead to, and be the source of, emotions with distinctive human characteristics" (Rodriguez Valls 2018, p. 213). In addition, he thinks that the human being as a psychological subject requires nature and culture. In this regard, "angst makes sense when we talk not of adaptation to the environment, but of man overcoming the natural cycle. Therefore, it belongs to the realm of culture, in as much as culture is born when man is born" (Rodriguez Valls 2018, p. 216).[14] Thus, he believes that anxiety and angst are mutually irreducible.

---

[13] The complexity of this entity increases if we distinguish between feelings, emotions, and affections as three different aspects in the psychological subject.
[14] He also thinks that the origin of those two emotions is different: in the case of anxiety, it is the emotion which motivates hazard identification; whereas in angst, it is the knowledge of my free condition – as human being – and the need to set up an existential project under finite conditions.

5 From Psychology to Psychiatry: Limits of Computational Psychology and the Role of Causes as Interventions in Psychiatry

Subsequent to the emphasis on epistemological issues, which are central concerning to scientific status of psychology and to the characteristics of the psychological subject, there are methodological issues on the limits of psychology, which are also particularly relevant. Part IV of this book deals with them in two directions: limits as *ceiling* in terms of research and limits as *frontiers* regarding other disciplines.[15] The former is at the core of chapter 8, devoted to "The Limits of Computational Psychology in J. Fodor" and prepared by Pedro Chacón, whereas the latter accompanies to chapter 9, on "The Interventionist Theory and Mental Disorders," where Raffaella Campaner takes into account the distinction between psychology and psychiatry.

Methodological issues are particularly relevant when the limits become the focus of research. Functionalist theories have occupied a prominent role in cognitive psychology. They are very keen of the computational model, but – as Chacón points out – there are problems, theoretical and empirical, that appear while dealing with consciousness, intentionality, *qualia*, or mental causation. Regarding the mind, Jerry Fodor has defended the functionalist framework and the computational model,

> considering it to be the only one which can be used to justify the autonomy of psychological explanations and the configuration of psychology as an independent science. Fodor, a disciple of [Hilary] Putnam and defender of [Noam] Chomsky's innatism, has been controversially defending the need to combine a computational theory of mind with a representational one for years (Chacón 2018, p. 222).

Chacón starts with the coordinates of Fodor's theoretical proposals, which connect concepts of the philosophy of language and those concerning mental processes and states. Then he discusses the internal demarcation of Fodor's model of psychological explanation, because it is related to themes such as learning theory and perception rather than other topics such as social psychology and developmental psychology. Thereafter, Chacón deals with language of thought and psychological explanations, because Fodor pays special attention to deliberate

---

[15] On the issue of the limits of science as frontiers and ceiling, from a general perspective, see Gonzalez (2016).

decision-taking, concept learning, sensory perceptions, and psycholinguistic processes.

Later on, the topic of structure of the human mind appears, due to Fodor's proposal of the modularity of the mind. This is followed by an analysis of the problems of the computational theory of mind and the epistemic boundedness of computational psychology. Finally, Chacón sees two important limits that Fodor establishes in his own explanatory model: a) the questionable legitimacy of his radical refusal to consider the possible extension of psychology to the central cognition processes; and b) its plausible congruence with the particular epistemological status of psychological knowledge.[16]

While Pedro Chacón considers the limits as *ceiling* of psychology, seen in terms of internal limits of a psychological proposal made by a philosopher, Raffaella Campaner takes into account the other side of the limits: the *frontiers* of the discipline, insofar as she moves towards psychiatry. She analyzes the interventionist conception of causality developed by Woodward and the issue of mental disorders. In this regard, she recognizes that mental illnesses are currently seen as a motley combination of variables at a number of different levels (genetic, biochemical, neurological, social, psychological, etc.). Consequently, many theoretical models of mental disorders include various disciplinary standpoints (clinical psychology, genetic psychiatry, behavioral neurology, pharmacology, etc.).

Campaner focuses on causal analyses and causal explanatory models of mental disorders, the collection of different kinds of evidence, and the variables involved and their interactions. She uses mental disorders as a significant test case for the interventionist theory of causation and causal explanation proposed by Woodward. His view is scrutinized in her paper in the light of its feasibility to address issues arising in attempts to integrate different perspectives on mental disorders. She starts with the relations between the interventionist theory and psychiatric explanations, and this is followed by the study of causal discourse on mental disorders. In this regard, she takes into account three main aspects: a) the gathering of evidence concerning interventions; b) the variables, with their levels and interactions; and c) what causes disorders and how.

Her view calls for a *broader picture* of the problem discussed, which includes more elements than those available in the present interventionist approach. Campaner makes a clear move in favor of pluralism. She maintains that

> the interventionist account needs to pay adequate attention to such elements as the actual modes of interactions among variables, their spatial and temporal dimensions, the role of

---

16 The details on these aspects mentioned here are in Chacón (2018, pp. 232–236).

observational evidence, and the background assumptions in the constructions of causal models of disorders. Only accounting for these aspects too can a proper understanding of mental disorder be pursued, and the rapprochement of different conceptions of causation and causal explanation be seen in the prospect of conciliating different disciplinary approaches to mental disorders (Campaner 2018, p. 264).

6 Origin of This Book

Most of the papers here have their roots in the search for new contributions to "The Philosophy of Psychology: The Conception of James Woodward." This was the title of a conference in his honor at the University of A Coruña, Ferrol Campus, held on 13–14 March 2014, where he delivered two papers. This event, *Jornadas sobre la Filosofía de la Psicología: La concepción de James Woodward*,[17] has its origins in the conversations with him at the University of Pittsburgh during the summer of 2012. I aimed for new developments on philosophy of psychology as special science using his ideas as a focal point, because these workshops at the University of A Coruña, which started in 1996, are conceived as a series of conferences focused on relevant issues in philosophy and methodology of science and in philosophy of technology.

Considering the final versions of the papers, the result is an even richer picture than expected. The reason is clear: this book offers a variety of contributions on causal explanation in terms of intervention and also on the psychological subject that go beyond Woodward's approach. On the one hand, this book stresses his contribution to causal explanation but also presents some critical remarks; and, on the other, there are quite interesting proposals about the psychological subject in a different direction, where the limitations of some versions of naturalism become clear. They suggest that the scientific status of the psychological subject requires a broader picture than the available versions of naturalism can offer.

For the readers interested in Woodward's approach, the first chapter of this volume offers a large amount of bibliographical information. It includes references of his publications as well as a selection of texts on his work and on these important philosophical issues: causal explanations and philosophy of psychology as special science. The aim of this information as well as of the book as a whole is clear: it discusses Woodward's approach in both areas, but seeks to con-

---

[17] This was the title of the *XIX Conference on Contemporary Philosophy and Methodology of Science*, a series of workshops coordinated by the author of this preface.

tribute to the philosophical solution of problems surrounding topics such as *causal explanations* and *the conception of the psychological subject*.

To conclude this preface my gratitude goes to James Francis Woodward and to all who have cooperated in the shared aim of this publication. Let me also express my recognition to the persons and institutions that cooperated in the original event. First, my appreciation to the speakers of the conference and the efforts made thereafter by the authors of the papers to make contributions to the topics discussed; and, second, my acknowledgment to the organizations that gave their support: the University of A Coruña (especially to the Rector of the University and the Vice-rector of the Campus of Ferrol and Social Responsibility), the City Hall of Ferrol, and the Society of Logic, Methodology, and Philosophy of Science in Spain.

In addition, let me point out that I am thankful to Jose Fco. Martínez Solano, Amanda Guillan, and Jessica Rey for their contribution to the edition of this book. Finally, my gratitude extends to the Centre for Philosophy of Natural and Social Sciences (CPNSS) of the London School of Economics (LSE). My stay at LSE as research visitor has made it possible to prepare my contribution to this volume as well as to carry out a substantial part of the task of edition of this book.

References

The bibliography directly related to the topics indicated here can be found in the following chapter: Gonzalez, W. J. (2018). "Configuration of Causality and Philosophy of Psychology: An Analysis of Woodward's Causality as Intervention and its Repercussion for Psychology." This volume, pp. 59–70. The references used for the present text are the following:

Ahn, W., Kalish, C., Medin, D., and Gelman, S. (1995): "The Role of Covariation versus Mechanism Information in Causal Attribution." *Cognition*, v. 54, pp. 299–352.
Campaner, R. (2018): "The Interventionist Theory and Mental Disorders." This volume, pp. 243–268.
Carnap, R. (1932): "Psychologie in Physikalischer Sprache." *Erkenntnis*, v. 2, pp. 107–142.
Chacón, P. (2018): "The Limits of Computational Psychology in J. Fodor." This volume, pp. 221–242.
García Sedeño, M. A. (2017): "Naturalization of Psychology and its Future as a Science." This volume, pp. 181–201.
Gonzalez, W. J. (2002): "Caracterización de la 'explicación científica' y tipos de explicaciones científicas." In: *Diversidad de la explicación científica*, ed. W. J. Gonzalez, pp. 13–49. Barcelona: Ariel.
Gonzalez, W. J. (2003): "Herbert A. Simon: Filósofo de la Ciencia y economista (1916–2001)." In: *Racionalidad, historicidad y predicción en Herbert A. Simon*, ed. W. J. Gonzalez, pp. 7–63. A Coruña: Netbiblo.

Gonzalez, W. J. (2006): "Novelty and Continuity in Philosophy and Methodology of Science." In: *Contemporary Perspectives in Philosophy and Methodology of Science*, eds. W. J. Gonzalez, and J. Alcolea, pp. 1–28. A Coruña: Netbiblo.

Gonzalez, W. J. (2013): "The Roles of Scientific Creativity and Technological Innovation in the Context of Complexity of Science." In: *Creativity, Innovation, and Complexity in Science*, ed. W. J. Gonzalez, pp. 11–40. A Coruña: Netbiblo.

Gonzalez, W. J. (2015): *Philosophico-methodological Analysis of Prediction and Its Role in Economics*. Dordrecht: Springer.

Gonzalez, W. J. (ed.). (2016): *The Limits of Science: An Analysis from "Barriers" to "Confines."* Poznan Studies in the Philosophy of the Sciences and the Humanities, vol. 109, Leiden: Brill/Rodopi.

Gonzalez, W. J. (2017): "From Intelligence to Rationality of Minds and Machines in Contemporary Society: The Sciences of Design and the Role of Information." *Minds and Machines*, v. 27, n. 3, pp. 397–424. DOI: 10.1007/s11023-017-9439-0.

Gonzalez, W. J. (2018): "Configuration of Causality and Philosophy of Psychology: An Analysis of Woodward's Causality as Intervention and its Repercussion for Psychology." This volume, pp. 21–70.

Martínez Selva, J. M. (2011): "Conceptual Changes in Biological Explanations of Behavior." In: *Conceptual Revolutions: From Cognitive Science to Medicine*, ed. W. J. Gonzalez, pp. 97–117. A Coruña: Netbiblo.

Martínez Selva, J. M. (2018): "Psychobiological Explanations in Decision-making and Neuroeconomics." This volume, pp. 139–157.

McCabe, K. A. (2008): "Neuroeconomics and the Economic Sciences." *Economics and Philosophy*, v. 24, n. 3, pp. 345–368.

Niiniluoto, I. (1993): "The Aim and Structure of Applied Research." *Erkenntnis*, v. 38, pp. 1–21.

Roessler, J., Eilen, N., and Lerman, H. (eds.) (2011): *Causation, Perception, and Objectivity: Issues in Philosophy and Psychology*, Oxford: Oxford University Press.

Simon, H. A. (1959): "Theories of Decision-making in Economics and Behavioral Science." *American Economic Review*, v. 49, pp. 253–283.

Simon, H. A. (1965): "Administrative Decision Making." *Public Administration Review*, v. 25, pp. 31–37.

Simon, H. A. (1979): "Rational Decision Making in Business Organizations." [The 1978 Nobel Memorial Prize in Economics Lecture]. *American Economic Review*, v. 69, pp. 493–513.

Simon, H. A. (1993): "Decision Making: Rational, Nonrational, and Irrational." *Educational Administration Quarterly*, v. 29, pp. 392–411.

Simon, H. A. (1997): "Expert Decision Making and the Managerial Future." *Monash St Eliza Business Review*, v. 1, n. 1, pp. 30–37.

Thagard, P. (ed.). (2007): *Philosophy of Psychology and Cognitive Science*. Amsterdam: Elsevier.

Wierzchoń, M. (2018): "Dynamic level interaction hypothesis – A new perspective on consciousness." This volume, pp. 159–177.

Woodward, J. (2003) [Paperback edition, 2005]: *Making Things Happen: A Theory of Causal Explanation*. New York: Oxford University Press.

Woodward, J. (2012): "Causation: Interactions between Philosophical Theories and Psychological Research." *Philosophy of Science* v. 79, n. 5, pp. 961–972.

Woodward, J. (2014): "A Functional Account of Causation; or a Defense of the Legitimacy of Causal Thinking by Reference to the Only Standard That Matters – Usefulness (as Opposed to Metaphysics and Agreement with Intuitive Judgment)." *Philosophy of Science* 81(5): 691–713.

Woodward, J. (2018a): "Normative Theory and Descriptive Psychology in Understanding Causal Reasoning: The Role of Interventions and Invariance." This volume, pp. 71–101.

Woodward, J. (2018b): "Causal Cognition: Physical Connections, Proportionality, and the Role of Normative Theory." This volume, pp. 105–137.

Yablo, S. (1992): "Mental Causation." *Philosophical Review* v. 101, pp. 245–280.

Part I: Causal Reasoning in the Context of Normative and Descriptive Psychology

Wenceslao J. Gonzalez
Configuration of Causality and Philosophy of Psychology: An Analysis of Causality as Intervention and Its Repercussion for Psychology

Abstract: Within the context of contemporary philosophy of science, this paper offers a configuration of causality and its place in philosophy of psychology as special science. The analysis focuses on the very influential conception developed by James Woodward, with alternatives given in those aspects that require more attention (diversity of explanations, prediction, historicity, pluralism, etc.). Thus, this paper considers his preference for causal explanations and his interest in psychological cases. This chapter points out that his naturalism is combined with elements of anti-naturalism, insofar as is open to hypothetical explanations and ideal interventions. In addition, his vision of naturalism (epistemological, methodological, and ontological) is embedded with components of pragmatism.

The analysis of scientific explanation goes from the types of scientific explanation to the kinds of causal explanation. In this regard, among the varieties of causality in contemporary philosophy of science, Woodward develops a manipulative or interventionist approach. Meanwhile, the paper proposes a broader perspective of causality, which includes three levels of scientific research (basic, applied, and of application) as a framework for causality in psychology and human affairs. Overall, the main strength of his approach is in the criticism of other theories of scientific explanation. But his positive alternative to them, insofar as it involves a special insistence on hypothetical experiments and ideal components, seems to me less persuasive for a characterization of causality, in general, and causal explanations, in particular. The philosophical analysis is then followed by an outline of his academic trajectory, the references of this chapter, the full set of Woodward's publications, and a bibliography on his philosophy.

Keywords: causality, philosophy, psychology, Woodward, naturalism, pragmatism, explanation, trajectory, bibliography.

Recent decades of philosophy of science, in general, and philosophy of psychology, in particular, have seen a renewed interest in causality.[1] Thus, causal explanations and reflections on their consequences for psychology as a science have been emphasized. Both aspects can be connected in many ways, due to the relevance of the topics surrounding causality for many events concerning individuals, groups, and society as a whole. Hence, the problems regarding causality are pertinent to philosophical discussions as well as to the research made in sciences such as psychology. But they are also crucial for other realms, such as law, where causal relationship is commonly taken into account in some legal spheres (especially regarding a possible sanction).[2]

Among the conceptions of causal explanation, the analysis made by James Francis Woodward (Chicago, 17 September 1946) on causality as an intervention has been influential worldwide. Since his book *Making Things Happen: A Theory of Causal Explanation* (2003a),[3] there has been an outpour of publications using his ideas in epistemological and methodological debates, both regarding science in general (mainly natural sciences, but also social sciences) and concerning special sciences such as psychology. This is the reason this paper is focused on his philosophical approach.

1 Preference for Causal Explanations and Interest in Psychological Cases

Actually, Woodward has worked on causality and causal explanations since his first publication (Woodward 1979). In addition, he has shown frequent interest in psychological events, considering experiences of folk psychology as well as contributions of scientific psychology. His focus of attention is commonly on causal

---

[1] In this regard, this paper includes many references, especially within the bibliographical information in section 13. Some of the views on causality are new versions of previous approaches, whereas others are clearly new, commonly due to the source of inspiration – the scientific case chosen as a model – on what "causality" is. This leads to epistemological, methodological and ontological differences between the conceptions of causality proposed.

[2] The problems regarding causality are central for law in fields such as criminal law, both in theoretical terms and in practical ones. On the one hand, the doctrines behind the legislation on penal law assume, in one way or another, a conception of causality connected by what is considered responsible for a crime. On the other hand, judges and juries have in mind some kind of approach to causality in order to evaluate beyond reasonable doubt the responsibility for a crime (either committed or an attempted).

[3] Here the references and quotations are from the book of 2003 reprinted in 2005 in paperback.

explanations, and psychological events are among the cases that he analyzes regarding causal relationships.[4] Their explanations, either of types or singular cases, are seen from the perspective of an interventionist conception of causality (see Woodward 2007b), although he also pays attention to counterfactual interpretations of causal relationships (cf. Woodward 2011).

Natural phenomena as well as social events are considered by Woodward according to a naturalist conception of causal explanation. In his philosophical approach, there is a continuity between ordinary phenomena and events and the scientific research on them, which is one of the leads of his book on the theory of causal explanation (2003a). Thus, he puts effort into

> showing how the apparatus of direct graphs and a manipulationist approach to causation can be used to reconstruct commonsense judgments about token-causal relationships (Woodward 2003a, p. 85).[5]

But his style of thought includes a relevant second step, which has more of a Kantian methodological flavor,[6] insofar as – for Woodward –

> to the extent that commonsense causal judgments are unclear, equivocal, or disputed, it is better to focus directly on the patterns of counterfactual dependence that lie behind them – the patterns of counterfactual dependence are, as it were, the "objective core" that lies behind our particular causal judgments, and it is such patterns that are the real objects of scientific and particular interest (Woodward 2003a, p. 85).

These contents can be in the realm of psychology, which Woodward sees as one of the "special sciences" (i.e., sciences considered as less consolidated than

---

4 Other cases that are of special interest for his philosophical analysis are phenomena from physics, biology, and neuroscience. See, in this regard, Woodward's publications in sections 13.2 and 13.3 devoted to his papers and chapters of books. It is particularly relevant Bogen and Woodward (1988).

5 On the concept of causation, see Woodward (2007a).

6 The Kantian methodological flavor is in how he uses the ideal components, understood as a kind of cornerstone of the philosophical process, to grasp the causal relations of natural phenomena. In Woodward's view, the ideal components (hypotheses, experiments, etc.) are crucial to the characterization of the causal relationship. This process includes "intervention as an idealized experimental manipulation," Woodward (2003a, p. 94). Thus, in order to characterize the real world, he uses procedures based on what is clearly constructed (ideal hypotheses and experiments, counterfactuals, etc.) and, therefore, his philosophical process is then revisionary rather than descriptive.

This style of thought, where there are elements of epistemological naturalism and methodological anti-naturalism, reminds me of some aspects of Peter Strawson's approach (cf. Gonzalez 1995 and 1998a).

physics and chemistry, where particular epistemological and methodological problems arise due to the kind of phenomena studied in them). Although he thinks of psychology as a special science, he looks for a methodological continuity between natural sciences and social sciences in terms of a naturalist approach. The characteristic topics of what Merrilee Salmon calls "interpretivism" or the "interpretative point of view" of the social sciences (1992, pp. 408–401, and 2002) have serious difficulties in going into Woodward's conception of psychology. Thus, within the framework of the *Erklären-Verstehen* methodological controversy,[7] his position is clearly closer to the first than to the second option.

As a consequence, the attention of this paper goes initially to naturalism as a crucial component of his philosophical approach. This analysis is accompanied by a set of specific features in his vision. Thereafter, the research goes to cause and scientific explanation as seen from a structural perspective, the varieties of causality in contemporary philosophy of science, and the manipulative or interventionist conception (as the viewpoint endorsed by Woodward). After these analyses, there are more considerations regarding causality in science, in general, and causality in psychology and human affairs, in particular. They are followed by the bibliographical information concerning his work and the topics discussed here.

2 A Naturalism Open to Hypothetical Explanations and Ideal Interventions

Following Woodward's approach, causality requires taking into account the concept of "causation" and the features of causal explanations. Initially, their study belong to the general approach to philosophy of science and, in principle, causation and causal explanations can reach any of the empirical sciences (either natural, social, or artificial).[8] In addition, it is assumed that they do not have a role within formal sciences, at least insofar as cause connects with intervention and "the notion of an intervention has not a role in mathematical proofs" (Wood-

---

[7] Nine views on the *Erklären-Verstehen* methodological controversy are available in Gonzalez (2015c, pp. 173–177).
[8] As is the case for very influential philosophers of science, Woodward takes into account natural sciences and social sciences. The sciences of the artificial, which were among the contributions made by Herbert Simon (see Simon [1969] 1996), are not among the topics of his habitual philosophical research, even though Woodward has special recognition for econometrics. See Woodward (2003a, pp. v, 39, 42, 48).

ward 2003a, p. 221). Thus, the explanations in logic and mathematics follow a different path from natural sciences[9] (this is the case even in strict finitist approaches, where mathematics is above all a human activity).[10]

Although Woodward is interested in how we use causal and explanatory claims, he recognizes that his project also has a significant *revisionary component*, which goes beyond such a descriptive attempt regarding the actual use of causal and explanatory claims (cf. Woodward 2003a, p. 7). On the one hand, it is revisionary in how causality is sometimes thought of in ordinary life and in certain scientific practices; and, on the other, it is also revisionary insofar as his approach offers guidance on how causality should be thought of, which underlines the role of hypothetical experiments and accepts ideal interventions.

Within this twofold philosophical project – descriptive as well as revisionary – there is a frequent intertwining of two kinds of elements: (i) some very detailed descriptions of causal relationships (e.g., in order to criticize the deductive-nomological model of scientific explanation),[11] and (ii) a frequent insistence on "hypothetical interventions" (cf. Woodward 2003a, pp. 57, 102, 146, *et passim*), including "hypothetical experiments" (see Woodward 2003a, pp. 49, 114–117, 129, *et passim*), in order to characterize causal relationships. Thus, the role of the realm of the *ideal* in Woodward's analysis is explicitly highlighted:

> My aim is to give an account of the content or meaning of various locutions, such as *X* causes *Y*, *X* is a direct cause of *Y*, and so on, in terms of the response of *Y* to a *hypothetical idealized* experimental manipulation or intervention on *X* (Woodward 2003a, p. 38, emphasis added).

Descriptive as well as revisionary aspects of the psychological issues appear when Woodward discusses psychology under the label of "special sciences." The descriptive component is available when causal relationships in the psychological field are in *empirical* studies – usually experiments – concerning "with how subjects (adults, but also small children and nonhuman animals) learn and reason about causal relationships" (Woodward 2012, p. 961). Meanwhile he accepts a second branch – "theoretical" – where the question at stake is "to explain how people ought to learn, reason, and judge regarding causal rela-

---

[9] Another matter is to think of the logical and epistemological configuration of the causal explanations. See, for example, von Wright (1973).
[10] See, in this regard, Gonzalez (1991a and b).
[11] In his book there is a whole chapter devoted to the causal explanations inspired by Carl Gustav Hempel's influential approach, cf. Woodward (2003a, ch. 4, pp. 152–186).

tions" (Woodward 2012, p. 961). This second branch, which he labels "normative," is where the revisionary has a lead.

These issues on what psychology actually is and what it ought to be need to take into account the philosophico-methodological status of this scientific discipline. In this regard, I think that there are reasons to consider that psychology is *scientifically dual*, insofar as it has a direct relation with epistemological and methodological problems of the natural sciences (e.g., in areas such as psychobiology, and specifically, in psychophysiology) and it also has an undeniable link to epistemological and methodological problems of the social sciences (e.g., in social psychology and psycho-pedagogy). In addition, psychology has a role regarding the sciences of the artificial, especially when discussing artificial intelligence and the similarities and differences between designed machines and human minds.[12]

When Woodward discusses psychological issues from the perspective of causal explanations, on the one hand, he aims to stress that theoretical and empirical approaches can be combined, since he sees them as complementary (which seems in tune with a naturalist continuity between science and philosophy). But, on the other hand, besides the "descriptive" level, he wants to add a philosophical reflection regarding the *ought to be* (i.e., the "revisionary" or "prescriptive" way), where the "traditional" conceptions on causation (such as, regularity, process theory, counterfactual, etc.) are replaced by his *interventionist* characterization of causality, where the sphere of the ideal is very important (cf. Woodward 2012, pp. 961–971). Moreover, the *ideal* has the status of being regulative in order to address causal relationships.

At the same time, his views differ from influential counterfactual approaches, due to his new views on causal explanation. Thus, he wants to offer an alternative to well-known conceptions on causality. Furthermore, he has put a lot of effort and details into his own philosophical approach, where the concept of "causation" and the features of causal explanations configure a *specific characterization* of a manipulative or interventionist conception. It includes thinking "of an intervention as an *idealized experimental manipulation* carried out on some variable X for the purpose of ascertaining whether the changes in X are causally related to changes in some other variable Y" (Woodward 2003a, p. 94, emphasis added). This conception is novel in several ways, and it is certainly different from those that he sees as defending ideas in line with his ma-

---

[12] See, for example, Simon (1991); and Simon (1995). The journal *Minds and Machines* is devoted to these kinds of issues. On Simon's views and the difference between Artificial Intelligence and human intelligence, see Gonzalez (2017).

nipulability theory of causality (Woodward 2003a, p. 12), such as R. Collingwood (1940) or G. H. von Wright (1971).[13]

According to his naturalist proposal, Woodward develops a philosophical conception of causality and its relation to explanation with continuity between ordinary cases and scientific observations and experiments. Thus, his attention goes to many ordinary examples of psychological interest and which are empirically testable. In this regard, he has made philosophical contributions to philosophy of psychology in two main directions at least: a) the nexus between psychology and other empirical sciences (mainly, natural ones, such as neurobiology) [see Woodward forthcoming a], trying to show how the psychological problems can be discussed in a clear scientific framework (i.e., psychology as special or diverse science, but scientific after all) [Woodward 2007b]; and b) the contribution of the empirical work made by psychology (mainly the group led by Alison Gopnik) to the study of philosophical problems addressed by philosophers (such as causality, which can be considered in toddlers) [Bonawitz et al. 2010].

3 A Naturalist Approach Combined with Components of Pragmatism

Naturalism is the common ground for Woodward's interest in causality and his philosophical reflection on psychological issues.[14] 1) His conception includes a semantic naturalism, insofar as he accepts two relevant aspects regarding language: (i) the terms used in language – ordinary and scientific – are well oriented and can grasp, in principle, what it is real; and (ii) there is an important continuity between ordinary usage and scientific practice (Woodward 2003a, p. 19). 2) There is a logical overlapping between explanations in science and in ordinary contexts, insofar as causal explanations in different areas of science can "share at least some structural features with causal explanations in more ordinary contexts" (Woodward 2003a, p. 19).

---

13 Explicitly, Woodward rejects conceptions such as von Wright's approach (as well as the views defended by Peter Menzies and Huw Price), where "the characterization of a manipulation (or intervention) makes essential reference to human agency or free choice, and the hope is that this can be somehow grasped or understood independently of the notion of causality," Woodward (2003a, p. 104). See Woodward (2009). On Menzies' and Price's positions, see Woodward (2003a, pp. 123–127).
14 On the varieties of naturalism in the recent philosophical conceptions on science, see Gonzalez (2006, pp. 1–28; especially, pp. 5–9).

3) His philosophical approach is very explicit in assuming an epistemological naturalism, which includes "the objectivity of causal relationships" (Woodward 2003a, p. 12). He accepts that, in principle, human knowledge is well oriented and assumes a continuity between science and philosophy. 4) Woodward's analysis of science, in general, and of psychology, in particular, follows the methodological tenets of naturalism when he assumes that the social world should be researched and tested according to methods valid, in principle, for natural sciences.[15]

5) There is, underneath his view, an acceptance of an ontological naturalism (see Woodward 2003a, p. 23), which is in tune with his vision of psychological issues in a non-dualist conception of the human being and an evolutionary explanation for the origin of mental states. According to his naturalistic and evolutionary perspective (see Woodward 2003a, p. 120, see also chapter 2 of his book [2003a]), there is no legitimacy of entities such as "mind" or "consciousness," if they are understood as suprasensible objects.[16] 6) Woodward's axiological naturalism is also clear when he accepts the values assumed by the scientists and admits a continuity of values in ordinary life and values in science.[17] They are not purely descriptive values because there might be prescriptive as well ("normative" in his terminology). 7) He also accepts ethical values according to a naturalist view open to normativity.[18]

As commonly happens in the conceptions endorsing some form of naturalism, there is a science or group of sciences used as the main source for philosophical inspiration.[19] In this regard, Woodward recognizes that his ideas have their roots in the long tradition of the work in experimental design and econometrics, which includes Ronald Fisher and Herbert Simon, that has been continued – at least, in some respects – by Clark Glymour[20] and Judea Pearl (2000).[21]

---

15 This leads to the emphasis on neuroscientific characterization of concepts such as causality: "as with other concepts, the acquisition of the concept of causality involves a complicated interaction between prespecified neural mechanisms and 'learning,'" Woodward (2003a, p. 126).
16 Certainly, Woodward is not a dualist, and he does not think that mind should be understood as some kind of non-physical object. Woodward, J., *Personal communication*, 13.10.2015.
17 Woodward maintains that his comprehensive account of causal explanation "applies to a wide variety of causal and explanatory claims in different areas of science and ordinary life," Woodward (2003a, p. 4). His "theory should allow us to evaluate explanations. It should help us to distinguish between better and less good explanations," Woodward (2003a, p. 23).
18 On his ethical views, see Woodward and Allman (2007).
19 See, in this regard, Gonzalez (2006, pp. 5–9).
20 On Clark Glymour's approach, see his contribution in Spirtes, Glymour, and Scheines (1993).
21 Judea Pearl tries to unify the probabilistic, manipulative, counterfactual, and structural conceptions of causality. He uses mathematical apparatus in order to study the relations between

What Woodward has done is "to take these ideas out of the social scientific and biomedical contexts for which they were originally designed and show how they may be generalized to other areas of science" (Woodward 2003a, p. v).

What is clear is his interest in econometrics (Woodward 2003a/2005, pp. 39, 42, and 48; and Woodward 1995). Thus, he pays attention to the kind of causality proposed by Clive Granger and the tests for this "Granger causality," which are widely used in econometrics for modeling and testing relationships between time series involving economic data. For Woodward (2014a, p. 700),

> Granger causality is the relationship that exists between two variables X and Y when the information about the value of X makes the values of Y more predictable, relative to some alternative in which information about X is absent (Granger 1969)." In this regard, it seems clear that "X can Granger cause Y even though the relationship between X and Y does not satisfy condition M, that is, even though interventions on X will not change Y – a point that Granger himself recognizes (Woodward 2014a, p. 700).

Consequently, Woodward's naturalist conception – the functional approach to causation – does not focus on the mere description of the "practices among econometricians but instead provides resources for asking critical questions about them" (Woodward 2014a, p. 700).

Complementary to the acceptance of diverse forms of naturalism, there are components of *pragmatism* in Woodward's philosophical conception. I) Language – with its cognitive content – is linked to a practice:

> we introduce concepts (including concepts of cause and explanation) because we want to *do* things with them: make certain distinctions, describe certain situations ... (Woodward 2003a, p. 8).

II) Epistemological contents, including causal relations and explanations, are connected to the primacy of the practice, due to "a highly practical interest human beings have in manipulation and control" (Woodward 2003a, p. 10). III) Methodologically, an important feature is the prominent role of the "instrumental" success when there is a comparison of competing theories of explanation (Woodward 2003a, p. 224). In addition, functional explanations should be seen in terms of usefulness (Woodward 2014a). IV) Ontologically, human beings appear as practical agents interested in changing the world: they should not be

---

statistical associations and causal connections. As Woodward sees his approach, Pearl defends "what might be described as broadly manipulationist or interventionist treatment of causation: Causal claims have to do with what would happen under ideal, suitably surgical experimental manipulations ('interventions')," Woodward (2003b, p. 321).

mere spectators or passive collectors of knowledge claims (Woodward 2003a, p. 25). V) Axiologically, there are scientific values whose relevance comes from scientific practice. A scientific value is, in principle, rooted in scientific practice rather than in an ontologically oriented alternative (Woodward 2003a, p. 224).

Overall, Woodward's philosophical approach is primarily naturalist regarding key issues of science (such as language, structures, knowledge, methods, activity, ends, and values). He also accepts components of pragmatism, due to his interest in practice, insofar as they can be combined with his naturalism regarding science (mainly basic science and application of science). In addition, he is open to forms of realism, such as a kind of *instrumental realism* connected with experiments (Woodward 2003c), or a version of *modest realism*, understood as an ontological support for causal relationships and scientific explanations (see Woodward 2003a, pp. 118, 120, and 202). But his emphasis on the role of the ideal (hypotheses, experiments, interventions as regulative, etc.) [cf. Woodward 2003a, p. 130] includes, *de facto*, the acceptance of a variety of anti-naturalist methodology,[22] which drives the revisionary trait of his theory of causal explanation.

4 Cause and Scientific Explanation: A Structural Perspective

After the central features of Woodward's philosophical approach – a naturalism open to hypothetical explanations and ideal interventions as well as to pragmatist components – the attention goes to the perspective on cause and scientific explanation. On the one hand, cause and explanation are connected in many ways both in general philosophy of science and special philosophy of science, which includes the *broad approach* as well as the *restricted conception*.[23]

---

[22] On the one hand, Woodward agrees that he is anti-naturalist insofar as naturalism about methodology is the view that one should only describe, not prescribe (Woodward, J., *Personal communication*, 13.10.2015), because he also wants to prescribe. But, on the other, he is also methodological anti-naturalist in his constant emphasis on the ideal components as being crucial to characterize causality. Methodologically, his philosophical research is more focused on *hypothetical* and *idealized* factors than on factual ones: "the response of Y to a hypothetical idealized experimental manipulation or intervention on X," Woodward (2003a, p. 38). The prescriptions that he seeks as well as the stress that he puts on the ideal components are in tune with the revisionary trait of his philosophical conception (cf. Woodward 2003a, p. 7).

[23] Within the context of the problem of methodological universalism, the different levels of analysis in philosophy of science are studied in Gonzalez (2012).

Thus, the connection between cause and explanation can be found in characterizations of the human undertaking of scientific research as well as in categorizations of the groups of sciences (natural, social, and artificial) and in singular presentations of specific features of a concrete science (such as psychology).

On the other hand, cause and explanation are not *eo ipso* bi-directional or co-implicative concepts, insofar as (i) there are non-causal explanations as well, and (ii) the notions of cause and explanation are "complex and multifaceted," which leads Woodward to the recognition that cause and explanation might not be fully captured by any single approach (cf. Woodward 2003a, p. v). This opens the door to a possible *pluralism* in cause and explanation,[24] where the manipulative or interventionist account of explanation and causation proposed by Woodward might be just *an account* that illuminates an important strand regarding the notions of causation and explanation.

Because Woodward's approach to cause and explanation is primarily epistemological and secondarily methodological, which tries to avoid ontological commitments (see Woodward 2014a), the possible pluralism in cause and explanation could lie in being open to conceptions more favorable to ontological commitments. This pluralism can be thought of mainly in terms of scientific realism rather than in terms of an explicit naturalism.[25] In addition, besides the mostly *structural perspective* on cause and explanation that he defends,[26] there might be elbow room for a dynamic approach that grasps historicity, which could lead to a clear role of cause link to historicity (in science, in groups of sciences, and in particular sciences) [see Gonzalez 2011 and 2013b].

Moreover, his perspective on cause and explanation is mostly structural insofar as Woodward includes a special attention to invariance.[27] Epistemologically, he considers that "the notion of *invariance* is closely related to the notion of an intervention" (Woodward 2003a, p. 15), which is one of the milestones of his approach to causal explanation. Methodologically, he makes explicit that "the notion of invariance-under-interventions is intended to do the work (the work of distinguishing between causal and merely accidental generalizations) that

---

[24] Even though Woodward is very explicit in his defense of an interventionist theory of causation (see Woodward 2003a, p. 93), I think it is not fair to claim that he is "very explicit about his anti-pluralistic stance in this project," De Vreese (2006, p. 6).

[25] In this regard, it is interesting that Woodward accepts a "kind of modest realism about causal and explanatory relationships," cf. Woodward (2003a, pp. 118, 120, and 202).

[26] This is also the case even when he discusses a science such as biology, which has a clear dynamic component. Cf. Woodward (2010). See also Woodward (2001).

[27] Invariance has a full chapter in his book on causal explanation: Woodward (2003a, ch. 6, pp. 239–314). See also Woodward (2000).

is done by the notion of a *law of nature* in other philosophical accounts" (Woodward 2003a, p. 16).²⁸

Contemporary philosophical conceptions on cause and explanation have commonly many nuances. This is the case of Woodward's approach that, when he wrote his book on *Making Things Happen*, makes explicit that "there is less consensus on the topics of explanation and causation in philosophy than there was three or four decades ago" (Woodward 2003a, p. 3). It seems to me that the outpour of papers on explanation and causation of recent decades makes it even harder to have something even close to the consensus obtained by Carl G. Hempel in his times, when the discussion focused on the deductive-nomological model of explanation (see Hempel and Oppenheim 1948, Hempel 1965, and Hempel 1966).

Certainly, the distinction between description and explanation is pervasive in science (cf. Woodward 2003a, p. 5). Moreover, it is needed in natural sciences (e. g., in biology: classificatory activities versus explanations of discoveries), in social sciences (e. g., in economics: description of statistical correlations versus explanations of causal links between events), and in the sciences of the artificial (e. g., in pharmacology: the description of the components of a medicine and the explanation of the causes of the cure of an illness). In this regard, it seems to me very important that psychology should not stop at the level of description of phenomena (including in control observations), because we need to reach the level of explanation in order to get actual science (in the contemporary meaning of the word) [cf. Gonzalez 2013a].

5 From the Types of Scientific Explanation to the Kinds of Causal Explanation

Diversity regarding the types of scientific explanation is central in Ernest Nagel's analysis of this topic. In his influential search for patterns of scientific explanation, he defended that "explanations are answers to the question 'Why?' However, very little reflection is needed to reveal that the word 'why' is not unambiguous and that with varying contexts different sorts of answers are relevant responses to it" (Nagel 1961, pp. 15–16).²⁹ Thus, he distinguished a non-exhaus-

---

28 According to Stathis Psillos "Woodward's notion of 'invariance under interventions' cannot offer an adequate analysis of lawhood, since laws are required to determine what interventions are possible," Psillos (2007, p. 104).
29 In this regard, see also Ruben (1990 and 1993).

tive list of answers that sometimes are called "explanations," which are four types: 1) the deductive model (where the deductive-nomological model is located), 2) probabilistic explanations (which is the place for the inductive-probabilistic type), 3) functional or teleological explanations, and 4) genetic explanations (where Nagel includes "historical inquires") [Nagel 1961, pp. 20–26].

Concerning these scientific explanations pointed out by Nagel, which can be useful to characterize Woodward's position, it seems clear that his approach varies noticeably from one option to another. Thus, he offers a strong criticism of the *deductive-nomological* (DN) model of scientific explanation developed by Hempel. Thus, in *Making Things Happen* Woodward tries to demolish the Hempelian proposal of DN explanations (Woodward 2003a, ch. 4, pp. 152–186; especially pp. 184–186). In this regard, although he sees some ideas of DN model (regarding objectivity, a unified treatment of explanations, and the interest in fitting with science), and considers they might be acceptable (Woodward 2003a, pp. 184–186), but stresses that they require a different framework: an interventionist causal explanation perspective instead of a "nomic expectability" in the coordinates of logical empiricism.

Meanwhile, concerning the *inductive-probabilistic* explanations, it is easy to see that Woodward also is very critical of Hempel's ideas of an "inductive-statistical" (IS) model of scientific explanation (or IS explanation). He grasps a common ground between the DN model and the IS model, and he explicitly criticizes the goal or rationale of the DN model and the IS model of scientific explanation. He considers that

> explanation is not even in part a matter of showing that an explanandum is nomically expectable, and the DN/IS models do not even state necessary conditions for successful explanation (Woodward 2003a, p. 155).

However, Woodward considers the relations between causes and probabilities within his interventionist framework of causal explanations (Woodward 2003a, pp. 52, 61–65, 88, *et passim*).

Even though Woodward considers probabilities and causes, it seems that he is commonly working on functional explanations or, at least, he works on a "functional" account of causation and explanation. Indeed, Woodward recognizes that he offers a "functional" account of causation and explanation,

> meaning by that term an account that focuses on the functions or goals of causal reasoning in order to understand causal notions. But this enterprise is different from offering an account of "functional explanations" in the sense in which that notion is used by [C. G.] Hempel, [E.] Nagel and others – functional explanations in this sense are thought to be expla-

nations with a distinctive structure that appeal to goals, teleology or functions possessed by some system.[30]

Causal explanations are then *functional explanations* for Woodward insofar as there are functions or goals in order to grasp the causal notions at stake. In this regard, his causal explanations take into account usefulness, because he thinks that usefulness is the standard that matters, rather than other kinds of criteria (either metaphysical or intuitive) [Woodward 2014a, pp. 691–713]. Thus, when he conceives the functional approach "in terms of the goals and purposes of causal thinking" (Woodward 2014a, p. 691), he is in tune with an *epistemic engineering*. This view is clearly different from the discussion around causality and teleology between Georg Henrik von Wright and Raimo Tuomela (see Gonzalez 2003, pp. 33–50; especially pp. 37–40).

Epistemic engineering involves thinking of causal cognition in functional terms. By "functional approach" to causation Woodward means

> an approach that takes as its point of departure the idea that causal information and reasoning are sometimes useful or functional in the sense of serving various goals and purposes we have. It then proceeds by trying to understand and evaluate various forms of causal cognition in terms of how well they conduce to the achievement of these purposes. Causal cognition is thus seen as a kind of epistemic technology – as a tool – and, like other technologies, judged in terms of how well it serves our goals and purposes (Woodward 2014a, pp. 693–694).

As for genetic explanations or a historical type of scientific explanation – especially after his defense of the epistemic engineering – it seems recognizable that these are not his focus of attention. Even though he mentions "causal history" (cf. Woodward 2003a, pp. 124, 127, 135), he is not usually thinking of it in terms of historicity but rather in terms of processes that can evolve. His focus of attention is regularly on invariance and invariant elements rather than factors that can change according to historicity in the *changes themselves* ("internal historicity") and in the *contexts* around those changes ("external historicity"). But both aspects of historicity are needed when we want to understand causal processes in events studied by social sciences and in research in the sciences of the artificial.

---

30 Woodward, J., *Personal communication*, 13.10.2015. For Nagel, "in many functional explanations there is an explicit reference to some still future state or event, in terms of which the existence of a thing or the occurrence of an act is made intelligible" (1961, p. 24).

Furthermore, besides the types of scientific explanations (such as deductive-nomological, inductive-probabilistic, functional or teleological, and genetic or historical, which Nagel thought of as possible ways to answer the question *why?* non-exhaustively), there are at least two kinds of scientific explanations: causal and non-causal. This is a distinction that is commonly assumed, and it was explicitly worked out by Wesley Salmon.[31] In this regard, following a functional type of explanation in the specific sense pointed out, Woodward is undoubtedly committed to causal explanations. Within this kind of explanation, he distinguishes between "total cause," "contributing cause," and "direct cause" (see Woodward 2003a, pp. 45–61; especially pp. 50–51, and 55).

Consequently, it seems clear that not every scientific explanation needs to be causal, and Woodward emphasizes that there are nuances in causality when dealing with the possible or actual effects and the way to obtain them. In addition, he pays attention to two relevant groups: a) explanations about "type-causation" (Woodward 2003a, p. 40) and b) explanations regarding cases ("singular causal explanation") [Woodward (2003a, pp. 209–220)]. Furthermore, he accepts a pragmatics of explanation in connection with the responses given to *w-questions* (*what-if-things-had-been-different-questions*):

> different choices of variables for theorizing are associated with different ways of carving up nature into possible alternatives, answers to different *w-questions*, and hence different explanations (Woodward 2003a, p. 233).

What I think is important concerning the *theoretical framework* for causal explanations is another epistemological and methodological difference, because there are *models* that belong to two main groups: descriptive and prescriptive. (i) Causality in descriptive models seek to reflect the empirical experience in everyday life (such as fire and smoke) and evidence in scientific research (such as a certain virus and a given disease). (ii) Causality within prescriptive models are causal explanations regarding what people, in general, and scientists, in particular, ought to do given some circumstances (e.g., regarding climate change, in the outbreak of a disease that might originate a widespread contagion or in the case of a predicted flood).

To the first group belongs the kind of empirical studies – in natural sciences, social sciences, and sciences of the artificial – where there is observation or experimentation in order to get a causal relation[32] (e.g., in the appropriate con-

---

[31] Wesley Salmon studied the difference between them, and he offered features of the non-causal explanation, cf. Salmon (2002a).
[32] On the different kinds of observations and experiments in science, see Gonzalez (2010).

sumption of natural resources and the ecosystem, in the decision-making of adults for financial investments, or in the effect of wind for accuracy in ballistics). The second group also appears in Woodward's reflection, but it does so under the label of "normative." For him, it is "normative in the sense that the theories in question purport to explain how people ought to learn, reason, and judge regarding causal relationships" (Woodward 2012, p. 961).[33]

But the term "normative," if its sense and reference are understood properly, involves "norms" or rules that, in principle, are compulsory or should be implemented in some given circumstances (such as traffic rules or not smoking in public buildings). Meanwhile, "prescriptive" is a broader term, which is related to recommendations, suggestions or indications that are open to variations and alternatives, according to the circumstances (such as a medical prescription that can be reduced as soon as there is some specific variation or there is a better alternative available for the patient).

Applied science is commonly in the sphere of prescriptions,[34] where "prescription" is understood in the sense of patterns of action to solve specific problems.[35] It is less frequent that applied science can be linked to *norms* (as in technology, where the processes have elbow room for variation once the objectives are well defined and the expected products – the artifacts – have a clear task and an expected price). Moreover, many of the problems of the application of science come from the possibility of alternatives in applied science. This can be seen in medicine, where physicians commonly make an application of scientific knowledge in cases where one or more alternatives are available according to this applied science.[36]

---

[33] Regarding this second group, Woodward maintains two things: a) he considers that we can propose models on how people *ought to learn and reason causally*; and b) the "normative models" often turn out to be descriptively useful (Woodward, J., *Personal communication*, 13.10. 2015).

[34] This can be seen in Herbert Simon's approach to applied science (cf. Simon 1990 and Gonzalez 1998b). See also Simon (2001).

[35] This use of "prescription" is different from the "normative" dimension of rationality – mainly, cognitive or epistemic rationality – which considers how *one ought to reason* (e. g., on causality). Certainly, when basic science gives explanations and predictions it goes beyond pure description. In this regard, the answers to the question why and the anticipation of the possible future require one to consider how one can give a reasonable explanation and grounded rational prediction instead of merely reflecting what has already been done. Meanwhile applied science includes predictions and prescriptions, where the former gives information about the future that can be used as a guide for the *patterns of action* of the latter.

[36] Applied economics and the application of economics represent two relevant examples of the prescriptive character rather than the normative status (cf. Gonzalez 2015a, ch. 11, pp. 317–341).

6 Varieties of Causality in Contemporary Philosophy of Science

For the contemporary analysis of causality, the main sources of reflection are scientific research and philosophical reflection.[37] To the first group belong conceptions of causality inspired by physics (such as Wesley Salmon's approach [Salmon 1971, 1984, 1990, 1998], which has direct repercussions in the work on social sciences developed by Merrilee Salmon [Salmon and Salmon 1979], and in the general approach due to Philip Dowe [2000]), by social sciences (such as Herbert Simon's perspective [Simon 1952 and 1955],[38] which was originally thinking of economics, and critically commented by Nicholas Rescher),[39] by statistics, econometrics, and computer sciences (Judea Pearl),[40] etc. Unquestionably, the list of contemporary options of this group can be enlarged (David Lewis, Patrick Suppes, Clark Glymour, Huw Price, Peter Menzies, etc.). Also their conceptions can be seen from a different angle, i.e., through the characteristic feature considered in thematic terms.

Henk W. de Regt has followed this line for some of these views with a simple example: someone hits a piano key and, usually, a sound is heard.

> While it may seem obvious that hitting the key (H) causes the sound (S), there is disagreement among philosophers about the content of this claim. [1] On the so-called regularly theory of causation, ascribed to Hume and espoused by empiricists such as Carnap and Quine, 'H causes S' merely asserts the regular succession of hitting piano keys and hearing sounds. [2] On Salmon's and Dowe's process theory, by contrast, 'H causes S' implies the existence of particular processes and interactions [...]. [3] On Lewis's counterfactual theory, causal claims reflect counterfactual dependencies: 'H causes S' means that there is a chain of counterfactually dependent events between H and S (if the key had not been hit, or the hammer had not been set into motion, etc., no sound would have resulted). [4] On the so-called agency theory of causation, defended by von Wright and more recently by Menzies and Price, 'H causes S' means that a free agent can bring about a musical sound by hitting the piano key. All these views reflect particular intuitions one might have with respect to causation (de Regt 2004, numbers added).

---

37 There are other sources of reflection such as technological innovation or the problems related to law and decision-making.
38 Thereafter, he published several papers on causality, where he returned to his interest for econometrics, see Iwasaki and Simon (1988).
39 Simon's conception was initially criticized by Nicholas Rescher (1953) and, thereafter, they reached a common ground on the topic (Simon and Rescher 1966).
40 On Judea Pearl's approach, see a detailed analysis of his book on *Causality*, published in 2000, in Woodward (2003b).

Unquestionably, to the second group of the contemporary reflection on causality belong the reflections made on "classical" philosophical problems, which have been renewed through philosophy of language and philosophy of mind. Among the exponents of this group is Michael Dummett, who has considered "backward causation."[41] In this regard, he points out: "the question remains whether, given that *in general* causality works in the earlier-to-later direction, we could not recognize a few exceptions to this general rule. If we find certain phenomena which can apparently be explained only by reference to later events, can we not admit that in these few cases we have events whose causes are subsequent to them in time? I think it is clear that we cannot" (Dummett [1954] 1978, p. 322).

If we do not think of "bringing about the past" but rather of the *relevance of the knowledge of the future* for the present, then there are interesting features concerning the relations between causality and prediction. Thus, the prediction about a future event can have a *causal relevance* on the present. This makes sense in a number of cases of ordinary life as well as in scientific contexts. It seems to me that Hurricane Katrina offers a clear example. In August 2005, the meteorologists predicted several days in advance that Hurricane Katrina was to hit the area of New Orleans severely. The American media – in particular, I recall ABC news – made it clear in the previous days that a substantial part of New Orleans would be flooded. The local authorities as well as the state of Louisiana urged the citizens to leave the city, which many did (because they were well aware of the damage that a hurricane can cause to the system of protection of the areas of New Orleans below sea level).

Even though this is not a case of "backward causation," insofar as the prediction occurs in time t and causes people to leave their homes at some time later, t+,[42] there is a *causal relevance* in the prediction made about the hurricane,[43] because once the prediction is known, people take action to save their lives or to avoid real physical damage. Thus, an anticipated phenomenon based on a reliable prediction originates a process of decision-making to leave one's house. In this regard, something that does not yet exist as such – a future event – is relevant for a collective action with a clear intentionality (e. g., to obtain a personal and familiar good).

Put differently, the *publication of the prediction* about the future, which leads to making decisions, seems to fit the core of the notion of causation: the depend-

---

41 His proposal can be found in Dummett (1954 and 1964).
42 Woodward, J., *Personal communication*, 13.10.2015.
43 It is a *causal relevance* rather than a *causal content* because the prediction made does not include an explicit causal claim.

ence between an event X and what generates or brings about Y (i.e., someone or something that makes it possible or changes some aspect[s] of its reality), given certain conditions and circumstances.[44] Moreover, the criteria based on counterfactuals can also be fulfilled with the publication of the prediction about the future: the effect (the social mobilization of the citizens of New Orleans) would not appear, or would be of different kind, without knowledge of the possible future and its consequences (the expected hurricane and its status as particularly dangerous).

Nevertheless, besides the causal relevance of prediction pointed out here, there is another relation between causation and prediction, which goes in the other direction. It is the use of causal relationships as a *support* for reliable predictions. This happens in natural sciences (physics, chemistry or biology offer many examples), but also in social sciences (demography) and sciences of the artificial (pharmacology). The existence of a known causal relationship between two natural phenomena or between two social or artificial events gives elements of stability or regularity (which Woodward commonly associates with invariance) in order to make a scientific prediction, which in principle increases the level of precision and accuracy of the prediction.[45]

Altogether, there are at least three aspects to consider in the interrelation between causality and prediction: a) the causal role of prediction (epistemological and ontological), b) the route from causation to prediction (epistemological and methodological), and c) the path from prediction to causation (methodological). In this regard, it happens in some disciplines that predictions made with accuracy are interpreted as criteria to validate causal inferences. Thus, there is a longstanding commitment in econometrics to validating causal inference through its predictive accuracy (which is related to Clive Granger's vision of causality).[46] In this regard, there is an analysis of causal inference from several disciplines made by M. E. Sobel (1995). However, the quality of prediction (of new data) is not the only means of testing a hypothesis, because a key question is also the appropriateness of the testing means to the terms and conditions of the hypothesis (see Gonzalez 2015a, p. 17, n. 35).

---

[44] It is interesting that Woodward accepts that "inferences from effect to cause are often more reliable than inferences from cause to effect," Woodward (2003a, p. 31).

[45] The present debate on the climate change and the reliability of the predictions made by the IPCC is related to this issue of when the relation is *causal* and when there is only a *correlation* between some factors without a causal linkage.

[46] On Granger's approach to causality, see Granger (2007). See also his important paper Granger (1969).

Scientific prediction can relate to causality in various ways: (i) knowledge of the possible future can bring about actions (an effect that can be total and direct) due to its causal component; (ii) the knowledge based on causal relationships can give good support for reliable predictions, which is particularly useful in some sciences, such as economics; and (iii) the knowledge regarding the success of some predictions can be used as a criteria for establishing causal relationships.[47] The existence of these possibilities makes it more difficult to accept that

> a concern with prediction doesn't explain why we make the distinctions we do between causal and noncausal relationships (Woodward 2003a, p. 31).

Underneath this claim – in connection to Woodward's constant association between causation and explanation – might be seen an implicit acceptance of the *asymmetry* – logical and methodological – between the scientific task of explaining and the scientific endeavor of predicting.[48] Constantly, his focus of attention is on explanation, and he seems to overlook the relevance of the relations between causation and prediction.[49] Even though he accepts a connection between both, insofar as causal claims can involve predictions regarding the outcomes of interventions,[50] this connection in his approach might often be understood as predictions in terms of "testable implications" involved in causal inferences rather than as genuine predictions of the future supported by causal claims.[51]

Predicting the future – with the epistemological, ontological and heuristic dimensions – is particularly important for science. In this regard, the relations

---

[47] On the issue of causality and its relation to scientific prediction, see Gonzalez (2015a, pp. 17n, 50, 64, 125, 128, 133, 135–138, 143–144, 276, 302).

[48] The logical asymmetry between explanation and prediction is connected with epistemological-methodological aspects of a science, either natural or social (or artificial). Nicholas Rescher sees this issue in the following way: "in adequate explanatory arguments the premises must support the conclusion firmly – if not with decisive certainty, then with very high probability – whereas with cogent predictive arguments we often do (and are entitled to) settle for much lower degrees of probability. For a perfectly cogent prediction can rest on considerations to the effect that the predicted outcome is substantially more likely than any other possibility within the pertinent range of alternatives. Thus between prediction and explanation there is not just a temporal difference but also a significant epistemic difference in the degree to which the causal linkage at issue must be evidentiated," Rescher (1998, p. 166).

[49] "Prediction" has not an entry in the subject index of the book by Woodward (2003a), and its presence in the volume is completely secondary.

[50] Woodward, J., *Personal communication*, 13.10.2015.

[51] See, for example, Woodward (2003a, p. 319). On the distinction between testable implications and predictions of the future, see Gonzalez (2015a, pp. 15n, 54, 107, 140, 157, 159, 205, 217–218, and 337).

between causation and prediction, which include the three ways indicated above on scientific prediction in its relations to causality, have consequences for basic science, applied science, and the application of science. They can occur when we are dealing with economic theory, applied economics, and the application of economics in different contexts.

Noticeably, in his approach on prediction and causality, Woodward stresses that a predictive relation between X and Y is not sufficient for X to cause Y:

> one can have information that is relevant to prediction (including prediction based on generalizations that many philosophers are prepared to regard as laws), or information about spatio-temporally continuous processes, or information that allows for the sort of unification and systematization that many philosophers have thought relevant to explanation, and yet lack the kind of information that is relevant to manipulation on which my account focuses (Woodward 2003a, p. 10).

Usually, in one way or another, the diverse conceptions of causal explanation deal with *generic patterns* of a phenomenon (in type-explanations) and with *specific episodes* of an event (in singular causal explanations). But Woodward recognizes that, in the second case, his approach has limitations:

> my intent is to show that the interventionist framework can be used to capture judgments about token causation in an interesting range of cases, but I make no claim to have provided an exhaustive treatment of all possible cases (Woodward 2003a, p. 75).

7 A Manipulative or Interventionist Approach

The motley variety of conceptions on causality and causal explanation mentioned in the first group, where Woodward is very relevant, commonly follow the route from science to philosophy and back again. Frequently, these conceptions think of scientific contributions in terms of inspiration, analysis, interpretation, and application. Regarding these conceptions it is possible to distinguish two main lines of thought: 1) *Causal monism*, where there is just one axis for causality, a criterion which is either determinist or probabilistic (usually based on deduction or supported by induction); and 2) *causal pluralism*, where there might be more options than an overall concept of causation and more possibilities on how to characterize the relations between causation and causal explanations.[52]

---

52 This option of causal pluralism assumes the existence of limits, i.e., there is no universal or

De facto, causal pluralism can be considered in different directions. First, it can be studied in the features of how the concept of "causation" is thought of in itself (epistemologically, ontologically, etc.) and in its relations with the notions of "condition" and "occasion."[53] Second, it can be contemplated in the types of causal explanations to deal with the diverse aspects of reality (natural, social or artificial), due to the differences in the aims, processes, and results of scientific research in each realm of reality.[54] Third, it can take into account the possibility of combinations of causes due to the complexity, either structural or dynamic, of the phenomena or events studied.[55] Thus, among these options is the defense of a main route on causation and causal explanation (e.g., interventionist or manipulationist, counterfactual, etc.), and being open to the possibility of additional axes for causality in order to fit with the structure and dynamics of the real world.

Explicitly, within his interventionist theory, Woodward is in favor of a broad notion of causal explanation, where "any explanation that proceeds by showing how an outcome depends (where the dependence in question is not logical or conceptual) on other variables or factors that counts as causal" (Woodward 2003a, p. 6). Thus, in order to avoid circularity (causal explanation includes what counts as causal), he points out that causal explanations "furnish information that is potentially relevant to manipulation and control" (Woodward 2003a, p. 6).

Prima facie, the criterion of manipulation or intervention fits better with the explanations in the social sciences than Wesley Salmon's idea of contact understood in a physical way (Salmon 2002a and b), but we know that Woodward does not see a distinctive goal or rationale for causal inquiry based on prediction (Woodward 2003a, p. 31), which is a limitation for social sciences that are developed as applied sciences (such as economics). Meanwhile "control" can include features quite independent of causal explanations, for example, when control is used in applied science (in connection with predictions and prescriptions) and in the application of science.

---

overriding criterion either in causation or in causal explanations. On the limits of science as frontiers and confines, see Gonzalez (2016).

53 One of the possibilities is to find differences between causality in natural phenomena and in human events.

54 In a scientific sphere like psychology, we can think of differences in the causal explanations in the cases of psychobiology and social psychology.

55 The existence of complexity is one of the main difficulties for a methodological universalism in science, cf. Gonzalez (2012).

Intervention is probably the touchstone of Woodward's approach to causation, especially as invariance-under-interventions. He makes it explicit that the notion of intervention in his characterization

> represents a regulative ideal. Its function is to characterize the notion of an ideal experimental manipulation and in this way to give us a purchase on what we mean or are trying to establish when we claim that X causes Y. We have already noted that for that purpose, it isn't necessary that an intervention actually be carried out on X. All that is required is that we have some sort of basis for assessing the truth of claims about what would happen if an intervention *were* carried out (Woodward 2003a, p. 130).

Ideal rather than actual is then the relevant feature of intervention in Woodward's approach to causal explanation, which accompanies his insistence regarding counterfactuals "that have to do with the outcomes of hypothetical interventions" (Woodward 2003a, p. 122, see also p. 132). But the emphasis on the ideal entails dealing with some philosophical issues, especially because he considers that "the notion of an intervention is already a causal notion" (Woodward 2003a, p. 104). However, it seems that

> causation has excess content over invariance-under-interventions. So there is more to causation – *qua* an intrinsic relation – than invariance-under-actual-and-counterfactual-interventions (Psillos 2007, p. 94).

(i) Epistemologically, he allows hypothetical interventions which could never occur in practice. In this regard, it seems more reasonable to limit interventions to such as might not have actually occurred in practice, but which certainly could have occurred in practice. This involves linking the concept of "causality" closely to what is *practically possible*.[56] (ii) Methodologically, the route chosen by Woodward involves an anti-naturalist path in a naturalist approach. The path is *anti-naturalist* insofar as it is precisely the *ideal* that can lead us to what causality actually is. This is not inconsistent if it is done, for example, in a similar form to Peter Strawson's, which proposes a constructive use of imagination. This involves imagining things differently from what they actually are (e.g., a world of sounds) as a way to understand better by contrast our real world (e.g., spatio-temporal) and our actual conceptual scheme.[57]

---

[56] I owe this idea to Donald Gillies. Cf. Gillies, D., *Personal communication*, 1.8.2014.

[57] This revisionary part of Strawson's approach is understood as a way of thinking of an alternative conceptual structure which, nevertheless, can shed light on our actual conceptual scheme, cf. Strawson (1959, pp. 117–134). On his characterization of human knowledge, see Gonzalez (1998a).

8 Causality at Three Levels of Scientific Research

Causality can be considered in science within a wider philosophico-methodological framework than causal explanation, because its task is not confined to the sphere of basic science or to some applications of science. Thus, causality can have a role at the three main levels of scientific activity: 1) basic science (explanation and prediction), 2) applied science (prediction and prescription), and 3) application of science (the use of scientific knowledge within the variable contexts).[58]

These levels characterize the orientation or style of *doing research* instead of being degrees or scales of science. This includes that the research does not necessarily follow a line that starts with basic science and ends up in the application of science. Most philosophers of science – Woodward included – have been centered on basic science (with special attention to theories from physics and biology); occasionally they have dealt with applied science (a tendency that is changing in recent times); and sometimes they have made deep analyses of the application of science (the most visible facet for society).[59]

a) In basic science, the aims, processes, and results of the research activity seeks to extend human knowledge to grasp a widening domain of reality as well as a more intense level of conceptualization of the world. b) In applied science, the focus is on the resolution of specific problems related to a practical domain (see Niiniluoto 1994 and 1995), which might be in the natural world, the social environment, or the artificial sphere. c) This applied knowledge is different from the actual *application of knowledge* (cf. Niiniluoto 1993, pp. 1–21; especially, pp. 9 and 19), which is the use made by the agents of applied knowledge within a diversity of settings and circumstances.[60] At each level we can see causality with a role, which is relevant for scientific research, in general, and for psychological research, in particular.

---

[58] On the features that are characteristic of these three levels, see Gonzalez (2013a, pp. 11–40; especially, pp. 17–19). On Woodward's views on basic science and applied science, see Woodward (2003a, pp. 11–12).

[59] When they do, it is mostly in the context of science, technology, and society, which is commonly driven by philosophers of technology rather than by philosophers of science. See Gonzalez (2005 and 2015b).

[60] Scientific creativity is then crucial for technological innovations. In this regard, "the returns to the application of scientific knowledge to invention might vary across technological fields," Fleming and Sorenson (2004, p. 926).

First, causality often has a role in basic science, which aims – among other things – to increase our scientific knowledge or to fill lacunas in our knowledge of nature, society, or the artificial world. The existence of causal explanations is the area of basic science constantly emphasized by Woodward. But causality also has a relation to *scientific predictions*. *De facto*, scientists use causes to anticipate possible futures. Moreover, causation is commonly seen as a key factor for the prediction of phenomena that we actually cannot control, such as the trajectory of a meteorite near a planet, the social consequences of the meteorological event "el Niño," or the obsolescence of some materials and the lifetime of radioactive products.[61]

Looking at the field of psychology as basic science, we can find causal relationships in psychological explanations as well as in psychological predictions. The first case has been a central issue in Woodward's research, in order to characterize his interventionist conception of causality as well as to validate it empirically (cf. Woodward 2007b and 2012). Meanwhile the second case can be found in the psychological studies connected to economic behavior. In this regard, particularly interesting is the context of bounded rationality of human agents, where the research is made on decisions concerning ordinary things (such as buying and selling).[62]

Second, causality also has a role in applied science, where the aim is to solve concrete problems in a finite number of steps (cf. Niiniluoto 1993 and 1994). Thus, causality can be connected to *predictions* of a possible future (in climate change, in business cycles or in new medicines needed for rare diseases), which are the contents of influence in *prescriptions* (i.e., the pattern for solving specific problems in a given milieu). This can be seen in sciences like economics, which needs predictions as a previous stage to state the prescriptions that can solve the specific problem [see Gonzalez 1998b] (such as inflation, unemployment, public deficit, etc.). In this regard, economics is a quite interesting case, because it is a social science (and can be related to psychology in terms of rationality) as well as a science of the artificial (cf. Gonzalez 2008).

Besides the role of causality for scientific prediction in the case of applied science, it seems clear that the prescription of what ought to be done commonly requires the acceptance of causality insofar as it is recognized as instrumental

---

[61] It can also be maintained that prediction is related to mathematics, insofar as this formal science is a human activity, cf. Gonzalez (1996). In this regard, the role of causality might be in the human process of learning mathematics in order to do calculations.
[62] See, in this regard, the works of Daniel Kahneman, based on empirical studies related to decision-making: Kahneman and Tversky (1973), Kahneman and Snell (1990), and Kahneman (2003).

rationality (the efficacy and the efficiency in the relation between means and ends). This presence of causality for prescription can be seen in the ongoing discussions on what should be done about climate change (in order to stop or reduce the predicted warmer climate that can damage the coasts of many countries), about the solution of the ongoing economic crisis in the European Union (which started around 2007) and about the regulation of radio-electric space after the extraordinary development of all kinds of artifacts related with waves (smart phones, electronic tablets, etc.).

Third, causality has a role in the area of *application* of science. It seems clear that, in many relevant cases, the use of scientific knowledge by agents in given conditions and circumstances is made under the assumption of a relation between causes and effects (as well as an instrumental rationality, where the means should eventually achieve some ends). The application of dispositions approved by international panels of climate change, the recommendations made by the World Health Organization regarding pandemics or the criteria approved by international institutions to regulate financial markets are commonly made based on the acceptance of causality.[63]

Pertaining to psychology, we can think of psychological therapy, which ought to be the application of the scientific knowledge available to a specific person or a given group, taking into account their circumstances. Psychological therapy assumes some version of causality, insofar as the means – medicines, conversations, changes in the patterns of behavior, etc. – should lead to a better situation than in the previous stages of a specific person or a given group. In the psychological therapy, such recommended means are conceived with a causal influence in the state of affairs (private or public) of the individual or the members of a group, which is able to give us the expected effects.

9 Causality in Psychology and Human Affairs

When causality looks at psychology, which is a discipline that Woodward has considered predominantly in two spheres (folk psychology and scientific psychology, with special interest in experiments),[64] two main directions appear: de-

---

[63] The variety of measurements the international institutions (IMF, ECB, UE, etc.) have taken since the beginning of the economic crises in order to fix it have in common the acceptance of some kind of causal relationships instead of a mere correlation of variables. The results of the application of each measure proposed are used, *de facto*, as the main criterion to evaluate the actual or presumptive character of such causal relationship.

[64] On his views on experiments, see Woodward (2014b).

scriptive and prescriptive, which he calls "normative." On the one hand, the descriptive research tries to offer,

> as a matter of empirical fact, how various populations (adult humans, human children of various ages, non-human animals) learn and (where appropriate) reason about and judge with respect to causal relationships (Woodward 2018a, p. 74 in this volume).

On the other hand, the prescriptive ("normative") research

> purports [to] say how we *ought* to learn and reason about a causal relationship and make causal judgments. This normative focus is perhaps most obvious in the case of theories of causal learning and inference from various sorts of data that have been developed in statistics and machine learning (Woodward 2018a, p. 71).[65]

Descriptions of causal relationships are made in the work conducted by psychologists, but Woodward also stresses that

> important portions of it can also be found in the literature on animal learning, comparative animal cognition, and, in some cases, in disciplines like anthropology (Woodward 2018a, p. 74).

Meanwhile, prescriptions on causal relations appear in theories that make proposals regarding which inferences to causal conclusions are justified (i.e., which inferences can lead reliably to the achievement of some epistemic goal such as truth). In this group, Woodward places approaches based on structural equations modeling, the ideas about causal reasoning developed by Pearl, the Bayesian treatments of causal inference, and other proposals about causal inference based on machine learning ideas (Woodward 2018a, pp. 71–72).

Psychological events related to causal relations can be analyzed by philosophy of science in terms of what they *are* and what they *ought to be*. This requires taking into account some historical aspects. Initially, psychology was heavily influenced by philosophy. In this "rational psychology," where there is a kind of universal *homo psychologicus*, the main link of causality was with mind and will of the individual, following a decision-making.[66] Thereafter, "empirical psychology" was developed, rooted in the observation of processes (ordinary or not)

---

[65] On the role of the normative theory, see Woodward (2018b).
[66] This configuration is also available in some contemporary approaches that are keen on a universal rationality, such as in one of the periods of Herbert Simon's approach (cf. Dasgupta 2003). It is also assumed in conceptions of philosophy of mind and psychological philosophy based on Wittgensteinian ideas (cf. Kenny 1979).

of individuals and groups.[67] Finally, "experimental psychology" was systematically acquired in laboratories, where a milestone was the work of Wilhem Wundt in Leipzig, which opened the door to a large number of contributions.

Nevertheless, for many years, psychology has struggled to configure its scientific status.[68] In this regard, since the second half of the nineteenth century, a number of conceptions (such as *Gestaltpsychologie*, psychoanalysis, behaviorism, cognitive psychology, etc.) have offered different theoretical foundations and practical solutions (which are often labeled as "paradigms," "research programs," etc.) for the problems addressed in psychology. Certainly, the psychological theories that Woodward considers are related to the present status of psychology (mainly in the United States and the Western countries), where conceptions such as *Gestaltpsychologie*, psychoanalysis, or behaviorism are seen as old psychological theories[69] (and in cases such as Sigmund Freud's approach as a lack of evidential support).[70]

Undoubtedly, Woodward is keen on folk psychology (cf. Horgan and Woodward 1985), which fits quite well with his epistemological naturalism. Folk psychology was also in the philosophy of psychology developed by Ludwig Wittgenstein (1982). But the difference is in the approach: Woodward assumes *de facto* an epistemological and methodological continuity between folk psychology and scientific psychology, where the observation and experimental methods of the latter can be used to revise the validity of the contents of the former. Wittgenstein, meanwhile, is focused on the language of action as a way of clarifying the psychological concepts (cognitive, volitional, and affective) connected to human actions (and not merely to observable behavior) [cf. Wittgenstein 1980a and 1980b], where mental acts (such as intentions) can have a role.

Following an emphasis on the psychological theories accepted nowadays (mainly in the United States), Woodward sees neuroscience as a key to explain psychological events, including concepts. Thus, neural mechanisms are central for the formation of concepts such as causality, which cannot be conceived

---

67 Even now present psychology linked to education relies to a large extent on control observations.
68 Even now, there are strong methodological approaches in quite different directions. One direction leads to seeing psychology as a natural science, where neuroscience can hold the key for central psychological issues (Thagard 2007). Meanwhile, a second direction stresses the character of psychology as a social science. Thus, it assumes the features of intentionality and social environment. Therefore, the conflicts of personality, family relations, social behavior, etc., require concepts that include understanding, interpretation, and application.
69 On his views on behaviorism, see Woodward (2003a, p. 34).
70 In this criticism Adolf Grünbaum has played an important role (cf. Grünbaum 1984).

just in terms of pure experience (see Woodward 2003a, p. 126). In this regard, if we consider his approach to psychology as a science, which gives a special relevance to neuroscience and to the continuity between humans and nonhuman animals, and we see it within the methodological framework of the controversy between *Erklären* and *Verstehen*,[71] then it seems clear that Woodward's position is closer to the former (explanation) than to the latter (understanding).

Human affairs can have causal explanations, but – in his approach – these explanations should avoid anthropomorphic elements regarding interventions.[72] Thus, causal processes that produce changes can be explained without the involvement of human actions that can qualify as "interventions" (Woodward 2003a, p. 127). Furthermore, in his view, in human affairs we should distance ourselves from the emphasis on singularity to find causality. Instead, he proposes that we should rather look at the kind of explanations that are open to *generalizations*. In this regard, he goes against philosophers influenced by the late Wittgenstein, such as Elisabeth Anscombe (1971),[73] insofar as Woodward maintains that "token or singular causal claims always should be understood as committing us to the truth of some type-level causal generalization" (Woodward 2003a, p. 72).

10 Advancements and More Pluralism

Looking back, there are advancements with his important contribution:[74] Woodward has built up a theory of causal explanation and has connected it with issues related to philosophy of psychology. Although there are previous conceptions of an interventionist perspective on causal relationships, his vision is different and original. Overall, I see the main strength of his approach in the criticism of other theories of scientific explanation, such as those related to

---

71 On the debate *Erklären* and *Verstehen* and the relations between causal explanations and teleological explanations, see Gonzalez (2003, pp. 34–40). On the repercussion for the methodology of scientific predictions, see Gonzalez (2015a, pp. 129–138).
72 In the more precise characterization of his interventionist view there are not anthropomorphic elements, cf. Woodward (2003a, p. 98). In addition, he maintains that "the important and philosophically neglected category of 'natural experiments' typically involves the occurrence of processes in nature that have the characteristics of an intervention but do not involve human action or at least are not brought about by deliberate human design," Woodward (2003c, p. 94).
73 On the same topic, see von Wright (1974).
74 Among these advancements is that he "shows that not all causal explanations should take the form of deductive (or inductive) arguments," Psillos (2007, p. 94).

well-known philosophers related to the analytic tradition: Hempel, Salmon, Lewis, Kitcher, etc.

But Woodward's positive alternative to them, insofar as it involves a special insistence on hypothetical experiments and ideal components, seems to me less persuasive for a characterization of causality, in general, and causal explanations, in particular. In this regard, Sthatis Psillos thinks that

> Woodward's theory highlights and exploits the symptoms of a good causal explanation, without offering a fully-fledged theory of what causal explanation consist in. Invariance-under-interventions is a symptom of causal relations and laws. It is not what causation or lawhood consist in (Psillos 2007, p. 106).

Of the four famous types of scientific explanation distinguished by Nagel, Woodward's rejection of the deductive-nomological model, the criticism of some inductive-probabilistic models, the explicit acceptance of a specific version of the functional conception, and the overlooking of the genetic type of explanation (especially if it is understood in terms of a historical model) are all clear. In my judgment, he is right when he inclines to accept pluralism on scientific explanation, but this requires being more open to explanations specific to the social sciences. Thus, although he recognizes explanations other than functional,[75] it seems to me that that he puts excessive emphasis on the functional account of causation (see Woodward 2014a). In addition, he should extend the scope of causal explanations beyond stable structures (which are the focus of his interventionist counterfactuals).

Pluralism seems to me necessary in scientific explanation in order to fit what science actually *is* and to consider what it *ought to be* to develop it more now and in the oncoming future. I think that more pluralism is required than a structural functionalist analysis can offer in this regard. Thus, besides explanations conceived in structural terms – where a key role is invariance – we need explanations able to grasp *dynamic* terms. This includes explanations where historicity can have a central role in order to be able to explain deep changes in history of science – in the kind of research made and in the criteria used for evaluation and acceptance of theories – as well as in the social, cultural, economic, and political events commonly considered "revolutionary" (which are studied by the social sciences and, in some cases, by the sciences of the artificial).

---

[75] Woodward, J., *Personal communication*, 13.10.2015.

Causal explanations need to deal with historicity of phenomena and events instead of only being focused on processes and evolution.[76] Many human and social affairs – including psychological events that happen daily to individuals, groups, and societies – cannot be explained without the notion of "historicity."[77] Many decisions are usually made thinking of historical changes, with the wish to change personal lives, group dynamics, and the current course of affairs of a whole country.[78] Social life is made up of complex systems, which are commonly open, that are interconnected in dynamic terms. A causal relationship is frequently involved in the changes made in such systems, either thinking of the past or looking for a better future, which requires a scientific explanation conceived in historical terms (and not merely in genetic terms).

An objective theory of causation seems to me particularly important, and Woodward has worked very hard in this sense. But we need a theory of causation able to grasp the *diversity* of features of causality in natural sciences, social sciences, and sciences of the artificial. This means a theory of causation with a structural dimension and a dynamic perspective, which cannot be reducible to just one version of the main types of explanations pointed out by Nagel. Such a theory should take into account the features of the basic science, applied science, and application of science. In that theory, besides the issues of causality related to scientific explanations, the problems regarding causation and prediction should be addressed. These aspects are relevant for psychology as a basic science (e.g., in psychobiology), as an applied science (e.g., in the context of psycho-pedagogy), and for the applications of this science (by the psychologist use of the therapies according to the needs of the patients and their environments).

---

76 On the features of the concepts of "process," "evolution," and "historicity," see Gonzalez (2013b, pp. 304–307, and 2011).

77 Historicity (*Geschichtlichkeit/historicidad*) is a trait of the agents themselves and their relations with other human beings (individuals, groups, or society) within a historical context. In addition, historicity is a feature of the relations between the human beings and the environment, which lies underneath debates such as "sustainable development" and the ongoing discussion on the climate change (where a key issue is how to change human habits in their dealings with nature).

78 "Historical" is a term that, from time to time, can be used in a deep sense, connected to human beings and societies, which certainly goes beyond the mere chronological dimension to embrace the possibility of radical changes, in addition to gradual changes or piecemeal modifications. Consequently, these variations can be richer than an "evolution," understood in terms of mere adaptation or conceived as the path for a mere mutation, in order to take in an actual facet of "historicity" pointed out. Contemporary history offers a good number of examples in this regard.

11 James Woodward's Trajectory

Through a large number of publications — some of them with other authors — Woodward is commonly associated with the philosophical research on causation and causal explanation. But his areas of research also include philosophy of psychology, where he has special interest in empirical psychology, mainly regarding learning and causal evaluation. In this regard, he has collaborated with a covenant of the McDonnell Foundation. In addition, he has devoted attention to psychology related to moral issues.

Woodward's influential academic career started at Carleton College, where in 1968 he got a B. A. in Mathematics, and continues at the University of Texas at Austin, where he defended his Ph. D. in 1977. The dissertation was entitled "Explanation in Science and History" and the supervisor was Edwin Allaire. Among his academic positions are his initial appointments at the University of Wisconsin-La Crosse (1976–1979); the College of Charleston, South Carolina (1980–1981); and the Memphis State University, now University of Memphis (1981–1983).

Subsequently, Woodward worked at the California Institute of Technology (1983–2010). He was Professor of the well-known Caltech from 1992 to 2001. This was followed by his appointment as J. O. and Juliette Koepfli Professor of the Humanities at the California Institute of Technology, from 2001 to 2010. Thereafter, from 2010 onwards, he has been Distinguished Professor of History and Philosophy of Science, at the University of Pittsburgh.

During his trajectory, he received an initial acknowledgment with the Mellon Post-Doctoral Instructorship at the California Institute of Technology, given to him in 1983. More important are two academic recognitions that Woodward received many years later. The first was related to his research on causality: the very prestigious Lakatos Award, in recognition of his book *Making Things Happen*, given in 2005. The second was institutional: his election as President of the Philosophy of Science Association, a position that he held from 2010 to 2012. During his term, the Hempel Award appeared, given to Bas van Fraassen by the Governing Board of the Philosophy of Science Association, "recognizing lifetime scholarly achievement in the philosophy of science."[79]

---

[79] The Governing Board of the Philosophy of Science Association, Official announcement on the inaugural 2012 Hempel Award, 25 September 2012. The Award was given at the PSA meeting in San Diego on 17 November 2012.

Acknowledgments: I am grateful to James Woodward for his comments on this paper as well as for the information he provided me. I am thankful to Donald Gillies for the conversations on this topic and his remarks on this paper.

12 References of this chapter

Some of the references in this section belong to volumes of the *Gallaecia Series. Studies in Contemporary Philosophy and Methodology of Science*. This collection deals with central topics in contemporary philosophy of science.[80] Thus, they are volumes that discuss issues connected to the problems addressed in the present chapter.

Anscombe, G. E. M. (1971): *Causality and Determinism*. Cambridge: Cambridge University Press.
Bogen, J. and Woodward, J. (1988): "Saving the Phenomena." *The Philosophical Review*, v. 97, n. 3, pp. 303–352.
Bonawitz, E. B., Ferranti, D., Saxe, R., Gopnik, A., Meltzoff, A. N., Woodward, J., and Schulz, L. E. (2010): "Just Do It? Investigating the Gap between Prediction and Action in Toddlers' Causal Inferences." *Cognition*, v. 115, n. 1, pp. 104–117. DOI: 10.1016/j.cognition.2009.12.001 (visited on 12.5.2017).
Collingwood, R. (1940): *An Idea of Metaphysics*. Oxford: Clarendon Press.
Dasgupta, S. (2003): "Multidisciplinary Creativity: The Case of Herbert A. Simon." *Cognitive Science*, v. 27, pp. 683–707.
de Regt, H. W. (2004): "Making Things Happen: A Theory of Causal Explanation." *Notre Dame Philosophical Reviews*, v. 7. https://ndpr.nd.edu/news/23818-making-things-happen-a-theory-of-causal-explanation/, visited on 29.7.2014.
De Vreese, L. (2006): "Pluralism in the Philosophy of Causation: Desideratum or Not?" *Philosophica*, v. 77, pp. 5–13.

---

80 As editor of the volumes, I summarize the titles and the years of publication: *Progreso científico e innovación tecnológica*, 1997; *El Pensamiento de L. Laudan. Relaciones entre Historia de la Ciencia y Filosofía de la Ciencia* 1998; *Ciencia y valores éticos*, 1999; *Problemas filosóficos y metodológicos de la Economía en la Sociedad tecnológica actual*, 2000; *La Filosofía de Imre Lakatos: Evaluación de sus propuestas*, 2001; *Diversidad de la explicación científica*, 2002; *Análisis de Thomas Kuhn: Las revoluciones científicas*, 2004; *Karl Popper: Revisión de su legado*, 2004; *Science, Technology and Society: A Philosophical Perspective*, 2005; *Evolutionism: Present Approaches*, 2008; *Evolucionismo: Darwin y enfoques actuales*, 2009; *New Methodological Perspectives on Observation and Experimentation in Science*, 2010; *Conceptual Revolutions: From Cognitive Science to Medicine*, 2011; *Scientific Realism and Democratic Society: The Philosophy of Philip Kitcher*, 2011; *Las Ciencias de la Complejidad: Vertiente dinámica de las Ciencias de Diseño y sobriedad de factores*, 2012; *Creativity, Innovation, and Complexity in Science*, 2013; *Bas van Fraassen's Approach to Representation and Models in Science*, 2014; *New Perspectives on Technology, Values, and Ethics: Theoretical and Practical*, 2015; *The Limits of Science: An Analysis from "Barriers" to "Confines,"* 2016; and *Artificial Intelligence and Contemporary Society: The Role of Information*, 2017.

Dowe, Ph. (2000): "Causality and Explanation." *British Journal for the Philosophy of Science*, v. 51, n. 1, pp. 165–174.
Dummett, M. A. E. (1954): "Can an Effect Precede Its Cause." *Proceedings of the Aristotelian Society*, v. 28 (supplement), pp. 27–44. Reprinted in: Dummett, M. A. E. (1978): *Truth and Other Enigmas*, pp. 319–332. London: Duckworth.
Dummett, M. A. E. (1964): "Bringing about the Past." *The Philosophical Review*, v. 73, pp. 338–359. Reprinted in: Dummett, M. A. E. (1978): *Truth and Other Enigmas*, pp. 333–350. London: Duckworth.
Dummett, M. A. E. (1978): *Truth and Other Enigmas*. London: Duckworth.
Fleming, L. and Sorenson, O. (2004): "Science as a Map in Technological Search." *Strategic Management Journal*, v. 25, nn. 8/9, pp. 909–928.
Gonzalez, W. J. (1991a): "Mathematics as Activity." *Daimon*, v. 3, pp. 113–130.
Gonzalez, W. J. (1991b): "Intuitionistic Mathematics and Wittgenstein." *History and Philosophy of Logic*, v. 12, pp. 167–183.
Gonzalez, W. J. (1995): "Strawson's Post-Kantian Empiricism." In: Hintikka, J. and Puhl, J. (eds.): *British Tradition in 20th Century Philosophy. Proceedings of the 17th International Wittgenstein Symposium*, pp. 249–257. Vienna: Hölder-Pichler-Tempsky.
Gonzalez, W. J. (1996): "Prediction and Mathematics: The Wittgensteinian Approach." In: Munevar, G. (ed.): *Spanish Studies in the Philosophy of Science*, pp. 299–332. Dordrecht: Kluwer.
Gonzalez, W. J. (1998a): "P. F. Strawson's Moderate Empiricism: The Philosophical Basis of His Approach in Theory of Knowledge." In: Hahn, L. E. (ed.): *The Philosophy of P. F. Strawson*, The Library of Living Philosophers, vol. 26, pp. 329–358. La Salle, IL: Open Court.
Gonzalez, W. J. (1998b): "Prediction and Prescription in Economics: A Philosophical and Methodological Approach." *Theoria*, v. 13, n. 32, pp. 321–345.
Gonzalez, W. J. (2003): "From *Erklären-Verstehen* to *Prediction-understanding*: The Methodological Framework in Economics." In: Sintonen, M., Ylikoski, P., and Miller, K. (eds.): *Realism in Action: Essays in the Philosophy of Social Sciences*, pp. 33–50. Dordrecht: Kluwer.
Gonzalez, W. J. (ed.) (2005): *Science, Technology and Society: A Philosophical Perspective*. A Coruña: Netbiblo.
Gonzalez, W. J. (2006): "Novelty and Continuity in Philosophy and Methodology of Science." In: Gonzalez, W. J. and Alcolea, J. (eds.): *Contemporary Perspectives in Philosophy and Methodology of Science*, pp. 1–28. A Coruña: Netbiblo.
Gonzalez, W. J. (2008): "Rationality and Prediction in the Sciences of the Artificial: Economics as a Design Science." In: Galavotti, M. C., Scazzieri, R., and Suppes, P. (eds.): *Reasoning, Rationality, and Probability*, pp. 165–186. Stanford: CSLI.
Gonzalez, W. J. (2010): "Recent Approaches on Observation and Experimentation: A Philosophical-methodological Viewpoint." In: Gonzalez, W. J. (ed.): *New Methodological Perspectives on Observation and Experimentation in Science*, pp. 9–48. A Coruña: Netbiblo.
Gonzalez, W. J. (2011): "Conceptual Changes and Scientific Diversity: The Role of Historicity." In: Gonzalez, W. J. (ed.): *Conceptual Revolutions: From Cognitive Science to Medicine*, pp. 39–62. A Coruña: Netbiblo.

Gonzalez, W. J. (2012): "Methodological Universalism in Science and Its Limits: Imperialism versus Complexity." In: Brzechczyn, K. and Paprzycka, K. (eds.): *Thinking about Provincialism in Thinking*, Poznan Studies in the Philosophy of the Sciences and the Humanities, vol. 100, pp. 155–175. Amsterdam/New York: Rodopi.

Gonzalez, W. J. (2013a): "The Roles of Scientific Creativity and Technological Innovation in the Context of Complexity of Science." In: Gonzalez, W. J. (ed.): *Creativity, Innovation, and Complexity in Science*, pp. 11–40. A Coruña: Netbiblo.

Gonzalez, W. J. (2013b): "The Sciences of Design as Sciences of Complexity: The Dynamic Trait." In: Andersen, H., Dieks, D., Gonzalez, W. J., Uebel, Th., and Wheeler, G. (eds.): *New Challenges to Philosophy of Science*, pp. 299–311. Dordrecht: Springer.

Gonzalez, W. J. (2015a): *Philosophico-methodological Analysis of Prediction and Its Role in Economics*. Dordrecht: Springer.

Gonzalez, W. J. (ed.) (2015b): *New Perspectives on Technology, Values, and Ethics: Theoretical and Practical*, Boston Studies in the Philosophy and History of Science, vol. 315. Dordrecht: Springer.

Gonzalez, W. J. (2015c): "From the Characterization of 'European Philosophy of Science' to the Case of the Philosophy of the Social Sciences." *International Studies in the Philosophy of Science*, v. 29, n. 2, pp. 167–188.

Gonzalez, W. J. (2016): "Rethinking the Limits of Science: From the Difficulties to the Frontiers to the Concern about the Confines." In: Gonzalez, W. J. (ed.), *The Limits of Science: An Analysis from "Barriers" to "Confines,"* Poznan Studies in the Philosophy of the Sciences and the Humanities, pp. 3–30. Brill-Rodopi, Leiden.

Gonzalez, W. J. (2017): "From Intelligence to Rationality of Minds and Machines in Contemporary Society: The Sciences of Design and the Role of Information." *Minds and Machines*, v. 27, n. 3, pp. 397–424. DOI: 10.1007/s11023-017-9439-0.

Granger, C. (1969): "Investigating Causal Relations by Econometric Models and Cross-Spectral Methods." *Econometrica*, v. 37, n. 3, pp. 424–438.

Granger, C. W. J. (2007): "Causality in Economics." In: Machamer, P. and Wolters, G. (eds.): *Thinking about Causes. From Greek Philosophy to Modern Physics*, pp. 284–296. Pittsburgh: University of Pittsburgh Press.

Grünbaum, A. (1984): *The Foundations of Psychoanalysis. A Philosophical Critique*. Berkeley: University of California Press.

Hempel, C. G. (1965): *Aspects of Scientific Explanation and Other Essays*. New York: Free Press.

Hempel, C. G. (1966): *Philosophy of Natural Science*. Englewood Cliffs, NJ: Prentice Hall.

Hempel, C. G. and Oppenheim, P. (1948): "Studies in the Logic of Explanation." *Philosophy of Science*, v. 15, n. 2, pp. 135–175. Reprinted in Hempel, C. G. (1965): *Aspects of Scientific Explanation and Other Essays*, pp. 245–295. New York: Free Press.

Horgan, T. and Woodward, J. (1985): "Folk Psychology is Here to Stay." *The Philosophical Review*, v. 94, n. 2, pp. 197–226.

Iwasaki, Y. and Simon, H. A. (1988): "Causal Ordering, Comparative Statics, and Near Decomposability." *Journal of Econometrics*, v. 39, pp. 149–173. Reprinted in Simon, H. A. (1997): *Models of Bounded Rationality*. Vol. 3: *Empirically Grounded Economic Reason*, pp. 13–42. Cambridge, MA: The MIT Press.

Kahneman, D. (2003): "Maps of Bounded Rationality: Psychology for Behavioral Economics." *The American Economic Review*, v. 93, n. 5, pp. 1449–1475.

Kahneman, D. and Snell, J. (1990): "Predicting Utility." In: Hogarth, R. M. (ed.): *Insights in Decision Making*, pp. 295–310. Chicago: The University of Chicago Press.

Kahneman, D. and Tversky, A. (1973): "On the Psychology of Prediction." *Psychological Review*, v. 80, pp. 237–251.

Kenny, A. (1979): *Action, Emotion and Will*. London: Routledge and Kegan Paul.

Kitcher, Ph. and Salmon, W. C. (eds.) (1989): *Scientific Explanation*. Minneapolis: University of Minnesota Press.

Nagel, E. (1961): *The Structure of Science. Problems in the Logic of Scientific Explanation*. New York: Harcourt, Brace and World.

Niiniluoto, I. (1993): "The Aim and Structure of Applied Research." *Erkenntnis*, v. 38, pp. 1–21.

Niiniluoto, I. (1994): "Approximation in Applied Science." In: Kuokkanen, M. (ed.): *Idealization, VII: Structuralism, Idealization and Approximation*, Poznan Studies in the Philosophy of the Sciences and the Humanities, vol. 42, Amsterdam: Rodopi, pp. 127–139.

Niiniluoto, I. (1995): "The Emergence of Scientific Specialities: Six Models." In: Herfeld, W. E., Krajewski, W., Niiniluoto, I., and Wojcicki, R. (eds.): *Theories and Models of Scientific Processes*, Poznan Studies in the Philosophy of the Sciences and the Humanities, vol. 44, Amsterdam: Rodopi, pp. 211–223.

Pearl, J. (2000): *Causality: Models, Reasoning, and Inference*. Cambridge: Cambridge University Press.

Psillos, S. (2007): "Causal Explanation and Manipulation." In: Persson, J. and Ylikoski, P. (eds.): *Rethinking Explanation*, pp. 93–107. Dordrecht: Springer.

Rescher, N. (1953): "Some Remarks on an Analysis of the Causal Relation." *The Journal of Philosophy*, v. 51, pp. 239–241.

Rescher, N. (1998): *Predicting the Future: An Introduction to the Theory of Forecasting*. New York: State University of New York Press.

Ruben, D. H. (1990): *Explaining Explanation*. London: Routledge.

Ruben, D. H. (ed.) (1993): *Explanation*. Oxford: Oxford University Press.

Salmon, M. H. (1992): "Philosophy of Social Science." In: Salmon, M. H. et al.: *Introduction to the Philosophy of Science*, pp. 404–425. Englewood Cliffs: Prentice-Hall.

Salmon, M. H. (2002): "La explicación causal en Ciencias Sociales." In: Gonzalez, W. J. (ed.): *Diversidad de la explicación científica*, pp. 161–180. Barcelona: Ariel.

Salmon, M. H. and Salmon, W. C. (1979): "Alternative Models of Scientific Explanation." *American Anthropologist*, v. 81, n. 1, pp. 61–74.

Salmon, W. C. (ed.) (1971): *Statistical Explanation and Statistical Relevance*. Pittsburgh: University of Pittsburgh Press. The book includes the contributions made by Richard C. Jeffrey and James G. Greeno.

Salmon, W. C. (1984): *Scientific Explanation and the Causal Structure of the World*. Princeton, NJ: Princeton University Press.

Salmon, W. C. (1990): *Four Decades of Scientific Explanation*. Minneapolis: University of Minnesota Press.

Salmon, W. C. (1998): *Causality and Explanation*. New York: Oxford University Press.

Salmon, W. C. (2002a): "Explicación causal frente a no causal." In: Gonzalez, W. J. (ed.): *Diversidad de la explicación científica*, pp. 97–115. Barcelona: Ariel.

Salmon, W. C. (2002b): "Estructura de la explicación causal." In: Gonzalez, W. J. (ed.): *Diversidad de la explicación científica*, pp. 141–159. Barcelona: Ariel.
Simon, H. A. (1952): "On the Definition of the Causal Relation." *The Journal of Philosophy*, v. 49, pp. 517–528.
Simon, H. A. (1955): "Further Remarks on the Causal Relation." *The Journal of Philosophy*, v. 52, pp. 20–21.
Simon, H. A. (1990): "Prediction and Prescription in Systems Modeling." *Operations Research*, v. 38, pp. 7–14. Reprinted in: Simon, H. A. (1997): *Models of Bounded Rationality*. Vol. 3: *Empirically Grounded Economic Reason*, pp. 115–128. Cambridge, MA: The MIT Press.
Simon, H. A. (1991): "Mind as Machine: The Cognitive Revolution in Behavioral Science." In: Jessor, R. (ed.): *Perspectives in Behavioral Science: The Colorado Lectures*, pp. 37–52. Boulder, CO: Westview Press.
Simon, H. A. (1995): "Machine as Mind." In: Ford, K. M., Glymour, C., and Hayes, P. J. (eds.): *Android Epistemology*, pp. 23–40. Menlo Park, CA: AAAI/The MIT Press.
Simon, H. A. ([1969] 1996): *The Sciences of the Artificial*, 3rd edition. Cambridge, MA: The MIT Press.
Simon, H. A. (2001): "Science Seeks Parsimony, not Simplicity: Searching for Pattern in Phenomena." In: Zellner, A., Keuzenkamp, H. A., and McAleer, M. (eds.): *Simplicity, Inference and Modelling. Keeping It Sophisticatedly Simple*, pp. 32–72. Cambridge: Cambridge University Press.
Simon, H. A. and Rescher, N. (1966): "Cause and Counterfactual." *Philosophy of Science*, v. 33, pp. 323–240. Reprinted in: Simon, H. A. (1977): *Models of Discovery*, pp. 107–134. Boston: Reidel.
Sobel, M. E. (1995): "Causal Inference in the Social and Behavioral Sciences." In: Arminger, G., Clogg, C. C., and Sobel, M. E. (eds.): *Handbook of Statistical Modeling for the Social and Behavioral Sciences*, pp. 1–38. New York: Plenum.
Spirtes, P., Glymour, C., and Scheines, R. (1993): *Causation, Prediction and Search*. New York: Springer.
Strawson, P. F. (1959): *Individuals. An Essay in Descriptive Metaphysics*. London: Methuen.
Thagard, P. (ed.) (2007): *Philosophy of Psychology and Cognitive Science*. Amsterdam: Elsevier.
von Wright, G. H. (1971): *Explanation and Understanding*. Ithaca: Cornell University Press.
von Wright, G. H. (1973): "On the Logic and Epistemology of the Causal Relation." In: Suppes, P., Henkin, L., Joja, A. and Moisil, G. C. (eds.): *Logic, Methodology and Philosophy of Science*, vol. 4, pp. 293–312. Amsterdam: North-Holland. Reprinted in Sosa, E. and Tooley, M. (eds.). 1993. *Causation*, pp. 105–124. Oxford: Oxford University Press.
von Wright, G. H. (1974): *Causality and Determinism*. New York: Columbia University Press.
Wittgenstein, L. (1980a): *Bemerkungen über die Philosophie der Psychologie/Remarks on the Philosophy of Psychology*, vol. 1, edited by G. E. M. Anscombe and G. H. von Wright, translated by G. E. M. Anscombe. Oxford: B. Blackwell.
Wittgenstein, L. (1980b): *Bemerkungen über die Philosophie der Psychologie/Remarks on the Philosophy of Psychology*, vol. 2, edited by G. H. von Wright and H. Nyman, translated by C. G. Luckhardt and M. A. E. Aue. Oxford: B. Blackwell.

Wittgenstein, L. (1982): *Letzte Schriften über die Philosophie der Psychologie/Last Writings on the Philosophy of Psychology*, vol. 1, edited by G. H. von Wright and H. Nyman, translated by C. G. Luckhardt and M. A. E. Aue. Oxford: B. Blackwell.
Woodward, J. (1979): "Scientific Explanation." *British Journal for the Philosophy of Science*, v. 30, n. 1, pp. 41–67.
Woodward, J. (1995): "Causality and Explanation in Econometrics." In: Little, D. (ed.): *On the Reliability of Economic Models: Essays in the Philosophy of Economics*, pp. 9–61. Dordrecht: Kluwer.
Woodward, J. (2000): "Explanation and Invariance in the Special Sciences." *British Journal for the Philosophy of Science*, v. 51, n. 2, pp. 197–254.
Woodward, J. (2001): "Law and Explanation in Biology: Invariance Is the Kind of Stability That Matters." *Philosophy of Science*, v. 68, n. 1, pp. 1–20.
Woodward, J. (2003a): *Making Things Happen: A Theory of Causal Explanation*. New York: Oxford University Press. Reprinted in 2005 in paperback.
Woodward, J. (2003b): "Critical Notice: *Causality* by Pearl." *Economics and Philosophy*, v. 19, n. 2, pp. 321–340.
Woodward, J. (2003c): "Experimentation, Causal Inference, and Instrumental Realism." In: Radder, H. (ed.): *The Philosophy of Scientific Experimentation*, pp. 87–118. Pittsburgh: University of Pittsburgh Press.
Woodward, J. (2007a): "Causation with a Human Face." In: Price, H. and Corry, R. (eds.): *Causation and the Constitution of Reality*, pp. 66–105. Oxford: Oxford University Press.
Woodward, J. (2007b): "Interventionist Theories of Causation in Psychological Perspective." In: Gopnik, A. and Schulz, L. (eds.): *Causal Learning: Psychology, Philosophy and Computation*, pp. 19–36. New York: Oxford University Press.
Woodward, J. (2009): "Agency and Interventionist Theories of Causation." In: Beebee, H., Hitchcock, Ch., and Menzies, P. (eds.): *The Oxford Handbook of Causation*, pp. 234–262. Oxford: Oxford University Press.
Woodward, J. (2010): "Causation in Biology: Stability, Specificity, and the Choice of the Levels of Explanation." *Biology and Philosophy*, v. 25, pp. 287–318.
Woodward, J. (2011): "Psychological Studies of Causal and Counterfactual Reasoning." In: Hoerl, C., McCormack, T., and Beck, S. R. (eds.): *Understanding Counterfactuals/Understanding Causation*, pp. 16–53. Oxford: Oxford University Press.
Woodward, J. (2012): "Causation: Interactions between Philosophical Theories and Psychological Research." *Philosophy of Science*, v. 79, n. 5, pp. 961–972.
Woodward, J. (2014a): "A Functional Account of Causation; or a Defense of the Legitimacy of Causal Thinking by Reference to the Only Standard that Matters – Usefulness (as Opposed to Metaphysics and Agreement with Intuitive Judgment)." *Philosophy of Science*, v. 81, n. 5, pp. 691–713.
Woodward, J. (2014b): "Causal Reasoning: Philosophy and Experiment." In: Knobe, J., Lombrozo, T., and Nichols S. (eds.): *Oxford Studies in Experimental Philosophy*, vol. 1, pp. 294–324. Oxford: Oxford University Press.
Woodward, J. (2018a): "Normative Theory and Descriptive Psychology in Understanding Causal Reasoning: The Role of Interventions and Invariance." This volume, pp. 71–101.
Woodward, J. (2018b): "Causal Cognition: Physical Connections, Proportionality, and the Role of Normative Theory." This volume, pp. 105–137.

Woodward, J. (forthcoming a). "Explanation in Neurobiology: An Interventionist Perspective." In: Kaplan, D. (ed.): *Integrating Psychology and Neuroscience: Prospects and problems*. Oxford: Oxford University Press.

Woodward, J. and Allman, J. (2007): "Moral Intuition: Its Neural Substrates and Normative Significance." *Journal of Physiology*, v. 101, pp. 179–202.

13 Woodward's Publications

Six sections are used to present James F. Woodward's publications here: 1) monograph, 2) articles on philosophy of science in journals, 3) chapters in edited volumes, 4) critical notices of some relevant books, 5) book reviews, and 6) other publications. The distinction between the critical notices and the reviews is due to the status of the former as a kind of article regarding a book, which explains why the critical notices are longer than the latter. The section on other publications aims to make explicit some papers on topics different from those addressed in this book on philosophy of psychology, which is focused on causality and psychological subject and develops new reflections on James Woodward's contribution.

13.1 Monograph

Woodward, J. (2003): *Making Things Happen: A Theory of Causal Explanation*. New York: Oxford University Press. [Reprinted in paperback edition: 2005.]

13.2 Articles in Journals

Woodward, J. (1979): "Scientific Explanation." *British Journal for the Philosophy of Science*, v. 30, n. 1, pp. 41–67.

Wolfson, P. and Woodward, J. (1979): "Scientific Explanation and Sklar's Views of Space and Time." *Philosophy of Science*, v. 46, n. 2, pp. 287–294.

Woodward, J. (1980): "Developmental Explanation." *Synthese*, v. 44, n. 3, pp. 443–466.

Woodward, J. (1981): "Why the Numbers Count." *The Southern Journal of Philosophy*, v. 19, pp. 531–540.

Woodward, J. (1982): "Paternalism and Justification." *Canadian Journal of Philosophy*. Supplementary volume 8: *New Essays in Ethics and Public Policy*, pp. 67–89. Reprinted in: Cragg, W. (ed.) (1987): *Contemporary Moral Issues*, 2nd edition, pp. 249-ff. Toronto: McGraw-Hill Ryerson Limited.

Woodward, J. (1983): "Glymour on Theory Confirmation." *Philosophical Studies*, v. 43, n. 1, pp. 147–152.

Woodward, J. (1984): "Explanatory Asymmetries." *Philosophy of Science*, v. 51, pp. 421–442.

Woodward, J. (1984): "A Theory of Singular Causal Explanation." *Erkenntnis*, v. 21, pp. 231–262. Reprinted in: Ruben, D. (ed.) (1993): *Explanation*, pp. 246–274. Oxford: Oxford University Press.

Horgan, T. and Woodward, J. (1985): "Folk Psychology Is Here to Stay." *The Philosophical Review*, v. 94, n. 2, pp. 197–226. Reprinted in: Lycan, W. G. (ed.) (1990): *Mind and Cognition: A Reader*, pp. 399–420. Oxford: Basil Blackwell. Also reprinted in: Greenwood, J. (ed.) (1991): *The Future of Folk Psychology: Intentionality and Cognitive Science*, pp. 149–175. Cambridge: Cambridge University Press. Also reprinted in: Christensen, S. and Turner, D. R. (eds.) (1992): *Folk Psychology and the Philosophy of Mind*, pp. 144–166. Hillsday, NJ: Lawrence Erlbaum Associates. Also reprinted in: Lycan, W. G. (ed.) (1999): *Mind and Cognition: An Anthology*, 2nd edition, pp. 271–286. Malden, MA: B. Blackwell; and in: Crumley, J. (ed.) (2000): *Problems in Mind: Readings in Contemporary Philosophy of Mind*, pp. 198–214. Mountain View, CA: Mayfield.

Woodward, J. (1986): "Are Singular Causal Explanations Implicit Covering-law Explanations?" *The Canadian Journal of Philosophy*, v. 16, pp. 253–279.

Woodward, J. (1986): "Explanation in Social Theory: Comments on Alan Nelson." *Ethics*, v. 97, n. 1, pp. 187–195.

Woodward, J. (1987): "On an Information Theoretic Model of Explanation." *Philosophy of Science*, v. 54, pp. 21–44.

Woodward, J. (1988): "Understanding Regression." *Philosophy of Science Association*, Supplementary volume 1, pp. 255–269.

Bogen, J. and Woodward, J. (1988): "Saving the Phenomena." *The Philosophical Review*, v. 97, n. 3, pp. 303–352.

Woodward, J. (1992): "Realism about Laws." *Erkenntnis*, v. 36, pp. 181–218. Reprinted in: Tooley, M. (ed.) (2000): *Analytical Metaphysic: A Collection of Essays*. Hamden: Garland.

Bogen, J. and Woodward, J. (1992): "Observations, Theories and the Evolution of the Human Spirit." *Philosophy of Science*, v. 59, pp. 590–611.

Woodward, J. and Goodstein, D. (1996): "Conduct, Misconduct and the Structure of Science." *American Scientist*, v. 84, n. 5, pp. 479–490. Reprinted in: Sherman, P. and Alcock, J. (eds.) (1998): *Exploring Animal Behavior*, pp. 9–20 (4th edition 2005). Sunderland, MA: Sinauer Associates.

Woodward, J. (1997): "Explanation, Invariance and Intervention." *Philosophy of Science Association*, supplement to v. 64. (=Proceedings of the 1996 Biannual Meeting of the Philosophy of Science Association, part II: Symposia papers), pp. S26–S41.

Woodward, J. (1997): "Explanation and Invariance (Abstract)." *Proceedings and Addresses of the American Philosophical Association*, v. 71, pp. 108–109.

Woodward, J. (1998): "Causal Independence and Faithfulness." *Multivariate Behavioral Research*, v. 33, n. 2, pp. 129–148.

Woodward, J. (1999): "Causal Interpretation in Systems of Equations." *Synthese*, v. 121, pp. 199–257.

Goodstein, D. and Woodward, J. (1999): "Inside Science." *The American Scholar*, v. 68, n. 4, pp. 83–90.

Hausman, D. and Woodward, J. (1999): "Independence, Invariance and the Causal Markov Condition." *British Journal for the Philosophy of Science*, v. 50, pp. 521–583.

Woodward, J. (2000): "Data, Phenomena, and Reliability." *Philosophy of Science*, supplement to v. 67, n. 3. (=Proceedings of the 1998 Biannual Meeting of the Philosophy of Science Association, part II), pp. S163–S179.

Woodward, J. (2000): "Explanation and Invariance in the Special Sciences." *British Journal for the Philosophy of Science*, v. 51, pp. 197–254.

Woodward, J. (2001): "Law and Explanation in Biology: Invariance Is the Kind of Stability That Matters." *Philosophy of Science*, v. 68, n. 1, pp. 1–20.
Woodward, J. (2001): "Causation and Manipulability." In: Zalta, E. (ed.): *Stanford Encyclopedia of Philosophy*, updated 2008, http://plato.stanford.edu, visited on 21.8.2015.
Woodward, J. (2002): "What Is a Mechanism: A Counterfactual Account." *Philosophy of Science*, supplement to v. 69, n. 3. (=Proceedings of the 2000 Biannual Meeting of the Philosophy of Science Association, part II), pp. S366–S377.
Woodward, J. (2002): "There Is No Such Thing as a *Ceteris Paribus* Law." *Erkenntnis*, v. 57, n. 3, pp. 303–328. This paper belongs to a special issue on *ceteris paribus* laws, edited by J. Earman, C. Glymour, and S. Mitchell.
Woodward, J. (2003): "Scientific Explanation." In: Zalta, E. (ed.): *Stanford Encyclopedia of Philosophy*, updated, 2008, http://plato.stanford.edu, visited on 21.8.2015.
Hitchcock, C. and Woodward J. (2003): "Explanatory Generalizations, Part I: A Counterfactual Account." *Nous*, v. 37, n. 1, pp. 1–24.
Hitchcock, C. and Woodward J. (2003): "Explanatory Generalizations, Part II: Plumbing Explanatory Depth." *Nous*, v. 37, n. 2, pp. 181–199.
Woodward, J. (2004): "Counterfactuals and Causal Explanation." *International Studies in the Philosophy of Science*, v. 18, pp. 41–72.
Hausman, D. and Woodward, J. (2004): "Modularity and the Causal Markov Condition: A Restatement." *British Journal for the Philosophy of Science*, v. 55, pp. 147–161.
Hausman, D. and Woodward, J. (2004): "Manipulation and the Casual Markov Condition." *Philosophy of Science*, v. 71, n. 5. (=Proceedings of the 2002 Biannual Meeting of the Philosophy of Science Association, part II), pp. 846–856.
Woodward, J. (2006): "Sensitive and Insensitive Causation." *The Philosophical Review*, v. 115, pp. 1–50.
Woodward, J. (2006): "Responses to Humphreys, and Sober." *Metascience*, v. 15, pp. 53–66. DOI 10.1007/s11016–006–0001–6, visited on 21.8.2015.
Woodward, J. (2006): "Some Varieties of Robustness." *Journal of Economic Methodology*, v. 13, pp. 219–240.
Woodward, J. and Allman, J. (2007): "Moral Intuition: Its Neural Substrates and Normative Significance." *Journal of Physiology*, v. 101, pp. 179–202.
Woodward, J. (2008): "Social Preferences in Experimental Economics." *Philosophy of Science*, v. 75, n. 5. (= Proceedings of the 2006 Biannual Meeting of the Philosophy of Science Association, part II), pp. 646–657.
Woodward, J. (2008): "Response to Strevens." *Philosophy and Phenomenological Research*, v. 77, n. 1, pp. 193–212.
Allman, J. and Woodward, J. (2008): "What Are Moral Intuitions and Why Should We Care about Them? A Neurobiological Perspective." *Philosophical Issues*, v. 18, pp. 164–185.
Woodward, J. (2010): "Causation in Biology: Stability, Specificity, and the Choice of the Levels of Explanation." *Biology and Philosophy*, v. 25, pp. 287–318.
Woodward, J. (2010): "Data, Phenomena, Signal, and Noise." *Philosophy of Science*, v. 77, n. 5, pp. 792–803.
Bonawitz, E. B., Ferranti, D., Saxe, R., Gopnik, A., Meltzoff, A. N., Woodward, J., and Schulz, L. E. (2010): "Just Do It? Investigating the Gap between Prediction and Action in

Toddlers' Causal Inferences." *Cognition*, v. 115, n. 1, pp. 104–117. DOI: 10.1016/j.cognition.2009.12.001, visited on 21.8.2015.

Henderson, L., Goodman, N. D., Tenenbaum, J. B., and Woodward, J. (2010): "The Structure and Dynamics of Scientific Theories: A Hierarchical Bayesian Perspective." *Philosophy of Science*, v. 77, n. 2, pp. 172–200.

Woodward, J. (2011): "Data and Phenomena: A Restatement and Defense." *Synthese*, v. 182, n. 1, pp. 165–179.

Woodward, J. (2011): "Counterfactuals All the Way Down?" *Metascience*, v. 20, pp. 27–33.

Woodward, J. (2011): "Mechanisms Revisited." *Synthese*, v. 183, n. 3, pp. 409–427.

Woodward, J. (2012): "Causation: Interactions between Philosophical Theories and Psychological Research." *Philosophy of Science*, v. 79, n. 5, pp. 961–972.

Woodward, J. (2013): "Mechanistic Explanation: Its Scope and Limits." *Proceedings of the Aristotelian Society*, Supplementary volume 87, pp. 39–65.

Woodward, J. (2014): "A Functional Account of Causation; or a Defense of the Legitimacy of Causal Thinking by Reference to the Only Standard that Matters – Usefulness (as Opposed to Metaphysics and Agreement with Intuitive Judgment)." *Philosophy of Science*, v. 81, n. 5, pp. 691–713.

Woodward, J. (2014): "Simplicity in the Best Systems Account of Laws of Nature." *British Journal for the Philosophy of Science*, v. 65, n. 1, pp. 91–123.

Woodward, J. (2014): "Interventionism and Causal Exclusion." *Philosophy and Phenomenological Research*, April, pp. 1–45, online: DOI: 10.1111/phpr.12095, visited on 21.8.2015. Print version: v. 91, n. 2, (2015), pp. 303–347.

Woodward, J. (2014): "From Handles to Interventions: Commentary on R. G. Collingwood, 'The So-called Idea of Causation.'" *International Journal of Epidemiology*, v. 43, n. 6, pp. 1714–1718.

Woodward, J. (2015): "Methodology, Ontology, and Interventionism." *Synthese*, v. 192, n. 11, pp. 3577–3599. DOI: 10.1007/s11229–014–0479–1, visited on 21.8.2015.

Hutcherson, C. A., Montaser-Kouhsari, L., Woodward, J., y Rangel, A. (2015): "Emotional and Utilitarian Appraisals of Moral Dilemmas are Encoded in Separated Areas and Integrated in Ventromedial Prefrontal Cortex." *Journal of Neuroscience*, v. 35, n. 36, pp. 12593–12605.

Woodward, J. (2016). "The Problem of Variable Choice." *Synthese*, v. 193, n. 4, pp. 1047–1072.

Woodward, J. (forthcoming). "Physical Modality, Laws and Counterfactuals." *Synthese*. Published online (2017), DOI: 10.1007/s11229–017–1400–5.

13.3 Chapters in Edited Volumes

Woodward, J. (1989): "The Causal/Mechanical Model of Explanation." In: Kitcher, Ph. and Salmon, W. C. (eds.): *Scientific Explanation*, pp. 357–383. Minneapolis: University of Minnesota Press.

Woodward, J. (1990): "Supervenience and Singular Causal Claims." In: Knowles, D. (ed.): *Explanation and Its Limits*, Royal Institute of Philosophy Conference, pp. 211–246. Cambridge: Cambridge University Press.

Woodward, J. (1993): "Capacities and Invariance." In: Earman, J., Janis, A., Massey, G., and Rescher, N. (eds.): *Philosophical Problems of the Internal and External Worlds: Essays Concerning the Philosophy of Adolf Grünbaum*, pp. 283–328. Pittsburgh: University of Pittsburgh Press.

Woodward, J. (1995): "Causality and Explanation in Econometrics." In: Little, D. (ed.): *On the Reliability of Economic Models: Essays in the Philosophy of Economics*, pp. 9–61. Dordrecht: Kluwer.

Woodward, J. (1997): "Causal Modeling, Probabilities and Invariance." In: McKim, V. and Turner, S. (eds.): *Causality in Crisis? Statistical Methods and the Search for Causal Knowledge in the Social Sciences*, pp. 265–317. Notre Dame: University of Notre Dame Press.

Woodward, J. (1998): "Statistics." In: *The Encyclopedia of Philosophy*. London: Routledge. https://www.rep.routledge.com/articles/statistics/v-1/, visited on 21.8.2015.

Woodward, J. (2001): "Probabilistic Causality, Direct Causes, and Counterfactual Dependence." In: Galavotti, M., Suppes, P., and Constantini, D. (eds.): *Stochastic Causality*, pp. 39–63. Stanford, CA: CSLI.

Woodward, J. (2001): "Explanation." In: Machamer, P. and Silberstein, M. (eds.): *Blackwell Guide to the Philosophy of Science*, pp. 37–54. Oxford: Blackwell.

Woodward, J. (2003): "Experimentation, Causal Inference, and Instrumental Realism." In: Radder, H. (ed.): *The Philosophy of Scientific Experimentation*, pp. 87–118. Pittsburgh: University of Pittsburgh Press.

Woodward J. and Cowie, F. (2004): "Is the Mind a System of Modules Shaped by Natural Selection?" In: Hitchcock, Ch. (ed.): *Great Debates in Philosophy: Philosophy of Science*, pp. 312–334. Oxford: Blackwell.

Woodward, J. (2005): "Prospects for a Manipulability Account of Causation." In: Hajek, P., Valdes-Villanueva, L., and Westerstahl, D. (eds.): *Logic, Methodology, and Philosophy of Science: Proceedings of the Twentieth International Congress*, pp. 333–348. London: King's College Publications.

Woodward, J. (2007): "Causal Models in the Social Sciences." In: Turner, S. P. and Risjord, M. K. (eds.): *Handbook of the Philosophy of Science*, Vol. 8 *Philosophy of Anthropology and Sociology*, pp. 157–210. Amsterdam: Elsevier.

Woodward, J. (2007): "Causation with a Human Face." In: Price, H. and Corry, R. (eds.): *Causation and the Constitution of Reality*, pp. 66–105. Oxford: Oxford University Press.

Woodward, J. (2007): "Interventionist Theories of Causation in Psychological Perspective." In: Gopnik, A. and Schulz, L. (eds.): *Causal Learning: Psychology, Philosophy and Computation*, pp. 19–36. New York: Oxford University Press.

Woodward, J. (2008): "Mental Causation and Neural Mechanisms." In: Hohwy, J. and Kallestrup, J. (eds.): *Being Reduced: New Essays on Reduction, Explanation, and Causation*, pp. 218–262. Oxford: Oxford University Press.

Woodward, J. (2008): "Invariance, Modularity, and All That." In: Hartmann, S., Hoefer, C., and Bovens, L. (eds.): *Nancy Cartwright's Philosophy of Science*, pp. 198–237. London: Routledge.

Woodward, J. (2008): "Explanation." In: Psillos, S. and Curd, M. (eds.): *The Routledge Companion to the Philosophy of Science*, pp. 171–181. London: Routledge.

Woodward, J. (2008): "Cause and Explanation in Psychiatry: An Interventionist Perspective." In: Kendler, K. S. and Parnas, J. (eds.): *Philosophical Issues in Psychiatry: Explanation, Phenomenology and Nosology*, pp. 132–184. Baltimore: Johns Hopkins University Press.

Woodward, J. (2008): "Comments on John Campbell's *Causation in Psychiatry*." In: Kendler, K. S. and Parnas, J. (eds.): *Philosophical Issues in Psychiatry: Explanation, Phenomenology and Nosology*, pp. 216–235. Baltimore: Johns Hopkins University Press.

Woodward, J. (2009): "Experimental Investigations of Social Preferences." In: Ross, D. and Kincaid, H. (eds.): *The Oxford Handbook of Philosophy of Economics*, pp. 189–222. Oxford: Oxford University Press.

Woodward, J. (2009): "Agency and Interventionist Theories of Causation." In: Beebee, H., Hitchcock, Ch., and Menzies, P. (eds.): *The Oxford Handbook of Causation*, pp. 234–262. Oxford: Oxford University Press.

Woodward, J. (2009): "Why Do People Cooperate as Much as They Do." In: Mantzavinos, C. (ed.): *Philosophy of the Social Sciences: Philosophical Theory and Scientific Practice*, pp. 219–265. Oxford: Oxford University Press.

Woodward, J. (2011): "Causal Perception and Causal Understanding." In: Roessler, J., Eilen, N., and Lerman, H. (eds.): *Causation, Perception, and Objectivity: Issues in Philosophy and Psychology*, pp. 229–263. Oxford: Oxford University Press.

Woodward, J. (2011): "Psychological Studies of Causal and Counterfactual Reasoning." In: Hoerl, C., McCormack, T., and Beck, S. R. (eds.): *Understanding Counterfactuals/Understanding Causation*, pp. 16–53. Oxford: Oxford University Press.

Woodward, J. (2011): "Causes, Conditions, and the Pragmatics of Causal Explanation." In: Morgan, G. (ed.): *In Philosophy of Science Matters: The Philosophy of Peter Achinstein*, pp. 247–257. Oxford: Oxford University Press.

Woodward, J. (2012): "Reciprocity: Empirical Evidence and Normative Implications." In: Kincaid, H. (ed.): *Oxford Handbook of Philosophy of Social Science*, pp. 581–606. Oxford: Oxford University Press.

Woodward, J. (2014): "Causal Reasoning: Philosophy and Experiment." In: Knobe, J., Lombrozo, T., and Nichols S. (eds.): *Oxford Studies in Experimental Philosophy*, vol. 1, pp. 294–324. Oxford: Oxford University Press.

Woodward, J. (2014): "Scientific Explanation." In: Sklar, L. (ed.): *Physical Theory: Method and Interpretation*, pp. 9–39. Oxford: Oxford University Press.

Woodward, J. (2015): "Empirical Investigations of Human Causal Judgment." In: Lombrozo, T., Knobe, J., and Nichols, S. (eds.): *Oxford Studies in Experimental Philosophy*, vol. 1, pp. 294–324. Oxford: Oxford University Press.

Woodward, J. (2016). "Causation in the Sciences." In: Humphreys, P. (ed.): *The Oxford Handbook of Philosophy of Science*, pp. 163–184. N. York: Oxford University Press. (There is a much longer version for the on-line volume.)

Woodward, J. (2016). "Unificationism, Explanatory Internalism, and the Autonomy of the Special Sciences." In: Pfeifer, J. and Couch, M. (eds.), *The Philosophy of Philip Kitcher*, ch. 5, pp. 121-ff. N. York: Oxford University Press.

Woodward, J. (2016). "Emotion versus Cognition in Moral Decision-making: A Dubious Dichotomy." In: Liao, M. (ed.), *Moral Brains: The Neuroscience of Morality*, pp. 87–119. N. York: Oxford University Press.

Woodward, J. (2017): "Intervening in the Exclusion Argument." In: Beebee, H., Hitchcock, Ch., and Price, H. (eds.): *Making a Difference: Essays on the Philosophy of Causation*, pp. 251–268. Oxford: Oxford University Press.
Woodward, J. (2017): "Interventionism and the Missing Metaphysics: A Dialogue. In: Slater, M. and Yudell, Z. (eds.): *Metaphysics and the philosophy of science*, pp. 193–228. Oxford: Oxford University Press.
Woodward, J. (2018): "Normative Theory and Descriptive Psychology in Understanding Causal Reasoning: The Role of Interventions and Invariance." This volume, pp. 71–101.
Woodward, J. (2018): "Causal Cognition: Physical Connections, Proportionality, and the Role of Normative Theory." This volume, pp. 105–137.
Woodward, J. (forthcoming a): "Explanation in Neurobiology: An Interventionist Perspective." In: Kaplan, D. (ed.): *Integrating Psychology and Neuroscience: Prospects and Problems*. Oxford: Oxford University Press.
Woodward, J. (forthcoming b): "Mechanisms and Causation in Biology." In: Waters, K., Travisano, M., and Woodward, J. (eds.): *Causal Reasoning in Biology*, Minnesota Studies in Philosophy of Science on Causation and Biology, vol. XXI. Minneapolis: University of Minnesota Press.

13.4 Critical Notices

Woodward, J. (1985): "Critical Review: Horwich on the Ravens, Projectability and Induction." *Philosophical Studies*, v. 47, n. 3, pp. 409–428.
Woodward, J. (1990): "Laws and Causes." *The British Journal for the Philosophy of Science*, v. 41, pp. 553–573. This is a review article of the books of Michael Tooley's *Causation: A Realist Approach* and James Fetzer (ed.), *Probability and Causality*.
Woodward, J. (1994): "Essay Review of Paul Humphreys' *The Chances of Explanation*." *British Journal for the Philosophy of Science*, v. 45, n. 1, pp. 353–374.
Woodward, J. (2003): "Critical Notice: *Causality* by Pearl." *Economics and Philosophy*, v. 19, n. 2, pp. 321–340.

13.5 Book Reviews

Woodward, J. (1985): "Paul Horwich: *Probability and Evidence*." *Erkenntnis*, v. 23, n. 3, pp. 213–219.
Woodward, J. (1985): "Rolf Sartorius, Editor: *Paternalism*." *Ethics*, v. 95, n. 2, pp. 353–354.
Woodward, J. (1985): "Peter Achinstein: *The Nature of Explanation*." *Ethics*, v. 95, n. 2, pp. 359–360.
Woodward, J. (1985): "Henry Kyburg: *Epistemology and Inference*." *Ethics*, v. 95, n. 2, p. 391.
Woodward, J. (1985): "D. M. Armstrong: *What Is a Law of Nature?*" *Ethics*, v. 95, n. 4, pp. 949–951.
Woodward, J. (1986): "Robert John Ackermann: *Data, Instruments and Theory: A Dialectical Approach to Understanding in Science*." *Philosophy of Science*, v. 53, n. 3, pp. 455–458.

Woodward, J. (1988): "W. Essler, H. Putnam and W. Stegmuller, eds: *Epistemology, Methodology and Philosophy of Science: Essays in Honour of Carl G. Hempel on the Occasion of his 80th Birthday, January 8th, 1985*." *Ethics*, v. 98, n. 3, p. 621.

Woodward, J. (1988): "William K Lowrance: *Modern Science and Human Values*." *Ethics*, v. 98, n. 3, pp. 630–631.

Woodward, J. (1988): "Wesley Salmon: *Scientific Explanation and the Causal Structure of the World*." *Nous*, v. 22, n. 2, pp. 322–324.

Woodward, J. (1993): "Paul Humphreys: *The Chances of Explanation*." *Philosophy of Science*, v. 60, n. 4, pp. 671–673.

Woodward, J. (1996): "David Ruben: *Explaining Explanation*." *Philosophy and Phenomenological Research*, v. 56, n. 2, pp. 477–482.

Woodward, J. (2002): "Ronald Giere: *Science without Laws*." *Philosophy of Science*, v. 69, pp. 379–384.

Woodward, J. and Adolphs, R. (2004): "Jean Changeux: *The Physiology of Truth*." *Science*, v. 306, p. 1684.

Woodward, J. (2012): "Samuel Bowles and Herbert Gintis: *A Cooperative Species: Human Reciprocity and Its Evolution*." *Journal of Economic History*, v. 72, n. 2, pp. 564–566.

13.6 Other Publications

Woodward, J. (1986): "The Non-identity Problem." *Ethics*, v. 96, pp. 804–831.

Woodward, J. (1987): "Reply to Parfit." *Ethics*, v. 97, n. 4, pp. 800–816.

Woodward, J. (1992): "Liberalism and Migration." In: Barry, B. and Goodin, R. (eds.): *Free Movement: Ethical Issues in the Transnational Migration of People and Money*, pp. 59–84. London: Harvester-Wheatsheaf.

Bogen, J. and Woodward, J. (2005): "Evading the IRS." In: Jones, M. and Cartwright, N. (eds.): *Correcting the Model: Idealization and Abstraction in Science*, Poznan Studies in the Philosophy of Science and the Humanities, pp. 233–267. Amsterdam: Rodopi.

Woodward, J. (2016): "Justice and Reciprocity: The Case for Non Ideal Theory." *Social Philosophy and Policy*, v. 33, pp. 122–154.

14 Bibliography on James F. Woodward

Clearly, recent years have shown an increasing interest in Woodward's philosophy and, in particular, in his conception of causal explanation. In addition to his interventionist theory on this topic, causality has had a sort of revival in philosophy, especially in philosophy and methodology of science. In this regard, the present bibliography offers a selection of the publications related to causal explanation and philosophy of psychology that can be connected to his philosophical approach.[81]

---

[81] I am thankful to José Francisco Martínez-Solano and Jessica Rey for their contribution to this bibliographical information.

Devoted to causality and causal explanation, there are several books where many additional references can be found, such as Beebee, H., Hitchcock, Ch. and Menzies, P. (eds.) (2009): *The Oxford Handbook of Causation.* Oxford: Oxford University Press; Beebee, H., Hitchcock, Ch., and Price, H. (eds.) (2017): *Making a Difference: Essays on the Philosophy of Causation.* Oxford: Oxford University Press; Hausman, D. M. (1998): *Causal Asymmetries.* Cambridge: Cambridge University Press; Psillos, S. (2002): *Causation and Explanation.* Chesham: Acumen (London: Routledge, 2014); McKay Illary, Ph., Russo, F., and Williamson, J. (eds.) (2011): *Causality in Sciences.* Oxford: Oxford University Press; Russo, F. and Williamson, J. (eds.) (2007): *Causality and Probability in the Sciences.* London: College Publications; and Roessler, J., Eilen, N., and Lerman, H. (eds.) (2011): *Causation, Perception, and Objectivity: Issues in Philosophy and Psychology.* Oxford: Oxford University Press.

Oriented to philosophy of psychology, there is a large number of publications, which pay attention to the scientific status of psychology and the most influential schools among psychologists. Among the recent books with extensive bibliographic information are Margolis, E., Samuels, R., and Stich, S. (eds.) (2012): *The Oxford Handbook of Philosophy of Cognitive Science.* Oxford: Oxford University Press; Mason, K., Sripada, Ch. S., and Stich, S. (2008): "The Philosophy of Psychology." In: Moran, D. (ed.): *Routledge Companion to Twentieth-Century Philosophy,* pp. 583–617. Abingdon: Routledge; Symons, J. and Calvo, P. (eds.) (2009): *The Routledge Companion to Philosophy of Psychology.* London: Routledge; Thagard, P. (ed.) (2007): *Philosophy of Psychology and Cognitive Science.* Amsterdam: Elsevier; and Weiskopf, D., and Adams, F. (2015): *An Introduction to the Philosophy of Psychology.* Cambridge: Cambridge University Press.

Previous works of interest are Block, N. (ed.) (1980): *Readings in Philosophy of Psychology,* vol. 1. London: Methuen, and (1985) vol. 2. London: Methuen; Carruthers, P. and Botterill, G. (1999): *The Philosophy of Psychology.* Cambridge: Cambridge University Press; Chisholm, R. M., Marek, J. C., Blackmore, J. C., and Hubner, A. (eds.) (1985): *Philosophy of Mind-Philosophy of Psychology.* Vienna: Hölder-Pichler-Tempsky; Haugeland, J. (ed.) (1997): *Mind Design II: Philosophy, Psychology, and Artificial Intelligence.* Cambridge, MA: The MIT Press; and Margolis, J. (1984): *Philosophy of Psychology.* Englewood Cliffs, NJ: Prentice Hall. In the present section the focus is on the works on philosophy of psychology that can be connected with the topics of the conception developed by Woodward.

Apel, J. (2011): "On the Meaning and the Epistemological Relevance of the Notion of a Scientific Phenomenon." *Synthese,* v. 182, n. 1, pp. 23–38.

Baumgartner, M. (2013): "Rendering Interventionism and Non-reductive Physicalism Compatible." *Dialectica,* v. 67, n. 1, pp. 1–27.

Bogen, J. (2002): "Epistemological Custard Pies from Functional Brain Imaging." *Philosophy of Science,* v. 69, n. S3, pp. S59–S71.

Bogen, J. (2010): "Noise in the World." *Philosophy of Science,* v. 77, n. 5, pp. 778–791.

Boumans, M. (2005): "Measurement outside the Laboratory." *Philosophy of Science,* v. 72, n. 5, pp. 850–863.

Cartwright, N. (2002): "Against Modularity, the Causal Markov Condition, and Any Link between the Two: Comments on Hausman and Woodward." *British Journal for the Philosophy of Science,* v. 53, n. 3, pp. 411–453.

Cartwright, N. (2003): "Two Theorems on Invariance and Causality." *Philosophy of Science,* v. 70, n. 1, pp. 203–224.

Cartwright, N. (2004): "Causation: One Word, Many Things." *Philosophy of Science,* v. 71, n. 5, pp. 805–820.

Cartwright, N. (2006): "From Metaphysics to Method: Comments on Manipulability and the Causal Markov Condition." *British Journal for the Philosophy of Science*, v. 57, n. 1, pp. 197–218.

Chinn, C. A. and Brewer, W. F. (1996): "Mental Models in Data Interpretation." *Philosophy of Science*, v. 63 (supplement), pp. S211–S219.

Collins, J., Hall, N., and Paul. L. A. (eds.) (2004): *Causation and Counterfactuals*. Cambridge, MA: The MIT Press.

De Vreese, L. (2006): "Pluralism in the Philosophy of Causation: Desideratum or Not?" *Philosophica*, v. 77, pp. 5–13.

Dowe, Ph. (2009): "Would-cause Semantics." *Philosophy of Science*, v. 76, n. 5, pp. 701–711.

Eberhardt, F. and Scheines, R. (2007): "Interventions and Causal Inference." *Philosophy of Science*, v. 74, n. 5, pp. 981–995.

Galavotti, M. C. (2010): "Probabilistic Causality, Observation and Experimentation." In: Gonzalez, W. J. (ed.): *New Methodological Perspectives on Observation and Experimentation in Science*, pp. 139–155. A Coruña: Netbiblo.

Galavotti, M. C., Suppes, P., and Costantini, D. (eds.) (2001): *Stochastic Causality*. Stanford: CSLI.

Gijsbers, V. and de Bruin, L. (2014): "How Agency Can Solve Interventionism's Problem of Circularity." *Synthese*, v. 191, n. 8, pp. 1775–1791.

Glymour, B. (2000): "Data and Phenomena: A Distinction Reconsidered." *Erkenntnis*, v. 52, n. 1, pp. 29–37.

Glymour, C. (2004): "Critical Notice: James Woodward, *Making Things Happen: A Theory of Causal Explanation*." *British Journal for the Philosophy of Science*, v. 55, pp. 779–790.

Glymour, C. (2007): "When Is a Brain Like the Plane?" *Philosophy of Science*, v. 74, n. 3, pp. 330–347.

Glymour, C., Danks, D., Glymour, B., Eberhardt, F., Ramsey, J., Scheines, R., Spirtes, P., Teng, C., and Zhang, J. (2010): "Actual Causation: A Stone Soup Essay." *Synthese*, v. 175, pp. 169–192.

Glynn, L. (2013): "Of Miracles and Interventions." *Erkenntnis*, v. 78 (supplement 1), pp. 43–64.

Gonzalez, W. J. (2010): "Recent Approaches on Observation and Experimentation: A Philosophical-methodological Viewpoint." In: Gonzalez, W. J. (ed.): *New Methodological Perspectives on Observation and Experimentation in Science*, pp. 9–48. A Coruña: Netbiblo.

Goodwin, W. (2013): "Quantum Chemistry and Organic Theory." *Philosophy of Science*, v. 80, n. 5, pp. 1159–1169.

Gopnik, A. (2012): "Scientific Thinking in Young Children: Theoretical Advances, Empirical Research, and Policy Implications." *Science*, v. 337, pp. 1623–1627.

Gopnik, A., and Schulz, L. (eds.) (2007): *Causal Learning: Psychology, Philosophy and Computation*. New York: Oxford University Press.

Hall, N. (2006): "Comments on Woodward, *Making Things Happen*." *History and Philosophy of Life Sciences*, v. 28, n. 4, pp. 611–624.

Halpern, J. and Pearl, J. (2005): "Causes and Explanations: A Structural-model Approach – Part I: Causes." *British Journal for the Philosophy of Science*, v. 56, pp. 843–887.

Halpern, J. and Pearl, J. (2005): "Causes and Explanations: A Structural-model Approach – Part II: Explanations." *British Journal for the Philosophy of Science*, v. 56, pp. 889–911.

Hanzel, I. (2008): "Idealizations and Concretizations in Laws and Explanations in Physics." *Journal for the General Philosophy of Science*, v. 39, n. 2, pp. 273–301.

Harris, T. (2003): "Data Models and the Acquisition and Manipulation of Data." *Philosophy of Science*, v. 70, n. 5, pp. 1508–1517.

Hiddleston, E. (2005): "James Woodward: *Making Things Happen*." *The Philosophical Review*, v. 114, n. 4, pp. 545–547.

Hitchcock, Ch. (2012): "Portable Causal Dependence: A Tale of Consilience." *Philosophy of Science*, v. 79, n. 5, pp. 942–951.

Humphreys, P. (2006): "Invariance, Explanation, and Understanding." *Metascience*, v. 15, pp. 39–44.

Imbert, C. (2013): "Relevance, not Invariance, Explanatoriness, not Manipulability: Discussion of Woodward's Views on Explanatory Relevance." *Philosophy of Science*, v. 80, n. 5, pp. 625–636.

Jansson, L. (2014): "Causal Theories of Explanation and the Challenge of Explanatory Disagreement." *Philosophy of Science*, v. 81, n. 3, pp. 332–348.

Jantzen, B. and Danks, D. (2008): "Biological Codes and Topological Causation." *Philosophy of Science*, v. 75, n. 3, pp. 259–277.

Karbasizadeh, A. E. (2008): "Revising the Concept of Lawhood: Special Sciences and Natural Kinds." *Synthese*, v. 162, n. 1, pp. 15–30.

Kistler, M. (2013): "The Interventionist Account of Causation and Non-causal Association Laws." *Erkenntnis*, v. 78 (supplement 1), pp. 65–84.

Leonelli, S. (2009): "On the Locality of Data and Claims about Phenomena." *Philosophy of Science*, v. 76, n. 5, pp. 737–749.

Leuridan, B. and Froeyman, A. (2012): "On Lawfulness in History and Historiography." *History and Theory*, v. 51, n. 2, pp. 172–192.

Malaterre, Ch. (2011): "Making Sense of Downward Causation in Manipulationism: Illustrations from Cancer Research." *History and Philosophy of the Life Sciences*, v. 33, n. 4, pp. 537–561.

Massimi, M. (2011): "From Data to Phenomena: A Kantian Stance." *Synthese*, v. 182, n. 1, pp. 101–116.

McAllister, J. W. (1997): "Phenomena and Patterns in Data Sets." *Erkenntnis*, v. 47, n. 2, pp. 217–228.

McAllister, J. W. (2010): "The Ontology of Patterns in Empirical Data." *Philosophy of Science*, v. 77, n. 5, pp. 804–814.

Menzies, P. (2006): "Making Things Happen: A Theory of Causal Explanation." *Mind*, v. 115, n. 459, pp. 821–826.

Mitchell, S. D. (2008): "Exporting Causal Knowledge in Evolutionary and Developmental Biology." *Philosophy of Science*, v. 75, n. 5, pp. 697–706.

Paslaru, V. (2009): "Ecological Explanation between Manipulation and Mechanism Description." *Philosophy of Science*, v. 76, n. 5, pp. 821–837.

Price, H. and Corry, R. (eds.) (2007): *Causation, Physics, and the Constitution of Reality. Russell's Republicanism Revisited*. Oxford: Clarendon Press.

Priest, G. (2013): "Lost in Translation: A Reply to Woodward." *Philosophy and Phenomenological Research*, v. 86, n. 1, pp. 194–199.

Psillos, S. (2004): "A Glimpse of the *Secret Connexion*: Harmonizing Mechanisms with Counterfactuals." *Perspectives on Science*, v. 12, pp. 288–319.

Psillos, S. (2007): "Causal Explanation and Manipulation." In: Persson, J. and Ylikoski, P. (eds.): *Rethinking Explanation*, pp. 93–107. Dordrecht: Springer.

Ramsey, J. L. (2008): "Mechanisms and Their Explanatory Challenges in Organic Chemistry." *Philosophy of Science*, v. 75, n. 5, pp. 970–982.

Reiss, J. (2005): "Causal Instrumental Variables and Interventions." *Philosophy of Science*, v. 72, n. 5, pp. 964–976.

Reiss, J. (2009): "Counterfactuals, Thought Experiments, and Singular Causal Analysis in History." *Philosophy of Science*, v. 79, n. 5, pp. 712–723.

Rosenberg, A. (2012): "Why Do Spatiotemporally Restricted Regularities Explain in the Social Sciences?" *The British Journal for the Philosophy of Science*, v. 63, n. 1, pp. 1–26.

Saatsi, J. and Pexton, M. (2013): "Reassessing Woodward's Account of Explanation: Regularities, Counterfactuals, and Noncausal Explanations." *Philosophy of Science*, v. 80, n. 5, pp. 613–624.

Schindler, S. (2011): "Bogen and Woodward's Data-phenomena Distinction, Forms of Theory-ladenness, and the Reliability of Data." *Synthese*, v. 182, n. 1, pp. 39–55.

Schindler, S. (2014): "Explanatory Fictions – for Real?" *Synthese*, v. 191, n. 8, pp. 1741–1755.

Sobel, D. M., Tenenbaum, J. B., and Gopnik, A. (2004): "Children's Causal Inferences from Indirect Evidence: Backwards Locking and Bayesian Reasoning in Preschoolers." *Cognitive Science*, v. 28, pp. 303–333.

Sober, E. (2006): "Invariance, Explanation, and Understanding." *Metascience*, v. 15, pp. 45–53.

Steel, D. (2006): "Comment on Hausman and Woodward on the Causal Markov Condition." *British Journal for the Philosophy of Science*, v. 57, n. 1, pp. 219–231.

Strevens, M. (2007): "Making Things Happen: A Theory of Causal Explanation." *Philosophy and Phenomenological Research*, v. 74, n. 1, pp. 233–249.

Tal, E. (2011): "From Data to Phenomena and Back Again: Computer-simulated Signatures." *Synthese*, v. 182, n. 1, pp. 117–129.

Teller, P. (2010): "'Saving the Phenomena' Today." *Philosophy of Science*, v. 77, n. 5, pp. 815–826.

Votsis, I. (2011): "Data Meet Theory: Up Close and Inferentially Personal." *Synthese*, v. 182, n. 1, pp. 89–100.

Waskan, J. (2011): "Mechanistic Explanation at the Limit." *Synthese*, v. 183, n. 3, pp. 389–408.

Waters, C. K. (2005): "Why Genic and Multilevel Selection Theories Are Here to Stay." *Philosophy of Science*, v. 72, n. 2, pp. 311–333.

Weber, M. (2008): "Causes without Mechanisms: Experimental Regularities, Physical Laws, and Neuroscientific Explanation." *Philosophy of Science*, v. 75, n. 5, pp. 995–1007.

Weslake, B. (2006): "Review of *Making Things Happen: A Theory of Causal Explanation*." *Australasian Journal of Philosophy*, v. 84, n. 1, pp. 136–140.

Weslake, B. (2010): "Explanatory Depth." *Philosophy of Science*, v. 77, n. 2, pp. 273–294.

Yablo, S. (1992): "Mental Causation." *The Philosophical Review*, v. 101, pp. 245–280.

Zwier, K. R. (2013): "An Epistemology of Causal Inference from Experiment." *Philosophy of Science*, v. 80, n. 5, pp. 660–671.

James Woodward
Normative Theory and Descriptive Psychology in Understanding Causal Reasoning: The Role of Interventions and Invariance

Abstract: This paper explores some relationships between, on the one hand, normative philosophical theories of causation and causal reasoning and, on the other hand, descriptive theories of causal cognition of the sort produced in psychology. These issues are discussed from the perspective of an interventionist account of causation. The focus is on what I call distinctions *among* causal relationships in terms of such features as invariance, specificity and proportionality and the psychological significance of these. It is argued that normative and descriptive theorizing about causation have a great deal to learn from each other.

Keywords: causation, interventionism, invariance, causal specificity, proportionality

1 Introduction: The Normative and the Descriptive

The burgeoning literature on causation and causal cognition (causal learning, reasoning and judgment) spans many different disciplines, including philosophy, statistics, artificial intelligence and machine learning, as well as psychology. But broadly speaking, this research may be divided into two categories, although the division is far from tidy and there is considerable overlap.

First, there is work that is primarily *normative* in character in the sense that it purports say how we *ought* to learn and reason about a causal relationship and make causal judgments. This normative focus is perhaps most obvious in the case of theories of causal learning and inference from various sorts of data that have been developed in statistics and machine learning. These theories make proposals about which inferences to causal conclusions are *justified* – that is, which such inferences lead reliably to the achievement of some epistemic goal (such as truth). I include in this category of normative causal learning theories conventional causal modeling techniques based on structural equations modeling, the constraint-based approach to causal inference developed by Spirtes, Glymour and Scheines (2000), the ideas about causal reasoning described in Pearl (2000), the many flavors of Bayesian treatments of causal inference (e.g. Griffiths and Tenenbaum 2009) and other proposals about causal inference based on machine learning ideas, such as those due to Bernhard Schollkopf and his collaborators (e.g. Janzig et al. 2012). It is perhaps less common to think of the various accounts of causation and causal reasoning found in the philosophical literature as also normative in aspiration, but in my opinion they may be usefully viewed in this way, although they may have other goals as well.[1] Virtually all such philosophical accounts may be viewed as recommendations for how we *should* think about causation or which causal concepts we should employ and, since these recommendations in turn entail particular causal judgments, also as normative proposals about the causal judgments we ought to make. For example, on this way of looking at matters, philosophical accounts of causation according to which so-called double prevention relations (see section 5 below) are not genuine causal relationships because of the absence of a connecting process linking cause and effect can be thought of as normative proposals about how we should conceptualize the notion of causation and which about causal judgments are correct or warranted when double prevention relations are present. From this perspective, we may think of someone adopting the view that double prevention relations without connecting processes are not causal as committed to the claim there is some normative rationale or justification, connected to goals associated with causal reasoning, for distinguishing dependence relationships with connecting processes from those lacking this feature. We can then ask what this rationale is and whether it justifies the distinction in question.[2] Implicit in this way of viewing matters is the idea that we have *choices*

---

[1] In my view, many philosophers working on causation tend to efface the normative dimensions of what they are doing by, e.g., describing their projects as providing an account of what causation "is" or as providing a "metaphysics" of causation. This may make it sound as their role is merely reportorial or descriptive (of "causal reality" or the ontology of causation) and has no normative content (beyond such description). But of course there are many different ways of correctly describing the world. (There is nothing incorrect, for example, about just reporting correlations). We thus face the question of why we should think causally at all and why, in doing so, we should employ some particular way of thinking about causation rather than any one of a number of possible alternatives. In my view, answers to these questions will inevitably have a normative dimension and will require reference to our goals and purposes.

[2] Again, this way of viewing matters contrasts with the more usual practice (especially among metaphysicians) of thinking of the issue as simply one of whether double prevention relations are "really" causal or not. What I am urging is that we should ask whether we *should*, given

about which causal concepts to adopt (and about what commitments should be carried by such concepts) and that these choices can be evaluated in terms of how well they serve our goals and purposes.

As another illustration, David Lewis' well-known counterfactual theory of causation (Lewis 1973) and the similarity metric characterizing closeness of possible worlds on which it relies may be regarded as (among other things) a normative proposal about which causal claims should be judged as true and about the considerations that are relevant to assessing their truth. According to this normative proposal, causal claims should be judged as true or false depending on whether they are related to true counterfactuals in they way that Lewis' theory describes. Moreover, the true counterfactuals are those that are judged as such by the particular criteria for judging similarity among possible worlds that Lewis endorses. As an alternative normative proposal, one might imagine an account that still links causal claims to counterfactuals but makes use of a different similarity metric which is judged to be superior in some way to the metric Lewis employs – perhaps because it is clearer or more closely connected to whatever goals we think should guide causal inference. It then becomes a reasonable question why we should use Lewis' metric rather than this alternative.[3] Finally, the "interventionist" account of causation that I favor is also normative, both in the sense that it makes recommendations about which causal claims should be judged true or false, and in other respects as well – for example, as I have tried to explain elsewhere (e.g. Woodward 2015), the interventionist account imposes restrictions on the sorts of variables that can figure in well-posed causal claims, embodies ideas about which variables it is appropriate to "control for" in assessing "multi-level" causal claims, what sort of evidence is relevant to assessing such claims and so on. The distinctions among casual claims (with respect to features like stability and proportionality) that I have explored in more recent work (e.g. Woodward 2010) and which are discussed in more detail below are also intended to be taken normatively – I claim these are distinctions that it is appropriate or rational to make, given our epistemic goals.

---

our goals and purposes, view such relations as causal, thus highlighting the normative aspect of this question.

3 I assume of course that it is not an adequate response just to say that the reason for adopting Lewis' metric is that it captures "our" concept of causation. This just raises the question of why we should use (or why we do use) "our" concept rather than some alternative. What is needed is a response that shows that "our concept" serves goals and purposes we have (cf. Woodward 2003, pp. 137 ff.).

Alongside of these normative ideas, there is also a very rich and rapidly growing body of research that is more descriptive in aspiration: it purports to describe, as a matter of empirical fact, how various populations (adult humans, human children of various ages, non-human animals) learn and (where appropriate) reason about and judge with respect to causal relationships. A great deal of this work is conducted by psychologists but important portions of it can also be found in the literature on animal learning, comparative animal cognition, and, in some cases, in disciplines like anthropology. Moreover, although many philosophers would probably prefer not to think about what they are doing in this way,[4] the philosophical literature on causation is full of what look, at least on first inspection, like empirical descriptive claims – for example, claims that appeal to what people "would say" or how they in fact would think or judge regarding the truth of various causal claims. Thus one finds philosophers claiming that ordinary folk do or do not judge relationships between two candidate events to be causal (at least strictly and properly speaking) when there is counterfactual dependence but no "connecting process" linking the two events. (Compare Dowe 2000 with Schaffer 2000). In addition, one also finds in the philosophical literature many claims that are naturally understood as implicit descriptive claims about the sorts of evidence and other considerations that people rely on in reaching causal conclusions. For example, many discussions of so-called probabilistic theories of causation (e.g. Suppes 1970) would make little sense if it were not true that people systematically make use of information about probabilistic relationships among events (and, at least for some versions of probabilistic theories, *only* such information) in reaching causal conclusions. Similarly, Lewis' discussion of causal asymmetry seems to rest on the idea that people's judgments of such asymmetry are somehow guided by or closely track

---

4 Philosophers who are inclined to deny that they are making descriptive empirical claims about the causal judgments that people in fact make but who nonetheless appeal to "what we think" often describe what they are doing in terms of reporting their (or other's) "intuitions" about causation (or something similar, even if the word "intuition" is not used). A standard line is that intuitions are distinguished from mere descriptive claims about what the intuiter or others think because intuitions (or at least "correct" or "veridical" intuitions) involve some special sort of epistemic access or insight into non-psychological subject matter – e.g., into "causation itself." Those who think, as I do, that such views about intuition are incredible will also be unimpressed by this supposed distinction between genuine intuitions and mere empirical psychological claims, describing what the philosopher or others think. In any case even the most unreconstructed intuiters usually recognize some constraints from empirical psychology – for example, they are usually troubled (as they should be) by empirical results showing large numbers of people don't share their intuitions. So even for inveterate intuiters, empirical research about how people in fact learn and reason causally ought to matter.

beliefs they hold about such matters as the number of "miracles" required to produce convergence and divergence between different possible worlds.

A natural question, which this paper will explore, has to do with the relationship between these two forms of theorizing about causation and causal cognition – the descriptive and the normative. Should we think of them as entirely independent, perhaps on the grounds that there is a fundamental and unbridgeable gulf between "is" and "ought" and that how people ought to reason about causation (or anything else) has no bearing on how they do reason, and conversely? Or should we think of these two enterprises as related and, if so, how?

This paper and a companion paper in this volume (Woodward 2018) will argue that although there is of course a difference between how people in fact reason causally and how they ought to reason, nonetheless the two enterprises just described are in many ways closely related and each can be fruitfully influenced by the other. This influence can take a number of different forms, which I will try to illustrate below. First, normative theories of causation can suggest descriptive hypotheses about causality and cognition, possible experiments for assessing such hypotheses, and possible interpretations of experimental results that researchers are unlikely to think of in the absence of normative theorizing. A key idea here is that normative theories can play this role in part because they provide benchmarks or ideals against which actual performance can be compared, measured and understood. That is, it is very often a good strategy, in attempting to construct a descriptively adequate theory of a subject's causal cognition to begin with a normative theory of how this cognition ought to be conducted and then ask, as a descriptive matter, to what extent the cognition in question conforms to the requirements of the normative theory. Similar strategies of using normative theories as benchmarks to guide empirical research have been employed very fruitfully in other domains, including vision research (with the use of "ideal observer" analyses), decision theory and the study of non-causal learning.[5] I suggest that they are similarly fruitful when applied to causal cognition.

A closely related idea which helps to provide motivation for this strategy of guidance by normative theory is that among the empirical facts that we want a descriptive theory to explain are facts about the extent to which the causal cognition strategies of various subjects are *successful* or not in learning about the causal structure of the world. To explain such success or failure, we require a

---

[5] A well known illustration involving non-causal learning is provided by computational theories of temporal difference learning which were originally introduced as normative proposals in computer science. These have been used very successfully in a descriptive vein to illuminate the behavior of dopaminergic neurons and their role in reward computation.

normative theory that characterizes success and failure and tells us which procedures for learning, reasoning and so on will lead to success (or its absence). In particular, in comparison with other animals, including other primates, human beings are remarkably successful in learning about causal relationships and their capacities for successful causal leaning develop and improve over time. In fact even very young children are better causal learners in a number of respects than other primates. One would like an adequate descriptive theory of causal cognition to (among other things) explain how this success is achieved, just as an adequate theory of visual processing should explain how (in virtue of what inference procedures) the visual system is able to extract reliable information about the distal visual environment from visual stimuli.[6]

A second point about the role of normative theorizing is this: by making explicit the logical relationships between various sorts of causal claims and other sorts of claims (about e. g., patterns of covariation), normative theories can constrain the interpretative conclusions drawn from empirical results in various ways. Suppose, for example, it is correct, as interventionists claim (see section 2), that causal judgments should be distinguished from judgments about patterns of covariation (causation is different from correlation) and that one of the distinguishing features of the former, in contrast to the latter, is that they have implications for what *would* happen if various interventions *were* to be performed. Consider the implications of this idea for the interpretation of experimental results based on differential looking times that are taken by many developmental psychologists to support strong conclusions about infant causal knowledge.[7] The question someone holding a normative version of interventionism will ask about such claims is this: What if anything in these results supports the conclusion that the infants have distinctively *causal* beliefs or knowledge as opposed to expectations based on experienced patterns of covariation? According to interventionism, to the extent infants have the former, they must have beliefs or expectations having to do with what would happen to such correlations

---

[6] None of this is to deny, of course, that people sometimes make mistakes in causal inference, hold confused or normatively inappropriate ideas about causation and so on. But the general position taken in this essay is that many humans (both adults and children) are more "rational" and more closely approximate normatively "good" behavior in learning and judgment than is often supposed. Relatedly, there is more continuity between the cognitive strategies of ordinary subjects, including children, and strategies adopted by scientific investigators and that we can often use our knowledge of the latter to illuminate the former. Whether and in what respects these claims are is a complex empirical matter, but for supporting evidence in the case of children see for example, Gopnik (2012).

[7] I have in mind here results of the sort reported in e.g. Baillargeon (2002) and Spelke et al. (2002).

were various actions or manipulations to be performed. In some cases such evidence may exist or be obtainable from other sources, but it does not appear to be provided just from the results of looking time studies, taken by themselves. To the extent that no such evidence is available, there are no grounds for interpreting looking time results as providing support for distinctively causal beliefs, when these are construed along interventionist lines.

As another illustration, in experiments discussed in more detail in Woodward (2018), Ahn et al. (1995) argue that as a descriptive matter, people's causal attributions very often rest on beliefs about "mechanisms" rather than covariational information, where they take these to be mutually exclusive alternatives. But both many normative accounts of mechanism information (including interventionist accounts, as in Woodward 2013) and Ahn et al.'s own examples of mechanistic information make it clear that such information *implies* claims about patterns of covariation. In particular, there seems no reason to doubt that the subjects in Ahn et al.'s experiments who cite mechanistic information take this to have implications about (and to be in part based on) covariational information. If so, one can't treat the hypotheses that the subjects rely on mechanistic information and that they rely on covariational information as competing and mutually exclusive alternatives and Ahn et al.'s results cannot be interpreted as showing that subjects rely on the former *instead* of the latter.

Just as normative theorizing can be helpful for the construction of descriptive theorizing, so also (I will suggest) empirical results often can be suggestive for normative theories. One way in which this can work is this: if we see that as a matter of empirical fact people's causal cognition and learning exhibits certain features F, it will often be a fruitful strategy to consider the possibility that some of these features F contribute to such success and thus are candidates for incorporation into normative theory. I will appeal to this strategy to provide partial support for some of the normative claims discussed below. Conversely, if in the course of defending a normative account of causal judgment, a philosopher (or whoever) appeals to empirical claims about features of the judgments most people make and the way in these contribute to success, and those empirical claims turn out to be false, then this suggests that the normative theory is either mistaken or needs to be supported in some other way.

This picture of the interaction between the descriptive and normative fits naturally with another idea which is implicit in what I have said so far. This has to do with the importance and fruitfulness, in carrying out both the descriptive and normative projects, of trying to understand causal learning, reasoning and judgment in (what I will call) *functional* terms.[8] This means thinking about causal cognition in terms of *goals* or *aims* it attempts to serve (its functions) and evaluating normative proposals about causal learning, judgment and so on in terms of how well they achieve those goals. In other words, in trying to understand causal reasoning, we should ask what we want to *do* with that reasoning and what aims or purposes we are trying to achieve. Causal reasoning should be understood as *for* various (non-trivial[9]) goals, and not just as an end in itself. It thus becomes crucially important to specify what those goals are (or might be).

As explained in section 2, interventionists think of these goals as having to do centrally with manipulation and control, but a functional approach to causation can be understood to encompass other possible goals – for example, another possible goal of causal cognition might be the representation of correlational information in a compressed and uniformed form or perhaps the representation of various facts about informational dependence and independence (as in Janzig et al. 2012). In what follows, however, I focus only on interventionist goals.

The remainder of this paper is organized as follows. Section 2 presents an overview of the interventionist account of causation and describes its extension to distinctions among different sorts of causal judgment that (I claim) make sense in the light of goals related to intervention. Section 3 then explores some possible psychological implications of the basic interventionist idea that causal claims can be understood as claims about the outcomes of hypothetical experiments. Sections 4 and 5 then discusses the normative role of invariance in causal judgment and its empirical implications, with a special focus in section 5 on judgments in double prevention cases, in which a physical connection between cause and effect is absent. The companion to this paper in this volume (Woodward 2018) continues the exploration of the normative and descriptive significance of invariance, focusing on cases in which a physical connection between cause and effect is present, on examples illustrating the importance of proportionality as a condition on causal claims, and on what happens when, contrary to the strategy I recommend, descriptive investigations are not guided by normative theory.

---

8 For a more extended defense of this idea, see Woodward (2015).
9 Of course it is possible to trivialize this idea about understanding causation in functional terms – for example by insisting that the goal of causal thinking is just stating the truth about the causal facts and nothing more. I take this to be a completely unilluminating move if only because this is a goal shared by virtually all accounts of causation.

2 Interventionism and Distinctions among Causal Relationships

I have described my version of the interventionist account in detail elsewhere (Woodward 2003) and will confine myself here to a short summary. In particular, my goal in what follows is not to provide a detailed defense of interventionism as a normative theory but rather to illustrate how the normative components of the theory might be related to various sorts of descriptive investigations. The starting point of the interventionist account is the idea that causal relationships are relationships that are exploitable in principle for manipulation and control. We can make this slightly more precise by means of the following principle:

(**M**) C causes E if and only if it is possible to intervene to change the value of C, in such a way that if that intervention were to occur, the value of E or the probability distribution of E would change.

Here an "intervention" is an idealized unconfounded manipulation of C, which changes E if at all only through C and not in some other way. From the point of view of the descriptive psychology of causal learning, it is an important fact that some human actions qualify as interventions and can be recognized as such, but the notion of an intervention itself can be specified without any reference to human beings or their activities. However, the notion of an intervention does require causal concepts for its specification – most obviously because an intervention on C *causes* a change in the variable intervened on. (See Woodward 2003 for more detailed discussion.) Note also that (**M**) does *not* say that the claim that C causes E is true only when C *is* changed via an intervention or that one can only learn about causal claims by performing interventions. According to (**M**), what matters for whether C causes E is whether interventions on C are possible and whether a counterfactual claim about what *would* happen to E if C *were* to be changed by an intervention is true, not whether C *is* changed by an intervention. (**M**) allows for the possibility that one can learn about causal relationships from many different sources, including passive observations not involving interventions, but implies that in all such cases the *content* of what is learned is captured by (**M**). In other words, when one learns that C causes E from passive observation (or from some other source not involving the performance of an intervention), one should think of oneself as having learned that E would change under some intervention on C, but without actually performing the intervention in question. If one's evidence is not sufficient to establish such claims about what would happen under interventions on C, one's evidence is not sufficient to establish that C causes E.[10]

(**M**) was originally intended as a normative criterion for distinguishing *between* causal relationships and relationships that are non-causal (because, e. g., they are merely correlational or fail to satisfy some other necessary condition for causation) and relatedly, as a principle that helps to clarify the content of causal claims (see below). Most philosophical theories of causation (whether counterfactual, probabilistic or regularity based) have as their aim providing distinguishing criteria of this kind. There is, however, another normative project concerning causation that has received much less attention and that is also worthy of pursuit. This second project also has a broadly interventionist motivation and is potentially fruitful from the point of view of empirical psychology. This project involves drawing distinctions that are normatively or descriptively important *among* causal relationships. This project asks the following question: suppose we have various relationships that are causal in the sense of satisfying (**M**). What further distinctions, if any, might it be useful or important to draw (either for normative or descriptive purposes) *among* these relationships. Here are some possible distinctions of this sort which I will discuss either in this paper or in Woodward (2018) – in each case causal relationships satisfying (**M**) can differ in the extent to which they possess the feature in question and this can have normative and descriptive significance.

Invariance: Causal relationships satisfying (**M**) can more or less *invariant* or stable. That is, they can differ in the extent to which they continue to hold under changes in background circumstances.

Proportionality:[11] A cause can satisfy (**M**) and be more or less *proportional* to its effect or be to a greater or less extent "at the right level" for its effect. Causal claims satisfying (M) are proportional to the extent that they are formulated in such a way that they capture or convey, either explicitly or implicitly, the full pattern of dependence of the values of the effect on the cause – that is, to the extent that they specify which and how changes in the values of the effect-variable are

---

10 It follows that we can evaluate proposed causal inferences on the basis of whether they provide evidence that allows conclusions to be reliably drawn about the outcomes of appropriate hypothetical experiments. Certain inferential procedures such as the use of instrumental variables or regression discontinuity designs satisfy this criterion particularly well, as discussed in Woodward (2015).

11 The characterization of proportionality that follows differs in some respects from my earlier in characterization in Woodward (2010). I have introduced changes that I hope address some of the criticisms that have been leveled at my earlier characterization (and similar characterizations by others).

associated with changes in the value of the cause-variable. In addition, causal claims should be judged as preferable to the extent that they do not claim or suggest the existence of patterns of dependence between cause and effect that do not in fact hold or represent values of the cause variable as relevant or difference-makers for the effect-variable when they are not relevant.

Specificity: Causes satisfying (**M**) can be more or less *specific*. A cause-effect relationship is specific to the extent that the cause has just one type of effect (among some range of possible types of effects) and the effect is the effect of just one type of cause (among some range of possible types of causes).

As already suggested, I see the project of exploring these distinctions as having both a normative and empirical component. On the normative side, we can ask whether it makes normative sense for people to make these distinctions among causal claims, given the goals they have or the functions ascribed to causal thinking. On the empirical/descriptive side, we can ask whether people in fact make distinctions among their causal judgments in terms of the features just described and whether and how these distinctions serve those goals. My view, which I will defend below, is that there is a normative rationale for each of the distinctions and that in each case this rationale is closely bound up with the interventionist idea that causal reasoning is closely connected to our concern with manipulation and control. In other words, not only does our concern with manipulation and control help to structure the distinctions that we make between causal and non-causal claims (captured, I claim, by (**M**)) but it also influences the above distinctions we make among causal relationships.

Before turning to details, there is another issue that I want to get on the table. Most accounts of causal learning and judgment, whether normative or descriptive, begin with a stock of variables (or properties or descriptive terms) which are assumed to be somehow antecedently available for the characterization of causal relationships or the data from which they are learned. However, typically no account is offered about where those variables come from. Moreover, it is a commonplace that this initial choice of variables heavily influences the results of any causal analysis. To take just one of the simplest possibilities, given two random variables X and Y, characterizing a body of data, with X and Y probabilistically independent, one can always transform these to different variables – e.g. Z = X + Y, W = X − Y – which are dependent. Thus the causal conclusions reached by any inference procedure that infers causal relationships from information about independence and dependence relations (and this is true of virtually all such inference procedures) will depend on the variables employed – e.g., the conclusion may be that either that X and Y are causally unrelated or, alternatively, that Z causes W, depending on which variables are employed. In a similar way, different choices of procedures for aggregating more fine-grained micro-variables into coarse-grained macro-variables will also influence conclusions about the causal relationships among those macro-variables. And for essentially the same reason, any philosophical account that tries to understand causation in terms of regularities, statistical relationships or counterfactuals will also produce results that depend on the variables employed. For example, given a situation which is correctly described as one in which Y counterfactually depends on X, one can always re-describe the same situation in terms of variables W and Z, definable from X and Y, where these variables are counterfactually independent.

On a normative level, this seems to imply that accounts of causal learning and judgment are incomplete unless accompanied by accounts of variable choice – that is by accounts which provide normative guidance about how to choose variables appropriately (or how to "improve" one's choice of variables given some initial starting point or how to learn new, better variables for the purposes of causal cognition). Similarly, on the level of descriptive psychology, an important project, if we are to fully understand casual learning and reasoning, is to understand where the variables or descriptions subjects employ come from – why subjects employ one set of variables rather than another, how they learn new or more appropriate variables and so on. It seems fair to say that, despite the importance of these issues, at present we know very little about either the descriptive or normative aspects of this problem.

Providing a satisfactory account of variable choice is far beyond the scope of this paper. Here I want only to suggest that the distinctions among causal claims causation that I will be discussing – the distinctions with respect to invariance, proportionality, and so on – have some role to play in understanding variable choice. Some choices of variables will be such that we can formulate relationships among those variables that score relatively highly along the dimensions of invariance, proportionality and so on, while other choices of variables will lead to the formulation of relationships that score less well along these dimensions. To the extent that there are normative rationales for valuing features like invariance and proportionality in causal relationships, it will make sense, normatively, to choose variables that facilitate these goals. To the extent that, as matter of empirical fact, a concern with these goals guides people's causal reasoning, we may also expect, as a matter of empirical fact, that their causal cognition will reflect these features. Thus an additional reason for paying attention to notions like invariance is that this may give us some help with the problems of variable choice. Section 4, in particular, will illustrate this idea.

3 Interventionist Interpretations of Causation: Normative and Descriptive Considerations

In this section my focus is on the interventionist account of causation, as represented by principle (**M**), and some empirical psychological claims that one can think of as "suggested" or "motivated" by this principle. To avoid misunderstanding, let me emphasize that it is certainly possible to regard (**M**) is a normative principle only, and to decline to consider whether as a descriptive matter, subject's behavior and cognition conform to anything like (**M**). Nothing in (**M**) construed as a normative claim *forces* us to connect it with empirical psychology.[12] On the other hand, for all of the reasons, suggested in section 1, exploration of such connections seems a potentially worthwhile endeavor, and in what follows I proceed on the basis of this assumption.

Let us consider, then, the prospects for interpreting (**M**) as part of a descriptive account of the causal cognition of adult humans and perhaps other subjects – that is, as characterizing aspects of how people think and reason about causal claims. I begin by remarking that although, as noted above, (**M**) does not claim that one can learn about causal claims *only* by performing interventions, it is natural to suppose, if (**M**) has any plausibility as a descriptive theory, that people will learn about causal relationships relatively readily and reliably if they are able to actually perform appropriate interventions and observe the results. In other words, if (**M**) is psychologically plausible one would expect that performing interventions should facilitate subject's causal learning in various contexts. In addition, if the normative theory associated with interventionism describes aspects of how subjects in fact reason, one might expect that subjects will be sensitive in their causal learning and judgment to various distinctions that are normatively important within an interventionist framework. For example, one can ask whether various subjects (human adults, human children of various ages, non-human animals) are appropriately sensitive to the normative difference between intervening and conditioning[13] and whether they respond in normatively

---

[12] By the same token, there is no logical inconsistency in holding that (**M**) is correct as a normative theory but that people's inferences usually fail to conform to anything like (**M**) – hence that people are mostly irrational. Of course this is not the view taken in this essay.

[13] For discussion of the contrast between conditioning and intervening see Woodward (2007). Given random variables X, Y and Z, one can ask, e. g., (i) whether X and Y are independent conditional on Z. This is a question about conditioning. One can also ask (ii) whether, e. g., X and Y would be independent under an intervention on X. This is a question about intervening. (i) and

appropriate ways to information suggesting that their manipulations are confounded and thus not true interventions. The empirical research on human causal learning done so far seems to suggest affirmative answers to all of these questions.[14]

Another empirical issue that is suggested by (**M**) is this: adult humans readily put together between what they learn about causal relationships on the basis of passive observation and what they learn on the basis of interventions – indeed, the adult human concept of causation is one according to which one thinks that the very same causal relationship can be present between X and Y, regardless of whether X is produced by an intervention of whether it is passively observed. Because adult human beings think about causal relationships in this way, they can use what they have learned about causal relationships from passive observation to design novel interventions: we can establish on the basis of passive observation that X causes Y and then use this information to bring about Y by intervening on X. One question this raises is whether there is a stage in the development of human causal cognition at which young children are not yet able to do this. The answer to this question again seems to be "yes" – although three year olds readily learn about causal relationships from observation of the results of their own (and others') interventions) in the absence of various facilitating conditions, they are unable to use correlational information from passive observation to design their own interventions. By contrast, five year olds presented with the same experimental stimuli are able to do this (Bonawitz et al. 2010). This represents one of many respects in which human causal concepts change over time in the course of development and learning.

There are also a number of philosophical criticisms that have been directed at (**M**) which raise interesting empirical as well as normative issues, meriting further exploration. One such philosophical criticism is that (**M**) is viciously "circular" because it claims to elucidate the notion of X's causing Y by appealing to a notion (that of an intervention) which is obviously itself causal in character. An adequate account of causation, the critics claim, must be non-circular – it must be "reductive" in the sense that it explicates what it is for X to cause Y in terms of concepts (like "regularity," "correlation" and so on) that are themselves entirely non-causal. According to the critics, (**M**), by contrast, in effect attempts to "explain causation in terms of causation" and they ask how can that possibly be illuminating. A second worry advanced by philosophical critics can be put this

---

(ii) are non-equivalent and it is what happens under interventions that is diagnostic of causation.

14 For more detail, see Woodward (2007).

way: when an experimental manipulation of X can actually be carried out, it is perhaps plausible (the critic says) that (**M**) provides a criterion for determining whether X causes Y. However, even in this case, the critic claims, this criterion is (at best) of purely epistemological significance. It doesn't tell us anything about the *semantics* or *metaphysics* of causation – what causal claims mean or what causation is or anything like that. Moreover, when an appropriate experimental manipulation of X is not or cannot be performed, it is even less clear how (**M**) could possibly be illuminating: (**M**) connects "X causes Y" to a counterfactual about what would happen if an intervention on X were to occur, but how can that counterfactual be of any use if we can't carry out the intervention in question?

These are complex questions. I won't attempt anything like a complete answer here,[15] but will instead focus on one strand or aspect of them, which illustrates my theme of the interaction between the descriptive and the normative. I begin with an empirical observation, although one that reports a frequently made normative claim. This is that many researchers in a number of different disciplines claim that it useful or illuminating to connect causal claims and the results of hypothetical experiments in something close to the way described by (**M**). For example, the potential response framework developed by Rubin, Holland and others (e.g. Rubin 1974) and now widely used in statistics, econometrics, and elsewhere in social science is organized around construing causal claims in just this manner. As another illustration, many historians are (at least officially) leery of making causal claims of any kind, but those historians who do make such claims (see, e.g. Davis 1968) again often insist on connecting such claims to counterfactuals, where these have a broadly interventionist interpretation. Researchers adopting this approach, in both history and social science, typically claim that it helps to clarify the content of causal claims and to understand what sort of evidence is relevant to their assessment if one associates them with appropriate hypothetical experiments and that this is so both when one can actually perform the experiment in question and, more interestingly, even when this is not possible (cf. Angrist and Pischke 2009). Of course it is possible for critics to respond that these researchers are simply confused – they think that this connection with purely hypothetical experiments is useful and illuminating when it is not – but I would advocate a more charitable approach in which we try to understand, at both a methodological and psychological level, how it is possible for this connection to be informative.

---

15 For more on how a non-reductive account of causation can nonetheless be explanatory, see Woodward (2003).

The first thing to note in this connection is that causal claims are often advanced in forms that are unclear or indeterminate. One of the things that can be accomplished by associating causal claims with hypothetical experiments in the manner described in (**M**) is to clarify what such claims mean ("mean" in the sense of what they commit us to[16]) and to make them more determinate and precise – we do so by making it explicit that they are to be understood in terms of some one particular hypothetical experiment (which we specify) rather than another such experiment. Doing this requires, among other things, that the variables that are taken to be causally related must be the sorts of factors that in principle can be manipulated or changed by interventions: they must be factors such that it "makes sense" to think in terms of manipulating them. It also requires that we make it explicit what the possible values of those variables are and that it be made explicit just how changing the cause-variable from one of its values to others leads to changes in the value of effect-variable. In the case of many causal claims of form "X causes Y" there will be a number of non-equivalent possible ways of doing this – that is different possible claims about the outcomes of hypothetical experiments that might be associated with the original causal claim. Thus indicating which such hypothetical experiment is intended can clarify or disambiguate the original causal claim.

As a simple illustration, consider the claim (cf. Glymour 1986) that

(3.1)   Smoking five packs of cigarettes a day causes a substantial increase in the probability of lung cancer.

One (uncharitable) way of associating this with a hypothetical experiment is to interpret (3.1) as claiming

(3.1*)   Any intervention that changes whether someone smokes five packs a day to some smaller number of packs (e.g. 4.9 packs) will substantially change the probability that person develops lung cancer.

Under this interpretation (3.1) is likely false. Another, more charitable interpretation of (3.1) – probably closer to what the speaker intended – is to interpret (3.1) as claiming that

---

[16] Or perhaps it would be better to say that (**M**) tells us what one *ought* to mean by causal claims or how such claims ought to be interpreted, if they are to be made clear and precise. Note that when understood in this way, (**M**) counts as a *semantic* proposal, even if it does not provide a reduction of causal claims to non-causal claims. In this respect, the criticism that (**M**) has no implications for the semantics or content of causal claims seems misguided.

(3.1**) An intervention that changes whether someone smokes five packs to that person not smoking at all, substantially changes the probability of that person developing lung cancer.

(3.1**) may well be true and is in any case obviously a different claim from (3.1*). Someone asserting (3.1) can clarify what is meant by indicating which of (3.1*) or (3.1**) is the intended interpretation.

As a second, considerably more controversial example, consider the claim

(3.2) Being a woman causes one to be discriminated against in hiring.

Again, interventionists are inclined to regard this claim as unclear and to think that it can be made clearer or disambiguated by making it explicit just which claim about the outcome of a hypothetical experiment is intended. From an interventionist perspective, the basic problem with (3.2) as it stands is that the notion of a manipulation of or intervention on "gender" or "being a woman" is unclear. One possible way of manipulating gender is to change the structure of an individual's sex chromosomes immediately after conception (substituting an X chromosome for a Y or vice-versa), Interpreted with this particular intervention in mind, (3.2) might be understood as claiming that (3.2*) such an intervention would change someone's probability of being hired for certain jobs. While this claim is (I assume) true, an alternative construal of (3.2) which I would guess comes closer to capturing what most of those asserting (3.2) intend to claim is this:[17]

(3.2**) Intervening to change an employer's beliefs about the gender of an applicant will change that person's probability of being hired.

Here (unlike 3.2*) the implication is that given two otherwise identical applicants (e.g., identical in qualifications) but differing only in gender and features like external sex characteristics, male applicants are more likely to be hired. Note that in this case, the variable which is viewed as the target of the intervention (and the cause) is "employer beliefs about gender" rather than gender itself. (This illustrates how the interventionist framework forces one to be more precise

---

[17] To see the difference between (3.2*) and (3.2**), note that (3.2*) would be true under a regime in which hiring is based entirely on the applicant's merit and qualifications as long as different genders develop different interests and abilities that cause them to be differentially qualified for various jobs. Presumably what is intended by (3.2) is some claim to the effect that hiring decisions involving women are not made on the basis of the applicant's merit and qualifications and that qualified women are not hired because of their gender. (3.2**) comes closer to capturing this.

about which variables are the intended causal relata.) (3.2**) is a claim that might be (and in fact has been tested) by, for example, submitting otherwise identical resumes in which only the gender of job applicants has been altered. In any case, the important point for our purposes is that (3.2) and (3.2**) are non-equivalent claims which may well have different truth-values. It does not seem controversial that it would be worthwhile for someone asserting (3.2) to think through which of these possibilities he or she has in mind.

These considerations suggest at least part of (or one component of) a story about how it is possible for a claim like (**M**) to be useful or illuminating in elucidating the content of causal claims, despite its apparent "circularity": Thinking in terms of (**M**) (and more generally interpreting causal claims as claims about the outcomes of hypothetical experiments) forces one to be more precise and explicit about what causal claims commit us to and how they might be tested. If correct, this would explain the observation made above – that researchers in many different disciplines find it helpful to associate causal claims with hypothetical experiments. Note also that nothing in this strategy requires that one be able to carry out a reduction of causal claims to non-causal claims.

If anything like this suggestion/speculation is correct, it suggests further empirical questions. For example, it would be worthwhile to investigate to what extent it is true (as the above story suggests) that various subjects (both experts and others) perform better at causal learning and reasoning tasks if they are prompted to associate causal claims with hypothetical experiments in the manner described.[18]

It would also be interesting to learn more about the psychological mechanisms that underlie whatever abilities are at work when we associate causal claims with hypothetical experiments. In an interesting series of papers (e.g. Gendler 2007), Gendler invokes dual systems theory to explain the apparent fact that we seem capable of learning from thought experiments. Very roughly dual systems theory claims that human psychological processing is organized into two systems. System 1 is fast, automatic, "intuitive," and often operates unconsciously while system 2 is slower, more deliberative and reliant on explicit, conscious processing. Gendler's idea is that often when we engage in a thought experiment we "run" or otherwise make use of information supplied by system 1 and plug it into or make it available for processing in a more explicit form by system 2. One can think, as I do, that the system 1 versus system 2 dichotomy

---

18 There is some evidence that experts in international relations who systematically entertain counterfactuals when advancing causal judgments are more reliable than experts who do not do this (cf. Tetlock 2005).

is vastly oversimplified, and yet still think that there is something right about Gendler's basic idea and that some version of it can also be used to help elucidate how associating causal claims with hypothetical experiments can be illuminating. The thought would be that when one entertains a causal claim like "X causes Y" not everything that is relevant to reasoning with the claim or testing is (at least initially) explicit and available for critical assessment. One can entertain the claim that "X causes Y" without thinking, at least very clearly and explicitly, about just what would be involved in changing or manipulating X or how one expects Y to change under various possible manipulations of X. Associating "X causes Y" with a hypothetical experiment forces one to be explicit about such matters and one often does this by drawing on information that one "has" in some sense (it is present in one's system 1), but which one has not previously integrated explicitly into one's causal judgment. Put this way, the idea underlying (**M**) is not so much that whenever one entertains a causal claim one is necessarily thinking of it or representing it as a claim about two possible states of the cause, the outcome of a hypothetical experiment and so on, but rather that one can clarify or make precise what one was initially thinking by expanding the causal claim along the lines indicated by (**M**). Again, this is a suggestion that might in principle be tested empirically.

4 Invariance/Stability: Normative and Descriptive Considerations

I turn now to a more detailed discussion of the distinctions among causal judgments described in section 2, with this section and section 5 focusing on the notion of invariance. Suppose that two variables are related in the manner described by (**M**): E is counterfactually dependent on C in some particular set of background circumstances Bi, where the dependence in question has an interventionist interpretation – that is, E would change under some intervention that might be performed on C in Bi. What I will call the *invariance* (stability, robustness, insensitivity) of this relationship has to do with the extent to which it would continue to satisfy (**M**) under other background circumstances different from Bi.[19] In other words, the invariance of the C → E relationship has to do

---

19 Think of "background circumstances" as having to do with conditions or circumstances that are distinct from both C and E.

with the extent to which the dependence of E on C continues to hold as background conditions change from those in the actual situation.[20]

I will first illustrate the basic idea by means of a pair of examples from David Lewis (1986) and then attempt to make it more precise. Suppose, first, that Lewis writes a letter of recommendation for a job candidate N which leads to N's getting a job she would not otherwise have gotten, which in turn leads to N meeting and marrying someone she would not otherwise have married, which then leads to the existence and eventual deaths of children who would not otherwise have existed. Whether or not those children exist and die (D) is counterfactually dependent on whether (W) Lewis writes the letter of recommendation, with the dependence in question being of the non-backtracking sort that according to Lewis is sufficient for causation. Moreover, the W → D relationship satisfies condition (**M**) and thus counts as causal within the interventionist framework. Nonetheless, informal surveys suggest that the claim that W *causes* D strikes many people as in some way odd, misleading, or defective.[21] One plausible diagnosis for this reaction is that although the W → D relationship satisfies (**M**), it is relatively non-invariant (relatively unstable or relatively sensitive). It is relatively non-invariant in the sense that if any one of a large number of the actually obtaining background conditions had been different even in relatively small ways (if, say, N had received an even better offer from another school or if she had lingered a little less long in that bar where she met her future spouse) the counterfactual dependence of D on W would no longer have obtained.

Contrast this with a second example: A shoots B through the heart with a very large caliber gun at close range and B dies. Not only is B's death counterfactually dependent on A's shooting him through the heart (their relationship satisfies (**M**)) but this dependence relationship is relatively invariant in the sense that under many non-science-fictionish variations in background conditions (consistent with A's shooting) this dependence would continue to hold.

---

20 See Woodward (2006) for additional discussion. What I am here calling invariance is called sensitivity in that paper – there are some differences in detail in comparison with the present paper.

21 Assuming that the claim that W causes D is defective in some way, little, if anything, will turn in what follows on exactly what we think this defectiveness consists in. If (**M**) is correct, the claim that W causes D is literally true and hence its defectiveness must involve something else besides its literal falsity – it may be either misleading (because so far from paradigmatically causal) or uninformative or unexplanatory or pragmatically inappropriate on the grounds of its non-invariance. A second possible view is that the claim is literally false, which would of course require revision of (**M**), so that some invariance requirement is incorporated into its sufficiency clause. I find the first view simpler, but think I need not insist that the second view is mistaken as long as defectiveness is linked to relative non-invariance.

Given that someone has been shot through the heart, there is not much, in ordinary circumstances, that we or nature can do to prevent death.

As these examples illustrate, citing relationships satisfying (**M**) that are relatively non-invariant or unstable tends, at least often, to strike us as in some way less satisfactory than citing relatively more invariant relationships also satisfying (**M**). The former are seen as less "good," less paradigmatic or less satisfactory examples of causal relationships. For reasons I have relegated to a footnote (footnote 21), I will not spend time trying to say more exactly what this the unsatisfactory character of the former consists in – perhaps it is a matter of the relatively non-invariant relationships being defective from the point of view of causal explanation or, alternatively, of their being misleading or uninformative some other way. From my point of view, the important fact is that our causal judgments seem (at least as far as the anecdotal evidence cited above goes) sensitive to the difference between relatively invariant and relatively non-invariant relationships satisfying (**M**). Moreover, this is not just a feature of ordinary folk thinking about causation, but seems to permeate a great deal of causal thinking in scientific contexts as well: scientists also seem to value relatively more invariant relationships, regarding them as more explanatory or otherwise more satisfactory.

To illustrate this last point consider the common preference in the biological sciences for "mechanistic" explanations. Just what makes an explanation "mechanistic" is an interesting question,[22] but one feature shared by many mechanistic explanations is this: One begins with some overall relationship between an input and an output (an I → O relationship) satisfying (**M**) (e.g., a stimulus and a response, a push on a gas pedal and the acceleration of a car, the presence of lactose in the environment of the E. Coli bacterium and its synthesis of an enzyme that digests lactose). One then explains why this I → O relationship holds by breaking it down into intermediate links or components; in the simplest case this may involve a chain of single links (I → C_1 → C_n → O) although in more complex cases the intermediate causes may involve branches and convergences. If appropriately executed, this process produces a feeling of enlightenment or an "aha" experience, a feeling that the "black box" associated with the rather arbitrary-looking and mysterious original I → O relationship has been opened up and made more intelligible.

Philosophical accounts of mechanistic explanation often stop at this point – they purport to tell us what a mechanism or a mechanistic description is, but not why it is explanatory or why it is a good thing to have such a description. It

---

[22] For a more detailed exploration of what makes an explanation mechanistic, see Woodward (2013).

seems to me that this is not satisfactory. What is needed is a treatment that places the proposed account of mechanistic description in the context of a more general account of causation and explanation and which helps us to understand why this filling in of intermediate links furnishes deeper causal understanding. My remarks above about invariance seem to me to go at least some way toward providing this. Very often (at least in contexts in which mechanistic explanation seems appropriate) the intermediate links uncovered in the mechanistic description are more invariant than the original I → O relationship. This feature contributes, I believe, to our sense that the mechanistic information about intervening links furnishes a deeper explanation; this information strikes us as deeper or more satisfying in part *because* it involves causal relationships that are more invariant.

Although I believe that examples like those discussed provide some intuitive motivation for the idea that we value invariance in causal relationships, both the normative and descriptive dimensions of the idea deserve much more exploration. On a normative level, I've talked of relationships being relatively invariant or not, or more or less invariant, but have said very little to make any of this talk this precise or to explain why, normatively speaking, people should care about invariance. On an empirical level, there is the following question: supposing that people in fact care in some way about the extent to which causal relationships are invariant, just what sorts of invariance do they care about and why?

Let me begin with the normative issue. First, as should be apparent from my remarks above, I believe it best to think of invariance as a matter of degree and as relative to some particular class of changes (in background conditions), rather than simply thinking in terms of relationships that are (absolutely) invariant or not. In particular, we want to capture the idea that some relationship R may be invariant with respect to one set of changes in background conditions but not with respect to some other set of changes. Thus I do *not* propose some single criterion for sorting relationships in terms of a simple dichotomy (e. g., highly invariant versus non-invariant relationships). Second, there is one special kind of situation in which comparisons of degree of invariance are completely unproblematic: when the set of changes over which generalization R is invariant is a proper subset of the set of changes over which a second generalization R' is invariant, then R' is of course more invariant than R. Much more commonly, however, this sort of basis for an ordering of degrees of invariance will not be available. In such situations, I suggest two other considerations that seem in fact (and arguably as a normative matter should – see below) affect judgments about invariance. (I leave open the possibility that other considerations may be relevant as well.)

The first consideration has to do with *typicality:* with how frequently various sorts of changes in background conditions occur or are thought to occur or, more generally, with how typical versus unlikely or far-fetched or science-fictionish such changes seem.[23] If, say, some relationship R of interest is invariant under changes in background conditions of a sort that frequently occur[24] but R is non-invariant under other sorts changes that are rarer or more far-fetched, we will regard R as relatively invariant; the opposite verdict will be reached if R is non-invariant under common or usual changes but stable under infrequently occurring changes. As an illustration, consider that the counterfactual dependence holding between ingesting a substantial amount of cyanide and death might be disrupted if the ingester were to immediate receive an antidote and state of the art medical treatment, but that receiving this treatment is at present a very rare occurrence; most people ingesting cyanide in a range of commonly occurring background conditions die. These considerations lead us to regard the cyanide ingestion → death relationship as relatively invariant/stable. By contrast, the relationship between Lewis' writing a letter of recommendation and the existence and death of the children is likely to be judged as relatively non-invariant not just because there are many possible changes from the actual background conditions that would disrupt that relationship but because those changes are of sorts that are extremely common or typical.

A second set of considerations (perhaps not sharply distinct form the former) that are relevant to assessments of invariance are subject-matter specific considerations – considerations having to do with the subject matter or content of the generalization of interest. The role of these considerations is particularly apparent in scientific contexts, although my conjecture is that something analogous is operative in other, more ordinary contexts as well.[25] To illustrate what I have in mind, consider the role of judgments of invariance in economics. Serious, principled economists do worry a lot about the extent to which the generalizations on which their models rely are relatively invariant (this is the central

---

[23] One might speculate that insofar as we are interested in scientific contexts, typicality may matter more in some sciences than others – e.g., it may matter more in biology and the social and behavioral sciences than in physics.
[24] Of course whether conditions occur frequently or not depends on the reference class or range of environments considered. What happens frequently right now on the surface of the earth may happen only very rarely in the universe taken as a whole. Biologists may be more interested in and influenced by the former, physicists by the latter.
[25] Thus, for example, one might conjecture that the background conditions that matter most for assessments of invariance in contexts involving folk judgments of psychological causation differ from the background conditions that are regarded as most relevant in folk judgments of physical causation.

issue in the so-called Lucas critique of many macro-economic generalizations) but they care most about invariance under particular sorts of changes that are regarded as especially important for or relevant to economics – changes involving certain kinds of "economics" variables. Thus, for example, economists will be particularly concerned about whether the generalizations on which they rely are invariant under changes in incentives or relative prices or information that is available to economic agents. Generalizations that fail to be invariant under these sorts of changes will be regarded as defective for explanatory or modeling purposes. On the other hand, most economists would be undisturbed to learn that the generalizations they employ fail to be invariant under, say, the ingestion of mind-altering drugs by most members of the modeled population – these are not seen as economically relevant changes, perhaps in part because they are regarded as unlikely but also because a concern with them is not seen as part of the subject matter of economics.

As a second example, illustrated in more detail below, in many biological contexts, the kind of invariance that is regarded as mattering most is invariance under changes in conditions that are "biologically normal" – normal" either in terms of conditions internal to the organism or in terms of the external environment. Thus within a cell or organism, relationships characterizing gene regulation and protein synthesis or characterizing the operation of the immune system will be judged relatively invariant to the extent that they are stable under a range of physiological conditions that are normal for the organism – that these would break down under very extreme physiological conditions (heating the organism to 100 °C) is regarded as less significant from the point of view of assessing invariance. Of course judgments of normality are influenced by what usually happens but they are also influenced by ideas about biological function, whether a condition is or is not pathological and so on.

Finally, we should note that the extent to which a relationship is invariant depends on which factors are included in or left out from that relationship, since the latter give us the "background circumstances" over which we make judgments of invariance. In particular, a relationship between factors characterized at a very detailed and fine-grained level of description but which is incomplete in the sense of omitting relevant factors may be relatively non-invariant in comparison with a relationship formulated in terms of more coarse-grained factors but which does not omit factors relevant at that coarse-grained level. If, say, one is given (C1) the exact momentum and position of 90 per cent of the molecules in a mole of gas at time 1 and asked to formulate a relationship between C1 and C2, the position and momentum of those same molecules a minute later, there will be no interesting stable dependency relationship between C1 and C2. (Calculational difficulties aside, C2 will depend on the exact states of *all* of the molecules of the gas at time 1 – the omission of information about the remaining ten per cent from C1 will make C2 effectively independent of C1.) One the other hand, if one is given the values of just a few macro-variables – e. g., values for such thermodynamic variables as pressure, temperature and volume – one can formulate a relatively invariant generalization in terms of these variables. As this example illustrates, upper level, macro- or coarse-grained relationships may be more invariant than relationships formulated in terms of more micro-level variables if (as is often, perhaps almost always, the case) the latter are incomplete in the sense of omitting some relevant factors. This is just one of several ways in which a concern with finding relatively invariant relationships can sometimes (but by no means always) lead to a preference for relationships formulated at a more macro-, as opposed to a more micro- or fine-grained level. More generally, it may turn out that it is possible to formulate relatively invariant relationships among one set of variables but not among some other set, even if both sets can be used to describe some system of interest. In this sense a concern with invariance can help to guide variable choice. In a similar way, suppose, for the sake of argument, that if one had sufficiently exact characterizations of a complete set of neuronal variables describing individual brains and unlimited calculational abilities, one could formulate highly invariant relations in terms of these. It might nonetheless be true that in more realistic scenarios in which one did not know all of these relevant micro-variables and/or was unable to measure them with arbitrary precision, any relationships one might be able to formulate among known and measurable variables would be very non-invariant. As in the case of the gas, one might be better off, from the point of view of finding invariant relationships, if one were to employ a much more coarse-grained set of variables and a representation with greatly reduced degrees of freedom.

But why is relative invariance in causal claims a virtue, methodologically speaking? Among other considerations, identification of a relatively invariant (in comparison with a less invariant) causal relationship provides better opportunities for manipulation and prediction. A relatively invariant relationship is more generalizable or exportable to new or different situations and we can be more confident that it will not break down when we attempt to so use it.[26] Similar considerations apply to the factors identified above as influencing assessments of invariance. If, for example, I want to use some supposed relationship to control and predict, than it is obvious why it should matter to me to what extent changes in background circumstances that are likely to disrupt that relationship are likely to occur (around here, in the present circumstances). This ex-

---

[26] For additional discussion see Woodward (2010) and Lombrozo (2010).

plains, at least in part, why typicality considerations should matter in the assessment of invariance.

So much for the general idea of invariance and its methodological rationale. Given this idea, a number of empirical questions of a sort that may be of interest to psychologists suggest themselves. First, and most obviously, although the examples from Lewis and others described above are suggestive, they are entirely anecdotal. It would be worthwhile to investigate more systematically whether subjects from various populations distinguish among various sorts of causal claims with respect to their invariance in anything like the way suggested above. With the disclaimer that I'm not a psychologist and have no training in experimental design, here are some suggestions about possible ways this might be done. First, given some scale for rating the extent to which a candidate relationship is a good or paradigmatic example of a causal relationship, or how "appropriate" it is to describe the relationship as causal (the rating scale employed by Lombrozo in experiments described below), it seems reasonable to expect (if what I have said above is on the right track) that, other things being equal, subjects will rate relatively invariant claims as more paradigmatically causal.[27] A somewhat more ambitious undertaking would be an investigation of whether, when subjects are given evidence of covariational or dependency relationships at different "levels" or described in terms of different variables, they prefer the level at which more rather than less invariant relationships are found – "prefer" in the sense that they learn more invariant relationships more readily, use them preferentially in explanations and for prediction as so on. (Results of this sort would be analogs of the results from the experiments concerning proportionality conducted by Lien and Cheng [2000] and discussed in Woodward [2018] but with the focus instead on the way in which invariance-based considerations influence variable choice or choice of level.)

In addition to the general question of whether subjects in fact distinguish among more or less invariant causal claims in the way suggested, there is the further empirical question (assuming that they do make such invariance-based distinctions at all) of just which factors influence such judgments. I described above two interrelated candidates for such factors, one having to do with the frequency or typicality with which changes in background conditions occur and the other with more subject-matter specific constraints. But these suggestions derive from nothing more than my armchair-based casual empiricism. Again, it would be worthwhile, in my view, to investigate all of this more carefully and systematically. Is it true, for example, as my suggestions imply, that given some causal rela-

---

27 This in fact is what is found in the particular class of cases investigated by Lombrozo below.

tionship R holding in conditions Bi but which would be disrupted by a change in background conditions to Bk ≠ Bi, manipulating information about the frequency with which Bk occurs affects subject's judgments about the invariance of R, assessed in the ways described above?[28]

5 Double Prevention and the Role of Invariance

A final set of empirical issues raised by the role of invariance in causal judgment is this: Can we use this notion to explain specific patterns in the causal judgments that people make? Here there has been some very interesting and suggestive experimental work on the significance of invariance for causation by double prevention – work to which I now turn.[29] In double prevention, if some event *d* were to occur, it would prevent the occurrence of a second event *e* (which would otherwise occur in the absence of *d*) and moreover the occurrence of a third event *c* prevents the occurrence of *d*, with the upshot that *e* occurs. In Ned Hall's well-known example (Hall 2004), Suzy's plane will bomb a target (*e*) if not prevented from doing so. An enemy pilot p will shoot down Suzy's plane (*d*) unless prevented from doing so. Billy, piloting another plane, shoots down p (*c*), and Suzy bombs the target.

In such cases there is an overall counterfactual dependence of *e* on *c* (with the dependence in question satisfying requirement (**M**) and also being the sort of non-backtracking dependence associated with causal relatedness on counterfactual theories of causation). Nonetheless, a common reaction of many philosophers is that cases in which *e* is related to *c* by double prevention are either not cases in which *c* causes *e* at all, or at least they are cases which lack some feature which is central to many other cases of causation. This is reflected in the resistance many feel to saying that Billy's shooting down the enemy plane *caused* Suzy's bombing. Hall himself at one point (2004) used this and other ex-

---

28 Note that the frequency of occurrence of some possible background condition (different from the actual background conditions) under which a causal relationship R would break down is a factor which it seems natural to regard as highly "extrinsic" to R itself. According to a number of philosophical accounts of causation, the causal relationship between two events must depend only on factors that are "intrinsic" to that relationship. My guess is that as a matter of empirical fact, people's causal judgments fail in various ways to respect this intrinsicness requirement, but this is again a matter that deserves experimental investigation. Insofar as it is normatively appropriate for invariance considerations to influence causal judgment, there will also be normative reasons why causal judgment should not be based entirely on "intrinsic" considerations.
29 As noted above, these experiments do seem to provide some support for the claim that invariance based considerations influence causal judgment, but only in a very specific context.

amples to motivate the claim that we operate with (at least) two distinct concepts of causation, one amounting to non-backtracking counterfactual dependence ("dependence") and the other involving what he called "production." I won't try to reproduce in detail Hall's characterization of this second notion but the basic idea is that, unlike dependence, production will satisfy some sort of locality constraint and at least in many paradigmatic cases a connecting process (e. g., one involving energy/momentum transfer) will be present linking cause and effect. Thus production is present when, for example, a thrown rock strikes a bottle and causes it to shatter. Hall suggests that dependence relations involving production tend to strike us as paradigmatically causal and that it is the absence of the features associated with production from the relation between Billy's action and Suzy's bombing that explains why we think of the double prevention relation as non-causal or at least not fully or paradigmatically causal.

If we think about these ideas about double prevention from the "functional" perspective recommended in this paper, several questions naturally suggest themselves. First, as a matter of descriptive psychology, how widely shared are these intuitive judgments reported by Hall and others about the causal status of double prevention? Second, to the extent that people distinguish between double prevention relations and dependence relations involving production, can we say anything about *why* people make this distinction (that is, what normative rationale, if any, there might be for this distinction)? What is special about production, such that people distinguish it from other sorts of dependency relations? Since I have discussed empirical research bearing on these questions in more detail elsewhere (Woodward 2012), I confine myself here to a brief summary. First, there is indeed evidence from both experiments conducted by Walsh and Sloman (2011) and Lombrozo (2010) that adult subjects distinguish between at least some cases of causal relations involving production and some cases involving double production, and are more ready to judge the former as causal or as more paradigmatically causal. Second, and more interestingly, evidence from Lombrozo shows that subjects distinguish *among* double prevention relations, regarding some (in particular those involving intentional actions, artifacts with designed functions and biological functions – hereafter having "functional status") as more paradigmatically causal than otherwise similar double prevention relations not involving these features.

Following a speculation in Woodward (2006), Lombrozo suggests an explanation for this last pattern: double prevention relations involving functional status are typically more invariant than otherwise similar double preventions relations lacking these features and this difference explains why the former are judged to be more paradigmatically causal. For example, when a double prevention relation involves a biological adaptation (as is the case for examples of genetic regulation involving double prevention, which are quite common) then this dependence relation, precisely because it is an adaptation, is very often well buffered or protected against ordinary changes in a cell's environment or internal physiology – the dependence relation will continue to hold in the face of such changes. By contrast, in the Billy/Suzy scenario described above, the dependence of Suzy's bombing on Billy's shooting down the enemy is very unstable/non-invariant under many very ordinary environmental changes. For example, this dependence relation would no longer hold if the enemy pilot received a message to return to base before having an opportunity to attack Suzy, if a second enemy fighter had been available to attack Suzy, and so on. On this view of the matter, the dependence present in the Billy/Suzy scenario is relevantly like the dependence present in the Lewis' letter of recommendation example. Both are relatively non-invariant and both are judged as less than paradigmatically causal (at least in part) for this reason.

Even if correct, however, this analysis still leaves open the question of why subjects tend to judge that dependence relationships satisfying (**M**) in which physical connections are present are more paradigmatically causal than dependence relations that in which no physical connections are present. Might we use the notion of invariance to explain this pattern in judgment as well? The companion to this paper in this volume (Woodward 2018) explores this question and a number of others.

Acknowledgments: The ideas in this paper have been greatly influenced by ongoing discussions with the members of the Initiative on Causal Learning funded by the James S. McDonnell Foundation, with Alison Gopnik as Principal Investigator.

References

Ahn, W., Kalish, C., Medin, D., and Gelman, S. (1995): "The Role of Covariation versus Mechanism Information in Causal Attribution." *Cognition*, v. 54, pp. 299–352.
Angrist, J. and Pischke, J.-S. (2009): *Mostly Harmless Econometrics: An Empiricist's Companion*. Princeton: Princeton University Press.
Baillargeon, R. (2002): "The Acquisition of Physical Knowledge in Infancy." In: Goshwami, U. (ed.): *Blackwell Handbook of Childhood Cognitive Development*, pp. 47–83. Oxford: Blackwell Publishing.
Bonawitz, E., Ferranti, D., Saxe, R., Gopnik, A., Meltzoff, A., Woodward, J., and Schulz, L. (2010): "Just Do It? Investigating the Gap between Prediction and Action in Toddlers' Causal Inferences." *Cognition*, v. 115, pp. 104–117.

Cheng, P. (1997): "From Covariation to Causation: A Causal Power Theory." *Psychological Review*, v. 104, pp. 367–405.

Davis, L. (1968): "And It will Never Be Literature – The New Economic History: A Critique." *Explorations in Enterpreneurial History*, v. 6, pp. 75–92.

Dowe, P. (2000): *Physical Causation*. New York: Cambridge University Press.

Gendler, T. (2007): "Philosophical Thought Experiments, Intuitions, and Cognitive Equilibrium." *Midwest Studies in Philosophy*, v. 23, pp. 68–89.

Glymour, C. (1986): "Comment." *Journal of the American Statistical Association*, v. 81, pp. 964–966.

Gopnik, A. (2012): "Scientific Thinking in Young Children: Theoretical Advances, Empirical Research, and Policy Implications." *Science*, v. 337, pp. 1623–1627.

Gopnik, A. and Schulz, L. (eds.) (2007): *Causal Learning: Psychology, Philosophy, and Computation*. New York: Oxford University Press.

Griffiths, T. and Tenenbaum, J. (2009): "Theory-based Causal Induction." *Psychological Review*, v. 116, pp. 661–716.

Hall, N. (2004): "Two Concepts of Causation." In: Collins, J., Hall, N., and Paul, L. A. (eds.): *Causation and Counterfactuals*, pp. 225–276. Cambridge, MA: The MIT Press.

Janzing, D., Mooij, J., Zhang, K., Lemeire, J., Zscheischler, J., Daniusis, D., Steudel, B., and Scholkopf, B. (2012): "Information-geometric Approach to Inferring Causal Directions." *Artificial Intelligence*, vv. 182–183, pp. 1–31.

Lewis, D. (1973): "Causation." *Journal of Philosophy*, v. 70, pp. 556–567.

Lewis, D. (1986): "Postscripts to 'Causation.'" In Lewis, D.: *Philosophical Papers*, vol. 2. Oxford: Oxford University Press.

Lien, Y. and Cheng, P. (2000): "Distinguishing Genuine from Spurious Causes: A Coherence Hypothesis." *Cognitive Psychology*, v. 40, pp. 87–137.

Lombrozo, T. (2010): "Causal-explanatory Pluralism: How Intentions, Functions, and Mechanisms Influence Causal Ascriptions." *Cognitive Psychology*, v. 61, pp. 303–332.

Pearl, J. (2000): *Causality: Models, Reasoning, and Inference*. Cambridge: Cambridge University Press.

Rubin, D. (1974): "Estimating Causal Effects of Treatments in Randomized and Nonrandomized Studies." *Journal of Educational Psychology*, v. 66, pp. 688–701.

Schaffer, J. (2000): "Causation by Disconnection." *Philosophy of Science*, v. 67, pp. 285–300.

Spelke, E., Breinlinger, K., Macomber, J., and Jacobson, K. (1992): "Origins of Knowledge." *Psychological Review*, v. 99, pp. 605–632.

Spirtes, P., Glymour, C. N., and Scheines, R. (2000): *Causation, Prediction and Search*. Cambridge, MA: The MIT Press.

Suppes, P. (1970): *A Probabilistic Theory of Causality*. Amsterdam: North-Holland.

Tetlock, P. (2005): *Expert Political Judgment*. Princeton, NJ: Princeton University Press.

Walsh, C. and Sloman, S. (2011): "The Meaning of Cause and Prevent: The Role of Causal Mechanism." *Mind and Language*, v. 26, pp. 21–52.

Woodward, J. (2003): *Making Things Happen: A Theory of Causal Explanation*. New York: Oxford University Press.

Woodward, J. (2006): "Sensitive and Insensitive Causation." *The Philosophical Review*, v. 115, pp. 1–50.

Woodward, J. (2007): "Interventionist Theories of Causation in Psychological Perspective." In: Gopnik, A. and Schulz, L. (eds.): *Causal Learning: Psychology, Philosophy, and Computation*, pp. 19–36. New York: Oxford University Press.

Woodward, J. (2010): "Causation in Biology: Stability, Specificity, and the Choice of the Levels of Explanation." *Biology and Philosophy*, v. 25, pp. 287–318.

Woodward, J. (2012): "Causation: Interactions between Philosophical Theories and Psychological Research." *Philosophy of Science*, v. 79, n. 5, pp. 961–972.

Woodward, J. (2013): "Mechanistic Explanation: Its Scope and Limits." *Proceedings of the Aristotelian Society*, Supplementary v. 87, pp. 39–65.

Woodward, J. (2014): "A Functional Theory of Causation." *Philosophy of Science*, v. 81, pp. 691–713.

Woodward, J. (2015): "Methodology, Ontology, and Interventionism." *Synthese*, v. 192, n. 11, pp. 3577–3599.

Woodward, J. (2018): "Causal Cognition: Physical Connections, Proportionality, and the Role of Normative Theory." This volume, pp. 105–137.

Part II: Causal Cognition and Psychological Explanations: Structural and Dynamic Aspects

James Woodward
Causal Cognition: Physical Connections, Proportionality, and the Role of Normative Theory

Abstract: This paper, like its companion in this volume, explores ways in which, on the one hand, normative (philosophical or theoretical) theorizing about causation and causal reasoning and, on the other, empirical psychological investigations into causal cognition can be mutually illuminating. I focus on the role of information about the presence of a "physical connection" between cause and effect in causal judgment, the considerations relevant to in choosing the appropriate "level" of explanation, and the role of mechanism information in causal judgment.

Keywords: causation, interventionism, proportionality, causal processes, actual cause judgments, level of explanation, causal mechanisms

1 Introduction

This paper, like its companion in this volume (Woodward 2018), explores ways in which, on the one hand, normative (philosophical or theoretical) theorizing about causation and causal reasoning and, on the other, empirical psychological investigations into causal cognition can be mutually illuminating. I focus on a variety of topics – the role of information about the presence of a "physical connection" between cause and effect in causal judgment (sections 2–4), the role of a consideration, much discussed in the philosophical literature, called proportionality (cf. Yablo 1992), in choosing the appropriate "level" of explanation (section 5), and the role of mechanism information in causal judgment, in the context of a paper by Ahn et al. (1995) (section 6). I begin, however, with some background and stage setting, first on the contrast (and relationship) between "actual cause" and "type-level" causal judgments and, second, on some of the ways that the presence of a "physical connection" can be involved in causal judgment, since both of these will play an important role in my subsequent discussion.

2 Type, Token, and Actual Cause Judgments

The following "interventionist" condition for causation was introduced in the companion to this paper (Woodward 2018) and is defended in more detail in Woodward (2003):

(**M**) X causes Y in background circumstances B_i if and only if there is some possible intervention that changes the value of X, such that if that intervention were to occur, the value of Y or the probability distribution of Y would change.

Here X and Y are *variables* – repeatable types that are capable of taking different "values," as when some object is characterized in terms of the variable "mass," which for that object might take such values as "5 kg" or "10 kg." The language of "events" or types of events which is the more familiar way of talking about causal relata among philosophers can be thought of as a particular case of this variable-based framework, with types of event represented by a binary or two-valued variable, which takes different values in different situations depending on whether a particular instance of the event-type in question occurs or not. For example, the type of event associated with the breaking (or not) of a kind of bottle might be represented by a variable B which takes the value $B =$ *breaks* if some bottle of that kind breaks and $B =$ *does not break* if some bottle of that kind does not break. Similarly the type of event corresponding to the occurrence or not of lung cancer might be represented by a variable C, which takes values {lung cancer present, lung cancer not present} for particular people (e. g. Jones) depending on whether that person has lung cancer.

M is a particular version of counterfactual theory of causation, with the counterfactual dependence relations used to characterize causation involving so-called *interventionist* counterfactuals, specifying the response of the candidate effect variable if interventions on the cause variable were to occur. **M** is intended to characterize what is sometimes called (misleadingly, in my opinion) a "type-level" causal notion linking repeatable types (of variables or events) as in

(2.1)   Smoking causes lung cancer.

Such type-level causal claims contrast with so-called "actual cause" judgments relating particular token events, as in

(2.2)   Jones' smoking caused his lung cancer.

These can also be given a broadly "interventionist" characterization but this characterization will differ in detail from that provided by **M** (cf. Woodward 2003).

As discussed in Woodward (2018) another distinctive feature of **M** is that a relationship can satisfy it and thus qualify as causal, even though the there is no "physical connection" between the specified cause and effect – all that **M** requires is that there be counterfactual dependence of the right sort between the values of X and Y, whether or not a physical connection of some kind is associated with this dependence relation. So-called double prevention relationships, discussed in (Woodward 2018) provide one illustration of this possibility of dependence without physical connection.

The previous paragraph introduced a distinction between "type cause" and "actual cause" judgments. What does this involve?[1] As several writers have noted, type causal judgments (including those captured by **M**) and actual cause judgments are often or even typically prompted by different inferential tasks. When one makes an actual cause judgment one is typically presented with a particular outcome whose occurrence is taken as known – e.g., it is known that Jones has lung cancer. The task is then to reason "backwards" from this occurrence to what caused it – was it Jones' smoking or something else such as his exposure to asbestos? In the case of so-called type causal claims, the direction of inference is often (but not always) the opposite. One begins with a candidate for a cause, characterized generically as a type of event or factor, and then reasons "forwards" from this candidate to ask whether it causes some type of effect – e.g., one begins by focusing on smoking and asks whether it causes lung cancer. This is the sort of inquiry that was pursued in the well-known U.S. Surgeon General's report of 1964 on the effects of smoking on lung cancer. Experimentation or statistical investigation using population wide covariational data are often directly relevant to establishing whether type causal claims are true, as (2.1) illustrates. By contrast, establishing an actual cause claim like (2.2) requires detailed information about a particular event or individual, although other kinds of information may also be relevant.

Actual cause claims are *sometimes* the focus of scientific investigation, as when researchers ask about the cause of the extinction of the dinosaurs (was it due to the impact of a large meteor, a massive volcanic eruption, or some combination of the two?), but in most areas of science the causal claims of most interest are type-level causal claims like those captured by **M**. Researchers are typically most interested in such questions as whether smoking causes lung cancer, whether there is a type-level or generic causal relation between motion through a

---

[1] The remarks that follow are heavily indebted to a number of conversations with Chris Hitchcock and reflect my understanding of ideas he has defended both orally and in print. Needless to say, however, the particular formulations advanced above (and any mistakes they embody) are mine – especially since Hitchcock does not make mistakes.

magnetic field and current in a conductor, or whether large increases in the money supply cause inflation. Corresponding actual cause claims are much less often targets of scientific investigation. Moreover, type causal claims also play a very important role in ordinary or common sense causal cognition. If I wish to manipulate some aspect of my physical environment, as in tool use, it is usually generic or type-level causal information that matters most. By contrast, as I note below, actual cause judgments very often reflect somewhat more specialized human practices and interests. In my view, we lack a generally accepted theory of these, but the practices in question often seem connected to generalized notions of blame, responsibility, and fault attribution. It is in part for this reason that (as I will suggest below) an exclusive focus on actual cause judgments seems a poor starting point if one wants to understand causal reasoning in scientific and many ordinary contexts.

A number of more or less formal theories of actual cause judgment, including theories that make use of broadly interventionist treatments of causation have been proposed,[2] including Halpern and Pearl (2005a and 2005b), Hitchcock (2001), and Woodward (2003). Although I believe that these accounts capture important aspects of actual cause judgment, I think it fair to say that none captures or reproduces anything like the full range of judgments people make. Moreover, as remarked above, we seem to lack a generally accepted normative account of such judgments – that is, an account of the point or purpose of such judgments that could be used to generate general standards for when such judgments are correct or incorrect. Instead, to a larger degree than is desirable, the construction of theories of actual causations seem to be guided by nothing more than the aim of agreement with particular judgments people find intuitive or acceptable. This contrasts with situation with respect to type cause judgments where (or so I have claimed) interventionist criteria like those represented by **M** provide a natural normative standard for whether particular type cause judgments are correct – a type cause claim that X causes Y for which it is not true that X and Y are associated under ideal experimental manipulations of X, is, in a straightforward sense, incorrect. As we shall see in section 6, this lack of a normative theory for actual cause judgments has important consequences for the empirical study of such judgments.

Although the distinction between (2.1) and (2.2) is real and important, one needs to take care that the terminology of "type" versus actual (or token)

---

[2] Without going into detail, such accounts evaluate actual cause claims of form c caused e by asking whether e counterfactually depends (in an interventionist sense) on c when certain other variables are held fixed at various values. This is the sense in which such accounts are "interventionist" in spirit.

cause does not mislead. To begin with, in most cases "type" causal claims are not really plausibly interpretable as literally true claims about causal relations between types of events, at least in any sense of "type" that contrasts with "token." Instead the units, so to speak, over which type causal claims range, are really "tokens." For example, when it is claimed that (2.1) "smoking causes lung cancer" this should *not* be understood as the claim that the abstract type, "smoking" somehow has another abstract type (lung cancer) as its effect, independently of whether these are instantiated or present (as tokens) in particular individuals. Instead, what (2.1) means or implies is that particular individuals, who are left unspecified, either will or may be caused to develop lung cancer if they smoke – e.g., if Jones smokes, then his smoking will or may cause him to lung cancer (a "token" causal relation), Smith's smoking will or may bear a similar relation to Smith's lung cancer and so on. In this sense, both type-level and actual cause claims are "about" or have implications for "token" events and their relationship – again, the units that are claimed to be causally related in both cases are tokens. Thus a better way of thinking about type-level causal claims is to regard them as something like 'generalizations over some set of not further specified actual or possible token causal relations.' This phrase is obviously cumbersome, however, and for this reason (and because the terminology is so entrenched) I will retain the language of type versus token in what follows, while asking the reader to bear its limitations in mind.

A second and more important observation about the type versus token framework is that it seems to have encouraged, in both the philosophical and portions of the psychological literature, a tendency to exaggerate the centrality of actual cause judgments in understanding causation and causal reasoning at the type level, through a failure to distinguish between the general notion of token-level causal information and the much more specific information that is reported in actual cause judgments.[3] In particular, the following line of thought has been influential, perhaps especially among philosophers who are interested

---

[3] To put the point in a slightly different way, we should distinguish the issue of what the "units" are which involved in a causal relationship from whether the judgments we are making about that relationship are "actual cause" judgments and what standards govern those judgments. In the case of smoking and lung cancer in a particular population, the relevant units are individual people who smoke or not and who develop lung cancer or not and this is so whether we are making type-level causal judgments about that population or instead actual cause judgments about the causation of lung cancer in particular people in that population. When we make the latter judgments we are not just treating particular people as the relevant units (again, that is common to both type and token judgments); we are also invoking some very specialized standards concerning fault or responsibility ascription that characterize "actual cause" as opposed to other sorts of causal judgments.

in the "metaphysics" of causation: causal claims, including type-level claims, in some way involve or rest on relations between particular token events. (True, in the sense described above.) Our practices of actual cause ascription directly track or reflect information about such token relations and only such information. (A misleading idea, in my view.) Hence actual cause judgments are central to all kinds of causal judgment and getting clear about such judgments is the key to understanding causation more generally. (Also mistaken.)

In contrast to this line of thought, I believe that our practices concerning actual cause judgments have much less to tell us than many suppose about other varieties of causal judgment and reasoning that occur at the type level, including those that are important in science and for our practical manipulative activities. I've already alluded to one reason for this: Although some progress has been made in constructing general accounts of actual cause judgments, I believe it is often the case that such judgments reflect, in addition to the features captured in these general accounts, very complex and specific practical and normative concerns and principles concerning the attribution of blame, responsibility, and fault – concerns that are not operative (at least to the same extent or in the same way) when other sorts of causal reasoning and judgment are employed.[4] (By "blame," "responsibility," and "fault," I have in mind extended senses of these notions which encompass both attributions of moral and legal responsibility, as when we ask whether the blow struck by Jones caused (= was responsible for) Smith's death and attributions of fault in which biological structures and designed objects don't behave as they "should," as in "the failure of the O-rings at low temperatures caused the Challenger disaster.") Very roughly, when we make an actual cause judgment regarding some occurrence, we attempt to trace back the causal history or etiology of the occurrence with an eye to finding some action or natural occurrence which we can hold "responsible" for the occurrence. The "natural home" of many actual cause judgment thus includes, for example, contexts involving legal reasoning (did A's action cause

---

4 Glymour et al. (2010) describe a large number of examples involving actual cause judgments and argue convincingly that none of the available normative theories returns judgments about all these examples that accord with what seems "intuitive." (I'll add that I at least have no clear "intuitions" regarding some of their cases.) They also argue, again convincingly, that given the enormous number of possible examples, especially when one considers cases involving large numbers of variables, there is no reason to suppose that any method that proceeds inductively, attempting to constructing a theory that covers just the examples that happen to occur to the theorist, is likely to be successful – there will be no grounds for confidence that there do not exist additional counterexamples that have not yet been thought of. They note as well, as I have, the difficulty of making progress with this problem in the absence of a generally accepted normative theory.

the damage to B's property?), moral and prudential reasoning, medical diagnostic or forensic reasoning (what caused the patient's/victim's death?), and fault detection in engineering contexts (e. g., in circuit design). This picture is supported both by common sense observation and by numerous studies suggesting that in these contexts, subject matter specific norms, including ideas about normal or designed functioning and normatively prescribed or proscribed behavior are among the influences on actual cause judgment.[5] Moreover, when we move outside such contexts, at least sometimes we seem to loose our grip on what the standards of correctness are for actual cause judgments – again, this is connected to the observation above, that we seem to lack a compelling general theory of the aim or point of actual cause judgments.

One way of underscoring these points is to note that actual cause judgments often appear to be underdetermined by associated "type cause" information, even when this is accompanied by information about which particular token events have occurred and other sorts of token-level information about connecting processes – what I called "token-level information" above. Consider a well-known illustration due to McDermott (1995). A baseball is headed in the direction of a window and would shatter it if nothing is in the way. In fact, a strong, impenetrable brick wall is in between the ball and the window. However, before the ball can reach the wall, a fielder leaps and catches the ball. Did the action of the fielder prevent the window from breaking? That is, is it true that

(2.3)   The fielder's catch caused the window not to break.

This is a question about an "actual cause claim" and we seem pulled in two different directions. On the one hand, it is tempting to argue as follows: because of the presence of the brick wall, whether or not the fielder caught the ball made no difference to the breaking of the window – the window would not have broken regardless of whether caught the ball. Hence the fielder did not prevent the window from breaking. On the other hand, McDermott argues as follows: Something prevented the ball from breaking the window. Which was it – the fielder or the wall? When the question is put this way, it is tempting to respond that it was the fielder who prevented the window from breaking – perhaps in part because she made physical contact with (interacted with) the ball, and the wall did not.

This example suggests several points.[6] First, it is far from obvious how one might go about resolving, even in principle, the question of whether (2.3) is true.

---

5 See for example Hitchcock and Knobe (2009).
6 Admittedly, this is just one example but I believe that similar conclusions are supported by many other examples involving actual cause judgment, including a number of the examples in Glymour et al. (2010).

Indeed, it is hard to identify what is even at stake in trying to decide whether (2.3) is true – what turns on deciding the issue one way or another. A natural thought is that whatever rules or standards govern actual cause judgment in other contexts don't dictate, at least in any obvious way, which judgments are "correct" in connection with this example. Second, and relatedly, whether or not (2.3) is true seems to be underdetermined even by the *conjunction* of information about the type causal relations present in the example and by the token-level information – or at least it is not obvious how to determine from this information whether (2.3) is true. The description of the example seems to specify all the relevant information at the type level – e. g., what the effect of the ball's hitting the window would be, what would happen if the fielder missed catching the ball and so on. The description of the example also seems to specify all the obviously relevant information at the token level – we know that the fielder caught the ball, that it did not come into contact with the wall and so on. Yet all of this information does not settle, at least in any obvious way, whether (2.3) is true. Putting this in terms of the distinction between, on the one hand, token- (and type-) level causal information and, on the other hand, conclusions about the relationships reported in "actual cause" judgments, it appears we know all about the former but remain uncertain about the latter. An obvious explanation of how this is possible is that actual cause judgments are influenced by considerations (e. g., having to do with responsibility attribution) that are at least in part independent of token- and type-level causal information. If this is what is going on, a close examination of our practices with respect to actual cause judgment is not necessarily going to be a helpful entry point into understanding other forms of causal judgment and reasoning that are more type-like in character. I will return to this point below in section 6 in connection with a discussion of some experiments on causal attribution by Ahn and colleagues.

3 Connecting Processes and Causal Judgment

What is the role of the presence of a physical connection (or a connecting process) between cause and effect in causal judgment? Woodward (2018) noted that both armchair observation and more careful psychological research support the contention that subjects tend, ceteris paribus, to judge that dependence relationships among token events of the general sort described by **M** in which physical connections are present are more paradigmatically causal than dependence relations among token events in which no physical connections are present. For example, the shattering of a bottle by the impact of a thrown rock (with the trajectory of the rock and its impact serving as the physical connection between the throw and the shattering) is judged by almost everyone to be a paradigmatically causal interaction. If the presence of a barrier would block the trajectory of the rock, the shattering of the bottle also counterfactually depends (in accordance with **M**) on whether or not the barrier is present, but the relationship between the *removal* of the barrier and shattering is judged as less than paradigmatically causal, presumably because there is no "physical connection" between the absence of the barrier and the shattering.[7] Moreover, at a normative level, several well-known philosophical accounts of causation, including the "causal process" theories of Salmon (1984) and Dowe (2000) treat the presence of an appropriate sort of connecting process as a necessary and sufficient condition for genuine causation, at least at the token level. These observations prompt several questions pursuant to our overall project of understanding the interaction between descriptive and normative considerations in causal reasoning. First, as a descriptive matter, can we provide more detail about the role played by physical connection in causal judgment? Second, as a normative matter, what justification, if any, is there for assigning the presence of a physical connection an important role in causal judgment? How can we usefully approach the *normative* question of whether Salmon and Dowe are right in the role they assign to connecting processes?

As a point of departure, some general remarks about the ways in which information about connecting processes can enter into different sorts of causal judgments, including type and actual cause judgments, will be helpful. As a number of writers have noted and is illustrated by the example immediately above, the question of whether a connecting process is present or not seems have its most direct and straightforward application when we are dealing with actual cause claims (or at least claims that explicitly relate particular specified token events) rather than with more generic type-level claims. This is because connecting processes are naturally viewed as the sorts of things that can be present between particular, spatio-temporally located events or particular instantiations of variable values: a particular throw or trajectory of a rock can be physically connected or not to a bottle and perhaps to some event involving the breaking of the bottle, but it appears that the associated type of event or variable which within an interventionist framework takes values like {throwing a rock or not} is not itself physically connected to anything. Whatever role physical connection has in connection with this type causal claim is in some (presumably rather complex) way derivative from the role of physical connection in the asso-

---

[7] See Walsh and Sloman (2011) for reports of results from psychological experiments involving similar scenarios that provide empirical support for this claim.

ciated token causal relationships. This is reflected in the fact that philosophical theories like Salmon's and Dowe's that emphasize the role of physical connections in causation focus almost entirely on token, rather than type-level, causal relations.

Bearing this in mind, we see, when we turn to characterizing the role of physical connection information in type causal judgments, that matters are rather subtle. Suppose that, in accord with **M**, one wishes to represent a type-level causal relation ($R \rightarrow S$) between whether or not a rock is thrown in such a way that it strikes a bottle (represented by variable R) and whether or not the bottle shatters (S). When R takes the value = rock is thrown, there will be a physical connection between the instantiation of this value by some particular rock-throwing and the shattering of the bottle. But when the rock is not thrown, there will of course not be any such physical connection between the instantiation of the value R = rock not thrown and the instantiation of the value S = non-shattering of the bottle. That is, as far as the type-level $R \rightarrow S$ relation goes, there is a "physical connection" associated with one pair of values of these variables but not for the other pair of values. Similarly, if we consider a putative example of causation by omission involving a gardener who fails to water the flowers with the result that they die, it is very natural to regard this as a case in which there is no physical connection between the gardener's omission and the death of the plants, so that if this is a case of causation at all, it is a case of causation without a connecting process. However, this view of the example comes from focusing just on the token-level judgment that the gardener's omission caused the death of the plants. If we focus instead on the type-level judgment that whether or not the plants die causally depends on whether the gardener waters them, one of the values of the variable representing whether or not the gardener waters (the value corresponding to gardener watering) will of course involve a physical connection to the plants and the other value, corresponding to the gardener's failure to water, will not.

Thus when we consider the role of physical connections in type-level causal judgments what we really have in mind, at least often, are cases in which physical connections will hold between some particular realized values of the cause variable and the effect variable and not for others. For this reason, it would be highly problematic to demand that when variable X causes variable Y *all* instances or possible particular realizations of X must be physically connected to instances or realizations of Y. Or at least this will be a wrong-headed requirement for those causal claims which relate variables that can take values corresponding to absences or non-occurrences.

So far we have been considering cases in which one or more instantiated values of a candidate cause variable are physically connected to instantiated values of the effect variable and other values are not. However, there are of course other kinds of cases in which *no* values of the candidate cause variable are so connected to the effect. This is true, for example, of the double prevention cases described in Woodward (2018), when these are considered at a generic or type level: if the enemy fighter will shoot down Suzy's bomber unless the fighter is shot down by Billy, then there is no connecting process running either from Billy's shooting down the enemy plane to Suzy's dropping the bombs or from Billy's failure to shoot down to Suzy's failure to drop the bombs. Arguably, a similar point holds for putative cases involving causation between events or variables that are not usually represented as physical or for which we lack any clear idea about what would serve as the relevant connecting process. We may be tempted to claim that Jim's desire for beer causes him to open the refrigerator door on one occasion and perhaps that his lack of desire causes him not to open the door on another occasion but in neither case is there in any obvious sense a connecting physical process between these candidate causes and effects. If these are genuine cases of causation, they are cases of causation without a connecting process for *either* value of the variables D = {desire for beer, no desire for beer}, R = {opens door, does not open door}.

Insofar as there is any overall empirical pattern concerning the influence of the presence of a connecting process on causal judgments among ordinary subjects, either with respect to type or actual cause judgments, it seems to be something like this: First, the presence of a physical connection between particular token events (or more generally, particular instantiations of values of variables) realizing a generalization satisfying **M** is very often judged to be *relevant* to whether the relationship between these token items is paradigmatically causal, in the sense that the presence of such a process tends to boost the judgment that the relationship is causal or a good or clear example of causation: When (3.1) Billy's thrown rock hits the bottle and it shatters this is regarded as a paradigmatically causal interaction; subjects may disagree about whether (3.2) Billy's failure to throw causes the bottle not to shatter, but even those accepting this causal claim are likely to regard the relation in (3.2) as less clearly or paradigmatically causal than in (3.1). Similarly, the presence of a connecting causal process is also regarded as *relevant* to type-level causal judgment: as we saw in Woodward (2018), at least some double prevention relations (which lack the presence of a connecting process) are not judged as paradigmatically causal.

Second, despite the *relevance* of the presence of a physical connection, the presence such a connection does not seem to be treated, at least by many subjects, as a *necessary* condition for causation. This is shown by the fact, also reported in Woodward (2018), that subjects accept some double prevention relations as causal, the willingness of many subjects to regard mental causation as genuine causation, and by many other examples. Interestingly, neither pure causal process views like those associated with Salmon and Dowe nor versions of counterfactual theories (including **M**) that assign no significance at all to whether a connecting process is present adequately explain this pattern of judgment. Pure causal process theories are inconsistent (among other things) with the judgment that some relations of dependence not involving connecting processes are causal and pure dependence theories, including **M**, offer no explanation of why people often regard the presence of a connecting process as relevant to (even if not decisive for) whether that relationship is causal or paradigmatically causal.[8]

We should also note another empirical generalization about the judgments people seem willing to make: physical connectedness in the absence of any kind of counterfactual dependence is not regarded as *sufficient* for causation, even in cases in which other pre-empting or over-determining causes are absent. This is shown by many familiar examples; when a tennis ball is thrown against a brick wall, there is a connecting physical process that transfers energy and momentum to the wall, but the impact of the ball does not cause the wall to remain intact and standing. When a baseball strikes a window and the window shatters, there are also physical process involving incident photons and molecules in the surrounding air that collide with the window at the moment of shattering. Nonetheless this is not a case of causal over-determination; it is the impact of the baseball alone and not (also) the impact of the photons or nitrogen molecules that causes the shattering. Intuitively, this is because the impact of the tennis ball or the photons is not of such a character to make a difference between whether the wall stands up or collapses or whether the window shatters or not; the latter events do not depend on the former and the former are not causally relevant to the latter.

This suggests that to formulate an adequate theory, either descriptive or normative, which captures the role of connecting processes in causal judgment, we must also incorporate difference-making or counterfactual elements into the account: in particular, when the presence of a connecting process is relevant to whether a causal relationship is present, this connecting process must be of

---

[8] This is a reflection of the fact that virtually all of the best known philosophical accounts of causation, including **M** are dichotomous in the sense that they claim to classify relations into the categories of causal versus non-causal, but provide no account of *gradations* in causal judgment – that is, in subject's willingness to regard some candidate relations as more paradigmatically causal than others. The combination of **M** with other considerations like degree of stability and proportionality, which are graded, represents my attempt to capture aspects of such graded judgments.

such a character that it (and the candidate cause) makes a difference to the effect or such that whether or not the effect occurs counterfactually depends on whether the connecting process is present. In other words, the theory will need to *conjoin* some additional condition like **M** reflecting whether counterfactual dependence is present with some condition having to do with the presence of a physical process.[9]

In the following section, I explore a possible explanation for the observations about the role of connecting process just described. This explanation exploits and extends an idea introduced in Woodward (2018) – namely, that dependence relations satisfying **M** can differ in their degree of stability or invariance and that more stable relations are generally regarded as more paradigmatically causal. The further twist I will now offer is that dependence relationships that are associated with the presence of physical connection tend, other things being equal, to be more stable than those that lack this feature and that this explains (at least in part) both why they are regarded as more paradigmatically causal and provides a normative justification for why they are so regarded. In other words, physical connection matters to causation (insofar as it does) at least in part because of its connection with stability.

4 Connecting Processes and Stability

Before developing this idea in more detail, however, I want to underscore just what I am attempting to do. As explained in Woodward (2018), I advocate think-

---

[9] In this connection, it is also worth noting that taking physical connectedness by itself not to be sufficient for causation and requiring in addition that some relation of counterfactual dependence be satisfied has the advantage that it yields a concept that has an obvious use or function, since counterfactual dependence (when understood along the interventionist lines that I favor) is a feature of relationships that may be used for manipulation and control. By contrast, a concept of causation that took the mere presence of physical connectedness (of any kind) to be sufficient for causal relatedness is unlikely to be a useful concept, at least for many human purposes. This is because such physical connections are ubiquitous and indiscriminate; photons interacting with objects subsequently interact with many others and similarly for other subatomic particles, molecules making up the atmosphere etc. Indeed, all or almost all objects and events are "physically connected" in some way with all or most objects or events in their backward light cone, again implying that if physical connection is sufficient for causation, such relations are everywhere. This suggests that what is likely to be of interest to most human cognizers is not physical connectedness per se but something more like certain restricted kinds of physical connectedness – e. g., those that are also accompanied by counterfactual dependence or something similar.

ing about causation in *functional* terms, focusing on the functions or goals or purposes that underlie our thinking about causal relationships in the way that we do. Thinking about the present issue in this way immediately raises the following question: *why* do people distinguish in the way that they apparently do between (at least some) cases in which counterfactual dependence plus a physical connection is present and cases in which counterfactual dependence is present but no physical connection? That is, can we identify some further goal or aim or function, associated with causal reasoning, which such a distinction might serve? What does the presence of a physical connection give us in terms of satisfaction of these goals in comparison with cases of counterfactual dependence without physical connection? What if anything would be lost, from the point of view of goals and purposes associated with causal reasoning, if we were to adopt a conception of causation according to which the only relevant considerations in judging whether a relationship is causal have to do with some variety of counterfactual dependence characterized along the lines of **M**? Of course, some philosophers may wish to say that this question has a very simple (and trivial) answer: the presence of a physical connection between two events or, more plausibly (see above), the presence of such connection plus counterfactual dependence is just what causation *is* so of course people distinguish between cases in which these features are present and cases of dependence in which they are absent. From my point of view this is an unsatisfying answer because it affords no insight into (i) *why* we think about causation in this particular way and (ii) what justification (if any) there is for this – that is, it affords no insight into whether there is any *normative* rationale for the role that, as an empirical matter, physical connection plays in causal judgment.

I believe that any plausible candidate for a complete answer to (i) and (ii) will be complex, involving a number of different considerations, but in what follows I will focus very selectively on just one kind of consideration having to do with the relationship between invariance/stability and the presence of a physical connection in causal relationships. In particular, I want to consider the following possibility, which I label **PC** (for Physical Connection):

PC 1) Type-level relationships of (non-backtracking or interventionist) counterfactual dependence (that is, relationships that satisfy **M**) involving physical connections between the putative cause and effect tend, ceteris paribus, to be more invariant and stable than relations of counterfactual dependence that are not accompanied by physical connections. (Here "involving physical connections" means that there are physical connections between *some* values of the putative cause and the putative effect variables, but not necessarily *all* such values – the reason for this qualification is explained above.)

2) Actual cause judgments involving physical connections between cause and effect tend, ceteris paribus, to be more stable than actual cause judgments for which there is no associated connecting causal process. (Here "physical connection" means that such a connection is present between the particular token events represented in the actual cause judgment – e.g., such a connection is present when it is claimed that the gardener's watering caused the plants to survive and absent when it is claimed that the omission of watering caused the plants to die.) Moreover, the presence or not of a physical connection in such cases is a fairly reliable indicator of when such actual cause connections are stable – that is, such actual cause connections typically hold across those circumstances in which a physical connection is present.

Recall from Woodward (2018) that a type-level relationship satisfying **M** in background circumstances B_i is stable or invariant if that relationship would continue to hold across changes in background circumstances different from B_i. Analogously, let us say that an actual cause claim of form c caused e holding in circumstances B_i is stable to the extent that c would also cause e in other background circumstances different from B_i in which the physical connection between c and e continues to hold. (For more on what this means, see the examples below.) Recall also from Woodward (2018) that it is normatively appropriate that more stable relationships are judged as more paradigmatically causal because, ceteris paribus, the identification of more stable dependence relations better serves goals of causal thinking – such relationships are more usable for purposes of manipulation and prediction.

If **PC** is correct, this would help to explain why subjects often tend to regard dependence relationships in which physical connections are present as more paradigmatically causal than dependence relations in which such connections are absent. This would also show why (and in what respects) it is rational or normatively appropriate for us to judge in this way.[10]

---

[10] A clarificatory comment: There are of course many, many cases in which, as an empirical matter, the presence of a physical connection of the appropriate sort between at least some values of X and Y is necessary for Y to be counterfactually dependent on X and for the relationship between Y and X to satisfy **M**. For example, in ordinary circumstances, for a relationship satisfying **M** to be present between the position of the handle of a screwdriver and the position of the head of the screw, the tip of the screwdriver must be in physical contact with the head, at least for some values of the variables figuring in that relationship. Again, for a relationship satisfying **M** between the throwing (or not) of a rock and the shattering (or not) of a bottle to be present, the rock must, in ordinary circumstances, come into physical contact with the bottle. When whether **M** holds between two variables is dependent on whether an appropriate physical connection is present, it is completely unmysterious why we should care about whether or not the appropriate physical connection is present and want to understand the details of its operation,

But is (**PC**) correct? I think that (**PC**) is plausible for a significant range of cases, although (as reflected in the "ceteris paribus" clause in my formulation) it does not hold in all circumstances. In other words, the presence of a physical connection is an imperfect and defeasible but nonetheless useful indicator of the presence of a relatively stable relationship. Consider again a paradigmatic example of causation involving physical connection: a rock, thrown by Suzy, striking and breaking a glass bottle. Assume, for simplicity, that there are no other backup causes of bottle shattering present in the situation. Here the breaking is counterfactually dependent on Suzy's throwing and the "physical connection" between Suzy's throw and the breaking (that is, the situation in which the variable T describing whether or not Suzy throws takes the value = Suzy throws and the variable B describing whether the bottle breaks takes the value = breaks) just involves the trajectory of the rock through space until it comes into contact with bottle. In ordinary cases of this sort, the dependence of B on T will continue to hold for some considerable range of variations in background circumstances, provided of course that the right sort of physical connection continues to be present – that is, provided that the rock thrown by Suzy actually comes into contact with the bottle. The fact that $B \to T$ relationship continues to hold under many such changes in background conditions (provided the relevant physical connection continues to be present) illustrates what I have in mind by describing that relationship as stable or invariant. For example, if we displace Suzy and the bottle ten feet to the right, then in many usual circumstances whether the bottle shatters will continue to depend on whether Suzy throws, again assuming that the relevant physical connection is present. Similarly for rock throwings that occur at different times from the actual time, rocks thrown by different people and so on. More generally, for ordinary bottles and throws, different throws involving strikings will likely vary in the exact momentum with which the rock strikes the bottle and other physical details of the exact way in which the rock strikes the bottle, but variations in these factors, at least over a large range, are unlikely to affect whether the shattering counterfactually depends on the throw and impact, again as long as the appropriate physical connection is present.

A similar point holds for many other ordinary variations in the background environment such as changes in air temperature, pressure, presence of various

---

since this information is highly relevant to our interest in manipulation and prediction. The issue explored in the text above is different from this: it has to do with why we should distinguish in the way that we do between cases of counterfactual dependence in which a physical connection is present and cases of counterfactual dependence (e.g., double prevention) in which no physical connection is required for the dependence to be present.

other objects in the background, as long as they don't interfere with the physical connection. Put differently: If you have a rock which is big enough and thrown hard enough to shatter a bottle (assuming that it strikes it) in the actual background circumstances and a bottle which is fragile enough to shatter if there is such an impact, you generally don't have to worry that small variations in those background circumstances (or for that matter in the momentum of the throw) will make such striking ineffective in producing shattering. Hitting the bottle with a thrown rock is likely to be a fairly reliable and stable way of producing shattering, across a range of background circumstances, if it can produce shattering in the actual circumstances. I believe that a similar observation holds for many other causal relationships involving physical connections – pushes, pulls, tools that put the user in physical contact with some target object and so on. These all involve not just dependence relationships satisfying **M** but dependence relationships that are relatively stable across many ordinary environmental variations as well as many variations in the fine-grained values of the causally relevant variables (exactly how much force you exert on the chair in lifting it and so on). By contrast, although as the discussion in Woodward (2018) shows (see also Woodward 2006), it is certainly possible for a counterfactual dependence relationship not involving a physical connection to be relatively stable as a matter of empirical fact, many such dependence relationships seem to be relatively unstable – they often depend on a very precise arrangement of environmental circumstances and will be disrupted if these change.[11] Thus, at least for a range of cases, it will make sense, if one cares about the stability of a dependence relationship (or whether a dependence relationship in the sense of satisfying **M** is present at all) to focus on whether a physical connection is present – this is often a pretty good, albeit fallible, indicator of the stability of the dependence relation.[12]

Although it thus seems plausible that the presence of a physical connection and stability often seem to go together, it also seems clear, as already intimated,

---

[11] The Billy/Suzy scenario mentioned above and also discussed in Woodward (2018) and in Hall (2004) is a case in point.
[12] To put the point slightly differently: When E counterfactually depends on C in accord with **M** in the actual background circumstances or is known to depend on C in circumstances like those obtaining at present *and* the presence of a physical connection between C and E is necessary for this dependence relation to hold, then it is often a good heuristic to assume that this dependence relation will continue to hold as long as the physical connection is maintained. Thus, for example, the presence or absence of contact (a physical connection) is a good indicator of when we can generalize the rock thrown → bottle breaks dependency relation to other circumstances. This is non-trivial because (as observed above) the presence of a physical connection does not guarantee in general the presence of a dependency relation satisfying **M**.

that this association is far from perfect. In particular it seems perfectly possible for there to be cases in which physical connectedness (and counterfactual dependence satisfying **M**) between X and Y to be present but in which this dependence is not stable. This will happen, for example, in cases in which there is physical connection and dependence between X and Y but where the dependence of Y on X depends in a very delicate way on various background contingencies. An illustration is perhaps provided by a variant on the golf ball examples once popular in discussions of probabilistic causation: a golfer hits a golf ball (C) which strikes a tree limb, rebounds off, is kicked by a squirrel, and rolls into the cup (E). Here there is a physical connection linking C to E – one that may be readily recognizable and perceptually salient. Suppose that, given the actual circumstances, the ball's going into the cup (E) is counterfactually dependent on the ball striking the limb in the particular way that it did. In this case, it seems likely, as an empirical matter, that despite the presence of the physical connection between C and E, the dependence of E on C is highly unstable: if the squirrel had not kicked it in that particular way, if it had hit the limb at a slightly different angle, if the wind had been a bit different and so on, the ball would not have gone into the cup. My discussion above in effect assumes that although scenarios like the one just described are possible, they are unusual, not just in the obvious sense that they involve a series of unlikely coincidences but also in the further sense that they are not representative of the usual association between stability and physical connection.

It would be very interesting to learn more about the causal judgments of subjects about cases having this sort of structure. Would they judge such relationships to be less than paradigmatically causal because of their instability? My sense is that many philosophers would endorse the contrary judgment that in such cases the relation between C and E is clearly and unambiguously – even paradigmatically – causal and would take this to suggest that the presence of a physical connection influences causal judgment in a way that is at least in part independent of considerations of stability. Perhaps this is correct but, interestingly, unpublished experimental data from Rose, Danks, and Machery (in preparation) does suggest that adult subjects regard relationships of the sort just described as less than paradigmatically causal, despite the presence of a physical connection. This suggests that stability considerations affect causal judgment even when physical connection is present.

5 Proportionality and Finding the Right Level of Causal Description/Explanation

In this section I want to switch gears and focus on some issues having to do with the choice of level of description and explanation in causal judgment. As noted in Woodward (2018), this is a normative issue that has engendered a great deal of discussion in both the philosophy of science literature and in the literature in many areas of science. Within our framework the issue might be put this way: True causal claims satisfying (**M**) concerning some system of interest can be framed at many different possible "levels" of description – such claims can relate variables that are e.g., more or less detailed or fine-grained (or micro- or lower-level) or more or less general or abstract or macro. (These are not the same distinctions of course). For example, the causal principles governing the operation of a brain might be described either at a very fine-grained neuronal level or at a more general, coarse-grained level making use of concepts from cognitive science. Sometimes such descriptions of causal relationships at different levels can seem complimentary and not in competition with each other, but this is not always the case. Sometimes, some choices of level of description seem methodologically *better* or more appropriate than others, depending on empirical facts about the system being modeled. This raises the question of what principles or considerations do or should govern such choices of level of description. This question has particular resonance because of a widespread view in some philosophical circles (especially those with a more "metaphysical" orientation) that one particular level of description – in particular, one involving maximal detail – is always best in principle.

I argued in Woodward (2018) that one set of considerations having to do, both descriptively, and normatively, with the choice of an appropriate level of causal analysis derives from the notion of stability/invariance. Depending on the empirical characteristics of the system under study and what it is that we are interested in explaining, causal relationships at some levels may be more stable/invariant than others and hence provide a preferred level of description. In this section, I will discuss another, at least partially distinct set of considerations that also bear, both descriptively and normatively, on the choice of levels of causal explanation. These have to do with *proportionality,* a notion that I take (with some non-trivial modifications) from Stephen Yablo (1992) and that, as we shall see, has echoes in empirical research conducted by Patricia Cheng (Lien and Cheng 2000).

To illustrate the idea as originally introduced by Yablo (1992), consider a pigeon that has been trained to peck at red targets of any shade and *only* at red targets. Suppose that the pigeon is presented, either once or (if you like) on a series of occasions, with a target of particular shade of scarlet and that the pigeon pecks.

Now consider the following causal claims:[13]

(5.1)   The fact that the target was scarlet caused the pigeon to peck it.

(5.2)   The fact that the target was red caused the pigeon to peck it.

Yablo contends that, given the facts specified in the example, most people will (and, as a normative matter, should) prefer claim (5.1) to (5.2). Yablo links this preference to the idea that causes should be "proportional" to their effects; containing neither too little (where "too little" means being inappropriately narrow and omitting crucial elements) nor containing "too much" (where this means being overly broad and containing superfluous elements). On Yablo's view, (5.1) fails to satisfy this proportionality requirement because it is inappropriately narrow, omitting the information that other shades of red besides scarlet would lead the pigeon to peck. On the other hand, a causal claim that attributes the pigeon's pecking to the target's being colored (rather than being red) would be overly broad. By contrast, the causal description in (5.2) is "just right" in terms of balancing narrowness and broadness – it satisfies the intuition behind "proportionality."

Yablo tries to explain our preference for proportional causes in terms of metaphysical considerations having to do with "event essences" and the like. In what follows I will put these aside and focus instead on the methodological thesis suggested by (5.1) to (5.2) which is that some levels of description of causes and effects can be "better" or "more appropriate" than others and, in particular, that (5.2) is at a more suitable level of description or abstraction than (5.1), given the facts that Yablo specifies.

This thesis raises a number of questions that further illustrate some of the claims in Woodward (2018) about the interrelations between descriptive and normative issues. First, as a descriptive matter, is it true, as Yablo claims that subjects exhibit a preference for causal judgments framed at certain levels of description as opposed to others – in particular that they prefer claims like (5.1) to (5.2) given empirical circumstances like those specified above? Second, again as a descriptive matter, what principles govern (and what factors influence) such preferences? Third, is there some normative rationale or justification

---

[13] A parallel comparison can be framed between type-level claims: the redness of the target causes pigeon pecks vs the scarlet color of the target causes pigeon pecks. I frame the argument in terms of (5.1) and (5.2) in order to follow Yablo's exposition.

for the preferences that subjects exhibit? Both the second and third questions raise the issue of how one might best characterize a methodologically and descriptively fruitful notion of proportionality.

Essentially this question (among many others) is explored in a very rich paper by Lien and Cheng (2000). Compressing greatly, Lien and Cheng presented subjects with hypothetical soil ingredients that (they were told) were candidates for causes of plant blooming. These ingredients were described as varying in ways that fell into hierarchical structures or classes of increasing abstractness. For example, the ingredients varied as to color and these variations were represented at each of three levels of abstractness – particular shades of color (e.g., pine-green), general type of color (green), and (at a very general level) whether the color was "warm or cool." Similarly, the ingredients varied in shape and subjects were given information that represented these shapes both in highly specific ways (e.g., as a particular regular shape of certain dimensions), at an intermediate level of specificity (e.g., a type of shape), or in a still more abstract way (regular in the sense of rotationally symmetrical versus irregular). In addition, subjects were presented with information about the covariation between these ingredients, as described at these different levels of abstractness, and whether the plants bloomed. One of the tasks given to the subjects was to identify from such covariational information the causes of blooming and to predict on this basis how plants would respond to various soil treatments with the ingredients. The patterns of covariation were chosen in such a way that $\Delta p = Pr(E/C) - Pr(E/-C)$ was maximized when C was taken to be the most abstract category in the hierarchies. That is, Δp was maximized when blooming/non-blooming covaried maximally with possessing an irregular versus a regular shape or with possessing a warm versus a cool color (in both cases the maximally abstract characterizations of the ingredients). In contrast, blooming/non-blooming covaried less than maximally with more specific descriptions of the soil ingredients – that is, Δp was smaller when the soil ingredients were described in this way. Under these conditions, subjects preferred characterizations of the causes of blooming at the most abstract levels (rather than more specific levels) in the sense that they learned the abstract relationships from the covariational data more readily and used them, in preference to more specific relationships, to predict extent of blooming under new treatments.

These experiments provide an additional illustration of the interplay between descriptive and normative considerations in causal cognition that is one of the main themes of this paper and its companion. First, in agreement with Yablo's claims, the experiments show that subjects do sometimes prefer (learn and make use of) causal relationships or descriptions of causal relationships that are not characterized in a maximally specific or detailed way. Instead, they sometimes prefer more abstract characterizations. Second, as Lien and Cheng argue, the experiment suggests an obvious and very intuitive explanation/rationale for when and why subjects do this – thus suggesting that this preference is not a mistake or merely due to confusion. As already intimated, on Lien and Cheng's interpretation, the experiment supports the claim that (other things being equal) subjects favor characterizations of cause and effect at the level that maximizes the contrast $\Delta p = Pr(E/C) - Pr(E/\text{-}C)$ – that is, they prefer characterizations of the cause and the effect such that the arithmetic difference between the probability of the effect in the presence of the cause and the probability of the effect in the absence of the cause is maximized. Suppose, for example, that the presence of irregular shapes in the soil always leads to blooming and the presence of regular shapes never does, and that the presence of five-sided shapes increases the probability of blooming in comparison with the absence of five-sided shapes, but five-sided shapes do not always lead to blooming (only irregular five-sided shapes do) and the absence of five-sided shapes does not always lead to non-blooming (only regular non-five-sided shapes have this effect). That is, Pr (Blooming/Irregular shapes) = 1, Pr (Blooming/Regular shapes) = 0, and 1 > Pr (Blooming/Five-sided shapes) > Pr (Blooming/Non-five-sided shapes) > 0. Then the "irregular versus regular" level of description of the cause will be preferred to the description in terms of the contrast between five-sidedness and non-five-sidedness. An obvious normative rationale for this practice is that the more abstract level of description in this case provides more information about the conditions under which the effect will and will not occur than the more specific description; thus it provides more information that is useful for purposes of prediction and control.

Let us now apply the same analysis to Yablo's example in an attempt to explain why (5.2) is preferable to (5.1). As noted above, a limitation of (5.1) is that it fails to convey the information that the pigeon will peck at any red target, not just scarlet ones. By contrast (5.2) does convey this information. In addition, on a natural interpretation (5.1) misleadingly suggests that the pigeon will fail to peck at (all) non-scarlet targets, while (5.2) correctly suggests that the pigeon will fail to peck at all non-red targets. Lien and Cheng's account seems to capture these limitations fairly well. The contrast Δp between the probability of pecking given that the target is red and the probability of pecking, given that the target is not red is maximal – it is equal to 1. By contrast, although Pr (Pecks/target is scarlet) = 1, Pr (Pecks/target is not scarlet) is greater than zero. Thus Δp when the cause is characterized as "red" is greater than Δp when the cause is characterized as "scarlet" and on this basis, following Lien and Cheng's proposal, the characterization "red" is preferable. Of course, in a variant of Yablo's example in which the empirical facts are different, with the pigeon pecking at scarlet and only scarlet targets, (5.1) will then be preferable to (5.2) since the characterization of the cause at the level of scarlet/non-scarlet now maximizes the contrast between what happens in the presence and absence of the cause. This suggests, I think correctly, that which description of the cause is most appropriate in this sort of case depends on the empirical details of the case – there is no privileged level of description that is always most appropriate, regardless of which patterns of covariation are present. In any event, Yablo's discussion of the best causal description of pigeon behavior and Lien's and Cheng's experiment seem directed at very much the same problem and to have similar solutions

Lien and Cheng's proposal applies only to binary or dichotomous variables in which causes and effects are represented just in terms of two possible values – "present" and "absent." However the basic idea can be naturally generalized to variables that take many possible values and can be framed in terms of interventionist counterfactuals rather than conditional probabilities. This leads to the following formulation of proportionality. Causal claims satisfying the basic interventionist requirement (M) are proportional to the extent that they capture the full pattern of dependence of the values of the effect on the cause – that is, to the extent that they fully specify which changes in the values of the effect variable are associated with changes in the value of the cause variable and specify how such changes are associated. In addition, causal claims should be judged as preferable to the extent that they do not claim or suggest the existence of patterns of dependence between cause and effect that do not in fact hold or represent values of the cause variable as relevant or difference–makers for the effect variable when they are not relevant. For example, (5.1) fails to fully satisfy the proportionality requirement because it fails to capture the full range of cause values on which the effect depends (it fails to convey the information that the pigeon would peck at non-scarlet but red targets) and, on a natural interpretation, misleadingly suggests that the pigeon will not peck at such targets. By contrast, (5.2) correctly identifies (given the facts specified in the example) a fuller range variable values on which the effect variable depends.

As noted above, a number of writers, myself included, have appealed to considerations related to proportionality to argue that more general, less specific and detailed causal descriptions, both in common sense contexts and in various "upper level" sciences, are sometimes preferable to more specific and detailed descriptions found in "lower level" sciences. For example, Woodward (2008) argues (following Yablo 1992) that in situations in which an intention I to perform a certain movement B is multiply realized by several distinct patterns of neural activation n_1, n_2, and n_3, I (or more precisely the contrast between I and the absence of I – that is, *not I*) may better satisfy the requirement of proportionality with respect to B / *not B*, then any of n_1, n_2, or n_3. Thus, it is preferable from the point of view of proportionality to cite I rather than n_1, as a cause of B even on those occasions in which I is in fact realized by n_1. Of course this preference is also what is suggested by the advice to choose a level of description that maximizes Δp: in the envisioned circumstances $Pr\ (B/I) = 1$, $Pr\ (B/not\ I) = 0$, but $Pr\ (B/not\ n_1)$ is greater than zero (since B sometimes occurs in the absence of n_1). Critics have attacked such contentions, typically on the basis of metaphysical arguments that causal claims that provide more detail and specificity are always better and that the real causal action is always to be found at the level of such more detailed claims, with the upper level causal claims being epiphenomenal (or "excluded" by the lower level claims). Whatever one thinks about the details of such criticisms, we should note that the experimental results from Lien and Cheng show that subjects do in fact prefer levels of causal description that satisfy proportionality or maximize Δp and that, furthermore, it is easy to see how, as a normative matter, this preference serves (in terms of information provision) goals and purposes that people have, goals that would be less well served if one were to insist that more specific causal descriptions were always preferable. Assuming that people care about providing causal descriptions that better satisfy these goals, they thus seem to be behaving rationally when they are guided by considerations of proportionality in selecting causal descriptions. The question this raises for those who wish to claim that more specific descriptions of causes are always better is this: in what sense, if any, are those who prefer proportional but less specific causal descriptions (e. g. (5.2) to (5.1)) making a mistake?[14] Why should we be bound by some supposed metaphysical requirement

---

14 It is worth noting a possible response to these remarks that raises some interesting normative and empirical issues that have not to my knowledge been explored in any detail, especially on the empirical side. The response is to distinguish sharply between making a true causal statement (a claim that C causes E) and providing a satisfactory causal explanation. (Both Donald Davidson and David Lewis advance some version of this distinction, although in very different ways.) In particular, one might hold that some true causal claims are not explanatory (Davidson) and/or that some causal explanations do not involve citing true causal claims of form C causes E (Lewis). Thus making true causal claims and providing causal explanations are activities subject to different rules. One might then argue as follows: when subjects prefer the more abstract characterization they should be understood as supposing that this provides a better causal explanation of the effect of interest – a claim that may well be normatively correct. However, if we ask simply what *causes* the effect (rather than what best explains it) the more specific characterization is normatively correct (and perhaps, one might conjecture, as a descriptive matter, also the one that subjects prefer).

This sharp causal statement/causal explanation distinction raises a number of interesting issues. On a descriptive level, one might wonder whether it is true that subjects distinguish sharply between making true causal claims and providing causal explanations and judge these by different standards in the way claimed. On a normative level, one might wonder it is defensible to to provide maximally specific descriptions of causes if proportional descriptions are more informative about matters that we care about?

Before leaving this subject, let me try to correct a possible misinterpretation of my argument. A standard method employed by analytic philosophers discussing causation is to appeal to "intuitions" the philosopher has about the relationships present in various scenarios – both intuitions about whether those relationships are causal at all and about whether certain characterizations of those relationships are, causally speaking, "better" than others. Thus, a philosopher may report having the intuition that double prevention relations are "really" causal or that (5.2) is in some way preferable to (5.1). These intuitions are then taken as prima-facie evidence for various conclusions about causation. This is *not* the method or argumentative strategy that I have tried to follow above. I have not claimed, for example, that the preferences exhibited by Lien and Cheng's subjects should be interpreted as intuitions about causation and that these intuitions support or provide evidence for a proportionality requirement on causal judgment. Rather, I have argued as follows: as an empirical matter, people exhibit preferences for levels of causal description satisfying a proportionality requirement. Following the methodological strategy described in Woodward (2018) we should take seriously the possibility that these subjects are behaving reasonably and explore whether there is some normative basis for this preference. In fact, as we have seen, there is such a basis – one that appeals to the greater informativeness of causal descriptions satisfying proportionality. It is this normative basis and not anyone's intuitions (taken in themselves) that justifies adoption of proportionality.

6 Ahn et al. On the Role of Mechanism Information in Actual Cause Judgments

So far my focus has been on "success stories:" on mutually illuminating interactions between normative theorizing about causation, particularly within a broadly interventionist framework, and empirical psychological research about causal judgment. I turn next to a contrasting case: an influential experimental paper by Ahn et al. (1995), which illustrates what can happen when empirical investiga-

---

distinguish in this particular way between making true causal claims and providing causal explanations and why in particular, more detail and less abstraction is always preferable when making causal claims but that for some reason this preference is reversed when one provides explanations.

tion is *not* guided by any defensible normative theory. This paper is, in my opinion, relatively unsuccessful in large part *because* it does not make use of any defensible normative framework concerning causal reasoning and judgment. Ahn et al.'s paper also illustrates how experimental investigation can potentially benefit from the kind of analytical work and distinction-drawing that philosophers are good at and from a careful analysis (again informed by normative theory) of the *task* which subjects are asked to perform.

Ahn et al.'s experiments are premised on a supposed contrast between what they call "mechanism information" and information about "covariation." The authors present a series of experiments which they claim show that subjects appeal to mechanism information much more often than covariational information in making "causal attributions" (that is, "actual cause" judgments in which causes are ascribed to particular outcomes). They characterize mechanism information as follows:

> The mechanism information in causal reasoning specifies through which processes the event must have occurred (i.e., how a factor led to the consequence) by using vocabularies describing entities that are not presented in the event descriptions (Ahn et al. 1995, p. 309).

They contrast models of causal attribution which rely on this sort of information with models which instead "stress a general process involving the analysis of covariation between factors and effects."

The examples of mechanism information that Ahn et al. offer suggest that they are operating with a rather permissive notion of "mechanism." "Driving while drunk" is one of their examples (in the context of attributing a cause to an automobile accident); another example of "mechanism information" involves the information that a raccoon is in a cage (in the context of explaining why someone is unafraid of the raccoon). Their methodology for establishing the importance of mechanism information proceeds in the following way: Subjects are presented with a scenario in which, e.g., they are told that John had a car accident on route 7 last night. If, in deciding what caused the accident, subjects consider such questions as whether other people had accidents that night or whether John frequently has accidents, they are understood as making use of covariational information. If, instead, they consider such questions as whether John was drunk (or suggest that his accident was caused by drunkenness) this is taken to be an example of reliance on mechanism information. Ahn et al., find that subjects typically prefer to cite what they regard as mechanism explanation in advancing hypotheses about the causation of John's accident and are more interested in gathering mechanism information than in gathering covariational information in assessing such hypotheses. The authors report similar findings for the other scenarios they employ and it is on this basis that they reach their general conclusion that subjects rely more on mechanism information than covariational information in causal attribution.

I turn now to some general observations about the experimental tasks faced by Ahn et al.'s subjects. Note first that their experiments consisted merely in presenting subjects with verbal scenarios/queries and recording what responses subjects make and what information they seek in making them – as far as the experiments go, there is no fact of the matter about what caused John's accident and no basis for evaluating whether subject's responses are normatively correct.[15] Moreover, Ahn et al., do not attempt to provide any normative theory about what correctness in this context would consist in, which is not surprising, given the difficulty, noted above, of providing such an account. There is thus nothing analogous to the claim in Lien and Cheng's paper that choices of level of description that maximize Δp are normatively superior to alternative choices or to Lien and Cheng's strategy of comparing subject's actual behavior to this normative standard. Indeed, Ahn et al., even make use of nonsense scenarios ("the XB12 mimbled the wug at filmer") and record subjects' answer to these (e.g., the event occurred "because the XB12 resented the wug" [Ahn et al. 1995, p. 319]), classifying these answers as to whether they involve mechanism or covariational information – scenarios in which (one would suppose) there is no possible normative basis for assessing subject's answers.

Second, Ahn et al., asked their subjects to make one particular kind of causal judgment: "actual cause" judgments. Subjects were told that some particular event occurred (e.g. John had an accident) and were then asked to produce candidates for the or a cause of this event – e.g. John's drunkenness. Nonetheless the conclusions that are drawn (e.g., about the importance of mechanism information) from such examples are claimed to hold for casual judgment more generally, including various forms of type causal judgments. Although I earlier put aside the task of trying to provide a detailed normative account of actual cause judgments, it seems uncontroversial that to the extent that such judgments are correct or defensible, they will need to rely in part on particular facts about the effect-events we are trying to explain and the surrounding context. For example, particular facts about Jones and his car – e.g., that he was drunk and that his car suffered from no mechanical problems will be relevant to whether his

---

15 In other experimental set-ups there are a number of different possible criteria for correctness that can be appealed to. For example, if the experimental task is to learn from observational data which of several objects will activate a "blicket" detector, as in experiments conducted by Alison Gopnik, there is an obvious criterion for whether the subjects have selected the correct objects. My point is that there is nothing analogous to this in Ahn et al.'s experiments.

drunkenness caused the accident. Such facts are particularly likely to be regarded as relevant if subjects see the task as involving assessing whether Jones was "responsible for" or "to blame" for the accident. It is thus not surprising (and appropriate) that, as reported by Ahn et al., their subjects tend to focus on such particular facts and less on covariational information in addressing the experimental task. If instead the subjects had been asked what sort of information they regarded as relevant to such type cause questions as what causes automobile accidents or whether drunkenness plays an important role in causing accidents, it is a reasonable guess that they would have focused more on covariational information. Thus the experimental task Ahn et al., gave their subjects may have directed them away from regarding covariational information as relevant.

Independently of this, however, another general issue raised by Ahn et al., concerns their overall contrast between "mechanism" and "covariational" information. Again granting for the sake of argument that drunkenness is a possible "mechanism" of accident causation, it seems extremely likely that the subjects in their experiments believed that whether drivers are drunk covaries with their involvement in accidents. After all, this is an empirically well-supported correlation of which almost everyone is aware. Why not then think of the "mechanism information" associated with drunkenness as (at least in part) covariational information (or as closely associated with or as including covariational information) rather than as something which is different in kind from covariational information? In other words, when subjects invoke drunkenness as a cause of the accident, why not think of them as appealing to covariational information (among other things) even if this information is not presented in an explicitly covariational format (that is, in the form, "drunkenness covaries with accidents")?

In fact Ahn et al., seem to concede that mechanism information entails information about covariation (e.g. 1995, p. 306, where the authors make the very strong claim that mechanistic claims entail "deterministic" generalizations that "hold universally"). If I understand their view correctly, they hold that mechanism information differs from covariational information in that the former has additional content that goes beyond covariational information. They write:

> A mechanism is some component of an event which is thought to have causal force or necessity. [...] this approach treats events as composed of "surface" factors (John, Route 7) and one or more underlying responsible mechanism e.g. John's drunkeness, the failure of the brakes (Ahn et al. 1995, pp. 303–304).

Supposing that the covariational claim is that X covaries with Y, this additional content, as indicated in the passage quoted above, has to do with the fact that mechanistic information imports or involves the idea that X necessitates or determines Y, rather than just covarying with it. Ahn et al. make it clear elsewhere that mechanism information also involves information about intervening variables or processes leading from X to Y, and may involve the introduction of new terms or vocabulary besides X and Y, as when information about the covariation between John's driving and his involvement in accidents is supplemented by additional information about his habitual drunkenness.

On this understanding of mechanism information, Ahn et al.'s characterization of their results seems problematic. If mechanism information implies claims about covariation and if subjects who appeal to mechanism information are aware (as they typically seem to be) of the entailed covariational information, it is misguided to ask whether subjects prefer to rely on mechanism information rather than (or opposed to) covariational information, treating these as exclusive alternatives. Rather the issue is whether subjects rely on covariational information plus other information (which is what mechanism information involves on Ahn et al.'s account) or whether instead they rely purely on covariational information in making causal inferences. Ahn et al.'s experiments show at best that subjects do not rely on covariational information alone, but not that they don't rely on covariational information at all or that covariational information plays little role in their judgment, which is what Ahn et al., sometimes seem to suggest.

A related worry is that Ahn et al.'s characterization of mechanism information seems to conflate a number of different factors that may have different influences on causal judgment. It is apparent, both from the passage quoted above and elsewhere in their paper, that the authors think of the mechanism versus covariation contrast as having to do (among other things) with a contrast between, on the one hand, relationships that are genuinely causal and, on the other hand, relationships that involve "accidental" or spurious correlations or correlations that do not direct reflect causal connections. Indeed, they often seem to understand "covariational information" as information that simply reports a covariation, with no further indication about whether or not this is due to a correlation that reflects a direct causal connection. Thus the information that lung cancer covaries with yellow fingers apparently counts as covariational information, even though this covariation is due to the operation of a common cause (smoking) of both of these effects, and does not reflect any direct causal connection between lung cancer and yellow fingers.

Since on virtually any normatively plausible account of causation, including interventionism in the form of **M**, covariation (in this sense) underdetermines causal relationships, again it is hardly surprising that subjects tend not to rely just on covariational information (understood in this way) in causal attribution. This sort of behavior on the part of the subjects is normatively appropriate on any theory of causation that does not simply reduce causal claims to claims about covariation, regardless of whether the theory of causation assigns any special role to information that is distinctively about mechanisms, at least in any sense of mechanism that connects mechanisms with intervening processes and so on.

In addition, because Ahn et al.'s notion of mechanism mixes together the features of non-spuriousness, process and change of vocabulary and contrasts this just with covariational information, their finding that people prefer to make causal claims on the basis of the former, as opposed to the latter, even if correct, leaves it unclear just which features of the mechanism information are driving their judgments. For example, one highly relevant empirical question, not addressed in Ahn et al.'s paper, is whether subjects would be willing to make type causal judgments to the effect that Cs cause Es, on the basis of covariational information, in circumstances in which they have good reason to believe the C–E relation is not spurious, but without having information about the other features the authors associate with mechanisms such as process information connecting Cs to Es. As an illustration, if subjects were to believe that E covaries with C under interventions on C, would they be willing to judge that Cs cause Es (as an interventionist account of causation committed to **M** suggests they should) even if they had no information about processes leading from C to E? A great many experiments suggest an affirmative answer to this question, even though such subjects lack some information that Ahn et al. regard as crucial to knowledge of mechanisms. Once again more attention to what plausible normative theories have to say about the role of mechanism information in various sorts of causal inferences would have been beneficial for the design and interpretation of Ahn et al.'s experiments.

Finally, as Ahn et al.'s discussion makes clear, they are primarily interested in what people *usually* or *typically* when they make actual cause attributions. Unsurprisingly, they find that when given examples of outcomes such as automobile accidents for which people already have extensive beliefs about possible causes, people tend to make causal attributions by invoking candidates from this list rather than trying to discover new previously unknown candidate causes. But while it seems plausible that this is the most common pattern in actual cause judgment (and perhaps in causal judgment generally) and that "people do not very often start from scratch and go looking for novel causal relations" (Ahn et al. 1995, p. 308), it does not follow that *only* cases of this sort are interesting or important for understanding causal inference and judgment. After all at some point, subjects must *learn* the mechanism information to which (at least according to Ahn et al). they are appealing when they make actual cause judgments. Even if they learn it as a result of being told by others, at some point someone in this chain of communication must have learned it from other sources, which presumably include experiences of various sorts. So even if such learning from experience is statistically rare (in comparison with applying pre-existing causal knowledge to particular cases) it is still very important to provide an account of it, insofar as we think of our task as one of explaining why we are so successful at causal judgment. Ahn et al. have nothing to say about this issue, which is of central importance on normative accounts.[16]

7 Conclusion

Let me conclude with some meta-philosophical remarks. Although my primary purpose, both in this paper and its companion in this volume (Woodward 2018), has been to argue for the mutual relevance of normative (including "philosophical") theorizing about causation and descriptive empirical work to one another, I should, in the interest of full transparency, acknowledge a more general and ambitious (indeed subversive) purpose. As noted above, much of the philosophical literature on causation consists in the construction of theories based on a mixture of "intuitions" about particular cases and "metaphysical" ideas of various sorts about which are the acceptable building blocks to use (or the constraints that must be satisfied) in constructing an account of causation – for example, it is commonly assumed that these building blocks must not themselves make use of causal notions so that the resulting account is reductive in character. In addition it may contended that all true causal claims must be "grounded" in the laws of "fundamental physics," that "the" causal relation is an intrinsic relation between particular token events and so on. (Paul and Hall 2013 is a very recent example of this sort of enterprise.)

Judging from some of the critical reaction to my own work, I believe that many philosophers now assume that this sort of "metaphysical" project is the only project that it is legitimate or worthwhile for philosophers interested in causation and causal reasoning to engage in – if one is not doing the metaphysics of causation, one is not doing anything of any philosophical significance regarding causation. (Or at least one has failed to do an important part of what one should be doing – failed in one's philosophical duty, so to speak.) I have a very different view; I believe that there are other valuable and worthwhile projects – valuable

---

[16] It is a common place of post-Galilean science that reports of what happens for most typically or for the most part may tell us less about the underling structure of some domain than what happens in relevant special or artificial circumstances that occur only rarely.

both for philosophy and for disciplines outside of it – that are distinct from (and do not presuppose or rest on the results of) this metaphysical project. One such possibility is (I hope) illustrated by the approach taken and the ideas discussed in this paper and its companion. I would like to encourage philosophers to think of the project pursued in this paper and its companion as a viable alternative to more metaphysical projects.

At the risk of some repetition, I conceptualize the project I have been pursuing as involving a mixture of the normative and descriptive. At the normative level, the project involves investigating goals or functions associated with causal thinking and assessing various more specific causal concepts and sorts of causal judgment in the light of these goals and functions. Given these concepts and judgments, one also tries to uncover normatively good strategies for learning about and reasoning with the causal relationships represented in these judgments. These normative concerns then can be related to descriptive concerns in the manner described above – by investigating empirically to what extent subjects of various sorts conform to the requirements of the normative theories and by treating subject's reasoning and judgment as possible sources of normative ideas. As my discussion above illustrates, I believe one can engage in this sort of "functional" inquiry without providing a reductive account of causation and without entering into any detailed discussion of such questions as how causal claims in ordinary life and the special sciences relate to fundamental physical laws. My own sense (of course I am far from an impartial judge) is that such functional inquiries concerning causation have been very fruitful over the past few decades, both within philosophy and outside of it. It is important to create an intellectual space in which this non-metaphysical project is viewed as a valuable one to pursue.

References

Ahn, W., Kalish, C., Medin, D., and Gelman, S. (1995): "The Role of Covariation versus Mechanism Information in Causal Attribution." *Cognition*, v. 54, pp. 299–352.
Glymour, C., Danks, D., Glymour, B., Eberhardt, F., Ramsey, J., Scheines, R., Spirtes, P., Teng, C., and Zhang, J. (2010): "Actual Causation: A Stone Soup Essay." *Synthese*, v. 175, pp. 169–192.
Hall, N. (2004): "Two Concepts of Causation." In: Collins, J., Hall, N., and Paul, L. A. (eds.): *Causation and Counterfactuals*, pp. 225–276. Cambridge, MA: The MIT Press.
Halpern, J. and Pearl, J. (2005a): "Causes and Explanations: A Structural-model Approach – Part I: Causes." *British Journal of Philosophy of Science*, v. 56, pp. 843–887.
Halpern, J. and Pearl, J. (2005b): "Causes and Explanations: A Structural-model Approach – Part II: Explanations." *British Journal of Philosophy of Science*, v. 56, pp. 889–911.

Hitchcock, C. (2001): "The Intransitivity of Causation Revealed in Equations and Graphs." *Journal of Philosophy*, v. 98, pp. 273–299.

Hitchcock, C. and Knobe, J. (2009): "Cause and Norm." *Journal of Philosophy*, v. 106, pp. 587–612.

Lien, Y. and Cheng, P. (2000): "Distinguishing Genuine from Spurious Causes: A Coherence Hypothesis." *Cognitive Psychology*, v. 40, pp. 87–137.

McDermott, M. (1995): "Redundant Causation." *British Journal for the Philosophy of Science*, v. 46, pp. 523–544.

Rose, D., Danks, D., and Machery, E. (in preparation): "Actual Causation and Reliability."

Salmon, W. (1984): *Scientific Explanation and the Causal Structure of the World*. Princeton: Princeton University Press.

Walsh, C. and Sloman, S. (2011): "The Meaning of Cause and Prevent: The Role of Causal Mechanism." *Mind and Language*, v. 26, pp. 21–52.

Woodward, J. (2003): *Making Things Happen: A Theory of Causal Explanation*. New York: Oxford University Press.

Woodward, J. (2006): "Sensitive and Insensitive Causation." *The Philosophical Review*, v. 115, pp. 1–50.

Woodward, J. (2008): "Mental Causation and Neural Mechanisms." In: Hohwy, J. and Kallestrup, J. (eds.): *Being Reduced: New Essays on Reduction, Explanation, and Causation*, pp. 218–262. Oxford: Oxford University Press.

Woodward, J. (2010): "Causation in Biology: Stability, Specificity, and the Choice of the Levels of Explanation." *Biology and Philosophy*, v. 25, pp. 287–318.

Woodward, J. (2014): "A Functional Theory of Causation." *Philosophy of Science*, v. 81, pp. 691–713.

Woodward, J. (2018): "Normative Theory and Descriptive Psychology in Understanding Causal Reasoning: The Role of Interventions and Invariance." This volume, pp. 71–101.

Yablo, S. (1992): "Mental Causation." *Philosophical Review*, v. 101, pp. 245–280.

José María Martínez Selva
Psychobiological Explanations in Decision-making and Neuroeconomics

Abstract: Biological explanations of behaviour are aimed at establishing the relationships between different bodily functions, mainly those pertaining to the central nervous system, and certain behaviours. For this purpose, researchers choose a well-known behaviour, e.g., a decision-making task, together with a wide array of techniques (lesion, electroencephalography, functional neuroimaging, biochemical tests, among others). The research techniques are usually aimed at intensifying, interrupting or influencing in some way the activity of the region under study. The characteristics of the performance of the chosen behaviour are observed, explored and recorded to assess the effects of the technique employed. Sometimes the region under study is not altered but changes in its activity that occur at the same time or immediately before/after the actual behaviour develops are recorded. By combining different techniques, researchers are able to elucidate the degree of the involvement of a given brain region in the selected behaviour. This chapter describes how in the field of decision-making different techniques and approaches indicate that a given region of the brain – the ventromedial prefrontal cortex – is necessary to achieve a good performance in the Iowa Gambling Task, a decision-making task characterized by uncertainty and risk.

Keywords: psychobiological explanations, decision-making, neuroeconomics, behaviour

In this paper I present the results of various pieces of research on the biological factors that influence behaviour in decision-making, in particular, how different research techniques can provide data that allow us to state that a certain brain structure is intervening in decision-making processes.

We all make decisions continuously in our daily lives, about the most trivial and the most transcendental issues, from what studies to follow or what profession to choose, to whether to get married, to have children or not, whether to accept or turn down a job offer. It is frequently an automatic, routine process, but on occasions deep reflection is required, and in these cases decision-making in-

---

Research funded by grant PSI2008 – 04394/PSIC of the Spanish Ministry for Science and Innovation and by the FEDER programme.

volves great mental activity, including the consideration of the aspects and stimuli present in the situation, the memory of earlier experiences and, above all, the estimation of the possible consequences of the various options available. The decision is often postponed because of the difficulties in finding the best option. So we have a complex process, made up of a number of subprocesses, which takes in a wealth of varied information.

The study of decision-making is addressed mainly in the areas of psychology, neuroscience and economics, but also in other sciences such as medicine and law. As with all behaviour, decision-making may be influenced by many variables of a biological, psychological, social or cultural type. *Psychobiology* and other related scientific fields, such as *cognitive neuroscience*, offer biological explanations for behaviour that help us to know more about it and to predict it (cf. Bunge and Ardila 1988; Martínez Selva 1995; Rosenzweig, Breedlove, and Watson 2005). The biology of decision-making, that is what biological factors influence decision-making, is a current topic in psychobiology and cognitive neuroscience. There has been a wealth of studies recently on the brain mechanisms involved in decision-making, which have given rise to a new scientific field of study known as *neuroeconomics* (cf. Camerer 2003 and McCabe 2008). This is an interdisciplinary field, as is the decision-making from which it has arisen, in which psychologists and economists join forces with neuroscientists, i.e., researchers of the nervous system. *Neuroeconomics* describes the "networks" or neuronal systems activated when taking economic decisions, which may help to "explain" the decisions made by the economic actors and the relative weight of the variables involved. One of the main research techniques used is *functional magnetic resonance imaging* (fMRI), which reveals which areas of the brain participate in a specific behaviour or in a mental process, in this case decision-making. It is usual for many connected regions to be activated, thus leading us to refer to the whole as networks or neuronal systems. Nevertheless, the functions of each region may be different and can be studied separately through specific experiments.

1 Behavioural and Biological Variety and Complexity in the Study of Decision-making

Research in this area is carried out using tasks, which emulate or represent real daily situations which, therefore, allow some generalization or extrapolation. These tasks are performed in the laboratory under controlled conditions and are of limited duration. Since decision-making affects very different areas, there are different decision-making models, for example, economic decisions or moral decisions. Given that the cognitive and emotional processes intervening are also different, it is also possible to talk about a greater or lesser emotional or cognitive load and, therefore, tasks will differ in their complexity and the difficulty of performing them. In many decision-making situations, especially the more complex ones and those related to interpersonal behaviour, the consequences of the different options presented are not exactly known. So we can talk of tasks of *uncertainty*. Uncertainty, in turn, can come in two different forms: *risk* and *ambiguity*. In risk tasks the likelihood of a possible outcome of a choice can be estimated, while in ambiguity tasks this is not possible.

There are numerous biological variables under research that respond to the complexity of the tasks and mental processes involved as well as to the nervous system and other related systems, such as the endocrine system. Some examples of this wealth of biological variables can be seen in the following research questions currently being addressed:
- Which regions of the brain participate in decision-making?
- Do certain hormone levels affect decision-making?
- Is decision-making influenced by the changes that occur in the brain and other systems during development?
- Are there genetic components that intervene in decision-making?
- Are there changes in the brain or in the peripheral nervous system that precede the choices made in a task or that occur as a consequence of the choices made?

The first of these questions – the regions of the brain intervening in decision-making – is one of the most explored and is the subject of this paper. Different regions come into play and act together but with separable functions. They can be studied through several strategies and various techniques.[1] The most common procedure is to instruct the experimental subjects to perform a decision-making task while exploring their brain activity through techniques such as fMRI or *electroencephalography* (study of the brain's electrical activity, EEG) among others. Many experiments use patients with brain lesions or patients suffering psychopathological disorders. The location of a lesion that is associated to a specific way of performing a decision-making task, which may be different from that of a non-lesion control group, will contribute important information about the

---

[1] In an earlier paper I describe the main techniques used in psychobiology and the different valorations to be made from their findings. See Martínez Selva (2011).

participation of the region affected in decision-making. I will now look at the characteristics and limitations of lesion techniques and other research strategies.

2 Causal and Correlational Methods for Locating Mental Functions in the Brain

The observation of changes in behaviour that follow damage to the brain has been used to locate functions in the brain, from the simplest to the most complex. The brain is the headquarters of behavioural and psychological processes and we can state that, in general, different regions of the brain regulate or control different behaviours. In a broad sense, psychological processes and behaviours are considered brain functions. The basic idea is that the regulation of behavioural and psychological processes is located in brain regions that are heavily interconnected; the regions that control or regulate a specific psychological process or behaviour are usually described as *neuronal networks* or *distributed brain systems*. Therefore, brain lesions may alter to a greater or lesser degree behaviour and psychological, cognitive and emotional processes. These alterations mean we can talk about functions or behaviours being *located* in one or more regions of the brain. These disorders and the behaviours associated with them (language, attention, memory or decision-making, for example) are examined through specific tests and groups of persons with lesions in different regions are compared with non-lesion subjects. The aim is to relate the changes in the function or behaviour studied with the lesion in a certain region or in a part of a neuronal network of the brain (see Kolb and Whishaw 2006; Tirapu-Ustáriz, Maestú, González-Marqués, Ríos-Lago, and Ruiz 2011).

Since the nineteenth century the study of the effects of brain lesions has increased our knowledge of brain functions, their location and of a number of psychopathological processes. In theory, a lesion in a region of the brain that causes deterioration of a function would mean that we can affirm that the region controls that function. The lesion means that there is a region of the brain that is the *cause* of a behaviour, since when it is destroyed, that behaviour deteriorates or disappears. However, the interpretation of the effects of a lesion and, therefore, the assignation of a function to a region of the brain, entails various problems. First there is the huge anatomic variability between individuals, since a lesion in the same place will produce different effects in different people (Brett, Johnsrude, and Owen 2002). Then, in many cases, some recovery of lost functions can occur thanks to a possible physiological reorganization and to cognitive plasticity. In addition, the number of subjects in an experiment is often quite small as it is not easy to get groups of patients suffering similar lesions; it depends on fortuitous circumstances and may take some years. In practical terms, if we are to compare effects of lesions in various patients the extension of the lesion needs to be determined as accurately as possible. This is normally done by anatomic techniques, usually structural magnetic resonance. So, a minimum number of similar cases is needed if valid conclusions are to be drawn.

A further problem relates to the *specificity* of the effects of the lesion. Given the distributed nature of many functions and the strong interconnection between the regions of the brain, the fact that a lesion in one structure is followed by a loss of a function does not mean that the lesion is necessarily located in the structure or the system that regulates that function. This structure may participate or intervene together with other brain regions in the function under study. Furthermore, cognitive alterations are usually interdependent, so failings in one function, for example, attention, may lead to failings in another, for example, memory, which means that it is difficult to interpret the effects of a given lesion.

It may also be that the lesion affects the connections between different areas of the brain. Indeed, many functions, such as language and decision-making, depend on distributed brain systems and need the participation of many regions of strong interdependence. If their joint participation is required for a certain behaviour, the interruption of the connections will lead to a loss of function. This cannot be attributed to any single area, which in isolation may be responsible for other functions.

The lesion technique can help to unravel which regions are participating in a behaviour, but not the relations between them. Other techniques, like fMRI or EEG, can provide better information about the relations between the different structures when a psychological process or a specific behaviour is activated. Hypotheses on the location of brain functions based on lesion data therefore need to be confirmed by other techniques and procedures. The integration of knowledge obtained from different data and techniques enables us to ascertain the location in the brain of functions.

Another *causal* technique is the drug, electrical or magnetic stimulation of a region of the brain, either to activate or to inhibit it. Observing the ensuing changes in behaviour can lead to our locating the region of the brain on which that behaviour depends. However, there are again difficulties similar to those encountered when using the lesion technique, including that of the *specificity* of the activation provoked. The stimulation of a structure, followed by a change in behaviour does not mean that the brain processes that originate it are located there. It may be that the stimulation activates the connection between different regions or that it activates several structures at the same time, so the changes noted in the behaviour may be the result of activity in various regions. Again, we need data obtained from other methods if we are to confirm the location in the brain of functions, especially the more complex ones.

Another set of techniques are known as *correlational* in that they inform about changes in the regions of the brain where the activity increases when a task is carried out. Among these are the already mentioned, fMRI and EEG, to which we can add *magnetoencephalography* and *positron emission tomography* (PET). fMRI, which is widely used in the study of decision-making, detects brain activity through the level of brain tissue oxygenation, i.e., from the changes in the levels of oxygen supplied by the bloodstream. It indicates the metabolic function of a large number of neurons and it is based on the idea that neuronal and haemodynamic activities are united (cf. Logothetis 2008).[2] It offers a very precise anatomical image and allows the direct integration of functional and anatomical data. The technique locates and shows the neuronal "network" or distributed brain system that is activated when a subject performs a task.

When interpreting the data obtained with this technique we need to take into account a series of factors. Higher metabolic activity in a structure (one of the main advantages of these techniques) may indicate either activation or inhibition, i.e., the structure that shows itself as being most active may in fact be inhibiting other regions. Distinguishing this is crucial from a functional viewpoint since it enables us to understand how the brain works while a task is being performed. It is difficult to know beforehand whether the metabolism manifested by a structure increases or decreases when it is inhibiting another. So other means are needed to ascertain the circuits and organization of the region of the brain under study. Observing greater activity in one region or structure says little, in principle, about the real nature of the relations between the different structures or within the system in which they are activated when a certain conduct is carried out.

Yet because of their very nature, they can show activation in other regions due to the physiological processes not related to those necessary for the realization of the behaviour being studied. The mere activation of a region while a task is being performed does not mean that this region is *necessary* for its performance. It may be activated because it is connected to a region that *is* necessary. On the other hand, there are regions that may be always active, regardless of the task, and involved in modulation functions, such as keeping the subject

---

[2] An analysis of the importance and significance of functional neuroimaging techniques in explaining behavior can be found in Martínez Selva (2011, pp. 97–117).

awake and active. If we compare the realization when resting and during the performance of a task, the activity may not be detected because only the activity that is different between both states is measured (Rorden and Karnath 2004). In some cases it could also happen that the combination of a high activation in neuronal excitatory and inhibitory connections within a single brain region or between two or more interconnected regions would result in an increased metabolic activity and, at the same time, the net behavioural effect of this activation would be nil. In this case, it could be erroneously concluded that the activated region or regions under study would have a significant behavioural relevance (cf. González-García, Tudela, and Ruz 2014).

As in the case of the *causal* techniques, there are underlying problems related to the differences in the brain between people and the complex functions that are distributed in its various regions.[3] The use of fMRI also has certain *specificity* requisites that allow one to affirm that one or more regions of the brain are invariably associated to a psychological process. Likewise, it is necessary to have a better description of the mental processes intervening in a given behaviour. Thus, processes like *working memory* may refer to different mental operations (conservation of information in the short-term memory, selection of mental operations to perform [Poldrack 2010]). The more complex the process, the more conducts can be related to it and the more difficult it will be to locate the region of the brain whose activity specifically corresponds to the process. Again, the conclusion is that when there is a coincidence of results from different techniques that points to the same structure or structures intervening in a psychological process, then we can be sure of their participation.

Electrophysiological techniques, like EEG and derived techniques can give us some more data about how the activity of different structures is related. The *EEG coherence* data provide temporal information about the brain's activity, so it is possible to know whether regions are simultaneously activated or if they follow a specific sequence, and this could throw up interesting information about the relation between regions. A similar approach can be adopted when employing the fMRI technique, since certain statistical analyses of the metabolic changes in the regions under study provide relevant information about the coherence and connectivity existing between them. These analyses also allow us to know how these interactions change during the performance of a task.[4]

To locate the decision-making in the brain, the direct strategy is to use a causal technique to activate or inhibit the regions of the brain that supposedly

---

[3] See in this respect the paper by Aue, Lavelle, and Cacioppo (2009).
[4] See in this respect the paper by Rubinov and Sporns (2010).

intervene and observe the results. The main problem with this strategy is the difficulty in manipulating the brain without causing any damage. There are techniques that enable the direct activation or inhibition of a region of the brain, for example, the aforementioned electrical or magnetic stimulation, but they have been used sparingly to date. It is more usual to employ indirect techniques: the study of the activity in a region, the exploration of patients with lesions in the same region, drugs that can affect systems that are relevant to the function of a region or the study of patients suffering from psychopathologies that may have disorders in that area. Ideally, we would get several research techniques and strategies to coincide in contributing data that guarantee the role that is attributed to a structure for a given behaviour. This is known as *convergent validation:* the results obtained from the different techniques or approaches confirm the same hypothesis. Other ways of guaranteeing that we have a good knowledge of which regions participate in a behaviour include *meta-analysis*, which works by grouping the findings of research using common methods and their statistical analysis, so giving a synthesis of the main findings.

The work of the researcher is not limited to verifying whether a hypothesis about the intervention of a particular region in the brain holds or not. It has to be valued, on the grounds of previous research, to see if it fits in with the general theories about this and other behaviours and on the basis of the novelty of the data and the advances it supposes. This usually includes the relation of the results obtained with the general functions attributed to the regions or structures studied.

I will now present a series of studies on a standard decision-making task – the *Iowa Gambling Task* (IGT). This is a complex economic task that entails a lot of uncertainty. It simulates real life short and long-term decision-making. The subject is presented with four decks of cards, from which he or she must choose one each time. Depending on the deck chosen in each trial, the subject is rewarded (winnings) or punished (losses) in symbolic monetary prizes. As the game progresses and choices are made, two of the decks will lead to losses, and the other two will lead to gains. Two of the decks are characterized by small frequent losses while the other two include less frequent but greater losses. Participants are instructed to try to win as much money as possible over 100 consecutive choices. Most begin by choosing the riskiest decks, with bigger gains and losses, and then change around trial 40 to the more advantageous decks that bring long-term gains. During the first part, up to about trial 40, there is a predominance of ambiguity, since the subject does not yet know which of the four decks will provide the biggest winnings. In the second part, it is risk that predominates, for the subject has, bit by bit, learnt to distinguish which choices are more advantageous. Consequently, the subject begins to take cards from the two more advantageous decks and winnings outstrip losses as the task advances.

Studies with different techniques report different regions of the brain to be participating in the performance of the IGT. Later on, we will examine some examples of the confluence of data or convergent validation that confirms the intervention of a key brain region in each task.

3 A Distributed Brain System Intervenes in Decision-making in the Iowa Gambling Task

The IGT is a complex task whose execution involves the participation of different regions of the brain. Lesion and functional neuroimaging studies, like fMRI and PET, indicate that a network of structures, located in different parts of the brain, is activated during decision-making:
- the ventromedial prefrontal cortex (VMPFC), which includes part of the orbitofrontal cortex (OFC);
- the dorsolateral prefrontal cortex (DLPFC);
- the anterior cingulate cortex (ACC);
- the anterior insular cortex;
- the superior parietal cortex;
- the brain's reward system, in particular, two of its most important regions: the accumbens nucleus and the ventral striatum (caudate, putamen);[5]
- the amygdala.

These structures are related to different psychological processes that participate in decision-making. The VMPFC and the ACC intervene in the integration of cognitive and emotional information. The DLPFC is involved in the working memory and the mechanisms that sustain voluntary attention, processes in which the superior parietal cortex is also involved. These structures enable the recovery of short-term memories for later use. Other regions are related to the processing and anticipation of motivational and affective stimuli of a rewarding or aversive nature, e.g., the ventral striatum, the nucleus accumbens and the amygdala. Finally, within the framework of Antonio Damasio's somatic marker hypothesis,

---

[5] We have reviewed the participation of different areas of the brain when performing the IGT and other economic decision-making tasks in two previous papers. See Martínez Selva, Sánchez Navarro, and Bechara (2010); Martínez Selva, Sánchez Navarro, Bechara, and Román (2006).

certain structures, like the anterior insula, assign affective values to the somatic changes (cf. Damasio 1994).

We will now focus on the experimental data obtained using different techniques that confirm the role of the VMPFC in decision-making.

4 The Ventromedial Prefrontal Cortex in Decision-making

The ventromedial region of the prefrontal cortex includes the medial ventral region of the prefrontal cortex and the medial sector of the OFC. One function generally attributed to the prefrontal cortex is the processing of stimuli associated to rewards and punishments and, therefore, of the emotional stimuli and the reactions to them. Several authors have proposed that the VMPFC, and especially the medial orbital sector, represent the coding of the relative value of the reward or punishment of the stimuli (Rolls, McCabe, and Redoute 2008). In decision-making tasks, it would process the favourable and unfavourable consequences of the different options. This function is directly related to *behavioural flexibility* or the capacity to adapt behaviour to the consequences, which may vary with time and, in turn, lead to changes in behaviour.

This region processes motivational and emotional stimuli or signals from outside, together with somatic signals coming from internal organs and systems. It can integrate and associate the somatic states with present information and that stored in the memory. It provides the substrate to integrate the relations learnt among complex situations and internal states, including those of an emotional nature, and which have been associated to such situations in earlier experiences. The activation of this region can be somatic and direct, provoked by information reaching the somatic sensory cortex, but also indirect, so that cortical activation without somatic changes can be produced. In this case, we would be talking about a mnesic reactivation or recovery aroused by context stimuli. These evoke somatic signals stored in the memory similar to those already experienced.

Somatic states, sensorial information and experiences are integrated in the VMPFC with information coming from other structures, specifically, the amygdala, the hypothalamus and other brainstem nuclei (cf. Bechara, Damasio, Damasio, and Lee 1999). The VMPFC exercises its influence on the vegetative and motor activity via circuits that are directed towards the amygdala, the hypothalamus and the corpus striatum, and from there to the brainstem nuclei.

5 Specific Functions of the Ventromedial Prefrontal Cortex in Decision-making: The Somatic Marker Hypothesis

The most complete description of the role of the VMPFC in decision-making is known as the *somatic marker* hypothesis, and it was put forward by neuroscientist Antonio Damasio (1994), according to whom the positive or negative consequences of a decision provoke somatic changes ("markers") of an emotional nature which people associate with the decisions they take. This association between decision-making and the somatic changes caused by the consequences is retained in the memory. As a result, these somatic markers would *anticipate* the consequences of certain options on the basis of earlier experiences, and would therefore guide the decision-making process. The brain receives information continually form the guts and from internal organs that influences mental processes. These signals provide unconscious indexes that precede, facilitate and contribute to decision-making, even before a person can explain why he or she has taken a decision. The role of the VMPFC would, according to the previous section, be to integrate the somatic and visceral signals already experienced when taking similar decisions, as well as other signals present in the situation. Thus, when one is going to take a decision, one "relives" or updates in the VMPFC the emotional states that appeared as a consequence of decisions taken in previous similar choices. In this way, one recovers the somatic state provoked by the situation, so influencing the decision to be taken.

In short, this region of the brain intervenes in the estimation of the long-term consequences of the decisions taken, thanks to the integration of the somatic states with key information proceeding from the situation itself or from one stored in the memory.

In the laboratory, somatic markers are measured through autonomic responses, such as changes in skin electrical conductance due to sweating, in heart rate or in the activity of some facial muscles. As mentioned, this somatic information is normally unconscious. According to Damasio, somatic markers support cognitive processes, they allow appropriate social conduct, contribute to favourable decision-making and slow down the tendency to seek immediate reward while facilitating the representation or anticipation of similar situations on the future (cf. Bechara, Damasio, Tranel, and Damasio 2005; Bechara and Damasio 1997). In contrast, the absence, alteration or debilitation of these markers leads to unsuitable or unfavourable decisions being taken. Healthy people that do not perform well in laboratory decision-making tasks, show fewer somatic changes than those who perform correctly. The deficiency is accentuated, as we will see below, in patients with brain lesions in the frontal cortex, in those who are incapable of properly experiencing emotions and of generating bodily responses to signals that anticipate harm or losses. This can also occur in substance abuse patients. All present problems of adjustment in their social lives.

6 Data Obtained from Patients with Lesions in the Ventromedial Prefrontal Cortex

The main source of data on the involvement of the VMPFC in decision-making is the study of patients with traumatic or surgical lesions in this region. These patients usually present alterations in social conduct, decision-making and emotional processing. They conserve a normal level of intellectual capacities, intelligence and memory along with other cognitive functions, but they experience difficulties in learning from mistakes, and this is shown when making decisions (cf. Bechara and Van der Linden 2005). In their social, work and economic lives they are prone to adopt conducts that are harmful to them. They are insensitive to long-term future consequences, be they positive or negative. They are mainly guided by immediate outcomes. They lose behavioural flexibility, they persevere in their mistakes and show problems in adapting to changes produced in the conditions of a task or a certain situation. They have difficulties in planning their daily and future activities, in choosing their friends and companions, and in their social life in general (cf. Bechara, Damasio, and Damasio 2000; Bechara, Tranel, and Damasio 2000). They seem to have lost the capacity to use feelings and emotions to guide their behaviour.

The most plausible hypothesis, put forward by Damasio and collaborators, to explain their behaviour is that the lesion prevents the effect of signals or somatic markers that indicate the alternatives available and their possible consequences. The proof is that patients with prefrontal ventromedial lesion do not perform well in the IGT and do not develop anticipatory skin conductance responses from disadvantageous choices (cf. Bechara, Damasio, Tranel, and Anderson 1998). In other words, their somatic markers are deficient. In contrast, these patients experience somatic reactions to the consequences of the decisions they take regarding losses and gains, just like healthy subjects or those with no lesion in this region, although their responses are of a lower intensity. Their lesions impede or interfere in the use of the of the somatic signals set off by the amygdala, the hypothalamus and the nuclei of the brainstem, which are involved in future decisions and are necessary for taking appropriate decisions. The impression is that patients with ventromedial lesion, despite knowing which decks carry most punishments, do not make use of their experience when taking decisions, and show no anticipatory somatic reactions when faced with a new decision-making situation, which leads them to make disadvantageous choices.

Lesion to frontal regions upsets decision-making in situations of ambiguity or insufficient information (cf. Tanabe, Thompson, Claus, Dalwani, Hutchison, and Banich 2007; Koechlin and Hyafil 2007). When the OFC is the region affected, insensitivity towards uncertainty is produced, which means patients do not cope well in situations where there is a lack of information about the options available. The result is that they make choices that are not influenced by the level of risk or ambiguity and, therefore, the consequences are unfavourable.

The above experiments coincide in showing the role of the VMPFC when performing a complex decision-making task like the IGT. Yet, as stated earlier, the studies of lesions often show problems of interpretation for various reasons. Another aspect to consider here is the need to carry out studies of psychological functions (for example, intelligence, memory, attention, linguistic capacities) that can also suffer alterations. Alterations in complex behaviours like decision-making may be due to a deterioration of these functions and not be specific to decision-making.

The problem of the specificity of the lesion on decision-making has been highlighted by various researchers. Despite the worsened performance of the IGT provoked by the lesion in the VMPFC, it has been mooted that this effect is not specific to that location, but to more diffuse lesions (Manes, Sahakian, Clark, Rogers, Antoun, Aitken, et al. 2002). This is compatible with the findings that show that performance of the IGT depends on the wholeness of the VMPFC. When patients present lesions in the VMPFC that extend to adjacent regions, like the DLPFC, other cognitive functions (like working memory) that are necessary for the IGT may also be affected. In such cases, the deficits in the IGT could be due to these alterations and not to the ventromedial lesions. There is, therefore, a dissociation between the functions of the VMPFC and those of the DLPFC, since decision-making is specific to the VMPFC, but the lesions of the DLPFC impede both working memory and decision-making behaviours. Other authors also report nonspecific effects in the performance of the IGT in patients with frontal lesions (Fujiwara, Schwartz, Gao, Black, and Levine 2008). In particular, the deterioration in the performance of the task has been related to the volume of grey matter lost in the superior medial frontal regions. The superior medial frontal cortex may be more related to cognitive demands, such as those deriving from working memory and general attentional functions. More recent data suggest that broad frontal lesions that take in the OFC lead to increases in the amounts of the stakes in other economic decision-making tasks, which would translate into higher losses in the IGT (Clark, Bechara, Damasio, Aitken, Sahakian, and Robbins 2008).

Studies on lesion do not tell us so much about *causality*, in the strict sense, but more about the *need* for the VMPFC for "appropriate" or advantageous decision-making. It is therefore a case of a relation of limited causality. The participation of this cortical region seems to be *specific*, since only lesions here lead to alterations in decision-making tasks. It also tells us *how this structure is acting:* integration of external and internal signals ("somatic markers") that mark the favourable and unfavourable consequences of possible choices according to experience. The deterioration of this region affects decision-making selectively. Likewise, the integrity of other structures like the DLPFC and those mentioned above is also necessary, since they affect brain processes and functions that intervene not only in decision-making but in other behaviours, too. These studies offer us more insights into how the brain works and how different structures participate in complex behaviour. They often do this as a distributed brain system, in which different structures with different functions act in connection with each other.

In line with section 2, functional neuroimaging studies can complete or confirm earlier data and increase our knowledge of the role of this structure when carrying out the IGT and, therefore, in complex decision-making in general.

7 Functional Neuroimaging (Magnetic Resonance) Studies on the Role of the Ventromedial Prefrontal Cortex in the IGT

Data from functional neuroimaging also show the involvement of the VMPFC in the IGT, since performance of the task is accompanied by increases in the activity of this brain region (cf. Rogers, Owen, Middleton, Williams, Pickard, Sahakian, et al. 1999; Lawrence, Jollant, O'Daly, Zelaya, and Phillips 2009). The studies that establish a positive correlation between activation of the prefrontal medial cortex and the scores obtained in the decision-making tasks indicate that the higher the value of a variable (greater activity in that region), the better the task is performed (cf. Fukui, Murai, Fukuyama, Hayashi, and Hanakawa 2005). Similarly, the VMPFC shows activation associated with expected reward in many different tasks (cf. Rushworth and Behrens 2008). Other neuroimaging studies share the idea of the relevant role that the OFC also plays in decision-making, and find greater activation in the reward processing and when there is a competition between short and long-term response trends (cf. Elliott, Rees, and Dolan 1999;

Knutson, Fong, Bennett, Adams, and Hommer 2003). One function of the OFC would be to connect the information from the stimulus that can be recovered from the memory with the value of its reward.

These findings have also been confirmed by meta-analysis studies, many of which use fMRI (cf. Krain, Wilson, Arbuckle, Castellanos, and Milham 2006). Other researchers report a positive correlation between activation of this region on making an affective judgement and that produced by performing the IGT, which leads them to conclude that the greater the activity in the VMPFC, the better the IGT will be performed (cf. Northoff, Grimm, Boeker, Schmidt, Bermpohl, Hell, et al. 2006).

Data obtained by means of PET also give support to the role of this brain region in the IGT. Several studies show an increase in the metabolic activity of the OFC sector of the VMPFC, together with other brain areas, during IGT performance (see Bolla, Eldreth, Matochik, and Cadet 2004; Ernst, Bolla, Mouratidis, Contoreggi, Matochik, Kurian, et al. 2002).

8 Interpretation of Lesion and Functional Magnetic Resonance (fMRI) Data

We can talk of a coincidence of the data from lesion techniques and from functional neuroimaging, although their meanings are different. Apparently, the data provided by fMRI "explain" or rather show what the brain and its various regions are doing and, therefore, what system of structures (in this case the VMPFC) regulate or govern a behaviour (in this case the IGT), giving the impression that we "know" what is going on in the brain and that we can identify the mechanisms behind such a behaviour. It is a correlational technique in the sense that it shows what is happening in the brain at the same time as a behaviour occurs. Elsewhere, lesion techniques indicate the "necessity" of the VMPFC for appropriate decision-making to be produced in the task cited. To some extent we can talk of its "causal" nature. In contrast, fMRI does not point towards "causes," it rather signals and confirms that the VMPFC participates in the decision-making task, so helping to locate the structures that regulate or control this process. The correlational nature of neuroimaging limits its explanatory power in any "strong" sense, i.e., that of causal relation or necessity.

In summary, fMRI locates rather than explains. It is a great tool for obtaining data but needs to be complemented by other techniques, such as lesion, PET, EEG activity and, as much as possible, by more molecular studies on neuronal activity and the neurotransmission systems involved.

9 Conclusions: Functions of the Ventromedial Prefrontal Cortex in Decision-making

The VMPFC and its orbital sector play a crucial role in decision-making, as studied using the IGT. The structure takes in both emotional and cognitive information. It is involved in decision-making in ambiguous situations where there is insufficient information. It means that people can anticipate the size of the reward associated with the various options and the likelihood of their occurring (expected value) on the basis of experiences. It gives behaviour flexibility and allows, for example, ceasing to do something, or changing to another, more interesting or rewarding option (Koechlin and Hyafil 2007). In this sense, it represents the behavioural flexibility or the capacity to update the changing reward value of the stimuli, to make appropriate comparison and act accordingly. It allows the integration of cognitive and emotional signals, especially somatic ones, which are associated and which anticipate the consequences of decisions. Lesions would lead to a preference for risky decisions. Performing the complex IGT also requires the participation of simpler or more general processes and the participation of other regions of the brain. Thus, lesions to the DLPFC, which directly affects attention and working memory processes, also have, on account of their nonspecific nature, adverse effects on the performance of this and other tasks.

Much remains to be learnt about the biological bases of decision-making processes. Research should continue to address diverse tasks, of which we have seen just one example, as well as the participation of other structures. The use of more research techniques will enrich and complement the data obtained from lesion and fMRI studies. Finally, we need to move towards more detailed or molecular approaches and methods that will take us to the cell and neurotransmitter level. Combining research techniques and strategies brings more reliable, more consistent data which give more detailed knowledge of the exact biological mechanisms that enable and influence decision-making.

References

Allegri, R. F. and Harris, P. (2001): "La corteza prefrontal en los mecanismos atencionales y de memoria." *Revista de Neurología*, v. 32, pp. 449–453.

Aue, T., Lavelle, L. A., and Cacioppo, J. T. (2009): "Great Expectations: What can fMRI Research Tell Us about Psychological Phenomena?" *International Journal of Psychophysiology*, v. 73, pp. 10–16.

Bechara, A. and Damasio, H. (1997): "Deciding Advantageously before Knowing the Advantageous Strategy." *Science*, v. 275, pp. 1293–1295.
Bechara, A., Damasio, H., and Damasio, A. R. (2000): "Emotion, Decision-making and the Orbitofrontal Cortex." *Cerebral Cortex*, v. 10, pp. 295–307.
Bechara, A., Damasio, H., Damasio, A. R., and Lee, S. W. (1999): "Different Contributions of the Human Amygdala and Ventromedial Prefrontal Cortex to Decision-making." *Journal of Neuroscience*, v. 19, pp. 5473–5481.
Bechara, A., Damasio, H., Tranel, D., and Anderson, S. W. (1998): "Dissociation of Working Memory from Decision Making within the Human Prefrontal Cortex." *Journal of Neuroscience*, v. 18, pp. 428–437.
Bechara, A., Damasio, H., Tranel, D., and Damasio, A. R. (2005): "The Iowa Gambling Task and the Somatic Marker Hypothesis: Some Questions and Answers." *Trends in Cognitive Science*, v. 9, pp. 159–162.
Bechara, A., Tranel, D., and Damasio, H. (2000): "Characterization of the Decision-making Deficit of Patients with Ventromedial Prefrontal Cortex Lesions." *Brain*, v. 123, pp. 2189–2202.
Bechara, A. and Van der Linden, M. (2005): "Decision-making and Impulse Control after Frontal Lobe Injuries." *Current Opinion in Neurobiology*, v. 18, pp. 734–739.
Bolla, K. I., Eldreth, D. A., Matochik, J. A., and Cadet, J. L. (2004): "Sex-related Differences in a Gambling Task and Its Neurological Correlates." *Cerebral Cortex*, v. 14, pp. 1226–1232.
Brett, M., Johnsrude, I. S., and Owen, A. M. (2002): "The Problem of Functional Localization in the Human Brain." *Nature Reviews Neuroscience*, v. 3, pp. 243–249.
Bunge, M. and Ardila, R. (1988): *Filosofía de la Psicología*. Barcelona: Ariel.
Camerer, C. F. (2003): "Strategizing in the Brain." *Science*, v. 300, pp. 1673–1675.
Clark, L., Bechara, A., Damasio, H., Aitken, M. R. F., Sahakian, B. J., and Robbins, T. W. (2008): "Differential Effects of Insular and Ventromedial Prefrontal Cortex Lesions on Risky Decision-making." *Brain*, v. 131, pp. 1311–1322.
Damasio, A. R. (1994): *Descartes' Error: Emotion, Reason, and the Human Brain*. London: Putnam.
Elliott, R., Rees, G., and Dolan, R. J. (1999): "Ventromedial Prefrontal Cortex Mediates Guessing." *Neuropsychologia*, v. 37, pp. 403–411.
Ernst, M., Bolla, K., Mouratidis, M., Contoreggi, C., Matochik, J. A., Kurian, V., et al. (2002): "Decision-making in a Risk-taking Task: a PET Study." *Neuropsychopharmacology*, v. 26, pp. 682–691.
Fujiwara, E., Schwartz, M. L., Gao, F., Black, S. E., and Levine, S. (2008): "Ventral Frontal Cortex Functions and Quantified MRI in Traumatic Brain Injury." *Neuropsychologia*, v. 46, pp. 461–474.
Fukui, H., Murai, T., Fukuyama, H., Hayashi, T., and Hanakawa, T. (2005): "Functional Activity Related to Risk Anticipation during Performance of the Iowa Gambling Task." *Neuroimage*, v. 24, pp. 253–259.
González-García, C., Tudela, P., and Ruz, M. (2014): "Resonancia magnética funcional: Análisis crítico de sus implicaciones técnicas, estadísticas y teóricas en Neurociencia humana." *Revista de Neurología*, v. 58, pp. 318–325.
Jódar-Vicente, M. (2004): "Funciones cognitivas del lóbulo frontal." *Revista de Neurología*, v. 39, pp. 178–182.

Knutson, B., Fong, G. W., Bennett, S. M., Adams, C. M., and Hommer, D. (2003): "A Region of Mesial Prefrontal Cortex Tracks Monetarily Rewarding Outcomes: Characterization with Rapid Event-related fMRI." *Neuroimage*, v. 18, pp. 263–272.

Koechlin, E. and Hyafil, A. (2007): "Anterior Prefrontal Function and the Limits of Human Decision-making." *Science*, v. 318, pp. 594–598.

Kolb, B. and Whishaw, I. Q. (2006): *Neuropsicología humana*, 5th edition. Madrid: Panamericana.

Krain, A. L., Wilson, A. M., Arbuckle, R. Castellanos, F. X., and Milham, M. P. (2006): "Distinct Neural Mechanisms of Risk and Ambiguity: A Meta-analysis of Decision-making." *Neuroimage*, v. 32, pp. 477–484.

Lawrence, N. S., Jollant, F. O'Daly, O., Zelaya, F., and Phillips, M. L. (2009): "Distinct Roles of Prefrontal Cortical Subregions in the Iowa Gambling Task." *Cerebral Cortex*, v. 19, pp. 1134–1143.

Logothetis, N. (2008): "What We can Do and What We Cannot Do with fMRI." *Nature*, v. 453, pp. 869–878.

Manes, F., Sahakian, B., Clark, L., Rogers, R., Antoun, N., Aitken, M., et al. (2002): "Decision-making Processes Following Damage to the Prefrontal Cortex." *Brain*, v. 125, pp. 624–639.

Martínez Selva, J. M. (1995): *Psicofisiología*. Madrid: Síntesis.

Martínez Selva, J. M., Sánchez Navarro, J. P., Bechara, A., and Román, F. (2006): "Mecanismos cerebrales de la *Decision-making*." *Revista de Neurología*, v. 42, pp. 411–418.

Martínez Selva, J. M. and Sánchez Navarro, J. P. (2007): "Decision-making and the Emotional Brain." In: Lynch, T. E. (ed.): *Psychology of Decision-making in Medicine and Health Care*, pp. 113–141. New York: Nova Science.

Martínez Selva, J. M., Sánchez Navarro, J. P., and Bechara, A. (2010): "Un sistema cerebral distribuido para la *Decision-making*." *Salud (i) Ciencia*, v. 17, pp. 409–413.

Martínez Selva, J. M. (2011): "Conceptual Changes in Biological Explanations of Behaviour." In: Gonzalez, W. J. (ed.): *Conceptual Revolutions: From Cognitive Science to Medicine*, pp. 97–117. A Coruña: Netbiblo.

McCabe, K. A. (2008): "Neuroeconomics and the Economic Sciences." *Economics and Philosophy*, v. 24, n. 3, pp. 345–368.

Northoff, G., Grimm, S., Boeker, H., Schmidt, C., Bermpohl, F., Hell, D., et al. (2006): "Affective Judgement and Beneficial Decision-making: Ventromedial Prefrontal Activity Correlates with Performance in the Iowa Gambling Task." *Human Brain Mapping*, v. 27, pp. 572–587.

Poldrack, A. R. (2010): "Mapping Mental Function to Brain Structure: How Can Cognitive Neuroscience Succeed?" *Perspectives on Psychological Science*, v. 5, pp. 753–761.

Rogers, R. D., Owen, A. M., Middleton, H. C., Williams, E. J., Pickard, J. D., Sahakian, B. J., et al. (1999): "Choosing between Small, Likely Rewards and Large, Unlikely Rewards Activates Inferior and Orbital Prefrontal Cortex." *Journal of Neuroscience*, v. 20, pp. 9029–9038.

Rolls, E. T., McCabe, C., and Redoute, J. (2008): "Expected Value, Reward Outcome, and Temporal Difference Error Representations in a Probabilistic Decision Task." *Cerebral Cortex*, v. 18, pp. 652–663.

Rorden, C. and Karnath, H.-O. (2004): "Using Human Brain Lesions to Infer Function: A Relic from a Past era in the fMRI Age?" *Nature Reviews Neuroscience*, v. 5, pp. 813–819.

Rosenzweig, M. R., Breedlove, S. M., and Watson, N. V. (2005): *Psicobiología. Una introducción a la Neurociencia Conductual, Cognitiva y Clínica*. Barcelona: Ariel.

Rubinov, M. and Sporns, O. (2010): "Complex Networks Measures of Brain Connectivity: Uses and Interpretations." *Neuroimage*, v. 52, pp. 1059–1069.

Rushworth, M. F. S. and Behrens, T. E. J. (2008): "Choice, Uncertainty and Value in Prefrontal and Cingulate Cortex." *Nature Neuroscience*, v. 11, pp. 389–397.

Tanabe, J., Thompson, L., Claus, E., Dalwani, M., Hutchison, K., and Banich, M. T. (2007): "Prefrontal Cortex Activity is Reduced in Gambling and Nongambling Substance Users during Decision-making." *Human Brain Mapping*, v. 28, pp. 1276–1286.

Tirapu-Ustáriz, J., Maestú, F., González-Marqués, J., Ríos-Lago, M., and Ruiz, M. J. (2011): "Visión histórica y concepto de Neuropsicología." In: Tirapu-Ustáriz, J., Ríos Lago, M., and Maestú Unturbe, F. (eds.): *Manual de Neuropsicología*, 2nd edition, pp. 1–32. Barcelona: Viguera.

Michał Wierzchoń
Dynamic Level Interaction Hypothesis – A New Perspective on Consciousness

Abstract: Identifying the neurobiological and cognitive mechanisms of consciousness is one of the biggest challenges of modern science. This task is difficult because we need to simultaneously describe the mechanisms that enable access to conscious content and cause the subjective nature of the experience of this content. Previously proposed scientific models of consciousness seem to be limited to visual perception and focus on investigating the threshold of (most often visual) awareness rather than the problem of the subjective character of conscious experience. Thus, despite a growing number of experimental studies of consciousness, there is still no widely accepted, wide-ranging theory that describes these mechanisms' underlying access not only to visual content, but also to other types of conscious content (i.e., related to all kinds of perception and memory). There is also no widely accepted theory that addresses the problem of the subjective characteristics of conscious content. It seems that a theoretical model is needed that will compromise the philosophical and neurobiological approaches that are trying to address both issues. Here, I propose that this could be achieved with a unification of theories and methods proposed in the context of (neurobiological) cognitive studies of consciousness and I offer a new hierarchical model: a dynamic level interaction hypothesis that proposes an integrative view on the subject.

Keywords: consciousness, conscious access, subjective experience, metacognition, models of consciousness, hierarchical models of consciousness, dynamic level interaction hypothesis

One of the biggest challenges of modern science is to identify the neurobiological and cognitive mechanisms of consciousness (Miller 2005). The task is difficult because we need to simultaneously describe the mechanisms of access to the content of consciousness (and thus to determine the differences between conscious and unconscious information processing), and, at the very same time, propose what causes the subjective nature of the experience of this content

---

Preparation of this paper was supported with SONATA BIS grant, funded by National Science Centre, Poland (Grant 2012/07/E/HS6/01037) The research was developed at the Consciousness Lab, Institute of Psychology, Jagiellonian University, Krakow, Poland.

https://doi.org/10.1515/9783110576054-006

(i.e., why each of us experiences the same world differently, in our own way). Philosophers are still proposing new theoretical frameworks for consciousness discussing both issues in context of e.g., mind-body, binding or qualia problems (e.g. Bunge 2010; Chalmers 1996; Dennett 2001; Searle 1998). However, most of recent and influential scientific models of consciousness seem to focus on investigations of the threshold of awareness and its correlates, but do not really deal with the problem of the subjective character of conscious experience (e.g. Crick and Koch 1990; Dehaene and Naccache 2001; Dehaene and Changeux 2011; Lamme 2003; Lamme 2010; Tononi 2008).

Most of recent theories in the field are even more limited, as they investigate mechanisms of conscious experience related to only one modality, namely visual perceptual awareness (see e.g. Crick and Koch 1990; Dehaene and Changeux 2011; Lamme 2010). However, the research on the subject concerns a broad spectrum of different types of content, both perceptual (e.g., awareness of tactile information [see Froese, McGann, Bigge, Spiers, and Seth 2012] or interoceptive awareness [see Garfinkel, Seth, Barrett, Suzuki, and Critchley 2014]) and stored in memory (e.g., awareness of learning and memory representation [see Mealor and Dienes 2013; Wierzchoń, Asanowicz, Paulewicz, and Cleeremans 2012]). As a consequence, despite growing interest in experimental studies of consciousness and the large amount of data already available, there is still no widely accepted theory simultaneously describing mechanisms underlying conscious access to different types of content and addressing the problem of subjective characteristics of this content. There is a need for a theoretical model that will compromise the philosophical and neurobiological approaches trying to address both issues. Here, I claim that this could be done by integrating achievements and methods from neurobiological and cognitive studies on awareness and I propose the dynamic level interaction hypothesis to tackle this challenge.

1 Conscious Access and Subjective Experience

The challenges of describing mechanisms responsible for the access to conscious content and those responsible for the subjective character of experience are often discussed in context of the distinction between two forms of consciousness, i.e., access consciousness and phenomenal consciousness (Block 1995 and 2011). There is also an on-going debate whether they are related to separate neuronal and cognitive mechanisms (see e.g. Lamme 2010). Some researchers even discuss whether both of them describe consciousness, and thus, which of them should be investigated (Cohen and Dennett 2011). I will come back to this distinction in the next section of this chapter and will argue that a successful model of consciousness should take both features in to the account. However, before that a theoretical and an operational definition of awareness should be proposed. This is important, as the theories I will refer often use one definition, but then apply a measurement method that does not fit with the theoretical assumptions of a theory. This is also important, as we need to know not only what the conscious experience is, but also how we can access conscious content in order to propose some experimental settings allowing to investigate it.

From the theoretical point of view, we now need to discriminate two different approaches to consciousness. The first of them focuses on conscious content itself. According to this view, *awareness is related to subjective, direct access to the conscious experience* (see e.g. Overgaard and Sandberg 2012) that is often described as intrinsic, private and thus ineffable quale (see Dennett 1988 for the review). In this approach, verbal reports on consciousness content investigated in most of the research on awareness are inaccurate, as they do not allow investigating phenomenal content of awareness. The proponents of this approach often claim that we should focus our investigations on experience itself. The problem is that, if one wants to measure not only the access to awareness but also its subjective variability, verbal reports are, at least to some extent, unavoidable. Thus, we should at least avoid the interpretative level of description associated with verbal reports (e.g., judgements of the visibility, etc.) and question more primary levels of experience (e.g., visibility itself). This may be done with so-called first- and second-person methods (see e.g. Froese, Gould, and Barrett 2011), that are based on the phenomenological methods. Here, the idea is to distil the direct experience from the first-person introspection or second-person reports (see e.g. Heavey and Hurlburt 2008). In other words, to separate a direct experience from judgements, evaluations, or interpretations of this experience. This idea seems to be related to the phenomenological method of "eidetic" reduction, which aims to reach an essence of a phenomenon (Husserl [1913] 1982; Zahavi 2003). Some researchers argue that the challenge may be also tackled and to some extent quantified with subjective measures of awareness (Overgaard and Sandberg 2012). However, this is possible only when the measures focus on the experiential properties of an experience (e.g., visibility as measured with Perceptual Awareness Scale [see Ramsøy and Overgaard 2004]), but not the judgement of this experience (see Wierzchoń, Paulewicz, Asanowicz, Timmermans, and Cleeremans 2014).

On the other hand, one may claim that awareness is necessarily related with knowing that one is aware of a given content (e.g. Lau and Rosenthal 2011; Rosenthal 2012). For example, hierarchical models of consciousness assume, that a person is aware of a given content only if this content is re-represented by the higher-order representation (see also Cleeremans 2011 for the computational version of this model). This higher-order representation is often (but not necessarily – see the transitivity principle in Rosenthal and Weisberg 2008 and the next section of this paper) related to *metacognitive awareness*, awareness that we are aware of a given content (Lau and Rosenthal 2011). Here, it is not clear what we actually study when measuring awareness within the hierarchical theories: metacognition or awareness. Thus, it seems problematic to distinguish between awareness of a given content, and metacognitive judgement that is not necessary related to awareness (see Overgaard and Sandberg 2012).

Interesting approach to the problem of a distinction between direct experience (consciousness) and judgement of the experience (introspection) was proposed within the classical phenomenology framework (see Brentano [1874] 2015). Phenomenologists postulated we indeed should investigate direct experience rather than the (metacognitive) interpretation of this experience. However, they also assumed that both are, at least to some extent, inseparable. For example, Brentano ([1874] 2015) claimed that each act of consciousness has two objects. One is a common object of an act of consciousness (e.g., a sound of a bell). However, each act of consciousness has also access to itself. Thus, the second object of an act of consciousness is an act of accessing a content of awareness (e.g., perceiving I hear a bell). Phenomenological approach also postulated the direct experience might be investigated with the phenomenological methods that are based on first-person observation of our own mental states. The difficulty is how to test the conscious content to receive reports on direct experience rather than metacognitive interpretation of this experience. This again can be done e.g., within phenomenology methodology (see: 'eidetic' reduction).

Knowing all of that, we now can take a closer look at the current empirical theories of consciousness and see to what extent they can describe both the mechanism responsible for access to a given content and for diversity of conscious experience assumed by most of the modern philosophical theories of consciousness.

2 In Search for the Interdisciplinary Perspective on Consciousness

Most of the current experimental studies on consciousness focus on the difference between conscious and unconscious processing, identifying neurobiological mechanisms of awareness. This is clearly visible when we take a closer look at any study investigating neural correlates of consciousness (see e.g. Block 2005 and Rees, Kreiman, and Koch 2002). In a typical experiment, researchers register neural processing when people are aware of a given content (using EEG, fMRI or other psychophysiological or neurobiological methods), and compare it to a situation when the very same content is potentially available (e.g., the same stimulus is presented), but people are not aware of it. Such studies usually suggest a set of brain areas that seems to be responsible for awareness in a sense that the activation of those structures are necessary if one is about to became aware (unfortunately, each type of stimulus is usually associated with other neural correlate of consciousness simply because other parts of the brain are engaged in the processing a given content [see Rees, Kreiman, and Koch 2002]). Binocular rivalry is a well-known example of a research paradigm that is used to investigate neural correlates of awareness.

In this paradigm, participants are exposed with two conflicting stimuli (e.g., a house and a face), each presented separately to corresponding locations of the two eyes (Blake 2001; Blake and Logothetis 2002; Rees, Kreiman, and Koch 2002). Interestingly, participants do not integrate both stimuli in a single percept. Conversely, the conscious perception alternates between the stimuli on the regular bases. At a given moment, only one stimulus is accessible, whereas the other one is supressed (Ling and Blake 2009). Binocular rivalry enables us to investigate the neural and cognitive mechanisms of cognitive access. Multiple studies done in this paradigm investigate under what conditions people became aware of one of the conflicting stimuli, and what extrinsic factors (related with the features of stimuli) determine binocular rivalry rate and strength (see Blake and Logothetis 2002). However, far less is known about intrinsic factors that determine the effect (see Miller, Hansell, Ngo, Liu, Pettigrew, Martin, and Wright 2010) and virtually no studies consider variables that may explain individual differences in the experience of rivalry (but see Lack 1969).

In the same vein, most of the scientific models of consciousness are focused on the neural mechanism that enables conscious access to a given content. For example, in the classical neurobiological theory of consciousness (Crick and Koch 1990) researchers tried to identify a brain mechanism responsible for visual awareness. The theory claims that visual awareness can have two forms: a vague experience based on very fast, sparse, and abstract coding of visual information in the iconic memory that contains only a concise, general "meaning" of what is perceived (see also gist perception: Fei-Fei, Iyer, Koch, and Perona 2007; or phenomenal awareness: Block 2005 and Lamme 2003), and more detailed experience related to attention and short-term memory engagement. Crick and Koch (1990) proposed the neural mechanism for the second form, suggesting that it is related to coherent and synchronous oscillations of neurons engaged in the perception of a given object (i.e., all those neurons, whose activity is related to the relevant features of an object – e.g., shape, colour, movement, etc.).

The model suggested that the oscillations are responsible for feature binding (and that the binding is one of the function of awareness) but do not really explain why it may "feel" different to perceive a given object for each of us (i.e., why the same process might correlate with different experience [see e.g. Chalmers 1996]). In other words, the model proposes a neural mechanism for conscious access, but does not deal with the problem of subjective character of the experience. It seems also important to note that the model assumes a none-or-all character of conscious access: either the set of relevant neurons were synchronised (and then a person became conscious), or no conscious access was observed. Thus, no variability in conscious experience is authorised by the model – a person might be either aware or unaware. However, subjectively this seems not to be a case. We subjectively experience our consciousness as a variable characterised by gradual changes of intensity. We will come back to this feature of awareness in the next section of this paper.

The subjective aspect of consciousness seems to be also neglected by more recent theories. For example, the neural global workspace theory (Dehaene and Naccache 2001; Dehaene, Changeux, Naccache, Sackur, and Sergent 2006) claims that a visual stimulus is consciously perceived when it activates a set of "global workspace" neurons in the parietal, prefrontal and cingulate cortices. According to the theory, this cluster of neurons is internally synchronised in a reciprocal and long-lasting manner. Additionally, long-distance connections between the 'global workspace' and other brain regions enable broadcasting information to many distant areas responsible for specific cognitive functions. Importantly, an activation of such a single distant area does not result in conscious availability of the information that is processed by this structure. For that, activation of the 'global workspace' is necessary. Similarly to the proposal of the neural correlates of consciousness, the model assumes the all-or-none character of conscious access. Either the 'global workspace' is activated and a person became aware of a given content, or no awareness is observed (see Del Cul, Baillet, and Dehaene 2007; Sergent and Dehaene 2004).

Interestingly, according to the neural global workspace theory, the function of awareness is to enable communication between specialised brain areas (see also "fame in the brain" [Dennett 2001]; the theatre of consciousness [Baars 2001]), so whenever we need to reinterpret the activation in the specialised brain area in context of information stored in a different brain region, awareness of a given content becomes necessary. This seems to open a possibility to propose a mechanism responsible for inter-subjective differences in a subjective content of awareness, that is, to claim it may stem from individual differences in the information stored in the brain. However, the theory has little to say about the subjective character of 'global workspace' content. The studies run within the 'global workspace' theoretical framework focus rather on variables (often extrinsic) that may cause conscious all-or-none access (see Dehaene et al. 2006).

Similarly, Lamme (2003 and 2010) proposes that visual awareness is an effect of recurrent interactions between early visual areas and higher brain areas. Depending on the areas of visual system that are engaged in the recurrent processing, the model provides a possible neural mechanism for phenomenal awareness (related to the iconic memory) or access awareness (that is related to working memory [see Block 2005 and Crick and Koch 1990]). As a consequence, the model proposes that function of awareness is to provide a content on which attention can operate. In other words, awareness means broadcasting information that might be later accessed by the higher cognitive functions. Thus again, the theory focuses on investigating why some information reach consciousness but have little to say about inter- and intra-individual differences in the content of conscious experience. This is especially interesting, as the model aims to describe the mechanism for phenomenal awareness (see critical commentary by Cohen and Dennett 2011). The model also assumes, at least to some extent, an all-or-none character of consciousness (although the theory is not really clear about this, permitting gradual access for phenomenal consciousness (see Windey, Vermeiren, Atas, and Cleeremans 2014), but proposing all-or-none mechanism for access consciousness).

All of those deficits might be partially explained by the scope of the research providing empirical evidence for the theories, as all models focus on neurobiological level of analysis and do not really take into the account the phenomenal level of experience (see Cohen and Dennett 2011). They of course make use of verbal reports (to provide a test of awareness under a given experimental conditions) but do not take a closer look at the content and variability of those reports. For this, a more interdisciplinary model addressing the problem at the multiple levels of analysis seems to be necessary.

Indeed, a dynamic development of interdisciplinary theoretical models connecting neuroscientific, cognitive and computational perspectives has been recently observed (see e.g. Cleeremans 2011; Kouider, de Gardelle, Sackur, and Dupoux 2010; Lau 2007; Oizumi, Albantakis, and Tononi 2014). Interestingly, most of the models accept and extend, more or less directly, the assumptions of the hierarchical models of consciousness (Armstrong 1981; Dretske 2006; Lau and Rosenthal 2011; Rosenthal 2005). The models from this group assume that we become consciously aware of a given content only when the representation of this content in the cognitive system (first-order representation) becomes the subject of another, higher-order representation (or metarepresentation) that re-describes first-level representation. Both representation levels are necessary for consciousness and may influence characteristics of the content of experience (at least according to some of the hierarchical models [see Carruthers 2000 and Cleeremans 2011]). Let us consider an example of visual perception. Here, the first-order representations ("located" mainly in the visual cortex) enable the automatic identification of a visual stimulus, whereas the second-order representations ("located" in the prefrontal cortex) enable the interpretation of the first-order representations (Lau and Rosenthal 2011).

Importantly, this interpretation is based on information available for the system and thus enables us to assess a certainty in the stimulus identification. In this sense, higher-order representations have similar function to the 'global workspace,' as they give access to local representations for the more general system that connects them with other local representations (Cleeremans 2011). However, in contrast to the neural global workspace theory that suggests all-or-none access to awareness, at least some of hierarchical models assume that access to conscious content is gradual (Anzulewicz, Asanowicz, Windey, Paulewicz, Wierzchoń, and Cleeremans 2015). This is because the fact of having become aware is a consequence of activation of a higher-order representation. Thus, the quality of the higher-order representation may influence the accessibility of conscious content (Cleeremans 2011).

It seems worth noting that the empirical evidence of hierarchical approach is, at least to some extent, based on the distinction between perceptual awareness and introspective awareness proposed by Armstrong (1981). However, the current versions of the hierarchical models do not necessarily agree that higher-order representations activation needs to be related to introspection (that is defined here as explicit knowledge about one's own mental state, e. g., knowing that I see, etc.). It is clearly visible in higher-order thought theory (Rosenthal 2005), which explicitly assumes that for introspective awareness one will need to activate a third-level representation that will re-describe second-order representation and make it available for consciousness (see transitivity principle, Rosenthal and Weisberg 2008). Thus, when only a second-order representation is activated, people have conscious access to a conscious content, but they do not have a metacognitive awareness of this content, i.e., they do not know that they are aware that they see, they just experience a visual content.

It is important to note that accepting the hierarchical models assumptions affects the way we test whether someone is aware or not. The hierarchical models of awareness connect awareness to the metacognition and thus the empirical evidence in favour of the models is mainly based on metacognitive measures of awareness (see Seth, Dienes, Cleeremans, Overgaard, and Pessoa 2008), such as confidence ratings or post-decision wagering (Lau and Rosenthal 2011; Sandberg, Timmermans, Overgaard, and Cleeremans, 2010; Wierzchoń et al. 2012).

This is because the higher-order representations should enable access to the current state of awareness (e.g., enabling the estimation of certainty – but see: Rosenthal and Weisberg 2008).

Similar assumptions on the multi-level representations responsible for conscious awareness are also made by the radical plasticity thesis (Cleeremans 2011). The theory holds that consciousness arises in a hierarchical, multi-level system. Additionally, the theory proposes that the first-order and higher-order representations are both shaped in the course of learning that is responsible for representation formation. Thus, according to the radical plasticity thesis, we became conscious in the course of representation formation (Cleeremans 2011). The theory also holds that individual differences in learning history are responsible for the differentiation of conscious experience (see problem of qualia). However, this particular assumption of the theory has not been systematically tested experimentally.

To sum up, consciousness seems to be the very popular subject of both empirical and theoretical investigations, but the current experimental evidence is focused on the mechanisms explaining how people become aware, rather than on the mechanisms explaining the subjective character of conscious experience (but see Cleeremans 2011). Hierarchical models of awareness seem to be the most promising attempt to deal with the second problem questioning the variability of participants' metacognitive access to an experience, but even those models still leave the subjective character of the experience undetermined. The models also failed to test their main theoretical assumption (i.e., transitivity principle) experimentally. This is because it was suggested that hierarchical organisation of cognitive system enabling awareness does not necessary imply metacognitive access to conscious content (Rosenthal and Weisberg 2008). However, the metacognitive measures of awareness are usually used to test theoretical assumptions of the hierarchical models (see Lau and Rosenthal 2011). Thus, how can we explain what mechanisms underlie the subjective nature of conscious content and how information reaches awareness threshold?

3 Dynamic Level Interaction Hypothesis

Here, I propose a dynamic level interaction hypothesis – a theoretical framework that aims to tackle the problem of inter – and intra-individual variability of consciousness, i.e., the subjective nature of the content of consciousness. The framework aims to define the levels of cognitive system hierarchy involved in the process and to describe the dynamical changes of representations responsible for the subjective character of conscious content. It starts from a critique of a transitivity principle (Lau and Rosenthal 2011; Rosenthal 2005) and list other variables (aside of the learning process – see Cleeremans 2011) that may contribute to conscious content formation. As a main principle, the model assumes that *a unique interaction between first-level representations and higher-order representation observed at a given moment may serve as a cognitive mechanism for subjective character of conscious experience*. It also claims that the very fact of re-representation (i.e., the fact that higher-order representation re-represents lower-level representation) makes information available for consciousness. Thus, the hypothesis allows us to explain what mechanisms underlie the subjective character of a given content and the access to a given content within the same theoretical framework. In other words, I propose that the interaction between first-level and higher-level representation give rise to subjective experience and can also explain its subjective character. The assumptions go beyond what was proposed by the current hierarchical models of awareness.

Dynamic level interaction hypothesis enables us to avoid the problem of the transitivity principle operationalisation. The activation in brain regions related to metacognitive processing (e.g., prefrontal cortex) differs depending the subjective ratings of certainty, but is not affected by the sensitivity of the visual system to visual information (see e.g. Rounis, Maniscalco, Rothwell, Passingham, and Lau 2010). This suggests that awareness, as measured with subjective ratings, is related to metacognition (see also Lau and Rosenthal 2011). Importantly, no activation was observed that could be associated with third-level of representation that is, according to transitivity principle, necessary for metacognitive awareness. Visual cortex activation seems to be related to low-level representation and prefrontal cortex activation seems to be related to high-level representation. There is no other specific activation that may serve as a neural source of third-level of activation assumed by the transitivity principle. From a methodological point of view, it is also hard to imagine a study in which participants would report their subjective experience in a way that would avoid any judgements of this experience at all (i.e., reports resulting from activation of visual cortex only [see Cohen and Dennett 2011]). This might be related with the inseparability of content of consciousness and act of accessing the conscious content (see Brentano [1874] 2015, as described in a previous section of this chapter).

Turning into the list of variables that may contribute to conscious content formation: most of hierarchical models of awareness assume that a re-description of a first-level representation underlies conscious access to a given content. However, the models do not explicitly predict the influence of other information stored in the cognitive system. This assumption seems to be consistent with one-source models of evidence accumulation (Del Cul, Dehaene, Reyes, Bravo, and Slachevsky 2009), proposing that awareness is based exclusively on the low-level representation processing (e.g., according to the models, only visual evidence determines the metacognitive awareness of visual content). As a consequence, the theories usually assume that one variable explain the variability of the subjective experience of a given content. For example, according to the radical plasticity hypothesis variability of experience is a result of individual learning history.

Here, I propose that in order to describe not only the mechanism of conscious access, but also the subjective variability of a given content, we should investigate the more complex system of conscious experience formation. We should define the list of variables that may contribute to metacognitive awareness aside of the strength of representation of a given content. In other words, aside of the re-representation of low-level representation, high-level representation integrates other available information and thus enables to differentiate conscious experience. Similar assumptions are made by dual-source models of accumulation suggesting that metacognitive judgements might be influenced by different kinds of processes, such as error detection, somatosensory cues or memory cues (see e.g. Resulaj, Kiani, Wolpert, and Shadlen 2009; Ullsperger, Harsay, Wessel, and Ridderinkhof 2010). According to those models, the metacognitive judgements are based on results of separate stage of evidence accumulation that is partially independent on the accumulation of evidence process as described above. The list of variables influencing higher-order representation and thus metacognitive awareness include: information from different perceptual modules, information from the motor reaction (including error detection), interceptive information and memory cues that are all to be integrated with the experience thanks to higher-order representation.

Finally, it seems reasonable to propose a similar list of variables that may influence lower-level processing. Here, the manipulations will simply influence the strength of the first-level representation of a given subjective content. In other words, the second list will include variables that influence bottom-up attention and thus vary the strength of evidence included in the formation of a conscious content. Having those two lists, we should be able to show that any manipulation that influences one of the levels of the hierarchy necessarily differentiates participants' subjective experience. Again, the main principle is that a unique interaction between first-level representations and higher-order representation (that both can be influenced by the variables listed above) occurring at a given moment underlies subjective character of conscious experience. Thus, the dynamical changes of multi-level representation system are responsible for the subjective character of conscious content. Let me consider an example of experimental studies that might serve as an evidence for such a theoretical model.

In a backward masking task participants are usually exposed with stimuli under conditions that disturb their visibility (e.g., masked stimuli are presented for a very short time), which results in decreased awareness (e.g. Sandberg et al. 2010; see Figure 1).

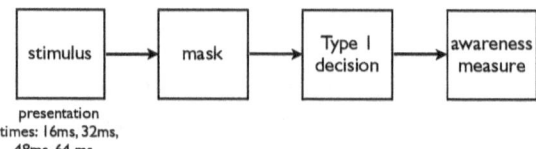

Figure 1. Diagram of experimental procedure of backward masking task with presentation time manipulation. At each trial a participant is presented with a target stimulus (e.g., geometric figure, face, etc.) that is then masked with a stimulus that prevents the previous one from being perceived (including target stimulus afterimages). Then, an identification/recognition test is usually applied (e.g., what figure was presented, what was a face gender, etc.). Finally, participants are usually asked to rate awareness of identification/recognition on an awareness measure (the most often used are confidence ratings, post-decision wagering and perceptual awareness scales – see: Sandberg et al. 2010). In order to vary stimulus visibility, manipulation of the target stimulus presentation time may be introduced.

We can, to some extent, track the subjective variability of awareness in the task using the subjective measures of consciousness.[1] For example, different presentation times result in different level of awareness observed with confidence ratings (Sandberg et al. 2010). This effect is clearly related with the quality of first-level representations (or strength of perceptual evidence) that are activated by the stimulus presentation. Thus, such studies confirm that variability of first-level representation may cause differences in subjective experience of a stimulus. An evidence for the similar effect of higher-level representation is more problematic. There is only indirect evidence collected with the backward masking task, suggesting that a selective deactivation of brain regions that are believed to be responsible for the higher-order representations (i.e., transcranial magnetic stimulation, TMS, to the prefrontal cortex) results in changes in subjective reports and impaired visual awareness (see Rounis et al. 2010, note that TMS does not affect type 1 decision accuracy, i.e., first-level representation quality

---

[1] Note that such methods are not very sensitive for the variability of conscious experience, as the subjective scales of awareness usually use some kind of predefine categories and thus do not allow participants to report freely what they experience. However, those methods clearly give us more information about the variability of awareness that is measured in most of the studies on neural correlates of consciousness (see e.g. Overgaard, Fehl, Mouridsen, Bergholt, and Cleeremans 2008).

seems to be intact under the stimulation). Those studies suggest that deactivation of higher-order representation may substantially change awareness reports, but do not really prove that more moderate changes in higher-order representations may also cause some differences in conscious experience. Manipulation of the higher-order representations in a backward masking task will be very difficult, but seem to be easier in context of other cognitive tasks used to investigate consciousness. This was, to some extent, done in case of binocular rivalry (see below), but the effects of first-level and higher-level representations manipulations have never been systematically investigated and compared.

Aside of the main principles, the dynamic level interaction hypothesis is based on three other important assumptions. Firstly, it assumes that the *processes underlying consciousness are universal*, that is, the mechanisms of subjective experience should be revealed in a wide spectrum of cognitive processes. In other words, it proposes that the subjective experience of visual, memory or somatosensory stimuli results from the dynamic interaction between first- and second-order representations. Thus, we should expect that the proposed mechanism of experience variability should be observed in context of different types of material. This assumption allows a connection between various traditions of research searching for the neural and cognitive mechanism of different types of conscious experience. Particularly, hierarchical models were proposed not only in context of visual awareness, but also have recently become very popular in context of bodily awareness studies (see Blanke and Metzinger 2009; Tsakiris 2010). Surprisingly, those studies have never been systematically compared and unified with studies investigating visual awareness or accessibility of memory trace.

Secondly, the dynamic level interaction hypothesis proposes that in order to explain the mechanism of subjective experience formation, it is necessary to assume the *graded character of conscious awareness* (Anzulewicz et al. 2015; Ramsøy and Overgaard 2004; Overgaard, Rote, Mouridsen, and Ramsøy 2006). In a broader context, the model assumes that we should accept that the successful theoretical framework for consciousness should go beyond comparison of conscious and unconscious processing and test the variability of experience. Importantly, the variability related with the level of awareness (in opposition to the variability of experience qualities, i.e., qualia) enables us to test the subjective experience with quantitative methodology. This is has been recently intensively investigated with the subjective scales of consciousness (see Dienes and Seth 2010; Overgaard and Sandberg 2012; Wierzchoń et al. 2012; Wierzchoń et al. 2014).

Finally, the model proposes that *the content of metacognitive representations is not necessarily subjectively accessible*, and thus we sometimes have problems with subjective experience variability verbalisation. It may even be that people are indeed constantly dealing with a subjective illusion of direct access to conscious content. This illusion might be caused by the transparency of higher-order representations (in analogy to transparent model of self-representation proposed by Blanke and Metzinger [2009]), which might be an effect of their automatisation (see Cleeremans 2011). In other words, when we are aware of a given content, we do not necessarily have a detailed and complete knowledge of what we see, know or feel. We simply experience the content of awareness without knowing that a higher-order representation of the experience is always involved. However, this experience is illusory, as higher-order representations are necessary involved in conscious experience formation and thus, the experience resulting from first-order representation and higher-order representation are, at least to some extent, inseparable within a conscious content.

4 How To Test Dynamic Level Interaction Hypothesis

Dynamic level interaction hypothesis is based on the assumption that the mechanisms of conscious experience formation are rooted in the continuous, dynamic interaction between two types of representations – first-order representations and higher-order representations (see also Cleeremans 2011 and Rosenthal 2005). It is assumed that first-order representations enable the automatic processing of visual/memory/somatosensory stimuli recognition and that the higher-order representations enable the interpretation of the first-order representation in context of other available information. It was also assumed that the continuous and dynamic interaction between the levels of representations results in subjective differentiation of an experience, thus that it explains inter- and intra-individual differences in the content of consciousness (this can be measured by variability related to the level of awareness or variability of experience qualities). Accepting those assumptions, one should propose manipulations by which the levels of representation might be modified independently to each other – i.e., the same representation would be interpreted differently depending on higher-order representation modification, or the first-order representation change will result in changes of conscious experience. To test these assumptions, experimental manipulations aim to selectively modify first- or higher-order representations should be proposed.

An interesting approach to this challenge was proposed by Aru, Bachmann, Singer, and Melloni (2012). They designed a task at which they manipulate visibility of stimuli with masking (sensory evidence manipulation) as well as with cues acquired by previous presentation of some of the masked stimuli (memory cues manipulation). They found that both manipulations influenced awareness ratings. In context of the theoretical model proposed in this chapter, masking may serve as an example of low-level representation manipulation, and memory cues may serve as high-level representation manipulation. However, the results show only that the manipulation of both levels of awareness influence sensory evidence, but not necessary the changes in subjective experience. That might be, that both manipulations simply influence sensitivity to the stimuli (i.e., awareness threshold). Thus, to test the assumptions of the proposed model one should manipulate both levels of representation more systematically. Interestingly however, the high-level representation manipulation used by Aru and colleagues (2012) is to some extent related to learning (of a certain subset of stimuli). Thus, turn our attention towards Cleeremans (2011) radical plasticity thesis assumptions.

Assuming that the learning can modify both levels of representation (Cleeremans 2011), we should be able to selectively train people in order to modify first-order or higher-order representations. We tested those assumptions in binocular rivalry, where we asked participants to control the frequency of switches between the stimuli (higher-order representation manipulation) or change the salience of one of the stimuli, influencing the activation of its first-level representation. Both manipulations should independently influence the subjective experience of rivalry. Interestingly, both manipulations were reported in the literature. In particular, Lack (1969) showed that practice of binocular rivalry under the instruction suggesting slower or faster rate of changes between the images resulted in changed paste of alternations (decreased on increased respectively). The effect clearly shows that higher-order control can affect conscious experience of rivalry, but surprisingly has never been replicated. In contrast, Freman and Nguyen (2001) study may serve as an example of a lower-level representation manipulation. They showed that the successive manipulation applied to one of the stimuli (consecutive changes in the stimulus salience) might result in equivalent changes in the experience of rivalry (alternations forced by changes in salience of the stimulus). Dynamic level interaction hypothesis is still only a preliminary theoretical model that requires a lot of testing. However, it provides a schema for the systematic investigations of the variables that might influence the subjective experience of a content of awareness. Importantly, as the model assumes that mechanisms underlying conscious experience of different contents are universal, the model might be tested in a wide spectrum of cognitive tasks. This is promising for understanding consciousness beyond the context of visual awareness.

References

Anzulewicz, A., Asanowicz, D., Windey, B., Paulewicz, B., Wierzchoń, M., and Cleeremans, A. (2015): "Does Level of Processing Affect the Transition from Unconscious to Conscious Perception?" *Consciousness and Cognition*, v. 36, pp. 1–11. DOI: 10.1016/j.concog.2015.05.004, visited on 8.5.2017.

Armstrong, D. M. (1981): *The Nature of Mind and Other Essays*. Ithaca: Cornell University Press.

Aru, J., Bachmann, T., Singer, W., and Melloni, L. (2012:. "Distilling the Neural Correlates of Consciousness." *Neuroscience and Biobehavioral Reviews*, v. 36, n. 2, pp. 737–746. DOI: 10.1016/j.neubiorev.2011.12.00, visited on 8.5.2017.

Baars, B. J. (2001): *In the Theater of Consciousness: The Workspace of the Mind*. New York: Oxford University Press.

Blake, R. (2001): "A Primer on Binocular Rivalry, Including Current Controversies." *Brain and Mind*, v. 2, n. 1, pp. 5–38.

Blake, R. and Logothetis, N. K. (2002): "Visual Competition." *Nature Reviews. Neuroscience*, v. 3, n. 1, pp. 13–21. DOI: 10.1038/nrn70, visited on 8.5.2017.

Blanke, O. and Metzinger, T. (2009): "Full-body Illusions and Minimal Phenomenal Selfhood." *Trends in Cognitive Sciences*, v. 13, n. 1, pp. 7–13.

Block, N. (2005): "Two Neural Correlates of Consciousness." *Trends in Cognitive Sciences*, v. 9, n. 2, pp. 46–52. DOI: 10.1016/j.tics.2004.12.006, visited on 8.5.2017.

Brentano, F. ([1874] 2015): *Psychology from an Empirical Standpoint*. New York: Routledge Classics.

Bunge, M. (2010): *Matter and Mind: A Philosophical Inquiry*. New York: Springer.

Carruthers, P. (2000): *Phenomenal Consciousness: A Naturalistic Theory*. Cambridge: Cambridge University Press.

Chalmers, D. (1996): *The Conscious Mind. In Search of a Fundamental Theory*. Oxford: Oxford University Press.

Cleeremans, A. (2011): "Frontiers: The Radical Plasticity Thesis: How the Brain Learns to Be Conscious." *Frontiers in Consciousness Research*, v. 2, n. 86, pp. 1–12.

Cohen, M. A. and Dennett, D. C. (2011) "Consciousness Cannot Be Separated from Function." *Trends in Cognitive Sciences*, v. 15, n. 8, pp. 358–364. DOI: 10.1016/j.tics.2011.06.00, visited on 8.5.2017.

Crick, F. and Koch, C. (1990): "Towards a Neurobiological Theory of Consciousness." *Seminars in the Neuroscience*, v. 2, pp. 263–275.

Dehaene, S. and Changeux, J. P. (2011): "Experimental and Theoretical Approaches to Conscious Processing." *Neuron*, v. 70, n. 2, pp. 200–227.

Dehaene, S., Changeux, J. P., Naccache, L., Sackur, J., and Sergent, C. (2006): "Conscious, Preconscious, and Subliminal Processing: A Testable Taxonomy." *Trends in Cognitive Sciences*, v. 10, n. 5, pp. 204–211. DOI: 10.1016/j.tics.2006.03.00, visited on 8.5.2017.

Dehaene, S. and Naccache, L. (2001): "Towards a Cognitive Neuroscience of Consciousness: Basic Evidence and a Workspace Framework." *Cognition*, v. 79, nn. 1–2, pp. 1–37.

Del Cul, A., Baillet, S., and Dehaene, S. (2007): "Brain Dynamics Underlying the Nonlinear Threshold for Access to Consciousness." *PLoS Biology*, v. 5, n. 10, p. e260. DOI: 10.1371/journal.pbio.0050260, visited on 8.5.2017.

Del Cul, A., Dehaene, S., Reyes, P., Bravo, E., and Slachevsky, A. (2009): "Causal Role of Prefrontal Cortex in the Threshold for Access to Consciousness." *Brain: A Journal of Neurology*, v. 132, n. 9, pp. 2531–2540. DOI: 10.1093/brain/awp111, visited on 8.5.2017.

Dennett, D. (1988): "Quining Qualia." In: Marcel, A. and Bisiach, E. (eds.): *Consciousness in Modern Science*, pp. 42–77. Oxford: Oxford University Press.

Dennett, D. (2001). "Are We Explaining Consciousness Yet?" *Cognition*, v. 79, nn. 1–2, pp. 221–237.

Dienes, Z. and Seth, A. (2010): "Gambling on the Unconscious: A Comparison of Wagering and Confidence Ratings as Measures of Awareness in an Artificial Grammar Task." *Consciousness and Cognition*, v. 19, n. 2, pp. 674–681.

Dretske, F. (2006): "Perception without Awareness." In: Gendler, T. S. and Hawthorne, J. (eds.): *Perceptual Experience*, pp. 147–180. Oxford: Oxford University Press.

Fei-Fei, L., Iyer, A., Koch, C., and Perona, P. (2007): "What Do We Perceive in a Glance of a Real-world Scene?" *Journal of Vision*, v. 7, n. 1, pp. 1–29.

Freeman, A. W. and Nguyen, V. A. (2001): "Controlling Binocular Rivalry." *Vision Research*, v. 41, n. 23, pp. 2943–2950.

Froese, T., Gould, C., and Barrett, A. (2011): "Re-Viewing from Within – A Commentary on First – and Second – Person Methods in the Science of Consciousness." *Constructivist Foundations*, v. 6, n. 2, pp. 254–269.

Froese, T., McGann, M., Bigge, W., Spiers, A., and Seth, A. (2012): "The Enactive Torch: A New Tool for the Science of Perception." *IEE Transactions on Haptics*, v. 5, n. 4, pp. 363–375.

Garfinkel, S. N., Seth, A. K., Barrett, A. B., Suzuki, K., and Critchley, H. D. (2014): "Knowing your Own Heart: Distinguishing Interoceptive Accuracy from Interoceptive Awareness." *Biological Psychology*, v. 104, pp. 65–74. DOI: 10.1016/j.biopsycho.2014.11.00, visited on 8.5.2017.

Heavey, C. L. and Hurlburt, R. T. (2008): "The Phenomena of Inner Experience." *Consciousness and Cognition*, v. 17, n. 3, pp. 798–810. DOI: 10.1016/j.concog.2007.12.00, visited on 8.5.2017.

Husserl, E. ([1913] 1982): *Ideas Pertaining to a Pure Phenomenology and to a Phenomenological Philosophy*. The Hague: Nijhoff.

Kouider, S., de Gardelle, V., Sackur, J., and Dupoux, E. (2010): "How Rich Is Consciousness? The Partial Awareness Hypothesis." *Trends in Cognitive Sciences*, v. 14, n. 7, pp. 301–307.

Lack, L. C. (1969): "The Effect of Practice on Binocular Rivalry Control." *Perception and Psychophysics*, v. 6, pp. 397–400.

Lamme, V. A. F. (2003): "Why Visual Attention and Awareness Are Different." *Trends in Cognitive Sciences*, v. 7, n. 1, pp. 12–18.

Lamme, V. A. F. (2010): "How Neuroscience Will Change our View on Consciousness." *Cognitive Neuroscience*, v. 1, n. 3, pp. 204–220. DOI: 10.1080/1758892100373158, visited on 8.5.2017.

Lau, H. C. (2007): "A Higher Order Bayesian Decision Theory of Consciousness." *Progress in Brain Research*, v. 168, pp. 35–48.

Lau, H. C. and Rosenthal, D. (2011): "Empirical Support for Higher-order Theories of Conscious Awareness." *Trends in Cognitive Sciences*, v. 15, n. 8, pp. 365–373.

Ling, S. and Blake, R. (2009): "Suppression during Binocular Rivalry Broadens Orientation Tuning." *Psychological Science*, v. 20, n. 11, pp. 1348–1355. DOI: 10.1111/j.1467-9280.2009.02446, visited on 8.5.2017.

Mealor, A. D. and Dienes, Z. (2013): "The Speed of Metacognition: Taking Time to Get to Know One's Structural Knowledge." *Consciousness and Cognition*, v. 22, n. 1, pp. 123–136. DOI: 10.1016/j.concog.2012.11.00, visited on 8.5.2017.

Miller, G. (2005): "What Is the Biological Basis of Consciousness?" *Science*, v. 309, n. 5731, p. 79.

Miller, S. M., Hansell, N. K., Ngo, T. T., Liu, G. B., Pettigrew, J. D., Martin, N. G., and Wright, M. J. (2010): "Genetic Contribution to Individual Variation in Binocular Rivalry Rate." *Proceedings of the National Academy of Sciences of the United States of America*, v. 107, n. 6, pp. 2664–2668. DOI: 10.1073/pnas.091214910, visited on 8.5.2017.

Oizumi, M., Albantakis, L., and Tononi, G. (2014): "From the Phenomenology to the Mechanisms of Consciousness: Integrated Information Theory 3.0." *PLoS Computational Biology*, v. 10, n. 5, p. e1003588. DOI: 10.1371/journal.pcbi.100358, visited on 8.5.2017.

Overgaard, M., Fehl, K., Mouridsen, K., Bergholt, B., and Cleeremans, A. (2008): "Seeing without Seeing? Degraded Conscious Vision in a Blindsight Patient." *PloS One*, v. 3, n. 8, p. e3028. DOI: 10.1371/journal.pone.000302, visited on 8.5.2017.

Overgaard, M., Rote, J., Mouridsen, K., and Ramsøy, T. Z. (2006): "Is Conscious Perception Gradual or Dichotomous? A Comparison of Report Methodologies during a Visual Task." *Consciousness and Cognition*, v. 15, n. 4, pp. 700–708.

Overgaard, M. and Sandberg, K. (2012): "Kinds of Access: Different Methods for Report Reveal Different Kinds of Metacognitive Access." *Philosophical Transactions of the Royal Society of London. Series B, Biological Sciences*, v. 367, n. 1594, pp. 1287–1296. DOI: 10.1098/rstb.2011.0425, visited on 8.5.2017.

Ramsøy, T. Z. and Overgaard, M. (2004): "Introspection and Subliminal Perception." *Phenomenology and the Cognitive Sciences*, v. 3, n. 1, pp. 1–23.

Rees, G., Kreiman, G., and Koch, C. (2002): "Neural Correlates of Consciousness in Humans." *Nature Reviews. Neuroscience*, v. 3, n. 4, pp. 261–270.

Resulaj, A., Kiani, R., Wolpert, D. M., and Shadlen, M. N. (2009): "Changes of Mind in Decision-making." *Nature*, v. 461, n. 7261, pp. 263–266. DOI: 10.1038/nature0827, visited on 8.5.2017.

Rosenthal, D. M. (2005): *Consciousness and Mind*. Alderley: Clarendon Press.

Rosenthal, D. M. and Weisberg, J. (2008): "Higher-order Theories of Consciousness." *Scholarpedia*, v. 3, n. 5, p. 4407. DOI: 10.4249/scholarpedia.4407, visited on 8.5.2017.

Rounis, E., Maniscalco, B., Rothwell, J. C., Passingham, R. E., and Lau, H. (2010): "Theta-burst Transcranial Magnetic Stimulation to the Prefrontal Cortex Impairs Metacognitive Visual Awareness." *Cognitive Neuroscience*, v. 1, n. 3, pp. 165–175. DOI: 10.1080/1758892100363252, visited on 8.5.2017.

Sandberg, K., Timmermans, B., Overgaard, M., and Cleeremans, A. (2010): "Measuring Consciousness: Is One Measure Better than the Other?" *Consciousness and Cognition*, v. 19, n. 4, pp. 1069–1078.

Searle, J. R. (1998): "How to Study Consciousness Scientifically." *Philosophical Transactions of the Royal Society of London. Series B, Biological Sciences*, v. 353, n. 1377, pp. 1935–1942.

Sergent, C. and Dehaene, S. (2004): "Is Consciousness a Gradual Phenomenon?" *Psychological Science*, v. 15, n.11, pp. 720–728.

Seth, A. K., Dienes, Z., Cleeremans, A., Overgaard, M., and Pessoa, L. (2008): "Measuring Consciousness: Relating Behavioural and Neurophysiological Approaches." *Trends in Cognitive Sciences*, v. 12, n. 8, pp. 314–321. DOI: 10.1016/j.tics.2008.04.008, visited on 8.5.2017.

Tononi, G. (2008): "Consciousness as Integrated Information: A Provisional Manifesto." *Biol Bull*, v. 215, n. 3, pp. 216–242.

Tsakiris, M. (2010): "My Body in the Brain: A Neurocognitive Model of Body-ownership." *Neuropsychologia*, v. 48, n. 3, pp. 703–712.

Ullsperger, M., Harsay, H. A., Wessel, J. R., and Ridderinkhof, K. R. (2010): "Conscious Perception of Errors and Its Relation to the Anterior Insula." *Brain Structure and Function*, v. 214, nn. 5–6, pp. 629–643. DOI: 10.1007/s00429–010–0261–1, visited on 8.5.2017.

Wierzchoń, M., Asanowicz, D., Paulewicz, B., and Cleeremans, A. (2012): "Subjective Measures of Consciousness in Artificial Grammar Learning Task." *Consciousness and Cognition*, v. 21, n. 3, pp. 1141–1153. DOI: 10.1016/j.concog.2012.05.01, visited on 8.5.2017.

Wierzchoń, M., Paulewicz, B., Asanowicz, D., Timmermans, B., and Cleeremans, A. (2014): "Different Subjective Awareness Measures Demonstrate the Influence of Visual Identification on Perceptual Awareness Ratings." *Consciousness and Cognition*, v. 27C, pp. 109–120. DOI: 10.1016/j.concog.2014.04.00, visited on 8.5.2017.

Windey, B., Vermeiren, A., Atas, A., and Cleeremans, A. (2014): "The Graded and Dichotomous Nature of Visual Awareness." *Philosophical Transactions of the Royal Society of London. Series B, Biological Sciences*, v. 369, n. 1641, p. 201282. DOI: 10.1098/rstb.2013.028, visited on 8.5.2017.

Zahavi, D. (2003): *Husserl's Phenomenology*. Stanford: Stanford University Press.

Part III: **Scientific Status of Psychology and the Psychological Subject**

Manuel Antonio García Sedeño
Naturalization of Psychology and Its Future as a Science

Abstract: The development in the field of neuropsychology is supporting reductionist approaches. They endorse explanations of causation of behaviour where mental phenomena are a mere consequence of brain processes. These advocates of eliminativism and physicalism believe that there is no actual science in folk psychology, i.e., the explanations made in terms of desires, beliefs, mind, etc. In its more radical expression, this conception can lead to brain solipsism. This paper does not accept these reductionist approaches and, especially, the brain solipsism. Thus, it is in opposition to these views, including the mereological perspective on psychology. This study analyzes the whole process of physicalization of psychology. It considers the main reasons underneath those views and takes into account three positions on psychology of recent decades: naturalistic, cognitive and social. This paper offers a vision of psychological science that is able to relate the components of the objective world to the subjective meanings. Thus, the object of psychology must be the explanation for the formation and development of human cognition as a social product. In this process, the neurological structure has an important role to explain human behaviour, which is not exclusive. Therefore, psychology should be understood as a science with a phenomenological component as well as a hermeneutical factor.

Keywords: neuropsychology, physicalism, eliminativism, science, folk psychology, phenomenology, hermeneutics

1 From Mental Phenomena to Neural Processes: Eliminativism in Psychology

Philosopher Patricia Churchland, according to studies that aim to explain mental phenomena as a result of neuronal processes, ponders that psychology is dying (see Churchland 1986). She considers that it is not possible to speak of the mind and brain as separate elements for they are the same thing; so it would be better to focus on the neurological dimension to understand this binomial and erase all the references to mental components from psychology. In the same way, other philosophers such as Eric Kandel, James Schwartz, and Thomas Jessell (2001); Gerhard Roth (2003); Wolf Singer (2003); Zack Lynch (2009); Michael Gazzaniga (2008); Antonio Damasio (2010); and Paul Churchland (2012) share this materialist view about the mental issue. They defend the identity theory, in which mind and matter are manifestations of the same entity, which are the brain and its neural architecture.

Nevertheless, they state that their point of view does not include psychology as a whole but just that one called "folk psychology." This kind of psychology is used by people based on the concepts built on their own experiences, aiming to understand, explain and predict some behaviour and mental states of one's own and those of someone else's. In this psychological approach each subject ascribes the causes of behaviour to mental states that rise from ideas, beliefs or feelings.

This psychological approach is shaped as an empirical theory, but is false and defective because of its inability to offer acceptable explanations to mental phenomena. Nevertheless, the very definition that it's offered of this folk psychology enables its reviews to extend as well to the psychology we know as "scientific."

The eliminativist arguments are supported by plenty of empirical data collected in the latest years of neurobiological investigation, such as the ones by Francis Crick (1994, 2003) and Gerald Edelman (2004), and their followers Gilulio Tononi (2000), Jean-Pierre Changeux (2002), Vernon Mountcastle (2005), Michael Gazzaniga (2005), Vilayanur Ramachandran (2006), and Antonio Damasio (1994, 1999, 2003). They accept the existence of a neurological determination in human behaviour as a consequence of the anatomical physiology of the neural engines. Psychology, as they state, only can explain the mind based on itself. They appeal to biology, thus they consider the mind in a natural context, biological-evolutionary. They do so in order to offer the scientific explanations that look for to match scientific theories with their evidences.

This stance leads them to consider the ontological and functional nature of the human mind from the perspective of neural networks structure. If we follow this way, where the neural networks are the only existing reality, then knowledge of the mind and its running would be compromised by the knowledge we have about the nervous system and its functional architecture. In this perspective, psychology depends on neurology. This tendency emphasizes the role that insular cortex plays on the mental process.

In recent years, the main role on the explanation of many mental functions linked to the inner corporal states (such as emotions, self-consciousness and even the effect of social interaction) has been placed in this cerebral structure (Bechara and Naqvi 2004; Craig 2009; Ibanez, Gleichgerrcht, and Manes 2010). In addition, this is also considered the key to explain more specific processes, such as subjective emotions (love, hatred, resentment, self-confidence or shame), and many behaviour disorders, either psychiatric or regarding personality.

Taking into account the relevance of this eliminativist approach to psychology, the present paper deals with two clearly different topics, which are related to each other. First, it seeks to show that the process of physicalization is dangerous, insofar as psychology is being absorbed *de facto* by neurology, and consequently psychology can find itself in danger of extinction. Second, this paper tries to show the existence of a genuine scientific psychology, which is epistemologically and methodologically autonomous regarding neurology. This scientific field, as far as I conceive it, includes elements of science in several directions, such as a natural component, open to a phenomenological aspect and with a hermeneutical factor. All together make psychology more complex than what the mere neurological approach claims.

2 The Physicalization of Psychology: Some Historical Keys

In order to understand how we have arrived to the situation of eliminativism and physicalization of psychology, we need to go back to the 60s. On the one hand, there was interest in the neopositivist claims regarding the preference for methods of natural sciences for social phenomena; and, on the other hand, the study of cognition in psychology using empirical methods similar to natural methods encouraged the birth of cognitivism. This new conception of cognition led to a new psychological approach to intelligence and thinking. The focus was on studying human mind in order to understand how the mind of any subject interprets, processes and stores the information in memory. It was a new cognitive science whose main goal was to discover how human mind is able to think and learn based on empirical methods.

In addition to this empirical approach, a new element was the development of Artificial Intelligence. In this new field the approaches to mathematical logic and new computation languages have particular influence. Thus, authors such as Turing, von Neumann, and Simon knew quite well the contributions made in the past by Frege, Russell, and Whitehead (Muggleton 2013).

The views on how to conceive the human mind in comparison with a machine opened new lines of research. In this regard, the contributions made by McCulloch and Pitts "were especially relevant: they proved that the operations realized by a nervous cell and its connections with otherneurons can be represented by a logical model" (García Vega and Moya Santoyo 1993, p. 338). Artificial Intelligence (AI) is therefore patterned following two approaches: the neurological and the symbolic one.

This neurological approach to AI was influential for a while. In this regard, Shannon and Wiener developed along these lines concepts like information, circuits, relay and commutation. Besides their contributions, there were other views, such the cybernetic theory developed by physiologist Berstein, who propose a transmission model of the information in the neuron which transcends the idea of the reflex arc (Whithing 1984). A feature shared by different approaches to AI was the emphasis on the empirical contribution to science. Thus, they assumed that learning is produced by the representation of what is obtained by experience. Following this criterion, what really matters is discovering the way these representations of the world are acquired, how they are stored and how are brought back from memory. This is a contemporary effort to give empirical basis to answers regarding old epistemological questions (Gardner 2006). These questions were those that are linked to knowledge of nature, its elements, sources, evolution and dissemination. This preference for empirical bases of cognition leads to cognition as an integration of all the processes by which sensorial input is transformed, reduced, elaborated, stored, recovered and used.

Under the influence of AI, the computational aspects were highlighted. The key point was the characterization of cognition in comparison with what a machine does. Cognition was seeing involved in every human activity and every psychological phenomenon. This was considered by Fodor, who many years after the contributions made in the 60s, considered cognition in this context of mind versus machine. This led to computational intelligence. It appears "as a computational system where information is encapsulated, an inferential mechanism with an access to the inborn information restricted by general aspects of the cognitive architecture" (Fodor 1983, p. 69). His work on modularity had a positive influence on the development of AI expert systems, for the creation of functional brain maps of cognitive neuroscience and for the study of the components of grammatical theory in linguistics and the growing interest in psychology for the investigation of vertical faculties (in specialized cognitive domains).

After the influence of logical positivism towards empirical basis for psychology and all the contributions made around AI – in terms of neurons and in terms of signs or symbols – the cognitive paradigm was influential in psychology. The cognitive vision followed two different lines of thought: constructivism and neuropsychology.

According to constructivism, the main contributions of prominent authors inside psychology field (Piaget, Ausubel, Bruner, and Vygotsky, etc.) confer importance to social and cultural aspects on the explanation of cognitive development. From this perspective, subject and object are mutually related at different levels of ontogenetic construction, because subject extends itself into the object, acting and reacting over it (Carretero 2009).

Following the lines of neuropsychology, there were diverse options. They thought of cybernetics, computation and neurophysiology. They were, enforced by the ideas of philosophers like Fodor (1983) or neurologists like McCulloch (1974). This author defended the possibility of elaborating an epistemology considering just the information coming from central nervous system. He offered a "hard" version of cognitivism, which was based on neuropsychology (Weiner and Shade 1965). According to this second path, cognitivism evolves to models in which the neurological aspects acquire progressively more importance as an explanatory element. Because of the constant advances of neuroimage techniques, it will look forward to reduce the psychological dimension to exclusively neurological and biochemical processes (Leahey 2008). This neuropsychology evolves with the contribution of neuroscience and contemporary psychology and suggests as a main subject studying the relationships existing between cerebral activity and high level mental functions (gnosias, praxias, language, memory, ...).

Currently, one of the most representative authors of this tendency is Antonio Damasio (2010). This psychologist, from the review of the case of Phineas Gage, has defended that in order for the mind to exist the body must first exist. Under his approach, mind should be considered a subproduct of the brain, which is shaped as elementary impressions that represent our basic sensorial experiences. This is what he calls *qualia,* merging with the brain in one whole thing.

The impact of this neurological perspective regarding psychology has been very strong. Moreover, it has been presented as the perfect approach to look for a "scientific" explanation to psychological capacities of the human being. In this regard, Francis Crick has developed models in order to maintain that consciousness is a banal fusion of neurons of the brain. Thus he thinks that joy, sadness, memories, ambitions, personal identity and free will are not more than the behaviour of a compound of nervous cells and the molecules associated to them.[1] In conclusion, he maintains that human consciousness should be understood like something belonging exclusively to the brain, like an epiphenomenon, a product of a specific neuronal architecture. Thus, it cannot be explained just by

---

[1] James D. Watson and Francis Crick were the first scientists to affirm openly that soul is within the brain (1953, pp. 737–738). In this work they state that the soul is a mere fusion of neurons of the brain that also allows the conscience to appear.

the study of the different parts of the brain nor from their interaction, but by the whole structure of the system.

Following a similar view, biologist and Nobel Prize-winner in medicine Gerald Edelman formulated a theory with the central idea of the selection and creation of groups of neurons (Theory of Neuronal Group Selection, TNGS) (see Edelman 2004). He considers that it is from experience that some neuronal structures can be born, and they ensure and control the physiological functions needed for living. They are full of connections linked to the pertinent points in the layers of the receptive cells, which able the representation of the world.

Despite of introducing the idea of the interaction between the environment and the body, the last one plays a secondary role because the explanation devolves upon the nervous system. Edelman (2004) claims that the outside world seems more like an excuse to the development of the brain capacity of self-organization and recognition of patterns, while the body would be almost an orthopaedic-biological extension of the hypostasised brain, needed to manipulate the environment.

Also physiologist Rodolfo Llinás (2001) maintains that the brain possess a structure that allows for the receiving of information, stores it, transforms it, and transmits it in different ways that go from movements into emotions. Like this, consciousness is just the result of the phylogenetic evolution of the nervous system.

Roger Penrose (1989) has offered one of the concepts of these physicalist theories of the consciousness.[2] Both he himself and his team members are focused on the quantum mechanics. In their explanation of the consciousness, and considering neurons are too big to find on them its origin, they descend to a lower level to look for it – to the cytoskeleton. The cytoskeleton is a part of the neuron that contains little structures called microtubules, full of water, which travel through those microtubules, that are responsible for the representation and, therefore, for the consciousness.

Penrose's hypothesis is this: consciousness is the addition of large amount of waves, formed in the microtubules inside the brain, merging into a one big wave, leading to the creation of an identity out of millions of individual cells. This way, every neuron influenced by this wave would modify its synapsis, the combination of the cerebral calculation of the nervous impulses and lastly, big-scale microtubular coherence producing consciousness (Monsterrat 2000).

All of these eliminativist models begin with the understanding of the brain as the basis of consciousness. They assume that the difference between mind

---

[2] See also his contribution in Penrose, Shimony, Cartwright, and Hawking (1997).

and body is not ontological but merely epistemological. In this regard, human mind is conceived as a quality or property of the brain. It is seemed as the result of its microstructure.

Despite of the predominance of the materialist monism and its many supporters nowadays, there are also other dualist approaches, such as the one maintained by neurologist John Eccles (1980), Nobel Prize in medicine. According to this author, the brain is not a structure complex enough to contain the phenomena related to consciousness. Thus, it should be admitted the autonomous existence of a self-conscious mind different from the brain. This is conceived as a non-material reality (i.e., it is not an organic reality) that carries out a superior function of interpretation and control of the neuronal processes.

His model follows the philosophy of the three worlds maintained by him and the famous philosopher Popper (see Popper and Eccles 1977) with the intention of looking for the ontological basics that support the concept of a self-conscious mind. This self-conscious mind works in a selective way (voluntary), mainly by the discriminative processes of the attention, on the neuronal machine. A self-conscious mind, with a nature capable of high level mental experiences like knowing the knowledge (Eccles 1980).

Eccles bases this aforementioned dualist hypothesis on ideas, such as the experiences of the self-conscious mind, are related with the neuronal processes that take place on the associative areas of the neocortex. This relationship is the product of the interaction between mental processes and cerebral processes, but not like an identity relationship. Following this way, the information coming from sensorial organs is transmitted to the brain. But, when it crosses the border between associative cerebral cortex and mind, then the information is transformed into the experiences of our perceptive world, which are different from cerebral processes.

In this process, the self-conscious mind reads the messages of many cerebral centres with highest levels of activity, like the associative zones of the dominant hemisphere, acting on these centres, modifying dynamic space-temporary patterns of the neuronal processes. So, self-conscious mind works as an interpreter and controller of neuronal processes.

Eccles demonstrated the existence of brain areas, where each one is responsible for a different specific function. This goes from being a mere object of reflection to have an issue of experimental evidence. Thus, the scientific and experimental neuropsychology is created (Barcia-Salorio 2004, p. 668).

Psychoneurological models have some trouble explaining certain phenomena and this contributes to the development of many theories that consider mind as an epiphenomenon of the brain. One of these theories comes from an emergentist vision, where there is the mind/body issue but it maintains that mental states are not the same as cerebral states. Thus, they cannot be reduced to them, but they are not independent from each other either (Searle 1997).

Under this light, mental processes – conscious or unconscious, even if cerebral processes cause them – cannot be reduced to them. They are autonomous phenomena or properties that rise from neurophysiological systems at some point in the long evolutionary process of the species. Therefore, mental processes such as perceiving, feeling, remembering, imagining, desiring, thinking, etc., are then emergent properties of neurological systems that cannot be explained by the analysis of its components. They require starting from different descriptive levels of the brain, such as: the structure and functioning of the neurons (microproperties) or from the structure and functioning of mental processes (macroproperties).

Because of this distinction between mental and neurological, it is possible to distinguish between mental processes (such as those that psychology studies when has an independent status) and cerebral processes (just those that neuroscience analyses). Moreover, they do not need to reduce the first to the second ones and, on the contrary, maintain a good relationship between the two levels (mental and neurological).

As already stated, I observe the narrow relationship established between cognitive psychologists and neurologists. Data obtained by neurological researches offer a solid methodology to cognitive psychology to sustain its models. I observe as we the close relationship established between cognitive psychologists and neurologists. The data obtained by neurological research offer a firm methodology for cognitive psychology to sustain their models. Nevertheless, neurology also seeks to develop its own methods capable of creating alternative theories to the psychological ones. This is a tendency that becomes stronger when psychological theories are ineffective.

There might be a fusion of psychology and neurology in terms of cognitive neuropsychology. It has been creating new models of process of information, shaped as flow diagrams linked to specific cerebral regions. These diagrams do not attempt to represent connections between different brain centres, but rather connections between different components of the cognitive system that end up in neural networks able to explain mental functions.

Despite the proposal of connexion between those two disciplines and the resulting unification of physical dimension and the mental component, the facts have proved exactly the opposite: the progressive annulation of mental side. It has gone from the consideration of the structure and functioning of the nervous system initiated by Ramón y Cajal to the notion of *qualia*, and from it to self-consciousness, voiding any psychological theory. A reductionist vision of psychology has been developed due to an inductive methodology in the neurology field, supported by the techniques of neuroimage and brain dissection on animals. This approach has led to the formulation of theories *ad hoc* to resolve questions still not resolved nor corroborated.

The dimension of this approach is so big that it seems necessary to establish other ways to develop a scientific psychology. It can be adopted a way similar to Popper's three worlds theory in which neurological issues belong to world 1 and, exceptionally, to world 2. Meanwhile, the human mind uses language as its main tool in world 3 (the one about mental processes where objective knowledge is produced).[3] Because of this, psychology has to be considered as an independent science, different from neurology.

3 The Post-historical Turn and Its Repercussion in Scientific Psychology

Regarding the foundations of a scientific psychology as independent from neurology, we can start from Quine's philosophical thought. Although he was a logical empiricist in many ways, his naturalization of epistemology was relevant for the development of the issue of a different approach to psychology. In this regard, it is particularly important his criticism of the fundamental ideas of logical positivism of the Vienna Circle. Thus, in his work *Two Dogmas of Empiricism* (Quine 1969) he attempts to destroy the distinction between the analytical and the synthetic. This also involves a criticism of the kind of reductionism proposed by the neopositivist philosophers of the Vienna Circle.

Quine considers that the criticism to metaphysics by logical positivists is just a linguistic turn. He thinks that they keep similar notions in their statements, especially when they are referring to the relation between linguistic aspects and sensorial experiences.

In light of this, he attempts to develop empiricism free of metaphysical concepts. In his view, the acquisition of knowledge of the world may be understood as a product of man, due to his own experience, where statements do not have a concrete and straight connection to the empirical fact. Following his epistemological position, the term "empirical" implies a socially elaborated process. For Quine, epistemology itself must become a natural science. Summarizing, he thinks all knowledge can be derived from terms which describe the sensitive experience.

---

[3] This idea of the three worlds has been developed by Popper in other of his works, such as *Unended Quest* (1976) and *Objective Knowledge* (1979).

Quine (1981) proposes a kind of naturalism focused on the pursuit of truth about the world. His epistemological conception emphasizes the traditional scientific procedures developed in a hypothetical-deductive method. In this method the limits are imposed just by science itself, as the fact of establishing references before knowing them. That means, asking about what there is before asking how we (do) know,

> as if we could build an infallible knowledge of sensitive data and then build our theory of the external world on the basis of that finished foundation in some way. A naturalist approach oriented to the explanation on how human beings build up a reliable theory about the outer world through our contact with it. But it is not an irrefutable epistemological theory, true and valid everywhere and every time but instead is able to be reviewed and submitted to readjustments and changes, where language is a relevant conditioning (Hernández Borges 2002, p. 70).

Quine's naturalist approach is oriented toward the explanation on how human beings build up a reliable theory about the external world through our contact with it. But, according to his view, it is not like the neopositivist position of an irrefutable epistemological theory, true and valid everywhere and every time. For Quine, knowledge can be reviewed and submitted to readjustments and changes. In this regard, language plays a key role as a relevant conditioning.

In addition, sensorial impressions have a central role in his view, because he thinks that formation of beliefs about the outer world is produced through a process that should not be prescribed but described through sensorial impressions.

This epistemological position leads to an approach to psychology based on language and sensorial impressions. Quine (1995) goes to see psychology among the natural sciences. For him, epistemology can be seen as a chapter of psychology and, therefore, of nature sciences. Epistemology is naturalized and psychology studies a natural phenomenon, which is "the physical human subject" (Quine 1974).

Within this strong line of naturalism, which stated by Quine, there are other conceptions. But there are also less strong views on naturalism, such as Ronald Giere's perspectivism and Philip Kitcher's combination of pragmatism and naturalism about social sciences. The role of the individuals plays an important role regarding epistemology as well as social factors, because Kitcher thinks of an epistemology socially embedded (Gonzalez 2011).

Giere, in his work *Explaining Science* (1988), conceives naturalism as an attempt of explaining decisions of scientists through the notion that these are agents with certain psychological abilities. This perspectivism leads him to the use of explanatory models that come from psychology. According to him, cognitivism should be considered as the most useful and reliable theory to formalize science (see Zamora Bonilla 2000).

With this position, Giere shows the ability of human and non-human beings to represent reality. They start a series of mechanisms that allow them to solve the problems that come throughout their relationship with the environment. This is an ability of the agents to build and create representations shaped as families of cognitive models about the environment. The ability allows the subject to assimilate and state hypotheses about the causal relations within him. Experience is going to be the mechanism that will allow the building of theories through its possibilities of application.

Kitcher gets deeper into the analysis of the epistemological concepts. Thus, he emphasizes on the necessity of describing the role of the individuals in the disciplines that are subject of study. He considers "levels of addition" of the different members that take part of it, their mental states, actions and abilities (Kitcher 1992 and 1993). These levels are focused on the individual practice and on the consensual practice. Therefore, human knowledge is understood as a consequence of the act of knowing in which the real belief is produced due to the social dimension of science.

From this social dimension comes in Kitcher the importance that is given to the contents (semantic, epistemic, methodological ...) of science. Thus, science works on upon contextual factors, which emphasizes the role of scientific activity. Kitcher agrees with Giere in considering psychology as the discipline able to allow formalization in science, for the value is focused on the cognoscente subject. Both share an interest in a cognitive approach based on naturalistic elements. It is a kind of cognitivism with a big isomorphism regarding the way the subject acquires his or her own knowledge.

These naturalist approaches are based on three perspectives: 1) the evolution of science as a Darwinian process, which provides it with an evolutionary character; 2) the inclusion of the cognitivist approach through the inclusion of models of representation; and 3) rationality and principle of symmetry, which Kitcher uses for the explanatory processes of rational and irrational beliefs (Zamora Bonilla 2000). This connection of rational and irrational beliefs is the consequence of considering the beliefs as cognitive states of the brain, which arise due to its interaction with the environment. This is something that psychology assumes completely.

Another kind of naturalism is in Laudan after leaving the emphasis in the historical approach. He proposes a view on naturalism focused on the empirical evidence that exists in the relation between the used means and the pursued ends (see Laudan 1998). This naturalist approach is presented as normative, insofar as is based in history of science, which show practices that gives us some norms about how to develop science.

Laudan also supports that rules for the advancement of epistemology. He proposes a normative naturalism whose key feature is the existence of normative rules of epistemology that must be understood as hypothetical imperatives which connect ends and means. These rules must be validated by empirical results through the association between such ends and means; thus, supported by facts. Axiologically, it also recognizes the value of history in order to know the changes in the values, purposes or epistemological goals.

To base this argumentation and to relate scientific activity, he proposes a reticulated model of scientific rationality which connects in circuit/in series theories, systems or sets of methodological rules (methods) and estimated epistemic values (ends or goals). In this framework, scientific methodology is of a naturalistic kind. For Laudan, axiology, methodology and the factual assertions are inevitably in a mutual dependent relationship. Thus, they are combined instead of been three of them as having a hierarchical configuration (Álvarez 1998, p. 120).

This vision of epistemology implies the existence of a methodology that contains a set of rules. They may be formulated in instrumental terms once the cognitive purposes of the research are recognized. Therefore, Laudan's normative naturalism tries to be a normative and empirical meta-methodology providing criteria to evaluate methodologies in competence. We are dealing with a methodological naturalism which leads to an ontological naturalism. This ontological naturalism considers existence through nature and what is focused solely on along with what is susceptible of being studied through the proper methods of science.

Although these versions of contemporary naturalism are different in many ways, they share the interest in cognitive aspects of the agents in order to understand scientific knowledge. In addition, there are authors that support cognitive psychology in a more explicit way. They are naturalists and cognitivists. Thus, they represent the "cognitivist turn" in philosophy of science, which is supported by Alvin Goldman (1999) and Paul Thagard (2005). They consider the possibility of relating the internal content of science with the elements of the social environment. Because mental representations are the mental shapes that the subject has about what is around us, the main aim of cognitive science will be to explain how humans think (Martínez Freire 1992).

The fundamental ideas of cognitivism, in particular, and cognitive science, in general, are also used as the base for the psychological science in these naturalists. Psychology can deal with the interdisciplinary study of how information is represented and transformed inside the mind through vital experience. But we should not forget about another line of thought inside cognitive science: constructivism.

According to constructivism, human being builds cognitive, social and emotional aspects schemes in the day-to-day life as a result of the relationship with the surrounding environment. Constructivism maintains that our knowledge is not based on correspondence with something external, but it is result of the construction of an observer who is not able to contact directly with their environment. Our world is a human world, a product of human interaction with natural and social *stimuli* that have achieved to process from our mental processing operations.

These naturalist and cognitivist approaches can be found in the so-called "social turn" with its conception of science as a social enterprise (Gonzalez 2006). This way, external values play a key role in science and technology, due to the fact that both of them are considered as a "social enterprise." This is a new vision of the objectives, processes, and results of scientific activities and technological doing, because the focus is on several of the aspects of science and technology that used to be considered secondary or even irrelevant. These three positions – the naturalist, cognitivist and social turn – appeared after the "historical turn," and they can be completed with scientific realism (Gonzalez 2006). It defends the use of a terminology capable of relating the components of the objective world with the subjective meanings not as an identity relation but through attributes that give to it some personal meaning and authenticity.

Finally, another interesting position at which to approach the subject of psychological science is hermeneutics. This conception can be based on the works of Gadamer ([1960] 1986 and 1989). This author considers that the knowledge is essential for the human existence. To the human being, all knowledge is a constant interpretation and, first of all, knowledge about himself. Each man or woman tries to understand his or her past, the origin of being, installed in a certain point of history. This leads him to understand his reality from a "determined hermeneutical position" not distinguished as a confrontation between man and situation but as "man being on it, being part of it" human mind can be defined as a construction that every human being makes within a context and understanding the action as its genesis. The experience is the path to human life with all it implies: illusions, frustrations, deceptions, pain (Gadamer [1960] 1986).

These views – naturalist, cognitivist, social, historical realism and hermeneutical positions – when they are seen in a global way, then human mind may be defined as a construction that every human being makes within a context, being the action itself the genesis of it. An action that is initially reflex, involuntary, triggered by external stimulation and that after repetition becomes voluntary. For hermeneutics the truth is the result of an interpretation.

In all this process, we find two capacities: thinking and feeling. The first one refers to the ability of processing information and all the processes that it implies (memory, attention, reflection, etc.) and the resulting construction of concepts. The second one refers to the perceptive processes where both external senses and internal organs are implied with experience itself. These abilities do not only favour the cognitive process but its absence affects negatively to the development of the construction of the mind.

Therefore, psychology should be understood as a discipline focused on studying the mind as a systemic set of processes of catching information, processing, using representation and language. This leads the subject to conceptualize himself as such, conceptualizing the world and operating inside him for his or her own personal development; ultimately: the subject is a being in the world.

Another important aspect in this process of construction of the mind – from an operative way rather than an actual ontological way – is its value inside of a context physical-social where it is located. Considering the mind as a personal construction, which the subject makes in a certain context, the elements that conforms that context (including the subject itself) will necessarily play a special role on it. This value will condition the way in which we accomplish the construction of the functioning of the mind and it is nothing less than what we understand as forms of expression of emotions in the Wallonian sense of this term:

> In the ontogenesis, emotion is the first to link the organism with the social environment, for the tissue of emotions is made of the fabric of its neurophysiological bases and the reciprocity that ensures exchanges with the environment. (...) In emotion and language we may find the keys that confer to men that their sings of identity; emotion and language have biological roots but also that they are configured and structured thanks to the social exchange. (...) Therefore, thanks to emotion and through it, the child turns from a biological being into a social one (Wallon 1939, p. 198).

Therefore, psychology is the discipline that is focused on the study of mechanisms of representation and conceptualization of the world (attention, memory, thoughts, reflections). For psychology, language is an essential and necessary tool. In addition, psychology should study emotions as that element that offers some coherence to this whole process of constructing the mind.

To sum up, the mind is a systemic organization between elements that allow the representation, language and emotions, where we face two levels to approach the study of psychology. The first one, in a molecular level, defined by the consideration of every capacity as an individual entity; this is, the study of nature of attention, memory, perception, language, etc., considered as elements.

On the other hand, the moral level, which considers in a global way the events experimented by the subject under the notion of fact or complex event, where its value comes from the meaning it has for him, inside his own mental development of cognitive, affective and social character. They are levels coming from the consideration of the human mind as something belonging exclusively to our species, which also allows to understand the great flexibility in human behaviour (Hare 2007).

In this way, psychology has been approaching to some different disciplines in its long road to achieve its status as a proper science. First, as a part of philosophy, psychology sought to conceptualize the term "psyche." Later, psychology tried to study behaviour from its exterior expression until its neurological nature. A long way where psychology has made meaningful contributions about the way we perceive, learn, think, act, behave with each other, fight, bring ourselves back together, organize socially and even destroy our habitat and planetary home.

In every moment psychology has used, not always successfully, natural science methods. This is so because psychology has always felt itself like a part of natural history, besides social and behaviour science. We should remind that, like Ardila (2002) has pointed out, psychologists work with problems that are related to the way we know the world, how we learn, how we process the incoming information, how we behave and relate with people different from ourselves, how we face our own existence, values, moral judgments, justice, unusual behaviour, work field, free time, ageing, death. These problems have great importance, and we have more questions than answers (Ardila 2002).

4 Final Remarks on the Naturalization of Psychology

Following the previous remarks, it is necessary to accept that, despite everything aforesaid and the strength of the arguments regarding naturalism, materialism is not free of ambiguities. Thus, it should be dismissed as an explicative model of mental phenomena. Its determinist and mereological nature leads to the explanation of mental phenomena through a single neurological point of view, forgetting any other approach that could intervene. Its vision of the human being, under neurological determinism, tends to consider him or her as a mechanical and isolated being.

Meanwhile, my approach goes in exactly the opposite way. It conceives men and women as a part of a natural environment that allows us to create a more coherent and solid structure to build up a scientific psychology. Kitcher (1993) and Goldman (1999) wrote about a contemporary naturalism in which functionalism and cognitivism are integrated. This has more advantages in order to obtain scientific explanations about the mind and its running than the purely materialistic vision of other naturalists.

According to my alternative point of view, we could also say that mentalist nature concepts do not have to be always considered metaphysical terms, for they occasionally constructions built with different techniques and adequate methodologies that support its validation as science. This is the case of causal models, through the use of structural equations, focused on the manipulation of variables and the acceptation of latent variables.

It seems to me that we can be against eliminativistic, materialistic and determinist approaches. In this regard, my alternative defends that psychology is conceived as a science that includes cognitive, social and hermeneutical elements. This is a psychology where the core concept is the "value of experience" as the consequence of processing the information of all the facts that build a certain situation, the degree of implication and the satisfaction that is produced in the present moment and its projection in the future. This value, consequence of the interpretation of the situation will be the cause that leads the subject to action and keeping certain patterns of behaviour, or to change to other ones more effective for keeping or eliminating it. Under this idea, facts are defined as elements of the world interpreted by emotions where language exerts a strong influence.

So, when trying to describe in psychological science the processes of representation of the world and, therefore, of cognition, the language used refers to the reality of the situation itself, to what is in the world and the meaning that the subject confers to it according to his values. Both things are real, independent, related to the subject according to the estimation of his interests. So, propositions have a kind of logical structure that reflects the kind of logic that the subject keeps with reality and his experience within it. This experience is understood not as individual sensations, facts and situations but as whole packages integrated by emotions as an essential component that came throughout the history of the subject. This is a concept somehow similar to the one of "qualitative class" of Carnap (1950) but more naturalized, where social and psychological context has a great importance.

Obviously, there is another language in the field of psychological science that refers to a previously mentioned molecular dimension, focused on mental functions and its measure. Since the beginning of experimental psychology, some studies about attention, memory, perception, language, sensations and feelings have been carried out in order to know the mechanisms that lie under the processes of construction of knowledge and resolution of problems. The physiological nature of all gains some value when it is related to experience, after we test its utility in our lives. So, terms such as expectations, motivation, beliefs, etc., accepted by folk psychology will be considered in the construction of a psychological science.

The employment of a hypothetical-deductive methodology has also allowed the development of psychological science in its early stages. In due course, the improvement in statistical techniques based on probability approaches has allowed the employment of causal models. These models are allowing the creation of theories with a higher ability, both explanatory and predictive, in probability terms; they are formulated through causal relations established between latent variables, different from traditional metaphysical concepts. This possibility allows the development of psychological science through empirical criteria, as recommended by methodological naturalism. But also, scientific psychology has been studying the development and utilization of a hermeneutical methodology focused on the narration of the subject, because it is considered it is the best way to obtain the keys to be able to know the value of experience; only this way adds the essential element that is the emotional value.

Concepts considered as metaphysical – like mind, consciousness, expectations, beliefs and similar elements – may be interpreted as constructions, not necessarily hypothetical, that came from the measurement of causal relations between phenomena or measured events in terms of observed variables. Categories of variables instead of metaphysical concepts like, for instance, defining consciousness as "ability of ..." So, scientific psychology will only accept observable and measurable realities in which their size and contextual value will be the key elements for its validation and the theories that support them.

In conclusion, despite of the efforts of neurology to melt with psychology to build up a new natural science, as neuropsychology, I consider that this simple union would affect negatively to the development of psychology as a science. Although the union seems convenient and plausible for the study of basic functions (attention, memory, language, etc.), the explanation and comprehension of them inside the existential space of the subject need more subjective processes like hermeneutics to complement nature science procedures. So we can, and we should, defend the existence of a psychological science with its own identity, independent from neurology and other similar sciences, whose object goal is the explanation of creation and development of human consciousness as a product coming from its own experience. (i) Psychology is a human, social and natural science, in which experience becomes the key for its understanding; that is the value of hermeneutics. (ii) Psychology is a science that has some characteristics to consider as it and that they can be analysed at different levels (semantic, logical, epistemological, methodological, ontological, axiological and ethical levels).

At the semantic level, we find psychological statements that refer to mental functions and states, based on practice and described in simple, proper and accurate language accepted by all the members of the community. At the epistemological level, this is a science that looks for a description and explanation of rational-emotive behaviours and the mechanisms used to solve all kinds of situations. It tries to achieve this aim through the combination of hypothetical-deductive methodology (methodological level), that provides causes; with hermeneutic that allows for its understanding. All of these aspects under the subject consideration, as a self with consciousness, are a part from the nature that interacts with it through a dyadic relationship (ontological level). There is also the level of values, what is worthy to be researched and the priorities in order to do the research (axiological level), which is followed by the ethical level, insofar as we deal with human beings that have a value in themselves and we should really care about how they are and what they actually need.

References

Álvarez, J. R. (1998): "El Naturalismo normativo y la Metodología de la Ciencia." In: Gonzalez, W. J. (ed.): *El Pensamiento de L. Laudan. Relaciones entre Historia de la Ciencia y Filosofía de la Ciencia*, pp. 117–132. A Coruña: Publicaciones Universidad de A Coruña.

Ardila, R. (2002): *La Psicología en el futuro*. Madrid: Editorial Pirámide.

Barcia-Salorio, D. (2004): "A Historical Introduction to the Neuropsychological Model." *Neurologia*, v. 39, n. 4, pp. 668–681.

Bechara, A. and Naqvi, N. (2004): "Listening to Your Heart: Interoceptive Awareness as a Gateway to Feeling." *Nature Neuroscience*, v. 7, pp. 102–103.

Braun, R. A. (2008): "El eliminativismo filosófico y su ataque a la Psicología." *Persona*, v. 11, pp. 51–87.

Carnap, R. (1950): "Empiricism, Semantics, and Ontology." *Revue Internationale de Philosophie*, v. 4, pp. 20–40. Reprinted in the Supplement to Carnap, R. (1956): *Meaning and Necessity: A Study in Semantics and Modal Logic*, enlarged edition. Chicago: The University of Chicago Press.

Carretero, M. (2009): *Constructivismo y Educación*. Buenos Aires: Paidós.

Changeux, J.-P. (2002): *L'homme de verite*. Paris: Odile Jacob. English translation by De M. B. Deboise (2004): *The Physiology of Truth: Neurosciencie and Human Knowledge*. Harvard: Harvard University Press.

Churchland, P. M. (2012): *Plato's Camera: How the Physical Brain Captures a Landscape of Abstract Universals*. Cambridge, MA: The MIT Press.

Churchland, P. S. (1986): *Neurophilosophy*. Cambridge, MA: The MIT Press.

Craig, A. D. (2009): "How Do You Feel Now? The Anterior Insula and Human Awareness." *Nature Reviews. Neuroscience*, v. 10, pp. 59–70.

Crick, F. (1994): *Astonishing Hypothesis: The Scientific Search for the Soul.* London: Simon and Schuster.
Crick, F. and Koch, C. (2003): "A Framework for Consciousness." *Nature Neuroscience*, v. 6, pp. 119–126.
Damasio, A. R. (1994): *Descartes' Error: Emotion, Reason, and the Human Brain.* London: Putnam.
Damasio, A. (1999): *The Feeling of What Happens: Body and Emotion in the Making of Consciousness.* New York: Harcourt Brace.
Damasio, A. (2003): *Looking for Spinoza: Joy, Sorrow, and the Feeling Brain.* New York: Harcourt.
Damasio, A. (2010): *Self Comes to Mind: Constructing the Conscious Brain.* London: William Heinemann.
Eccles, J. C. (1980): *Human Psyche.* Berlin/Heidelberg: Springer.
Edelman, G. M. (2004): *Wider than the Sky: The Phenomenal Gift of Consciousness.* New Haven: Yale University Press.
Edelman, G. M. and Tononi, G. (2000): *A Universe of Consciousness: How Matter Becomes Imagination.* New York: Basic Books.
Fodor, J. A. (1983): *The Modularity of Mind.* Cambridge, MA: The MIT Press.
Gadamer, H. G. ([1960] 1986): *Wahrheit und Methode.* Tübingen: J. C. B. Mohr (P. Siebeck).
Gadamer, H. G. (1998): *Praise of Theory.* New Haven: Yale University Press.
García Vega, L. and Moya Santoyo, J. (1993): *Historia de la Psicología II. Sistemas.* Madrid: Siglo XXI.
Gardner, H. (2006): *Multiple Intelligences: New Horizons in Theory and Practice.* New York: Basic Books.
Gazzaniga, M. S. (2005): *The Cognitive Neurosciences.* Cambridge: The MIT Press.
Gazzaniga, M. S. (2008): *Human: The Science of What Makes Us Unique.* New York: Ecco Books/Harper Collins.
Giere, R. N. (1988): *Explaining Science: A Cognitive Approach.* Chicago: The University of Chicago Press.
Goldman, A. (1999): *Knowledge in a Social World.* Oxford: Oxford University Press.
Gonzalez, W. J. (2006): "Novelty and Continuity in Philosophy and Methodology of Science." In: Gonzalez, W. J. and Alcolea, J. (eds.): *Contemporary Perspectives in Philosophy and Methodology of Science*, pp. 1–28. A Coruña: Netbiblo.
Gonzalez, W. J. (ed.) (2007): *Las Ciencias de Diseño: Racionalidad limitada, predicción y prescripción.* A Coruña: Netbiblo.
Gonzalez, W. J. (ed.) (2011): *Scientific Realism and Democratic Society: The Philosophy of Philip Kitcher*, Poznan Studies in the Philosophy of the Sciences and the Humanities, vol. 101. Amsterdam: Rodopi.
Guillaumin, G. (2008): "El naturalismo normativo y sus problemas (normativos)." *Signos filosóficos*, v. 10, n. 20, pp. 95–119.
Hare, B. (2007): "From Nonhuman to Human Mind: What Changed and Why?" *Current Directions in Psychological Science*, v. 16, n. 2, pp. 60–64.
Hernández Borges, M. R. (2002): "El naturalismo quineano o las limitaciones inevitables." *Laguna*, v. 10, pp. 69–80.
Ibanez, A., Gleichgerrcht, E., and Manes, F. (2010): "Clinical Effects of Insular Damage in Humans." *Brain Structure and Function*, v. 214, nn. 5–6, pp. 397–410.

Kandel, E., Schwartz, J., and Jessell, Th. (2001): *Principles of Neural Science*, 3rd edition. Norwalk: Appleton and Lange.

Kitcher, Ph. (1992): "The Naturalist Returns." *Philosophical Review*, v. 101, pp. 53–114.

Kitcher, Ph. (1993): *The Advancement of Science: Science without Legend, Objectivity without Illusions*. New York: Oxford University Press.

Laudan, L. (1998). "Naturalismo normativo y el progreso de la Filosofía." In: Gonzalez, W. J. (ed.): *El Pensamiento de L. Laudan. Relaciones entre Historia de la Ciencia y Filosofía de la Ciencia*, pp. 105–116. A Coruña: Publicaciones Universidad de A Coruña.

Leahey, T. H. (2008): *A History of Psychology. Main Currents in Psychological Thought*, 6th edition. Upper Saddle River, NJ: Pearson Education.

Llinás, R. (2001): *I of the Vortex. From Neurons to Self.* Cambridge, MA: The MIT Press.

Lynch, A. (2009): *The Neuro Revolution: How Brain Science is Changing Our World*. New York: Martin's Press.

Martínez Freire, P. (1992): "El giro cognitivo en Filosofía de la Ciencia." *Revista de Filosofía*, v. 10, n. 2, pp. 105–122.

McCulloch, W. S. (1974): "Recollection of the Many Sources of Cybernetics." *ASC Forum*, v. 6, n. 2, pp. 5–16.

Monserrat, J. (2000): "Pensamiento: Penrose y el enigma cuántico de la conciencia." *Revista de investigación e información filosófica*, v. 56, n. 215, pp. 177–208.

Mountcastle, V. (2005): *The Sensory Hand: Neural Mechanisms of Somatic Sensation*. Cambridge, MA: Harvard University Press.

Muggleton, S. (2013): "Alan Turing and the Development of Artificial Intelligence." *AI Communications*, v. 26, n. 3, pp. 3–10.

Penrose, R. (1989): *The Emperor's New Mind: Concerning Computers, Minds, and the Law of Physics*. Oxford: Oxford University Press.

Penrose, R., Shimony, A., Cartwright, N., and Hawking, S. (1997): *The Large, the Small and the Human Mind*. Cambridge, MA: Cambridge University Press.

Popper, K. R. (1976): *Unended Quest*. London: Fontana-Collins.

Popper, K. R. (1979): *Objective Knowledge*, revised edition. Oxford: Clarendon Press.

Popper, K. R. and Eccles, J. C. (1977): *The Self and Its Brain: An Argument for Interactionism*. Berlin: Springer.

Quine, W. v. O. (1969): "Epistemology Naturalized." In: Quine, W. v. O, *Ontological Relativity and Other Essays*, pp. 69–90. New York: Columbia University Press.

Quine, W. v. O. (1974): *The Roots of Reference*. La Salle, IL: Open Court.

Quine, W. v. O. (1981): *Theories and Things*. Cambridge, MA: Belknap Press.

Quine, W. v. O. (1995): *From Stimulus to Science*. Cambridge, MA: Harvard University Press.

Ramachandran, V. S. (2006): *The Emerging Mind*. London: Profile Books.

Roth, G. (2003): *Fühlen, Denken, Handeln. Wie das Gehirn unser Verhalten steuert*. Frankfurt am Main: Suhrkamp.

Searle, J. (1997): *The Mystery of Consciousness*. New York: New York Review of Books.

Singer, W. (2003): *Ein neues Menschenbild? Gespräche über Hirnforschung*. Frankfurt am Main: Suhrkamp.

Thagard, P. (2005): *Mind: An Introduction to Cognitive Science*, 2nd edition. Cambridge, MA: The MIT Press.

Wallon, H. (1939): *La Psychologie de l'enfant de la naissance à 7 ans*. Paris: Boyrrelier.

Watson, J. and Crick, F. (1953): "A Structure for Deoxyribose Nucleic Acid." *Nature*, v. 171, pp. 737–738.

Weiner, N. and Shade, J. P. (1965): *Progress in Brain Research. Cybernetics of the Nervous System*. London/New York: Elsevier.

Whiting, H. T. A. (1984): *Human Motor Actions: Bernstein Reassessed*. Amsterdam: North Holland.

Zamora Bonilla, J. P. (2000): "El naturalismo científico de Ronald Giere y Philip Kitcher." *Revista de Filosofía*, v. 13, n. 24, pp. 169–190.

Francisco Rodriguez Valls
The Emotional Subject in Philosophy of Psychology: The Cases of Anxiety and Angst

Abstract: Two emotions are analyzed in this paper: anxiety and angst. The idea is held that anxiety is a common emotion in animals and human beings having as an object a response in the face of indeterminate dangers. Angst, on the other hand, is properly an emotion of human beings resulting from the consciousness of freedom. The consequences of that idea in philosophy and in methodology of psychology are also analyzed looking for and proposing an interdisciplinary and bidirectional connection between them.

Keywords: fear, anxiety, angst, philosophy of psychology, neuropsychology of emotion

Since the abandonment of behaviorism and the rise of cognitivism, studies on emotions have experienced exponential growth, both in terms of empirical research and popularization. Clearly, when the whole psychology is described in terms of objective behavior, as behaviorism would have it, what one could feel or stop feeling "inside" is unimportant, since it does not conform to the third-person perspective that the approach founded by J. B. Watson (1913) and deepened by F. B. Skinner (1984) intended to impose.

However, if importance is given to other internal factors, as suggested by cognitivism, *emotions* become relevant. Because it is common experience that some of the behavior is determined simply to feel "at home" with ourselves or, otherwise, to follow our most natural internal inclinations. The internal inclinations are critical elements to establishing behavior. There is, in this sense, a more powerful argument which I intend to use later, and one that understands emotion as a kind of knowledge or, at any rate, derived from a kind of knowledge.

Paper presented at the Conference on Philosophy of Psychology (*Jornadas sobre Filosofía de la Psicología*), held at the Universidad de A Coruña (Spain), Campus of Ferrol, in March 2014. The author gratefully acknowledges valuable observations and remarks from Juan Arana, Concepción Diosdado and, particularly, Wenceslao J. Gonzalez to various stages thereof.

1 Two Main Options: Bodily Impulses and Cognitive Actions

There are two main options present in the most common trends in contemporary theory of emotion. They consider emotions a) as impulses from corporeality but qualifying the James-Lange hypothesis and having A. Damasio as its most conspicuous representative, especially in his works *Descartes' Error* (1994) and *Looking for Spinoza* (2004), or b) as strictly cognitive actions, position supported by outstanding authors such as R. Lazarus (1991) or M. Nussbaum (2001). This holds true even if they are unconscious emotions, as in the case of impulses and instinctive tendencies.

Since the eighties, the study of emotions in psychology grew more important, and much more so as from the nineties. D. Goleman's (1995) *Emotional Intelligence* popularized the research on emotions conducted by experimental psychologists such as J. D. Mayer and P. Salovey and grew an interest for psychology to deepen in such psychic phenomena. To said interest in emotions also contributed the rectification done by the study of emotions to the overly logical, cybernetic model of artificial intelligence, thus disputing its claim that human intelligent behavior should work along the lines of a computer. Authors such as R. Picard (1997) contributed to the view that rather than turning a human being into a logical automaton, we should learn to design emotional computers, so they would interact with humans in a way more consistent with the way we humans tend to behave.

Thus, what exactly constitutes an intelligent behavior for living beings, and particularly for us humans, was brought into question. In parallel, thought was given to the role that emotions play in the ordinary life of psychological subjects, in general, and the members of our species, in particular. Experimental psychology and philosophy of psychology were flooded with questions of this sort: What is it we call an emotion? Can emotions successfully lead the behavior of a living thing? Are there emotions specific to humans and, if so, where do they come from? Because of these reasons we must consider animals, including human beings, as *emotional subjects:* behavior cannot be understood fully and satisfactorily without considering the emotions they entail and that, in quite a good measure, influence action.

I believe emotions to be a key field of interdisciplinary interaction between experimental psychology and philosophy of psychology, one which may prove very fruitful. The philosopher must imbibe the results of the experimental discipline and the experimental psychologist ought to consider the proposals from philosophy and submit them to experimentation or, where appropriate, apply them to a comprehensive understanding of facts established through experience.

Dissertating on interdisciplinarity has become commonplace in contemporary epistemology. I think that in some respects philosophy can contribute even more so to designing more holistic strategies in psychology for the interpretation of data, as well as provide a broader view of data obtained by experimental psychologists in their laboratories. In this regard, studies conducted in recent years by James Woodward (2000, 2012) on causation are exemplary, and may ensure a complementary relationship between philosophy and experimental psychology.

This paper aims to contribute to said interdisciplinary interaction by exposing the case of two emotions which, although I hold to be noticeably different from each other, are commonly related in the practice of psychology; namely, anxiety and angst. The study hereby conducted implies a set of elements related to the difference between a naturalistic view and a non-reductionistic one (which might well be called "humanistic") of philosophy of psychology. Those elements, which cannot be developed in full here, will hopefully reveal themselves once my presentation reaches its conclusion.

As from here, my presentation will deal with the following topics: fear and anxiety as natural emotions (section 2), the philosophical treatment of angst: the metaphysical experience of emotion (section 3), similarities and differences between anxiety and angst (section 4), a clarification: is angst a type of anxiety? (section 5), and conclusion (section 6): the irreducibility between angst and anxiety.

2 Fear and Anxiety as Natural Emotions

In all likelihood, the authors who have more thoroughly studied the neurobiological basis of fear and anxiety, better defining what they are, have been J. LeDoux (1996) regarding fear and its association to various regions of the brain amygdala, and J. A. Gray and N. McNaughton (2000) regarding anxiety and the septal-hippocampal system. Since there are no major contradictions in their results, their research can be regarded as mostly complementary.

An assumption underlying their research – and one endorsed by the philosophy of psychology since time immemorial – is that these emotions are shared by animals and humans. Therefore, the results obtained in animal research can be transposed to the case of human fear and anxiety. As a matter of fact, their experiments are conducted primarily through animal experimentation and observation of behavior resulting from brain injury in the various areas under their study.

Obviously, for ethical reasons, these experiments cannot be performed on humans. However, the case stands that their results can be extrapolated to humans. Neither fear nor anxiety are emotions actually human; rather, it is man, as a biological system, who contemplates then in his own phylogenetic system. Obviously, they may acquire special conditions in humans due to the strong influence culture exerts on us: in humans, specific forms of fear and anxiety exist which demand a specific analysis.

In this sense, fear and ordinary anxiety can be said to have a common evolutionary origin. Its purpose is survival of the individual or the species, through the impulse of mechanical behavior and through feelings which spontaneously arise to various natural stimuli, and whose selection has been made by chance. Fear and anxiety can be explained from the common parameters of neo-Darwinism, a statement with which the whole naturalistic psychology would agree.

Both fear and anxiety are emotions that alert the psychological subject about danger. The difference usually drawn being that *fear* happens in the face of a particular danger, ranging in intensity from uneasiness to panic, while *anxiety* refers to an undetermined danger, a danger present and a real possibility we ought to care about.

To help differentiate the emotion of fear from that of anxiety, the example usually provided in experimental psychology (again, derived from animal experimentation) is that of the mouse entering a place where a cat can either be seen or smelled. In the former case, the natural emotion is fear, and it triggers three possible reactions, depending on the closeness of the determined and present danger: flight, laying still so as to go unnoticed, or facing confrontation once spotted in a desperate attempt to save its life.

In the latter, the emotion is the anxiety triggered by the detection of cat odor. The presence of danger is uncertain, although it is possible, creating an uneasiness about what may or may not be, that is, about a possibility which escapes our control, which is an element of anxiety. Having an uneasiness whose resolution "escapes our control" is a characterization of the state of anxiety. We might say that anxiety is a type of fear pending on finding out whether its object does really exist or a resolution in respect of which it is a certain passive subject, since it depends, as per the example above, on the confirmation of the cat being (or not being) in the same room as the mouse.

Both fear and anxiety can indeed be reactions either appropriate or inappropriate in respect to its object. They can lead to unwarranted panic attacks and to anxiety disorders, the latter extensively analyzed in psychiatry. I will focus only on the warranted emotions, or the so to speak "healthy" emotions. In this field, psychiatry has possibly devoted more attention to the patient suffering the condition than to acquiring knowledge about the behavior of the healthy. And rightly so, since it aims not that much to describe but rather to heal. Our study focuses more on the description of healthy behavior than on the pathology therapy. It is a study in philosophy of psychology, and not psychiatry, which is being conducted here.

Real danger as opposed to one potential and undetermined, that's what differentiates fear from anxiety. Conceptually, they are different phenomena, being the "situational map" implied by each different. In the former, the situation is clear and supports a set of answers phylogenetically defined; in the latter, the situational map is incomplete and requires a more active use of the cognitive faculties to better determine and evaluate danger, and to adopt a specific behavior.

Given the right stimulus, fear instinctively triggers a behavior that is, in many animals, "mechanical" and "automatic." Given the right stimulus, anxiety seeks to determine whether there is effectively a danger, preparing itself cognitively to provide an answer. In short, *anxiety* depends more on cognitive instances than fear might. When facing a situation, it is only natural that fear may turn into uneasiness when danger is undetermined and, therefore, the answer is not ready nor automatically triggered. This openness is related to intelligent behavior, in as much as it is proper to it to investigate what it does not know, and create responses not previously held when it discovers the cause for such uneasiness.

The thesis which can be proposed for experimentation is that anxiety is more likely to be found in higher animals than in those others whose actions are determined in every possible way by instinct. That may actually make sense, since anxiety requires an array of possible answers that, to put it in Zubiri's (1986) terminology, presuppose a dis-adjustment between the living being and its environment. Contrary to fear, anxiety lends itself to a behavioral indeterminacy which makes it closer to intelligent behavior than to fear. This situation of cognitive differences, in which we will inquire further on the following sections, would also render it understandable that, as has been advanced, the neurobiological basis of fear and anxiety may be different.

3 The Philosophical Treatment of Angst: The Metaphysical Experience of Emotion

Emotions (or "passions," using the classical terminology) have always had a place in the history of philosophy, especially as an intimate part of the analysis of the human structure, the human soul, and always in close relationship to ethics. It is part of rational, philosophical psychology, to study the influence of *passion* in human behavior.

A consideration which from ancient times enlightens its anthropological status is the claim that passions are morally indifferent, i.e., neither good nor bad *per se*. They are held, then, to be part of the animal confines of concupiscence or irascible appetites, while the part of the soul which directly refers to the good is neither of them, but the will. Being so, the will must control the appetites and use them to its advantage or constrain them, so as to advance towards the good and reject the bad. That is the position of Thomas Aquinas, who devoted an entire section of his *Summa Theologiae*, the *prima secundae*, to thoroughly address this issue.

A change in the ontological perspective on emotions (a departure from the way in which they were addressed in the past) springs precisely from the specific treatment of angst in S. Kierkegaard's *The Concept of Angst* ([1844] 1981). A change it is, because it presents a sentiment which is properly human by structure, which also implies that the response to it is indeed ethically relevant. And it is so to the utmost, since it may determine what might be considered an "authentic existence," as opposed to an "inauthentic" one (and therefore, not human, or, in other words, a failed human existence from the ontological point of view).

It is Kierkegaard's indisputable merit to let us see angst as a special case: it is not that man – out of his peculiar condition – may transform an animal feeling by transcending it, as it is the case with many other feelings, but that angst reveals itself as human from its inception, and as uniquely human. We may promptly wonder about the psychic origin of this emotion. We may wonder about the validity of the discovery of the Danish thinker, and especially about the *origin* that can be given to the emotion of angst.

In Kierkegaard we find the basic concepts which would be further explored by other angst theorists in the twentieth century, such as M. Heidegger ([1927] 2006 and [1929] 2006): and J. P. Sartre (1946). In them the following questions will become clear, questions which I structure on the basis of three ideas, so that their positions remain as points that I will explain later. I consider them to be crucial to the topic I want to address. 1) Angst is solely a human emotion, that can be defined as "vertigo in the face of freedom," 2) angst opens up in the presence of the possibility or, according to Heidegger, in the chasm of nothingness, when the only resource the human being can resort to is his own finitude, and 3) angst is an emotion that refers to the future, to the entire future of the subject in angst, and derives from the knowledge of having taken himself in his own hands, that is, from the responsibility of building himself up, of being something, or the possibility of failure and nothingness. Let us consider these three issues separately.

Proceeding in an orderly manner with the three issues outlined, we firstly find that the poetic image that both Kierkegaard and Heidegger establish to account for angst is the situation of the subject on the brink of abyss. That abyss, conceptually established, is none other than freedom, i.e., the fact that one depends upon himself and his own action to prevent falling. The condition of being free, of risking being or not being for having oneself and humankind in one's own hands produce a feeling of dizziness, narrowing, occlusion, of *angst*, which is exactly what angst itself is: self-knowledge as something which is at stake, and of one's own condition as the possibility which builds and causes a feeling.

It's a feeling that opens to the undetermined, and that makes you fear for yourself: one is at stake in free action and in his own choice of himself, having his own judgment as his sole guide. In these circumstances, and being aware of human contingency and limitation, fear for yourself and for the authenticity of everything which depends upon yourself is fully justified. The discovery of freedom exists only in what is human and, therefore, angst does not occur in any other animal species.

The discovery of freedom is what is specific to the human spirit, when he sees himself as his own cause, as a product of himself. Consequently, he escapes what Kierkegaard calls "naturalness," i.e., the spontaneity of the animal living in a circle of time whose axis is the present. In this sense, angst is not intended for the survival of the individual and the species, but for its authenticity, i.e., it has more to do with an ontological type of authenticity than with staying in time in mere terms of better or worse adaptation to the environment.

Secondly, when man discovers his own freedom he discovers it as essential, and as a phenomenon against which all is irrelevant, all appears as nothing: nothing is important other than the self facing itself. I would suggest, though possibly unnecessarily, that this position has nothing to do with a solipsistic attitude: it is not that the subject thinks only of himself and his sole fulfillment, regardless of the fate of all reality. That would be a question prior to that determination, which might be called selfish rather than solipsistic. And that is not the case. It is rather a question about the *condition of possibility* of my mission in the world and my meaning against the very existence of the world: I have only a mission in the world if I am able to be myself and, therefore, to exercise authentically my freedom.

The problem of freedom is that, to bridge the gulf of responsibility towards oneself, one can only tap into his own finitude. This contributes to angst as an emotion, since it raises the question of whether one will be able to succeed when facing his own possibility. It might certainly be possible to close our eyes to the abyss and build a banal existence, or jump into the abyss and, by committing suicide, avoid all responsibility. But those who accept angst, and take care of themselves, and care of the world as a result, those are the ones who are engaged in their human condition and live it bravely. In this sense, the discovery and understanding of freedom and of one's finitude, and therefore feeling angst at some point, defines human existence taken to the full or, at least, one that is aware of itself and of the true reality of the world in which the subject lives.

Thirdly, the future is the time axis to which angst opens us up to, i.e., angst gets to open us to the "totalization" (this word is key) of the subject's entire existence, presented as a project to be performed. All my potential I, what I can be and what will eternally constitute me as my reference, passes before my eyes and presents itself as a mission which affects my being and the being of the world. It is not a distant future that does not depend on me, but precisely the realization that what I will be depends on what I want myself to be and on the project being carried out on myself: angst presents all my time before me, and offers me the opportunity to develop it if I want to accept that possibility. What affects me is the "possibility as my own possibility" and, seeing that it is mine and that it is indeterminate, having to be determined by me, is what raises the responsibility that opens the feeling of angst.

The human being presents itself then as a project of existence, as having himself in contingent hands, which must risk in an existential plan that may succeed or fail.

A fourth issue should be clarified to avoid arriving at false conclusions. One thing is the feeling of angst being exclusively human and having the discovery of freedom as its source, and quite another the fact that, to be human, we had to be constantly in angst and, if you were not, humanity would be lost. In fact, that is not the case, and it has been Heidegger who has especially elaborated this issue of the rarity of the feeling of angst: angst is a feeling which only occasionally occurs in humans.

No one normal is eternally in angst. You cannot even say that, empirically, it occurs in all human beings, since not all live an authentic existence. Angst appears when I am aware of my own possibility, when I make the possibility mine and it becomes determined as an existential project. Therefore, angst is being put into practice, it fades and dissolves itself on the day-to-day building of myself. Only when the project is in crisis, when the possibility ceases to appear as mine, angst resurfaces strongly to establish the re-routing of the subject itself towards an end which the self believes to be ontologically valuable and which justifies the success of its own existence.

4 Similarities and Differences between Anxiety and Angst

Once the last two points have been established, a comparison, even if cursory, of the main similarities and differences between anxiety and angst would now seem proper. And the first similarity is that both are actual *emotions*. Admittedly, a precise approach to a definition of emotion requires a certain amplitude. But please allow me to simplify, since this is not the specific issue we have to deal with here.

Anxiety and angst are feelings which have, as any feeling, their endorsement in objective bodily sensations, and which expect the outcome of a certain action. As with any emotion, its presence can empirically be detected by means of organic quantitative measurements and, also, they entail an impulse to action. In this sense, emotions are not passive, they are not "passions," but they expect some action performed by the psychological subject.

Second, the reference of both anxiety and angst is something undetermined: a potential danger in the case of anxiety, and oneself's possibility in the case of angst. Both also have a special relationship with knowledge, since anxiety seeks to determine the object of danger and angst to determine one's own existential project. They also coincide in that anxiety occurs when there is either a fearful expectation of losing an advantageous situation, or an expectation of potentially improving one's situation: to the extent that the solution does not depend on himself, we can say that the subject is anxious. In the case of angst, uncertainty arises from the subject himself being at stake of winning or losing himself and, in this case, the action does depend on him.

However, to be exact, the results also depend on the particular set of factors that Ortega y Gasset termed "circumstance": "I am myself and my circumstance and, if I don't save it, I won't save myself either" ([1914] 2004). As it is well known, those circumstances comprise everything in between the subject's historical situation and the possibilities offered by our own corporeality. But that's more of a difference than a similarity.

The last statement makes us delve into the differences we may find between these two emotions. Certainly both of them refer to an unknown danger. But anxiety aims to identify the dangerous object itself, whether or not the cat is in the room (as in the example given in the second section), while angst aims to determine the nature of the subject himself or, better, build on a plan and design the subject's existential project.

Note that both activities are of a cognitive type: to determine or know something. But while anxiety can solve the mystery by means of instinctive procedures, as most animals do, the knowledge that produces angst needs to know how the subject is objectively and which is the end to which it should be re-directed. I mean, it is a knowledge that cannot be less than self-conscious and aware of one's own status as a subject, as well as of the structure it has.

Right because of that, the type of cognitive exercise undertaken differs in anxiety and angst. For the former, we only need a working memory until the object is determined on the axis of the present. Angst, however, requires to totalize the lifetime of the subject as a project and, therefore, its axis lies in the future: only the future will determine whether the project of myself that has been performed was successful or did fail. As regards to animal anxiety, there are automatic, unconscious repair mechanisms for imbalance. In the case of angst, though, it can only be remedied by exercising the conscience. That brings us to a conflicting point philosophically speaking, since, depending on the solution chosen, the resulting psychology will be of one kind or another and, consequently, there will be a certain vision of the human in general or quite another.

There is an observation to be made related to the nature of emotions and specifically their origin. From an evolutionary point of view, an emotion is a kind of subjective feeling arising from a phylogenetically successful behavior. In *The Expression of Emotions in Man and Animals* (1872), Darwin argued that the origin of those emotions was the repetition of different successful actions by individuals and, therefore, it did have knowledge somehow as its origin – even if it was just testing by trial and error.

Darwin's interpretation of the above is controversial from the synthetic theory of evolution's point of view, which turns what was (behavior-reinforcing) knowledge into a conduct coded by chance and subsequently selected because of its adaptive advantages. I do not intend to enter the debate, since the issue lies beyond the limits set for this work. But it is right to assert that, while anxiety may work within the neo-Darwinian model, the same can in no way be predicated of angst. On the contrary, it must be said that, in the case of angst, the knowledge of the subject's freedom is the conscious cause of the unconscious emergence of the emotion of angst.

In my view, only this may explain angst as a proper human emotion which, as Kierkegaard claimed, is rarely dealt with in psychology. In this respect, allow me to express a personal perplexity supporting Kierkegaard's claim. In the years I have spent on the study of emotions, I have had the chance to consult a few manuals of psychology of motivation and emotion. It has always struck me that, when they deal (usually at the end of thick volumes) with those emotions termed as "self-reflexive" emotions, theoretically corresponding to those linked to higher knowledge, they mention, for instance, pride or fault, which somehow could also be found in higher animals. But they fail to mention angst, which, according to contemporary philosophy, traditionally is the characteristic emotion leading to human self-possession.

Psychological experimentation must absolutely be made to interact with philosophical reflection, so as to avoid deficiencies like those I have just outlined. I consider this an urgent task, so that interdisciplinarity is not false and one-way only – from psychology to philosophy; indeed, the reverse is possible and effective. Therefore, I think we must make another urgent clarification, which I will discuss in the next section.

5 A Clarification: Is Angst a Type of Anxiety?

The psychologists I have studied do not deal with *angst*. Could the reason for that be that they consider it just a case of anxiety, a type of more intense anxiety? I guess that's exactly right. And it would be justified by the similarity of what is bodily felt in both instances. That reason warrants reconsideration; as a matter of fact, the proposal to review this issue purports to be the main contribution made by this paper. The confusion, I think, is a confusion of principles, and these I think should be made explicit.

The human being functions as a unit, but he is a complex entity. We must analyze the different layers that make up his structure. Philosophically, as I stated earlier, the classics consider passions as common to animals and men. That is essentially correct in most cases, as long as we realize that the specifics of what is human (e.g., the self-conscious exercise of the will) can lead to, and be the source of, emotions with distinctive human characteristics.

To wit, an emotion extensively considered by psychologists and philosophers. Who would deny that a dog feels love for its master? That is beyond doubt. The sense in which the term "love" is used in this case, though, clearly differs from the distinctive human love which implies the conscious construction of a shared future. Does the term *love* refer here to an emotion shared by dogs and humans, or is it simply a metaphor that relates them and which is used improperly? In the case of the dog there is submission and gratitude; in that of the human being, self-giving and freedom.

As Max Scheler understood well on establishing a gradation of feelings in his *Ethics* (1916), there is a specifically human dimension of emotion and value that applies only to man, and not to any other kind of animal. That, which does not come up in the customary handbooks of psychology, is what should be noted, limiting ourselves here to angst and anxiety, as those are the issues we are dealing with.

Thus, it could then be said that angst is to anxiety what human love is to a dog's love. Therefore, if both phenomena were accounted for when dealing with love generally, likewise dealing with anxiety would give account of angst, since the latter would only be the human form of anxiety – only more intense as an emotion. Well, that would be in my opinion a reductionism that must be overcome, because it leads to much confusion. In this special case rests the difference between a purely naturalistic psychology and a so to speak "non-reductionist psychology," which I propose to refer to as a "humanistic psychology."

Where would lie any potential difference in the field of emotion? At this point, we might appeal to abstract and difficult concepts of philosophical anthropology. But, since we are talking of philosophy of psychology, let me bring up a recent psychological theory reputedly very useful to understand the issue at hand. I refer to recent theories of *dual processes*. The most important book published about it so far, and one describing the state of the art, was edited by J. Evans and K. Frankish (2009) and published by Oxford University Press, entitled *In Two Minds: Dual Processes and Beyond*.

According to the theories of dual processes, two types of cognitive systems coexist in humans: one related to rapid and automatic action, allegedly unconscious and evolutionarily ancient, and another related to slow and conscious action, evolutionarily recent. These two cognitive systems usually complement each other to perfection, rarely colliding in a substantial way, and they form in humans a complex and well-designed structure that allows us to appropriately act in our environment. The neuroanatomy of the rapid-response system would be located in the primitive brain, while the new system would roughly correspond to the neocortex.

Evans and Frankish's book only tangentially deals with emotions. But still, I think the overall structure of the cognitive system they display can be applied to these psychic phenomena. The rapid and automatic action we may associate to instinct implies an impulse for action, which involves bodily features essentially identical to animal emotions. The slow and conscious action involves a feedback in the body, placing it as the cause of new emotions, this time properly human. It is in this scheme where you can distinguish animal emotion from human emotion: animal emotion is born in the system which might be called system I, the primitive one, and exerts its influence on system II, reaching the neocortex and setting the subject into action. The slow and conscious action, in turn, sends its impulses to the primitive brain, causing the body substrate of animal emotions. Were this the case, we could "feel" the same things, have similar emotions (e. g., love), but of a radically different causal origin. One would be caused by the animal instinct; the other by consciousness, being truly human. One would be a thrill of a living being; the other, exclusive of the living being defined as human.

This hypothesis has some experimental support in the case of fear. While working on the emotion of fear, J. LeDoux (2002, pp. 108–133) found that, regarding the visual system, there are two circuits: one goes from the optic nerve to the visual cortex, where that information is consciously processed, and the other directly leads from the optic nerve to the amygdala, which is the body part responsible for the emotion of fear. It has been found, additionally, that there is a direct connection between the visual cortex and the amygdala, so that there exists a mutual influence between those parts of the brain, which is obviously patent. What this American neurobiologist has done with fear could also be done, I think, with anxiety and angst. I do not know if the hypothesis I'm advancing has undergone experimental testing, so as to explore the relationship between the neocortex and the septo-hippocampal system. In my view, the verification of the theory of dual processes referred to emotions would warrant a study like the one I propose here.

Applying this to anxiety and angst, I think they should not be differentiated simply by their sensitive similarities, but by the causes defining each of them, and which turn them into different objects of study. From the point of view of sensation, there are obvious similarities, such as breathlessness and narrowing; from a causal perspective, though, they would totally differ: in anxiety the cause would be system I, while in angst it would plainly be system II.

This allows us to speak of the *causality* exerted by emotion upon consciousness, and also of that exerted by consciousness on body instances so as to awaken sensitive emotions. If we were to spouse a conclusion on why psychologists do not openly treat angst, it would be this: they identify the subjective states of anxiety and angst, and regard them as alike, without further inquiry into the underlying cause of the feeling. From our standpoint, in no way can angst be confused with anxiety, as discussed in the last two sections, despite both emotions sharing sensitive similarities.

6 Conclusion: Irreducibility between Angst and Anxiety

The issue at hand has methodological implications in the field of psychology which explain why anxiety is a subject often treated by what we might call "naturalistic psychology," while angst is dealt with only within the minority camp which I have proposed to call "humanistic psychology." Since anxiety admits an evolutionary explanation, which encompasses all living things, humans included, it is apt for experimentation, and allows for drawing conclusions from experiments with animals, in a way that humanistic psychology cannot aspire to.

Obviously, experiments cannot be performed – unless placed under many limitations – with humans. In this sense, it is much more difficult to empirically establish the specific difference between animal and human psychology and argue, as some epistemologists do, that consciousness or ethical value cannot be easily explained from an evolutionary point of view. I refer to the doubts expressed about it in the recent and controversial book of the philosopher of science T. Nagel, *Mind and Cosmos*, published by Oxford University Press in 2012.

Naturalistic psychology implies that human emotion is a further stage in evolutionary development and that, therefore, it can be explained basically by the same mechanisms that explain animal emotion. Humanistic psychology, on the contrary, sees a specificity in human emotion that makes it irreducible to any other more primary type of emotion. Angst as such is not a "ghost emotion" or a pseudo-problem, even if it is a human experience of a metaphysical value beyond evolutionary value, and one which deserves to be studied by a science seeking to account for every mental phenomenon, albeit exclusively human.

Personally, I do not know about experiments being conducted on angst. Rather, it seems to me that, as I have already pointed out, there is a confusion between those two emotions in psychology.

Humanistic psychology being always open to the naturalistic, the former consideration could be understood as an aid to experimental psychology from psychological positions closer to philosophy, to help it better understand the nature and specificity of the psychology of the human subject. This appeal to the complementarity of the two treatments precisely accounts for our talking here about anxiety and angst, within the reference framework set, which is not that of experimental psychology but, rather, that of philosophy of psychology.

The relationship between anxiety and angst is one more element in the wider debate between naturalism and humanism in today's philosophy of science generally, which has the overall aim to show either the reduction of man to, or his transcendence of, the spontaneity of nature. Humanistic psychology shows how, in the case of humans, not all phenomena can be derived directly from evolutionary stages: while anxiety plays a distinctive role in the survival of the individual and the species, angst only plays a role for existence in plenitude, understood under all cultural conditions that are irrelevant to the biological birth – growth – death cycle.

Angst makes sense when we talk not of adaptation to the environment, but of man overcoming the natural cycle. Therefore, it belongs to the realm of culture, in as much as culture is born when man is born. Furthermore, from my point of view, the origin of those two emotions is different: in anxiety, it is the emotion which motivates hazard identification; in angst, it is the knowledge of my free condition and the need for setting up an existential project under finite conditions. Therefore, I believe both to be mutually irreducible, which raises the perennial problem of dualism or monism in the structure of the human being. While this is a fundamental issue in philosophy, it is much more general than the problem that has brought us here.

References

Aquinas, Th. (1950): *Summa theologiae*. Turin/Rome: Marietti.
Damasio, A. (1994): *Descartes' Error: Emotion, Reason and the Human Brain*. London: Picador.
Damasio, A. (2004): *Looking for Spinoza: Joy, Sorrow, and the Feeling Brain*. London: Vintage.
Darwin, Ch. (1872): *The Expression of the Emotions in Man and Animals*. London: John Murray.
Evans, J. and Frankish, K. (eds.) (2009): *In Two Minds: Dual Processes and Beyond*. Oxford: Oxford University Press.
Goleman, D. (1995): *Emotional Intelligence*. New York: Bantam.
Gray, J. A. and McNaughton, N. (2000): *Neuropsychology of Anxiety: An Inquiry into the Functions of the Septo-hippocampal System*, 2nd edition. Oxford: Oxford University Press.
Heidegger, M. ([1927] 2006): *Sein und Zeit*. Tübingen: Niemeyer.
Heidegger, M. ([1929] 2006): *Was ist Metaphysik?* Frankfurt am Main: Vittorio Klostermann.
Kierkegaard, S. (1844): *Begrebet Angest*. Copenhagen: C. A. Reitzel. Translated into English as Kierkegaard, S. (1981): *The Concept of Angst*, edited by Reider Thomte, Princeton: Princeton University Press.
Lazarus, R. (1991): *Emotion and Adaptation*. Oxford: Oxford University Press.
LeDoux, J. (1996): *The Emotional Brain*. New York: Simon and Schuster.
LeDoux, J. (2002): "El aprendizaje del miedo: De los sistemas a las sinapsis." In: Morgado, I. (ed.): *Emoción y conocimiento*, pp. 108–134. Barcelona: Tusquets.
Nagel, T. (2012): *Mind and Cosmos*. Oxford: Oxford University Press. (Spanish translation and foreword by Francisco Rodríguez Valls (2014): *La mente y el cosmos*. Madrid: Biblioteca Nueva.)
Nussbaum, M. (2001): *Upheavals of Thought*. Cambridge: Cambridge University Press.
Ortega y Gasset, J. ([1914]/2004): *Meditaciones del Quijote*. In: Ortega y Gasset, J.: *Obras completas*, vol. 1. Madrid: Taurus/Fundación Ortega y Gasset.
Picard, R. W. (1997): *Affective Computing*. Cambridge, MA: The MIT Press.
Sartre, J. P. (1946): *L'existentialisme est un humanisme*. Paris: Éditions Nagel.
Scheler, M. (1916): *Der Formalismus in der Ethik und die materiale Wertethik*. Freiburg: Max Niemeyer.
Skinner, F. B. (1984): "The Operational Analysis of Psychological Terms." *Behavioral and Brain Sciences*, v. 7, n. 4, pp. 547–581.

Watson, J. B. (1913): "Psychology as the Behaviorist Views It." *Psychological Review*, v. 20, pp. 158–177.
Woodward, J. (2000): "Explanation and Invariance in Special Sciences." *British Journal of Philosophy of Science*, v. 51, pp. 197–254.
Woodward, J. (2012): "Causation: Interactions between Philosophical Theories and Psychological Research." *Philosophy of Science*, v. 79, n. 5, pp. 961–972.
Zubiri, X. (1986): *Sobre el hombre* (edited by I. Ellacuría). Madrid: Alianza Editorial.

Part IV: **From Psychology to Psychiatry: Limits of Computational Psychology and the Role of Causes as Interventions in Psychiatry**

Pedro Chacón
The Limits of Computational Psychology in J. Fodor

Abstract: There is no doubt that Fodor has been one of the most influential psychology philosophers in recent decades. He is also one of the most controversial. A heterodox disciple of Chomsky and Putnam, his theories in favour of innatism and modularity of mind, and his confrontation with Darwinian adaptationism and evolutionary psychology, have greatly marked the development of philosophical reflections about the possibility of a scientific psychology. His computational and representational theory was presented as the only one able to assure its achievement. However, Fodor never proposed it as a general theory of the human mind. This paper presents a revision of the limits he established, throughout his writings, for a computational psychology, including the ability to explain the most relevant processes, and perhaps the most interesting ones, of our cognitive activities. The reasons that take him to establish these are also analysed.

Keywords: Fodor, computational psychology, modularity of mind, functionalism, philosophy of psychology

There is a general consensus that in recent years functionalist theories have occupied a prominent or even predominant place in contemporary philosophy of mind and cognitive psychology. Just as widespread is the other consensus on the diversity, or at times confrontation, which must be acknowledged between the different theoretical proposals included in this generic term. Since the computational metaphor first appeared, shedding light on new paths for psychological research, many of the efforts in philosophy have focused on revising and refining the new theoretical model to make it more useful for empirical research and make it theoretically compatible with such unavoidable phenomena as consciousness, intentionality, *qualia* or mental causation.

For some philosophers, however, the problems of the incompatibility of the computational model with these phenomena were so important that they became good reasons for rejecting it. Even Hilary Putnam (1960 and 1988), the promoter of the functionalist theory of mind, felt obliged to reject it years later, considering it incompatible with an externalist conception of meaning.

1 Coordinates of Jerry Fodor's Proposal

Jerry Fodor (1968, 1975, 1983, and 2000) is one of the philosophers within the functionalist framework who have remained faithful to the computational model, considering it to be the only one which can be used to justify the autonomy of psychological explanations and the configuration of psychology as an independent science. Fodor, a disciple of Putnam and defender of Chomsky's innatism, has been controversially defending the need to combine a computational theory of mind with a representational one for years. His theoretical proposals have remained coherent, integrating concepts related to the philosophy of language with those concerning mental processes and states, and he is considered one of the most avid defenders of a cognitive psychology guided by the computational model referred to above.

Nevertheless, although perhaps for this very reason, hardly any of the theses that make up J. Fodor's theory on psychological explanation have been generally accepted and all of them have been sharply criticised. This is what happened with his vindication of a language of thought; with his Cartesian defence of the existence of representations loaded with semantic content; with his proposed modular conception of the human mind, apparently involving a renewed theory of the faculties; with his wide-ranging innatist concept of the cognitive capacities; with his ideas on strict content; with his concept of functional equivalence in the fullest sense of the word; with his adaptationist anti-Darwinism ...

Fodor himself, always controversial, has never stopped using his well-honed dialectic talents against other concepts, even those which might be considered close to his own approach. In this context, it is significant that the titles of Fodor's latest writings tend to signal the errors he intends to reveal in them: "Connectionism and the Problem of Systematicity: Why Smolensky's Solution Still Doesn't Work" (1990), *Concepts. Where Cognitive Science Went Wrong* (1998), *The Mind Doesn't Work that Way* (2000), and *What Darwin Got Wrong* (2010).

But this is not just a question of publicly airing his views or a mature critical attitude when faced with the criticism and opposing alternatives which have continued to grow. Back in 1968 in the Preface to his book on psychological explanation, after acknowledging the difficulties of the problems posed, Fodor admitted that he had arrived "at some views about what theories of psychological explanation *won't* work, however, and these include a number that are currently fashionable" (Fodor 1968, p. VII).

In fact, his philosophical career is defined to a great extent by his permanent struggle against the same demons, in particular logical behaviourism and the different forms of anti-mentalist materialism, which are the object of his criticism in this early book and continue to be so in his later works. And to behavioural and neurological reductionism he then added the externalist conception of meaning, environmentalism, semantic holism and adaptationist Darwinism.

Fodor seems to prove here what Bergson said early last century, when he claimed that the first step any philosopher takes is to reject some things, although this may later change to acceptance in some cases, but very seldom to denial. Although perhaps it would be more appropriate only to recognize in him a characteristic trait of the historical development of contemporary philosophy of mind: its markedly controversial character, and at the same time endorse the defence of the epistemic value of controversies in the advancement of knowledge, just as Mauricio Dascal (1995 and 1998) has been doing for years.

2 Internal Demarcation of Fodor's Model of Psychological Explanation

Fodor's criticism of other models of psychological explanation and the criticism of his approach by alternative theories in the philosophy of language and of mind have been the object of several monographic studies and continue to generate useful theoretical discussions (Dennett 1991, Loewer and Rey 1991, Segal 1996, and Wilson 2004). In this paper, however, I will not deal with any of these, but instead with a subject which in my opinion has not received due attention in spite of its relevance: the internal demarcation which Fodor establishes for his proposed model of psychological explanation, i.e., the boundaries and limits which mark the scope of the computational and representational theory of the human mind.

Our aim here will thus be to analyse the criteria and reasons justifying this self-restriction on the scope of the validity of this explanatory functionalist model by one of the philosophers who collaborated most closely in its rise and predominance. This is also an essential feature of the formulation itself of the theory Fodor devised, and an ever-present aspect of all his writings on this theme. For this reason, our analysis will follow the chronological order of publication to facilitate a better understanding of the modulations and extensions to this setting of limits.

At the beginning of his *Psychological Explanation. An Introduction to Philosophy of Psychology*, published in 1968, Fodor had already warned that in it he would only refer to a particular type of psychological explanation, which he identified generically as that intended to explain the behaviour of organisms according to their internal psychological state. This first position seems to include an important restriction affecting the theoretical proposals of the explanatory model: the need for it to include the existence and causal efficacy of the mental or psychic internal states of organisms. This was the only type of mentalist explanation which Fodor focused on to defend it from those who considered it erroneous, and to explain its conditions of possibility.

But, as Fodor himself admits, this approach is more appropriate for questions related to learning theory and perception than to other relevant wider areas of psychological theories and their applications, such as social psychology and developmental psychology. In addition, the type of psychological explanation analysed by Fodor, not only in this work but also throughout his later writings, is not put forward as the only relevant one if our aim is to be able to consider different human behaviours. There are other types of psychological explanations whose validity is not questioned, such as those which refer to "statistical regularities, to developmental norm, and so on," but about which Fodor admits in this same book "I shall have nothing at all to say" (1968, p. VIII).

Before going any further, perhaps we should emphasize here Fodor's general attitude to philosophy and psychology, and in particular to the way in which the relationship between them should be considered. The subtitle of the book cited above gives us a clue. This is a book on "philosophy of psychology," not on "philosophy of mind." In his opinion, a conceptual-linguistic analysis of the meaning and correct use of psychological terms are not needed here. This is an approach which Fodor has always kept faith with: in one of his latest books, published exactly fifty years after the first one, *Lot 2. The Language of Thought Revisited*, he still maintains that he did not see his philosophical project as

> a project in analytic philosophy, if that means analyzing either words, or concepts, or their uses. As far as I can tell, such projects have always failed, and my guess is that they always will (Fodor 2008, p. 22).

Fodor does not limit himself to rejecting logical behaviourism and the identification of mentalism with dualism that he attributes to Ryle and to Wittgenstein. He also adopts a very different approach to the work of the philosopher in the context of psychology. Instead of being limited to demonstrating e.g., the illegitimacy of a psychological explanation which implies confusion between motive and cause, in his opinion the task of philosophy compared with psychology should be similar to what happens in other more advanced sciences, i.e., aiming to describe the character and structure of the theories put forward and clarify the epistemological suppositions assumed in them.

The results of a philosophy of psychology would be those of a "psychological metatheory" (Fodor 1968, p. XIV), in Fodor's own words, in which speculative reflection is combined with empirical research and with theories put forward by the psychologists themselves. What is involved here, then, is an approach to the philosophy of a particular science without imposing homogeneously on it the general directives which supposedly characterize all scientific knowledge. As he continued to affirm in a much later text,

> There is probably no better way to decide what is methodologically permissible in science than by investigating what successful science requires (Fodor 1981b, p. 123).

As a result, the regulatory ideal of the philosophy of psychology devised by Fodor would be to justify an explanatory, rigorously scientific model of its own for psychology, while still guaranteeing its autonomy and protecting it from being reduced to explanatory types found in other sciences.

Seven years later, those initial, generic restrictions referring to Fodor's interest in a specific focus and psychological type of explanation were transformed into a reasoned rationale as to why the demands of a single explanatory model of scientific psychology impose severe restrictions on its scope of applicability. *The Language of Thought* (1975) is widely recognized to be the fundamental work in which Fodor explains his computational theory of mind (CTM) underlining its essential complementarity with a representational theory of mind (RTM) and vindicating the existence of an internal language. In this work he maintains that cognitive processes can only be adequately described as computational processes on symbolic mental representations, loaded with semantic content.

This conviction forms the central thesis of Fodor's functionalism and continues unaltered throughout the whole of his later philosophical development. As an example we can take the following statement in *Psychosemantics:*

> when one thinks about the constitution of mental processes, the connection between the idea that they are computational and the idea that there is a language of thought becomes immediately apparent (Fodor 1987, p. 25).

But what I want to emphasize here is that ever since he began to formulate the need for a computational and representational model of mind, Fodor has not limited himself only to vindicating the achievements and advantages which might be expected of this theoretical approach, but he has also repeatedly taken care to recognize clearly and explicitly its insurmountable limitations, identifying extensive, relevant fields of human behaviour and psychological processes which cannot be explained within its framework.

In coherence with the above approach to the philosophy of psychology, Fodor begins by assuming the most plausible theories on cognitive processes and recognizing as a fact that it is these theories which in different ways coincide in considering the processes as computational. As he admitted years later when he was working on *The Language of Thought* he was not aware that he was pressing for a new idea, but rather he was simply expounding what seemed to him a general consensus on the emerging interdisciplinary field of cognitive sciences and the topic of how minds work (Fodor 2008, pp. 3–4). As all computation implies a medium in which it is carried out, according to Fodor we must recognize a system of internal representations. What the mental processes compute are mental representations.

The task facing the philosophy of psychology is therefore defined as follows: to describe the representational system presumed to be the medium in which computational processes are carried out. And the path or strategy for carrying out this description can only be to attempt to infer this system from details of the psychological theories which are most likely to be true. It is, then, the prolificacy of the theories that the contemporary cognitive orientation of psychology has devised to explain the mental processes of organisms, and the fact that this orientation assumes a computational idea of these processes, that allows us in philosophical terms to legitimately defend the existence of internal representations, mentalism, and a functionalist response to the traditional body-mind problem. But that does not ensure that it is beyond dispute or permanent over time. Our philosophical loyalty to these convictions will be just as provisional as the validity of the psychological theories on which they are based. Its future will be linked to their destiny.

3 Language of Thought and Psychological Explanations

There are four areas where Fodor believes that he can demonstrate more clearly in *The Language of Thought* that psychological explanations presuppose a computational and representational theory of mind (CRTM): deliberated decision-making, concept learning, sensory perceptions and psycholinguistic processes. In his view, in these areas we inevitably have to recognize the existence of a private language, a mental language which cannot be identified with any natural learned language. In all these areas, mental states must be considered as relationships between the organism and its internal representations. In turn, causal relationships between mental states are adapted to the computational principles applicable to the representations.

Assuming this approach, Fodor has no doubt that cognitive psychology is the one in which human beings do our best for the rationality of mental processes at large. But he immediately adds that this descriptive model of psychological processes imposes severe restrictions. It is only applicable to those specific cases which can be adjusted to a formal system and those which fulfil a series of conditions:

> a) that there be some general and plausible procedure for assigning formulae of the system to states of the organism; b) that causal sequences which determine propositional attitudes turn out to be derivations under the assignment; c) that for each propositional attitude of the organism there is some causal state of the organism such that (c1) the state is interpretable as a relation to a formula of the formal system, and (c2) being in the state is nomologically necessary and sufficient for (or contingently identical to) having the propositional attitude (Fodor 1975, pp. 198–199).

According to Fodor, these conditions lead to limits to his proposed research programme. The mental states for which a psychological explanation can be given would only be those which are the result of the computation of internal representations. But evidently not all can be described in this way. Many of our ideas and events may be the effect of conscious or unconscious inferential psychological processes, but others may be derived from physiological causes. Cognitive psychology has to assume that there are mental phenomena which it cannot explain, as they are not computational. The problem is that some of these phenomena which are outside the scope of its domain are far from marginal or irrelevant. On the contrary, according to Fodor himself,

> some of the most systematic, and some of the most interesting kinds of mental events may be among those about whose etiology cognitive psychologists can have nothing at all to say (Fodor 1975, p. 200).

This disappointing conviction as to how little psychology can offer on the most relevant and significant themes of human existence persists in Fodor's mind and he links it to the general outcome which we can expect from the sciences in this context, for as he was to declare years later he was afraid that

> in psychology we can find a particular case of the general principle widely held in science, that the more interesting a phenomenon is for human beings, the less it seems to be something which can be examined scientifically (interview with García-Albea 1990, p. 18).

The psychological questions which Fodor mentions in *The Language of Thought* and which the computational model cannot cope with include: a) the aetiology of sensations, i.e., the causal explanation of our sensory representations from stimuli. These interactions are causal, not functional or computational and constitute the traditional object of psychophysical study differentiating it from cognitive psychology; b) perhaps also many of the mental activities which we evaluate as more creative and original, those which do not seem to be the result of processes governed by rules. Cognitive psychology can only engage in an explanation of mental states which have mental causes, but there are others, including very valuable ones, which may sometimes be the result of non-rational causes, as not every mental event has a mental cause (Fodor 1975, p. 203); and c) others which are the result of causal interactions between mental states, but not because of their semantic content, such as e.g., the undeniable effects exerted by the emotions on our perceptions and beliefs. Here again the explanatory tools of cognitive psychology are seen to be inadequate and a possible explanation must be left to psychobiology.

Fodor concludes his reflections on the limitations of the CRTM by showing that it is impossible to define them *a priori*. Restricted to the processes which can be analysed depending on semantic relationships between representations, this theory can be extended to all rational processes as he considers that these are identified with those which have mental causes. But how far it can occupy this domain will only be determined by empirical study and research. As a result of these restrictions, what can be achieved by a computational and representative approach will be considered disappointingly little by many. For Fodor, this is the price to be paid for a psychology which attempts to be scientific and not reductive. In any case, he adds,

> it would be a pretty irony if it proved to exclude quite a lot of what psychologists have traditionally worked on (Fodor 1975, p. 203).

The above comment may be more or less apt, but there is no call for alarm if this is in fact what happens. It would not be the first time that progress towards defining a scientific objective involves eliminating previous traditional questions, or that these are gathered up by other knowledge areas which may be completely new, or branches broken off from what was formerly a common field. In any case, what has caused most resistance to accepting the computational model is not that it is unable to explain everything, but rather how difficult it is to integrate traits which are considered essentials of the mind such as consciousness and *qualia*.

4 Restricted Modularity of Mind

In his writings analysed so far, Fodor limited himself to describing the theories underlying the psychological explanations derived from the consensual cognitive approach, but in *The Modularity of Mind* (1983) he took a bold step forward and presented his own theory on one of the traditional themes of psychology: the structure of the human mind. Right from the date of its publication, this provoked a shower of criticism and sparked off a lively argument which has still not completely died down.

In line with the aim of this paper, our analysis will focus on showing how it is precisely in a theory which plays a central role in his philosophical stance where Fodor is so interested in marking out its limits: the structure of cognitive modules is applicable to what he calls input systems, but not to the central systems of the mind. The reason is that only these are, to use his own expression, "encapsulated" and can be described computationally, which again implies an unattractive but unavoidable result: the higher mental processes, those traditionally linked to consciousness and thought, cannot be the object of explanation using the only model which ensures the autonomy of psychology as a science.

In *The Modularity of Mind* Fodor proposes establishing a functional taxonomy of psychological processes and the mechanisms which support them. Recovering traditional theories of psychological faculties and assuming the innatist Cartesian mentalism of Chomsky (1965), Fodor believes he can establish that the human mind is structured in three system classes, each with different functions and properties: input systems, central systems and output systems.

In this book Fodor deals with the first of these and, to a lesser extent, with the second, although without arriving in either case at a complete analysis of the structure of faculties understood as psychological mechanisms, and limiting himself to proposing it as a working brief for future empirical research. Those which are clearly shown to be modular are the input systems whose function is to analyse the sensory information from the stimuli. They are related to the traditional five senses and to language but are characteristically mechanisms linked to specific domain fields in each of them: e.g., in the case of vision, mechanisms of colour perception, mechanisms of analysis of form, mechanisms of three dimensional relationship analysis, and others such as those responsible for the visual control of bodily movements and facial recognition.

These highly specialized systems are "domain specific," and are characterized also by being linked to a fixed neural architecture and by their "informational encapsulation," by the non-interference of higher processes external to the system in how they function. The transformation of information which occurs in these processes can be computationally described, in contrast to what happens in the central processes, those traditionally associated with thought and problem solving, whose characteristic function is to establish beliefs and which are characteristically global rather than specific, because of their non-encapsulation, their isotropic and holistic (or "Quineian," as Fodor calls it) character which means that modularity cannot be attributed to these central systems. Similarly, and in contrast to what occurs in the input systems, according to Fodor there are no central processes whose function depends on specific neural structures, as they seem to be based on equipotential neural mechanisms.

From all of this, he believes he can deduce what he calls "Fodor's First Law of the Nonexistence of Cognitive Science" which he formulates in the following terms:

> the more global (e.g., the more isotropic) a cognitive process is, the less anybody understands it (Fodor 1983, p. 107).

And there is a corollary to this Law:

> *Very* global processes, like analogical reasoning, aren't understood at all (Fodor 1983, p. 107).

The final chapter of the book, "Conclusions and Warnings," is especially relevant as here Fodor clearly establishes the need to assume the limitations which are inevitably inherent in this modular conception of the structure of mind. First of all, these are non-contingent limitations in relation to our general cognitive capacity, the "epistemic boundedness," as in his own words,

> modular systems are, by definition, special purpose computational mechanisms. If the mind is a collection of such mechanisms, then there are presumably going to be at least some purposes for which the mind isn't fit (Fodor 1983, p. 120).

The second limitation is directly connected with the theme which is the object of our analysis as it refers precisely to the limits which, according to Fodor, can reasonably be expected when developing the computational programme of psychological processes. If the modularity thesis is correct, the difficulties which cognitive science has found in its advance in certain fields are understandable, while it has been able to reap relevant successes in others. In his opinion, even Artificial Intelligence has achieved spectacular advances in the simulation of relatively isolated and encapsulated processes, while its failure is evident in the simulation of globalizing intelligent behaviours. Cognitive psychology has been able to draw up plausible theories as to forms for coding sensory information but practically nothing is known about what happens after the information gets there. The ghost has been chased further back into the machine, but it has not been exorcised (Fodor 1983, p. 127).

The problem is that this modular structure would not only explain what is missing in what has been achieved so far, but it would set limits, we might even say *a priori*, to the future development of the cognitive sciences in general and of computational psychology in particular.

We can sympathize here with Fodor, appreciating how much can be achieved in clarifying local, modular mental processes, but we have to give up any hope that this computational model might be useful for understanding other more global processes which do not have a specific neural correlation and are not informatively encapsulated. It turns out to be impossible to devise computational models of these. Strictly speaking, Fodor does not deny the computational character of global thought processes, but as he confirmed years later, he found it very difficult to imagine how we can specify what the processes governing it are, e. g., understanding the relevance of behaviour to problem solving (García-Albea, 1990, p. 23).

5 Problems of the Computational Theory of Mind

Establishing the limits of a theory may mean that certain thematic areas cannot be approached from it, and also recognizes the difficulties involved when it is applied to others when attempting to find a satisfactory explanation for them. So, in general terms, there are two well-known problems which right from the early days of the computational theories of human mind were brandished by their opponents as fundamental obstacles to their acceptance.

The first problem is the *qualia*, the qualities which are present in the phenomenal experience, the wide qualitative spectrum of colours, flavours, feelings, etc. A merely functional description of mental states and processes leaves out this rich psychological domain. It seems evident that two different systems, although they meet Fodor's requirement of strict functional equivalence, may involve different *qualia*.

The second problem raised by the hopes pinned on functionalist theory was the content of mental representations and the propositional attitudes referring to them. A mentalist model of psychological explanation such as that proposed by Fodor in his computational theory of mind seems necessarily committed to recognizing that behaviour is linked to the meaning and semantic content of representations. But, again, a merely functional description and explanatory model which is limited to computational processes will encounter serious problems when it comes to integrating this semantic dimension and justifying the possibility of the intentional nature of the propositional attitudes.

With regard to the first of these problems, Fodor was clear from the start that the *qualia* necessarily fall outside the scope of any possible functionalist explanation. In the article he wrote with Ned Block, in 1972, "What psychological states are not," he analysed the "functional states identity theory" (FSIT), and after recalling the difference we must distinguish between dispositional states (beliefs, desires, inclinations ...) and states which occur (sensations, thoughts, feelings ...), he concluded by affirming that the "inverted spectrum" argument is strong enough to show that not all psychological states can be functionally identified.

From this irreducibility of the *qualia* to a possible functional explanation it can be directly deduced – as some critics have already done – that functionalism fails as it does not take into account a relevant part of mental states, so that it should be rejected as a model of psychological explanation. But others maintained that we should not lament the loss to science of these psychological qualities because, in spite of their importance in the subjective experience of the phenomenal subject, they are irrelevant to the aims of an explanatory theory of the processes which define the cognitive subject. Fodor and Block end the article acknowledging that

> these inverted (or absent) qualia cases in a certain sense pose a deeper problem for FSIT than any of the other arguments we shall be discussing (Fodor and Block 1972, p. 245).

Fodor's position on the problem posed by the *qualia* in relation to functionalist explanations cannot in strict terms be identified with any of the above mentioned: they do not constitute a proof of error, nor is the problem they pose solved by denying the psychological relevance of qualitative experiences: simply, we have to recognize that computational psychology is not capable of taking them into account. Functionalism can do many things, including some which other models are not able to do, for psychological explanations, but it is not able to construct an explanatory theory of the *qualia*.

Fodor then adds that there is not even a hint that functionalism or any other approach might make such a theory possible. There is no theory, and there are no clues as to what the conditions to construct it might be. Ned Block adopts a similar position where qualitative states do not form part of the domains of cognitive psychology; nothing we know about the psychological processes underlying our conscious mental life has anything to do with the *qualia*. According to the type of conceptual apparatus of psychology and our current approach to it, Block adds, it is inconceivable that it can offer an explanation of them. That is not to say that it is impossible, only inconceivable.

> All we have to go on is what we know, and on the basis of what we have to go on, it looks as if qualia are not in the domain of psychology (Block 1978, p. 85).

Years later, when Fodor summed up the capacity of the functionalist approach to throw some light on the traditional philosophical body-mind problem, he assumed what Pujadas (2002) called the "official history" of functionalism as the Hegelian *Aufhebung* of logical behaviourism and of identity theory, an integrated superseding of the best of each, the relational character of the former and the materialism of the latter. But in his article published in *Scientific American*, when analysing to what extent functionalism is responsible for non-mental traits, he again recognizes unambiguously that the qualitative content, key to the whole area of consciousness, poses a problem for functionalism, and after mentioning again the inverted spectrum argument, he concludes:

> As matters stand, the problem of qualitative content poses a serious threat to the assertion that functionalism can provide a general theory of the mental (Fodor 1981a, p. 122).

With reference to the second problem, that of intentional content, Fodor is much more optimistic. Computational functionalism is compatible with a representational theory of mind which recognizes that our propositional attitudes refer to representations which have semantic properties. In fact, it is not only compatible, but both theories, the computational and the representational, are mutually interdependent and complementary.

> Modern cognitive psychology rests largely on the hope that these two doctrines can be made to support each other (Fodor 1981a, p. 123).

Computational processes process symbols which in the case of the mind are representations with semantic content. And this content, as he continued to affirm in 1981, may be established through causal relationships, as it is the effect of specific stimuli, causing in turn specific behaviour and interacting with other beliefs. But the problems which the propositional attitudes pose for the computational model of psychological explanation are far from going away. In fact, the scope of the predominant philosophical preoccupations in Fodor's work in the years which followed centres on the aim of providing functionalism with a plausible theory of mental representation and semantic content. He considered that rather than continuing to attend to the different possible formulations of the Computational Theory of Mind he needed to clarify the problems involved in the admission of Representational Theory to the extent that it assumed the hypothesis of a Language of Thought.

Fodor therefore found himself obliged to unify his philosophical proposals on mind and his conceptions on language and the problem of meaning. Here it is relevant to mention his book *Psychosemantics. The Problem of Meaning in the Philosophy of Mind*, published in 1987 (see Bruner, 1990). New enemies of his proposal appeared on the scene, particularly "semantic holism." But Fodor's argumentative strategy did not undergo any important modifications. As A. Levine and M. H. Bickhard show in their defence of the computational theory of mental representations, ultimately Fodor does not hesitate to fall back on *"What else?"* to support its plausibility. We must also recognize that Fodor establishes a limit to his theories, in this case not referring to their extension, but to their possible epistemic rationale. As well as being based, as we already mentioned, on the supposition of the validity of empirical psychological explanations of cognitive orientation, the computational and representative theories of mind can in no sense be demonstrated or proved but simply, at most, proposed as the only ones compatible with established conditions. Thus, for example, "conceptual atomism has not been demonstrably proved, Fodor claims, but in the absence of any other candidate capable of meeting our demands, there is a presumption in its favor" (Levine and Bickhard 1999, p. 6).

The representational theory proposed by Fodor seems incompatible with semantic holism or the conceptual content of mental representations since, in his opinion, the idea that the identity or intentional content of a propositional attitude is determined by the totality of its epistemic relationships is mistaken. Here again an insuperable limit is established with the absolutist pretensions of a functionalist explanation of mind. If mental states and processes must be identified by their functional relationships with other mental states and processes, with *inputs* and *outputs*, that does not imply, and for Fodor is not admissible, that the content of a specific propositional attitude, e. g., of a belief, can be identified merely by its causal relationships. For Fodor's psychofunctionalism a functionalist theory of the content of beliefs is not possible. The powers of functionalism do not go as far as that.

However, with the aims of our analysis here we do not need to follow up each of the modulations and corrections which Fodor accumulated in his efforts to provide the RTM with an appropriate theory of meaning, especially those referring to "narrow content." It is enough just to emphasize that along with his consciousness of the limits of the computational approach, he became increasingly aware that in the cognitive realm all that glitters is not gold. Fodor's defence of functionalism as the most valid theory we have available is compatible with the increase in his internal criticism of what he judged to be mistaken deviations from its path.

As he said himself in *Concepts*, "something has gone badly wrong about how the program has been carried out;" or "the theory of concepts that cognitive science has classically assumed is a certain way seriously mistaken," but that this did not mean that we have to throw out "along with the baby: the bath, the bath towel, the bathtub, the bathroom, many innocent bystanders, and large sections of Lower Manhattan" (1998, p. VII). In the midst of the storm, Fodor, unlike Putnam, does not abandon (the functionalist) ship, and makes an effort to trim the sails and steer the boat without capsizing to calmer waters, but he makes no attempt to turn it into a transatlantic liner which can safely navigate in the deepest waters of the mind.

6 Epistemic Boundedness of Computational Psychology

The high point of Fodor's recognition of the limits of a computational psychology was undoubtedly the publication in 1997 of *How the Mind Works* by S. Pinker and *Evolution in Mind* by H. Plotkin, and the critical reviews of them Fodor wrote for the *London Review of Books*. Three years later he took up this criticism again in his work *The Mind Doesn't Work that Way* revealing the optimistic, exaggerated pretensions of the "new synthesis" between innatism, computational theory and Darwinism presented as an overall explanatory theory of the human mind. In spite of the relevance and controversial nature of the objections Fodor makes to the approaches which Pinker and Plotkin adopt to innatism and Darwinist adaptationism, our interest here is limited to the reasons he gives for a necessary self-recognition of the limits to the valid extension of the computational functionalist model in psychology.

Three of Fodor's comments are relevant here and all three are found in the introduction he wrote to the above, entitled "Still Snowing." First, although he considers that the computational theory of mind is "by far the best theory of cognition that we've got" and that therefore it is part of the truth, however, he has never thought that "it's a very *large* part of the truth; still less that it's within miles of being the whole story about how the mind works" (Fodor 2000, p. 1).

Fodor's second relevant commentary here refers to the different possible evaluations of the validity of the two theories which, as we have seen, demanded to be integrated into psychological explanation: the computational theory and the representational theory. In Fodor's opinion, the latter has continued to enjoy increasing success over fifty years of the development of cognitive science, while the attempts of the former to reduce thought to computation has had only varying success.

Thirdly and finally, Fodor explains the dimensions and reasons for this very different acceptance. The computational model has shown to be suitable for describing mental states which we describe as "intrinsically intentional," while it is not suitable for those which are "intrinsically conscious" (Fodor 2000, p. 4). The computational model is also fully appropriate for local and modular mental processes, while the central thought processes, those which seem most characteristic of human consciousness, due to their essentially global character cannot be captured by the functionalist networks. The alternative proposed by Pinker of an entirely modular, innate and evolutionarily adapted architecture of mind is not coherent with the global dimensions of abductive reasoning or by analogy even with common sense. In conclusion and once again in this history, we would have good reason to evaluate positively the processes achieved by which psychology has advanced along the computational path, but "the current situation in cognitive science is light years from being satisfactory" (Fodor 2000, p. 5). And not only that: there are solid reasons for presuming that it will continue to be so.

Although continuing to take up the same theoretical position is not always considered a good thing, Fodor acknowledges that in this case it may in fact have been so, as his ideas have not varied in this regard and he continues to think they are right. As we hope this overview of his work has shown, the advances made possible by computational psychology have always been limited to an area which in Fodor had well-defined boundaries. What may have changed, however, is the emphasis and importance he places in *The Mind Doesn't Work that Way* on the parts of his earlier books where he recognized the limits.

Fodor maintains that,

> It's the **main** point of the last chapter of *The Language of Thought* (1975) that the computational model is implausible as an account of global cognition. And it's a **central** theme in *The Modularity of Mind* (1983) that modular cognition is where Turing's computational story about mental processes is most likely to be true (2000, p. 7, my emphasis).

While we do not have an alternative theoretical model available and we have to assume that computational theory is only applicable to the modular systems of the human mind, the question of how a mental process may at one and the same time be mechanical and abductive remains a mystery and not only a problem.

> I think that, as things now stand, this and consciousness look to be the ultimate mysteries about the mind (Fodor 2000, p. 99).

But is this not perhaps too much? To admit that a specific theory cannot cope with sensations or feelings, deny that it can explain the intentional content of our mental representations, recognize that consciousness does not play a relevant role in it, admit that it has nothing to say about the higher processes with which we identify the cognitive superiority of human beings ... Is this not tantamount to acknowledging the failure of this theory? Would recognizing such wide-ranging limitations not in fact mean denying the validity of the computational model of mind as Putnam did in 1988? Among the arguments Putnam put forward was his rejection of the concept of narrow content proposed by Fodor. In Putnam's own words "meanings ain't in the head," and we should stop considering propositional attitudes as functional states.

But Fodor's position, although he was to revise his ideas later with regard to the intentional content of the mental representations, is not identical to that of his former maestro. As we understand it, his position fits better with the advice given by Pindar: *My soul, do not seek eternal life, but exhaust the realm of the possible*. Computational psychology would do well to exploit to the maximum the scope of its possibilities for understanding cognitive activities, but at least from the knowledge we have available, we cannot dream that it will become an integral theory of them. There is always a possibility that in the future someone may offer us fundamental ideas on knowledge, but until then we would do well to be content with how much we can and know how to do, while admitting that although cognitive science has been able to throw some light in part on the prevailing darkness

> what our cognitive science has found out about the mind is mostly that we don't know how it works (Fodor 2000, p. 100).

7 Final Remarks

I would like to end this review of the limits which Fodor establishes on his own proposed explanatory model by explaining two which I consider pertinent: the first concerns the questionable legitimacy of his radical refusal to consider the possible extension of psychology to the central cognition processes. The second refers to its plausible congruence with the particular epistemological status of psychological knowledge.

It is surprising that Fodor hardly mentions current empirical research on those central cognitive processes which fall under his sceptical convictions. What he himself defended, as we have recalled in relation to the orientation which the philosophy of psychology should adopt, which is the drawing up of a psychological metatheory closely linked to the achievements of scientific psychology to research on the suppositions of successful science, does not seem to hold up when he emphasizes that it is impossible for the computational cognitive approach to be successful in the attempt to clarify those processes, at least unless "new ideas" are put forward.

As Wilson points out, one characteristic of his arguments is that they are formulated *a priori* as the logical outcome of his rejection of massive modularity of mind, when to a considerable extent this is an empirical question (Wilson 2004, p. 3). Here, it is certainly significant that Fodor does not support his pessimistic theoretical conclusions with research results, limiting himself to establishing generic negative assessments of what has been achieved so far by cognitive science and artificial intelligence. And what may be even more relevant, he does not take into account or value the effective progress achieved in both developmental neuroscience and in cognitive research within a computational framework, of those same problems which he judged to be unapproachable from this perspective, especially those related with induction and inference processes (Thagard 2000, 2005, and 2011). A psychological metatheory should not only assume the achievements reached over recent years by research into cognitive mental processes such as perception or language acquisition. It is also appropriate here to remember that those pessimistic forecasts by Fodor have not prevented cognitive psychologists from continuing to attempt to clarify cognitive processes such as fixation of beliefs, inductive reasoning or analogical thought, using functionalist proposals for information processing.

"Psychology" is a term used to designate a motley and very heterogeneous group of different types of knowledge built up through the efforts of generations of psychologists with very different epistemic levels, obtained using different methodologies and dealing with heterogeneous objects. It is not just that different architects dispute with each other in their attempts to have the city built to their plans, but instead that within the common psychological city there are different epistemic inhabitants all with their own traits and life styles which live in different, widely separated districts, governed by their own idiosyncratic rules for living. Thus it is hardly surprising that any attempt to draw up a single theory of psychological explanation is bound to fail. The ideal of a "Unified Psychology" is only a legacy from the other ideal of a "Unified Science," but with an even greater likelihood of turning out to be just as unattainable and unproductive.

It is certainly true that the new cognitive approach – if that is used very generically to define taking into account the internal mental states of organisms to explain their behaviour – has affected much of the research in other areas. But, as Fodor acknowledged in his *Psychological Explanation*, the functionalist model which considers these mental states as computational states is hardly relevant at all to wide-ranging fields of psychology including what is known as evolutionary or developmental psychology and social psychology. And the "official history" of functionalism in psychology, which presents it as superseding logical behaviourism and the theory of identity, does not adapt either in the same way to the future outcome of each of these disciplines or bodies of psychological knowledge, and in any case much less than it might have done with regard to propositional attitudes. Thus, for example, the regularities on the extinction of an animal behaviour formulated by learning theory have not had to be integrated into a computational model of information processing, and advances in emotional psychology have gone along more with the causal explanations offered by biology and neuroscience than with functional descriptions. Finally, to sum up, it goes without saying that correlational and statistical methods have continued to demonstrate their effectiveness within the field of psychology, alongside experimental and simulation methodologies.

Even in the more restricted area of cognitive psychology, absolutist attempts to represent the functional architecture of the mind or the classic computational model or the connectionist model of parallel distributed processing are not justified. Even Fodor himself, who recognizes the limits of the first of these when designing a general theory of human mind, denies that the second may have some advantage here. But faced with the question of whether there may some sub-systems in the mind which function in connectionist mode, his reply is affirmative:

> Very likely, and there would be no point in not taking this possibility seriously (interview with García-Albea 1990, p. 30).

This means that it would be more reasonable, at least in my view, to assume the thesis of "multiplicity of mind" proposed by A. Clark who considers that

> the mind is best understood in terms of a multiplicity of virtual machines, some of which are adapted to symbol processing tasks and some of which are adapted for subsymbolic processing. For many tasks, our everyday performance may involve the cooperative activity of a variety of such machines (Clark 1989a, pp. 2–3).

This multiplicity of mind would demand a multiplicity of explanations, where each explanatory model would assume its own limits and the required complementarity of others. The rich internal variety of the mind with conscious states versus unconscious processes and propositional attitudes versus sensations, mean that the proposal of a single mechanism able to account for such diverse behaviour and competences is not plausible. Or to express it in more commonly used terms, a single theoretical framework will come up against important and apparently insurmountable difficulties to offer an architecture encompassing the whole of cognitive science, although scientists will continue to attempt to design it by drawing up partial blueprints (Ezquerro 1995).

In so far as the development possibilities of a cognitive psychology which conceives of the mental processes as computational processes are strictly limited by the modular character of these processes, their scope cannot include the central thought processes or higher cognitive activities of human beings. This was what Fodor forecast for the future of computational psychology and what he believed he could formulate as the "First Law of the Nonexistence of Cognitive Science." But it has always been very risky to attempt to set strict limits in philosophical terms for the progress of scientific knowledge. The history of science is riddled with cognitive results which had previously been declared impossible and with solutions to problems which had previously been considered a mystery.

The undeniable progress which has been achieved does not prevent us from admitting with Fodor that the day when we will be able to integrate all this knowledge into a general theory of the human mind still seems very far off, since as Angel Rivière points out, "there is not just one cognitive psychology (in the widest sense) but various. Knowledge can be explained psychologically in various ways, although these do share some minimum suppositions" (1991, p. 24). In the end, as Fodor admitted in an interview, cognitive science includes

> betting that the central problems of mind can be resolved – or at least that some progress can be made towards their solution – through the use of models based on the notions of mental representation and computational process. Whether this discipline will be successful or not depends on the result of the wager (interview with García-Albea 1990, p. 7).

At the present moment, it would also be unwise to make any forecast as to what the future holds for this sundry collection of knowledge we call psychology. As so often happens, progress may lead to an integration of theories or some may be absorbed into others. But, similar to what has occurred in other areas of scientific knowledge, it may also be that what awaits us in the future is the consolidation of different explanatory theories adapted to the scope of their specific domain, which cannot be integrated or reduced, but may at least be compatible. This seems to me the same wishful thinking with which Fodor ends his *Psychosemantics:*

> If Aunty's said it once, she's said it a hundred times: Children should play nicely together and respect each other's points of view. I do think Aunty's right about that (1987, p. 154).

References

Acero, J. J. (1995): "Teorías del contenido mental." In: Broncano, F. (ed.): *La mente humana*, pp. 175–206. Madrid: Trotta.

Blanco, A. (1980): "Información y computación en Fodor." *Anales del Seminario de Historia de la Filosofía*, v. 17, pp. 149–165.

Block, N. (1978): "Troubles with Functionalism." In: Savage, C. W. (ed.): *Perception and Cognition*, Minnesota Studies in the Philosophy of Science, vol. 9, Minneapolis: University of Minnesota Press, pp. 261–325. Reedited in: Block, N. (2007): *Consciousness, Function and Representation. Collected Papers*, vol. 1, pp. 63–101. Cambridge, MA: MIT Press.

Block, N. (2007): *Consciousness, Function and Representation. Collected Papers*, vol. 1. Cambridge, MA: MIT Press.

Botterill, G. and Carruthers, P. (1999): *The Philosophy of Psychology*. Cambridge: Cambridge University Press.

Broncano, F. (ed.) (1995): *La mente humana*. Madrid: Trotta.

Bruner, J. (1990): *Acts of Meaning*. Cambridge, MA: Harvard University Press.

Chomsky, N. (1965): *Aspects of Theory of Syntax*. Cambridge, MA: MIT Press.

Clark, A. (1989a): *Microcognition. Philosophy, Cognitive Science, and Parallel Distributed Processing*. Cambridge, MA: MIT Press.

Clark, A. (1989b): "Connectionism and the Multiplicity of Mind." *Artificial Intelligence Review*, v. 3, pp. 49–65.

Dascal, M. (1995): "Epistemología, controversias y pragmática." *Isegoría*, v. 12, pp. 8–43.

Dascal, M. (1998): "The Study of Controversies and the History and Theory of Science." *Science in Context*, v. 11, pp. 147–154.

Dennett, D. C. (1981): *Brainstorms. Philosophical Essays on Mind and Psychology*. Brighton: Harvester Press.

Dennett, D. C. (1991): "Granny's Campaign for Safe Science." In: Loewer, B. and Rey, G. (eds.): *Meaning in Mind: Fodor and His Critics*, pp. 87–94. Cambridge, MA: Blackwell.

Ezquerro, J. (1995): "Teorías de la arquitectura de lo mental." In: Broncano, F. (ed.): *La mente humana*, pp. 97–150. Madrid: Trotta.

Fodor, J. (1968): *Psychological Explanation. An Introduction to the Philosophy of Psychology*. London: Random House.

Fodor, J. (1974): "Special Sciences or the Disunity of Sciences as a Working Hypothesis." *Synthese*, v. 28, pp. 77–115.

Fodor, J. (1975): *The Language of Thought*. New York: Crowell.

Fodor, J. (1981a): *Representations*. Cambridge, MA: Cambridge University Press.

Fodor, J. (1981b): "The Mind-Body Problem." *Scientific American*, v. 244, pp. 114–123.

Fodor, J. (1983): *The Modularity of Mind*. Cambridge, MA: MIT Press.

Fodor, J. (1985): "Precis of the Modularity of Mind." *The Behavioural and Brain Sciences*, v. 8, pp. 1–42.

Fodor, J. (1987): *Psychosemantics. The Problem of Meaning in the Philosophy of Mind*. Cambridge, MA: MIT Press.

Fodor, J. (1998): *Concepts. Where Cognitive Science Went Wrong*. Oxford: Clarendon Press.

Fodor, J. (2000): *The Mind Doesn't Work that Way. The Scope and Limits of Computational Psychology*. Cambridge, MA: MIT Press.

Fodor, J. (2008): *Lot 2. The Language of Thought Revisited.* Oxford: Clarendon Press.
Fodor, J. and Block, N. (1972): "What Psychological States Are Not." *Philosophical Review*, v. 81, pp. 159–181.
Fodor, J. and McLaughlin, B. (1990): "Connectionism and the Problem of Systematicity: Why Smolensky's Solution Still Doesn't Work." *Cognition*, v. 35, pp. 183–204.
Fodor, J. and Piatelli-Palmarini, M. (2010): *What Darwin Got Wrong.* New York: Farrar, Strauss and Giroux.
Fodor, J. and Pylyshyn, Z. (1988): "Connectionism and Cognitive Architecture: A Critical Analysis." *Cognition*, v. 28, pp. 3–71.
García-Albea, J. E. (1990): "Funcionalismo y Ciencia Cognitiva, Lenguaje y Pensamiento, modularidad y conexionismo. Entrevista con J. A. Fodor." *Estudios de Psicología*, v. 45, pp. 5–31.
García-Albea, J. E. (2003): "Fodor y la modularidad de la mente (veinte años después)." *Anuario de Psicología*, v. 34, n. 4, pp. 506–516.
Gonzalez, W. J. (ed.) (2011): *Conceptual Revolutions: From Cognitive Science to Medicine.* A Coruña: Netbiblo.
Jackendoff, R. (2002): "Review of *The Mind Doesn't Work that Way.*" *Language*, v. 78, pp. 164–170.
Levine, A. and Bickhard, M. H. (1999): "Concepts: Where Fodor Went Wrong." *Philosophical Psychology*, v. 12, pp. 5–23.
Loewer, B. and Rey, G. (eds.) (1991): *Meaning in Mind. Fodor and his Critics.* Oxford: Basil Blackwell.
Martinez-Freire, P. (1995): "Wittgenstein y Fodor sobre el lenguaje privado." *Anuario Filosófico*, v. 28, n. 2, pp. 357–376.
Martinez-Freire, P. (2005): *La importancia del conocimiento. Filosofía y Ciencias Cognitivas.* Málaga: Servicio de Publicaciones de la Universidad de Málaga.
Pinker, S. (1997): *How the Mind Works.* New York: Norton.
Plotkin, H. (1997): *Evolution in Mind.* London: Alan Lane.
Pozo, J. I. (2006): *Adquisición de conocimiento.* Madrid: Morata.
Pujadas, L. M. (2002): *La ascensión y la caída de la teoría funcionalista de la mente.* Palma: Universidad de las Islas Baleares.
Rivière, A. (1991): *Objetos con mente*, Madrid: Alianza Editorial.
Segal, G. (1996): "The Modularity of Theory of Mind." In: Carruthers, P. and Smith, P. K. (eds.): *Theories of Theories of Mind*, pp. 141–157. Cambridge: Cambridge University Press.
Wilson, Robert A. (2004) "What Computations (Still, Still) Can't Do: Jerry Fodor on Computation and Modularity," in Stainton, R. J., Ezcurdia, M. and Viger, C. D. (eds.): *New Essays in Philosophy of Language and Mind.* Supplementary issue 30 of the *Canadian Journal of Philosophy*, pp. 407–425.

Raffaella Campaner
The Interventionist Theory and Mental Disorders

Abstract: The onset and development of mental illnesses are currently held to result from a combination of variables at a number of different levels (e.g., genetic, biochemical, neurological, social, psychological, etc.). Many theoretical models of mental disorders have been elaborated and embraced from many disciplinary standpoints (e.g., clinical psychology, psychoanalysis, psychiatry, genetic psychiatry, psychiatric epidemiology, behavioural neurology, pharmacology, etc.). This contribution focuses on causal analyses and causal explanatory models of mental disorders, the collection of different kinds of evidence, the variables involved and their interactions. Mental disorders are here taken as a significant test case for the interventionist theory of causation and causal explanation. On top of its major influence in the philosophical scenario, the interventionist view has attracted increasing interest from within investigations on many scientific topics, including cognition and mental illness. This view is considered here in the light of its feasibility to address issues arising in attempts to integrate different perspectives on mental disorders.

Keywords: interventionist theory, mental disorder, psychiatric explanations, causality

1 The Interventionist Theory and Psychiatric Explanations

Woodward's theory – which conjugates a manipulative core with the adoption of counterfactuals – has been one of the most successful theories of causation and causal explanation in the last decade or so. In the last few years, it has been regarded as especially suited to the so-called special sciences, to deal with highly variable and exception-ridden phenomena. Thanks to its stress on invariance under intervention, instead of general scientific laws, and its admitting of *degrees* of stability of generalizations, the interventionist theory has been held to fit various special sciences (see e.g. Woodward 2000), such as experimental biology (Waters 2007) and experimental epigenetics (Baedke 2012), and explanations of social behaviour (Henderson 2005).

Among others, psychology and psychiatry have been taken as disciplinary fields in which this approach can prove particularly fruitful. In what follows I will not address intersections between Woodward's theory of causation and psychology as far as research on causal learning, reasoning and representations is concerned (topics addressed, e.g., in Woodward 2007, 2012, and 2014; Bonawitz et al. 2010). I shall rather focus on interactions between the interventionist view and explanatory accounts of mental disorders. I shall point out some specific issues and methodological concerns emerging in investigations of mental illnesses from different disciplinary perspectives, and some possible merits and limits of the interventionist approach in tackling them.

From within psychiatry itself, an eminent scholar, Kenneth Kendler, has emphasized the merits of the interventionist account in the context of elaborating a philosophical framework for the discipline, which lies at the crossroads of medicine, psychology and various social sciences.[1] The relations between mind and brain and among different explanatory perspectives are regarded as some of the most important and challenging issues in psychiatry, which can benefit from interactions with philosophy of science. According to Kendler, psychiatry is irrevocably grounded in first-person experience, mind-brain dualism (which he labels as "Cartesian") is simply false, and biological reductionism is not to be preferred over other options. To grasp the complex aetiology of mental disorders, psychiatrists should abandon any monistic explanatory approach, and substitute the battle between alternative paradigms with explanatory pluralism and "patchy reductionism," striving for "piecemeal integration" and making sense of mental illness bit by bit.

Kendler regards the interventionist view as a very promising approach. In the first place, it repositions the mind-body problem and its series of endless disputes, which have attracted much attention from scholars in the field, but have led to little – if any – progress. In Woodward's account, causal relata are variables of different kinds, which can take different values. Which kinds of variables are involved in a causal relation has to do with the specific context at stake, and different kinds of variables can, in principle, be causally connected together. Kendler holds that mind-body disputes should just be got rid of as not genuinely relevant for psychiatry, metaphysically loaded and without actual practical import.

---

[1] These and the following reflections have a theoretical, and *not historical*, import, and do not consider the historical development of debates on mental disorders, their many facets and the numerous positions included.

In addition – and in contrast with any purely organicist approach to psychiatric disorders – Kendler stresses how psychiatry itself is inextricably "wedded to the mental world," and aims to alleviate human suffering resulting from "dysfunctional alterations in certain domains of first-person, subjective experience, such as mood, perception, and cognition" (Kendler 2005b, p. 433). So in dealing with mental disorders we cannot dispense with subjective experiences from patients' first-person reports. Progress in such fields as biological psychiatry, psychiatric genetics, epigenetics,[2] and the neurosciences should not ignore the world of human mental suffering as such, as a grounding element for both research and clinical activity.

However, an emphasis on first-person experiences should not deceive us as to what they are held to amount to. According to Kendler, first-person experiences emerge from and are entirely dependent upon brain functioning: "the mental world does not exist independently of its physical instantiation in the brain" (Kendler 2005b, p. 434). Still, mental processes, such as thoughts, feelings and impulses, occur within our subjective experience and do have causal efficacy. According to Kendler, mind-to-brain causality is to be admitted, because, although we do not fully understand it yet, we can observe mental processes "carrying critical causal information about human behaviour" (Kendler 2005b, p. 434).[3] Kendler's main concern is thus the need to overcome the die-hard dualism, in order to build up integrated accounts of mental disorders.

As a matter of fact, both conscious and unaware attitudes towards the nature of mind and brain and their relationship strongly influence any enterprise addressing mental disorders, whether it be performed by a researcher, clinician, nurse, family member, or social operator. Explicit and implicit models have a major impact both on lines of research pursued and on the kind of therapy adopted, and their role should not be underestimated.

One of the main reasons Kendler invokes to advocate interventionism has to do with its neutral attitude with respect to any ontological commitment. On the contrary, embracing a *mechanist* perspective requires us to specify which entities or parts constitute the systems under enquiry, which interactions and activities occur between them, and hence commits to some ontological level and some set of "bottoming-out" strategies. "Nested hierarchical descriptions of mechanisms typically *bottom out* in [...] the components that are accepted as relatively

---

[2] For some specific methodological reflections on psychiatric genetics, see Kendler (2005a and 2013); for some reflections on the impact of epigenetics on investigations of mental illness, see Thagard and Findlay (2011).
[3] Without discussing it in detail, Kendler recalls that his position is consistent with nonreductive materialism.

fundamental or taken to be unproblematic for the purposes of a given scientist, research group, or field." Bottoming out is relative. "Different types of entities and activities are where a given field stops when constructing mechanisms" (Machamer, Darden, and Craver 2000, p. 13), and any field is thus required to choose its fundamental level.

Woodward's interventionist theory has no specific interest in discovery mechanisms, but it is by no means incompatible with them: without playing a central role, causal mechanisms are admitted, and described as organized or structured sets of parts or components, governed by invariant generalizations (see Woodward 2002). The relationship between interventionism and mechanistic accounts of causation has been widely debated. On the one hand, the role of interventions in the identification of causally relevant variables for the construction of mechanistic models has been increasingly recognized in the last few years;[4] on the other hand, the role granted to mechanistic notions has been interestingly enhanced in Woodward's latest writings. In particular, his (2011) and (2013) acknowledge that mechanistic information plays an important part as *finer-grained* information on patterns of counterfactual dependence. Without opposing them, the interventionist view can do *without* mechanisms, and thus promises to do without any strong ontological commitment. Kendler sees this as a good reason to advocate an interventionist approach, since any sort of preliminary commitment to a given single – or just a few – levels could seriously limit the construction of a more articulate and adequate description and explanatory frameworks for mental disorders.

It needs to be stressed that the interventionist approach is not the only position Kendler refers to in addressing his concerns on psychiatry's methodology and conceptual tools. Promoting some form of explanatory *integrative pluralism*, Kendler correctly emphasizes that mechanisms can supplement the interventionist account. Relevant causal factors having an impact on mental illness can be present at both micro- and macro-levels, within the individual and outside her, and involve processes that can be best understood from biological, psychological, and sociocultural perspectives. According to Kendler (2008), mechanistic models can prove an adequate conceptual tool for psychiatry insofar as they allow portions of complex phenomena to be isolated and represented in schematic or sketchy ways.

Both the interventionist and mechanistic approaches are hence accorded some virtues.[5] With respect to the interventionist view, not only does it not com-

---

4 See e.g. Craver (2007), Glennan (2010), and Tabery (2009).
5 On explanatory pluralism in psychiatry, see also Campaner (2014).

mit to any specific set of basic entities, but it argues for a pick and mix of any kind of causal variables, at whatever level they stand, as long as the adequate invariant generalizations hold between them (see Woodward 2008). By admitting all kinds of variables, without privileging any level over the others, the interventionist approach can effectively represent causal investigations on mental disorders with a multidisciplinary and interdisciplinary character, responding to the need to intertwine various portions of relevant information. At the same time, the interventionist perspective does not force us to consider all elements as equally important. According to the field carrying on the investigation and the purpose at stake, explanations of mental disorders do – and must – focus on different levels according to a number of contextual matters, such as the field carrying on the investigation and the purpose at stake. For instance, "although humiliation is ultimately expressed in the brain, this does not mean that the basic neurobiological level is the most efficient level at which to observe humiliation" (Kendler 2005b, p. 436).

In principle, the interventionist perspective can equally admit causal claims concerning humiliation and loss as expressed in psychological terms and as expressed in terms of neurobiological entities and interactions, as long as they both reflect invariant under intervention relations. *Genuine* psychological variables can be admitted and recognized as causally relevant – and not mere epiphenomena of biological variables – as long as they can work as control variables for outcomes in human beings.[6] It is the context that dictates the most efficient level at which to operate a causal analysis; at the same time, it must not be forgotten that other levels are at play.

Finally, the interventionist model of causality connects causation with the *practical* purposes of all enquiries aimed at intervening to treat or, when possible, prevent illness. Moreover, the counterfactual dimension allows causal connections to be assessed, and to tell them from mere correlations, by referring to hypothetical situations. We can claim, for instance, that "national threats, such as the events of September 2011, can be considered to cause reduced rates of suicide in the threatened nations because, *had there been* an intervention to prevent those threats, the suicide rate *would not have changed*" (Kendler and Campbell 2009, p. 882). Once we know a genuine causal relation is in place, we can arrange various sorts of therapeutic and preventive strategies, by wiggling the causes and thus trying to produce or prevent given effects.

---

6 "The really difficult thing here is to find the right characterization of a psychological intervention" (Campbell 2007, p. 61).

In this section I have shown some of the respects in which the interventionist approach can address issues arising from causal investigations of mental disorders, referring to claims made by Kenneth Kendler, John Campbell, and Woodward himself. In the following section I shall tackle some more specific issues arising from different lines of scientific research and clinical practice dealing with mental disorders.

2 Causal Discourse on Mental Disorders

As is well-known, a major debate has been going on for years now on nosology, changing classifications of mental disorders, and the different versions of DSM – whose fifth edition recently appeared (DSM 5, 2013). Here let us just recall how *varying* definitions of mental disorders make it clear that problematic aspects arise with respect to the relations between physical and psychological features, and with respect to the relations between symptomatic diagnoses, etiological explanations, and treatments. Mental disorders are often viewed as

> a somewhat imprecise subclass of disorders or diseases, which differ from physical disorders primarily in their dominant symptoms. [...] Mental disorders involve behavioural or psychological features, rather than [just] the physical features of the person. This demonstrates that a disorder is classified as a mental disorder rather than a physical disorder on the basis of its symptoms, not its cause or aetiology (Gert and Culver 2004, p. 416).

Claims like this are controversial. It appears that causal investigations can be particularly important to shed light on what underlies symptoms, to obtain a deeper – and practically exploitable – understanding. Biological psychiatry, psychiatric epidemiology, genetic psychiatry, behavioural neurology, neuropsychology, clinical psychology, and others, call for a pathophysiological story for the disorders under enquiry, a story that consistently makes sense of different kinds of symptoms (physical, behavioural, psychological) and of a complex aetiology (e.g., genetic variations, structural neurological abnormalities, stressful events, ...). The following sub-sections consider a few issues arising from the search for causes of mental disorders, and related to the choice of causally relevant variables and their interactions.

2.1 Which Interventions? The Gathering of Evidence

The range of disciplines addressing mental disorders is very wide, and includes both fields dealing with strictly organic features and those focusing on non-bodily ones. The same disorder can be addressed by different fields, which relate it to different kinds of causal factors. For instance, according to neuropsychology, schizophrenia is a disease of the brain-mind system and is to be traced back to the cognitive system and the neuronal system on which the cognitive system depends. According to the systemic approach, it is a disease related to the network of relations and communication exchanges within the family, having to do with the rules holding within a family system. For psychoanalysis, schizophrenia's aetiology lies in distant infancy and unconsciousness, and that is where its causes must be sought. Causal constructs thus differ: the neurobiological position focuses on the prefrontal hypodopaminergy, clinical psychopathology on frontal lobe apathy symptoms and emotional alignment, clinical psychology on personality regression and cognitive deficits, and the public health discipline system on psychiatric invalidity.[7] Analogously, studies on Tourette Syndrome – a neurodevelopmental disorder – have largely focused on the neurotransmitter system and dopaminergic dysfunctions, but recent works also suggest a cognitive approach, based on the analysis of decision-making and reinforcement learning processes.[8]

Different views have very direct and practical implications with respect to the conceptualization of causal links and the interventions performed for therapeutic or preventive purposes, and consider and collect causal evidence in different ways. The interventionist account is grounded on invariance under intervention, which suggests experimentation – either actually carried out or just ideal – as the key to obtain causal knowledge. Woodward makes it clear that his view does *not* claim that causal relations can be assessed *only* through experimental interventions: "people may learn causal relationships from many sources, including passive observation." However, he remarks that also in such cases "the content of what is learned is given by [the following definition]: what one learns is what would happen were an intervention to be performed" (Woodward 2012, p. 965),[9] and randomized experiments can be taken as paradigmatic interventions.

The role of experimental and observational evidence in the assessment of causal relations is a problematic issue that can be taken, amongst others, as one of the aspects serving to draw distinctions between different disciplinary ap-

---

[7] See, e.g., Stoyanov (2009).
[8] Tics too are studied in neurobiological terms, but also in terms of emotions. On the state-of-the-art of investigations on Tourette Syndrome, see Cavanna (2013).
[9] Manipulability is the key-concept: *"No causal difference without a difference in manipulability relations, and no difference in manipulability relations without a causal difference"* (Woodward 2003, p. 61).

proaches to mental disorders. Some investigations carried on with a focus on strictly organic components (e.g., in neuropharmacology) largely appeal to randomized clinical trials, which – while presenting controversial features – have been broadly considered to provide the most reliable evidence available in the health sciences. On the other hand, clinical psychology, psychotherapy, cognitive-behavioural approaches and psychoanalysis tend to stress the role of evidence collected through first-person reports and individual colloquia. Gathering experimental and observational evidence on mental disorders both present problematic aspects. Let us recall a few of the problems emerging from research or clinical contexts.

> Experimental evidence is the most compelling evidence of causation. If it can be shown that experimentally (ideally randomly) inducing the causative agent consistently produces the outcome, at greater rates than in a nonexposed control sample, this is clear and compelling evidence of causation (van Reekum et al. 2001, p. 322).

However, "such evidence will be rare in neuropsychiatry" (van Reekum et al. 2001, p. 322) as in other disciplines dealing with mental disorders.

The most obvious concerns and limitations are ethical. Since forms of brain dysfunction cannot be experimentally induced in humans,[10] experimental approaches are hence largely applied to nonhuman species, but this practice too is increasingly considered to be ethically controversial, and might not even turn out to help much, given that nonhuman brains have major differences in structure and functions that may mislead investigators. Ethical issues also arise with respect to enrolling research subjects in a trial in cases in which they do not have the capacity, or have intermittent capacity, to consent. On the one hand, autonomy is regarded as one of the supreme principles in health care ethics; on the other, mental health autonomy may be limited by the pathology under examination, and still the enrolment of the patient may be desirable (e.g., for the patient's own sake; for her family; for the wider social context).

Further problematic issues have to do with the very design of the experimental settings and the identification of *homogenous* reference classes for causal enquiries on mental disorders. Many investigations performed in psychiatric epidemiology focus on twin studies, taken as particularly appropriate to disclose genetic causal factors, as well as the relative impact of genetic and environmen-

---

[10] "Transient alterations in brain function, such as with apomorphine or transcranial magnetic stimulation, are sometimes the exception to this ethical concern and may yield important results in the future" (van Reekum et al. 2001, p. 322).

tal factors.[11] However, these studies are usually restricted to genetic aspects, and can apply only if large enough samples of twins are available. In general, the selection of an appropriate sample and control group is one of the main challenges in research on mental disorders. The exposed group and the control group must share important features,

> but which [are the] variables to match on? The biopsychosocial model of behaviour suggests that variables to be considered include aspects of the medical history and examination findings, demographic and social variables, the individual's premorbid behavioural and family histories (van Reekum et al. 2001, p. 319).

That is an awful lot of variables, and awfully heterogeneous too.

Even if we were to determine uncontroversially which are the relevant variables to be represented in the reference class, the values of many of them might simply not be available. In particular, premorbid personal and collective histories are usually largely unknown, there being no reason to collect evidence on them before the onset of the disorder. Furthermore, it has been pointed out that adequate randomized controlled trials (RCTs) for mental disorders should be much more extended than they are and that, after being performed, they would need to be supplemented by large-scale observational follow-up studies. With respect to Alzheimer's disease, for instance,

> Saver and Kalafut calculate that 127 RCTs would have to be done in 63,500 patients over a 286-year period to determine the optimal combination of agents to treat this disease (Miller and Miller 2005, p. 71).

Follow-up studies have been employed, for instance, to investigate associations between traumatic brain injuries and many psychiatric disorders. With respect to the role of follow-up studies, investigations into the effects of treatments and drug reactions commonly appeal to observation and are concerned with *individual* clinical conditions, especially with respect to unintended effects, such as adverse drug reactions[12] and unpredictable immunological adverse effects – which very often take a long time and massive numbers of cases to occur. If in general counterfactual interventions can help address these points and orientate the use of causal models – by referring to just *hypothetical* experiments – it must be recalled that, in dealing with mental disorders, the whole experimental procedure,

---

[11] On the merits and limits of twin studies in psychiatric genetics, see e.g. Kendler (2013, p. 1058).
[12] Unexpected effects are not always adverse. They can also be beneficial, as, e.g., in the case of protection from ovarian cancer with use of oral contraceptives.

the identification of the experimental setting and the performance of the experiment are often extremely difficult even to hypothesize precisely.

It should also be stressed that evidence for the assessment of causal links underlying mental disorders is also collected in non-experimental contexts, and research methods can include observational studies, case studies, expert opinions, focus groups, and others. Without underestimating the role of RCTs, we shall recall that observation of individual symptoms, attitudes and reactions is fundamental in many approaches, especially on the clinical side. Not only does the encounter between the clinician and the patient with mental disorders start with the patient saying she is anxious, nervous, obsessed, …, but often no clear additional objective organic signs are present. In many cases, not only are the pathophysiological mechanisms underpinning most mental disorders unknown, but disorders are not characterized by objective findings on physical examination, medical imaging devices, or laboratory tests.

Often, instrumental examinations are of little significance on a clinical-diagnostic level, EEG (encephalogram) or CAT (computerized axial tomography) or PET (positron emission tomography) being mostly used for research rather than clinical purposes. The clinical causal discourse on mental disorders widely employs psychodiagnostic tests, which are not immune from epistemological concerns, mainly having to do with whether they tell us something about the patients' conditions or just about the patients' feelings (fear, anxiety, excitement, …) when they are being tested. "The observation takes place within the colloquium, and not after it, as it occurs in organic medicine" (Civita 1996, p. 17). Clinical psychology and psychotherapy collect much evidence from personal colloquia, reports, interviews, and observations of behaviour to infer information on the aetiology of what are regarded as abnormal behaviour and cognition.

"Like witness testimony in the courtroom, the most essential evidence in medicine is the patient's story" (Miller and Miller 2005, p. 72), and it is definitely so for clinical psychology and psychiatry. The patient's own account is not inherently unreliable per se. However, cognitive impairment may limit the validity of the subjects' responses. Affective and behavioural changes can be seen over the course of the disease: who is the appropriate informant of outcome status? If it is not the patient, second-person informants may not truly know what the subjects are experiencing, and it is often pointed out that the clinician's own intuitions and affective dimension play a role in truly getting to know the patient's condition.[13] In general terms, it is worth remarking that scientific causal discourse on

---

13 Up to the point that it has been stated, e.g., that "the history of schizophrenia says more in many ways about the perspectives of the observer than the observed" (Insel 2010, p. 187).

mental disorders is constructed differently in research and in clinical contexts. Clinically, causal evidence is less likely to be thought of in formal interventionist terms, being collected in settings which are far from strictly experimental, although some counterfactual causal thinking might still be in the background.

Unravelling different causes and effects is also thorny due to a high rate of comorbidity. This is often the case, for instance, in Tourette Syndrome, which is frequently accompanied by Attention Deficit Hyperactivity Disorder (ADHD), Obsessive Compulsive Disorder (OCD), rage attacks and depression.[14] The co-occurrence of different disorders makes it even more difficult to disentangle the relevant variables, their mutual dependence or dependence on some common cause; detect their precise temporal sequence; elaborate a prognosis and identify the best treatment. For research purposes, the modularity of pathologies can be assumed to decompose a complex system into isolated portions better suited to in-depth analysis.[15]

Modularity is not to be regarded as a property of the system itself, but as a tool allowing a simplified understanding of how the system functions. Tackling comorbidity can benefit from the assumption of modularity with heuristic purposes: given that more than one mental disorder can be present and simultaneously diagnosed, isolating modular causal relations can help disentangle them. This goes along the same lines suggested by Woodward:

> as I think of modularity, it is a feature of *representations* or *explanations* of the behaviour of systems, rather than a feature of the systems themselves (Woodward 2013, p. 51).

Modularity must then be bracketed when the time comes to treat the patient, when she is better considered and treated as a whole.[16]

---

14 See Kano et al. (2010), Gorman et al. (2010), Debes (2013).
15 In Wooward's theory, the parts of the system to which the causally-related variables C and E belong must operate independently enough to allow an exogenous cause to change the values of C without producing changes in other parts of the system which can influence the value of E independently of the manipulation of C. "A system of equations will be *modular* if it is possible to disrupt or replace (the relationships represented by) any one of the equations in the system by means of an intervention on (the magnitude corresponding to) the dependent variable in that equation, without disrupting any of the other equations" (Woodward 2003, p. 48).
16 "Even in the seemingly 'bodily' intervention of prescribing a psychoactive medication, a pill doesn't simply correct some somatic balance; more than this, it alters the way the patient thinks, feels or acts" (Sadler 2004, p. 165). Methodological dilemmas arise also in this respect. As far as pharmaceutical interventions are concerned, the overall effect on the system is largely unpredictable from local interventions. On the one hand, modelling of drug-target interactions finds it hard to reach up to systems' effects; on the other hand, enquiries into systems' effects can hardly be traced down to the molecular level of chemical drug testing (see e.g. Adam 2011).

In presenting modularity, Woodward also states:

> if a system consists of distinct causal mechanisms, then if one were to carry out *the right sorts of ideal interventions*, one could disrupt each of these mechanisms while leaving the others intact (2004, p. 67, italics added).

But how are "*the right sorts* of ideal interventions" to be identified? The very identification of *which* interventions are to be hypothesized to assess whether a link is causal is problematic. According to Woodward,

> the claim that X causes Y in itself commits us to nothing specific about *which* changes in X (produced by interventions) are associated with changes in Y (2010, pp. 290–291).

That is a pressing problem when the pathology we are confronting is little understood and its features controversial, as is the case with the majority of mental disorders. Many assumptions must be made, which depend on the specific disorder investigated and the field of inquiry. Identification of the appropriate interventions to be performed to unravel causal connections can only be achieved by embracing some specific model of the disorder under examination, which relies on already available knowledge. What is deemed the right sort of intervention depends on the model assumed. If the right kind of intervention is to be hypothesized, some preliminary – perhaps provisional and sketchy – model of the disorder, some conception of what the relevant variables and their basic features are, and of the way they work must be embraced. These aspects are crucial in actual investigations and should not be underestimated.

2.2 Which Variables? Levels, Variables and Their Interactions

Aetiological pathways leading to mental disorders are complex and interacting, constituting network-like structures. The heterogeneity of the elements involved in mental disorders makes the boundaries of investigations very flexible, and (alleged) complete accounts hardly possible, at least for the time being. Selecting variables depends on the disciplinary field. In the case of neurophysiology and neuropsychiatry, the knowledge of a few mechanisms is taken as the ground on which to build the disease's aetiology:

This is a well-known methodological problem for drug development in general, and an especially serious one when dealing with the mind-brain system.

neural models in psychiatry rely on the findings and theories of the divergent sciences of molecular biology, neurobiology, neuropharmacology, and psychiatric genetics to create a brain-based psychiatry (Garner and Hardcastle 2004, p. 365).

Mind and subjectivity are hence marginalized by neural models, and reductionism tends to prevail.[17] Instead, many psychology-oriented approaches tend to focus on the "mental" in the construction of causal models of mental illness: behavioural components, personal attitudes, and emotional aspects are held to be part and parcel of the disorder. Socio-economic aspects play an important role too, and are mainly the object of epidemiological investigations.

Stressful life events or cultural models, occupational conditions or the social environment are not properly grasped in a reductionist framework: while it can be reasonably argued that cultural models too ultimately exist as belief systems in the brains of individual members of a community, it is extremely unlikely that cultural elements shaping psychopathologies can be most efficiently understood at the level of basic brain biology. Even if one believes that high-order systems are completely constituted by lower-order elements, a lower, or the lowest, level might not be the most adequate at which to elaborate an explanation in a given context, nor the most efficient level at which to carry out an intervention.[18] While the causal role of neurobiological, neurochemical and genetic factors cannot be denied, a causal understanding of at least some disorders requires proper consideration of psychological and cultural factors *as such*. Psychiatric disorders include some sort and degree of psychological dysfunction, and a purely biological explanation alone is unlikely to suffice, at least in a clinical context.

The choice of a given set of variables has a number of implications. To start with, if the focus is put on the organic side, the patient tends not to be considered responsible for her "non-standard" behaviour – and this in turn can have serious legal consequences. Tracing the disorder entirely or mainly back to genetic or neurophysiological factors subtracts it from the realm of personal responsibility, placing it in the realm of misfortune. By contrast, if psychological factors are taken to play a prominent aetiological role, the patient will generally be held responsible. For this reason, many support groups strongly advocate biomedical models of psychopathology, claiming that, for instance, depression, social anxiety disorder, panic disorder, attention deficit hyperactivity disorder are ultimately medical problems – in a "hard," biomedical sense – and that patients are hence to be considered on a par with sufferers of such physical illnesses as can-

---

[17] On reductionism in psychiatry, see e.g. Schaffner (2013).
[18] More in general, the most adequate explanation in a given epistemic context is not necessarily the most detailed one.

cer, heart disease, and diabetes. The choice of variables also impacts on the sort of therapeutic interventions adopted (e.g., pharmacological, surgical, psychotherapeutic, ...), and on whether or not prevention strategies are promoted.

As we have seen, "the interventionist model can work independently of any underlying assumption about the specific causal mechanisms involved" (Kendler and Campbell 2009, p. 884), but it cannot be ignored that assumptions about the working components at stake are usually made when causal relations are sought. If we stick to the clinical context, a given therapeutic choice is made by deciding to act not only on a generic causal nexus, but on the *specific sort of variables* that are believed to be causally related. Mental processes are explained by a biochemical approach in terms of neurotransmitters, proteins and biochemical reactions, by a neural approach in terms of neurons, neural groups and synaptic connections, and by a cognitive approach in terms of mental representations, as concepts.

Even if we were to admit that ontological commitment is not necessary in the identification of causal relations, it is due – be it a commitment to the mental, neural, social or some other level – at least for causal models with therapeutic purposes. Whether a clinician opts for behavioural therapy, pharmacotherapy, or functional neurosurgery is unlikely to be independent of her ontological commitments. While the interventionist model can be accorded the merit of being neither reductionist nor anti-reductionist, it is arguable whether experts dealing with mental disorders are actually agnostic with respect to the entities they investigate and, even more, aim to control.

Causal variables involved in the occurrence of a pathology can be distant or proximate to its onset, specific or unspecific, and described at a lower or higher level of abstraction. Once identified, causal factors do not always count the same. In alcohol dependence (AD), for instance, risk factors can be psychological, social, economic, cultural and religious, and biological (aggregate genetic effects; molecular genetic variants; dysfunctional neural systems). Variants in aldehyde dehydrogenase (ALDH) gene strongly influence the risk for AD, are *highly specific*, *indirectly manipulable* (the effects can be stimulated pharmacologically by a drug, disulfiram), *not generalizable* (they have been detected only in the East Asia population), and, being expressed in the liver, *rather distal* from the brain, where the disease process takes place. Social norms responsible for expectations on pathological drinking behaviour, in turn, are *highly generalizable* as causal factors, *highly manipulable* and *quite distant* (see Kendler 2012). Causal variables can be evaluated along different dimensions, like causal strength, specificity, proximity, generalizability and manipulability, and will be judged differently according to what the explanation is going to be used *for*. A clinician, e.g., will evaluate specificity much higher than someone interested in public health who, aiming to reduce risks for broad areas of disorders, will rather look for factors with high generalizability. This does not make any explanation per se better than another, but all relative to the context at stake.

Problems also arise with regard to the very *identification* of the variables involved. *When* should outcome status be measured, and the relative causal variables sought? Can they be localized? Not only is the involvement of different variables relevant for a causal understanding of the disorder, but temporal dimension and location in place play an important part too. The *order* in which variables act can be crucial in the onset of the disorder, making it essential to render difference-making information in terms of spatiotemporally organized variables. Given, for instance, a predisposing genetic factor, the end of a marriage can be the triggering cause of depression if concurrent with a job loss, and not if occurring long before it. Causal understanding also requires that we know when the causative agent *first* appeared, and this is often very problematic. The use of neuroimaging has significantly favoured the tracing of temporal features of information processing and the spatial location of brain processes. For example,

> we now have evidence that the pathophysiologic changes underlying Alzheimer's disease (AD) may start well before the cognitive impairments become obvious. Late-onset depression, which occurs at a high rate in persons who later manifest AD, may appear, on the basis of the temporal sequence criteria, to be causative of AD. More likely, though, is the possibility that the underlying brain changes of AD first produce the late-onset depression, and thereafter the cognitive dysfunction typical of AD (van Reekum et al. 2001, p. 312).

The temporal order in which different variables interact in bringing about the disorder is relevant for their causal efficacy and for the overall behaviour of the disorder.

With regard to *spatial* features, location of brain lesions influences the impact of the lesion on the brain's functioning:

> lesion location is also important, so that small (e.g., subcortical) lesions disrupting neuronal circuits may produce dysfunction of large (e.g., cortical) areas of the brain similar to that seen with large lesions that directly affect the dysfunctional area. [...] Even within the realm of cerebrovascular disorders, important differences in outcome may depend on lesion location. The same loss of interest that is associated with depression in posterior strokes may represent the presence of an apathy state, and not depression, in strokes involving frontal systems (van Reekum et al. 2001, p. 323).

Temporal order and location may affect the onset of the disorder, the way in which it develops, and its clinical course during treatment. For example, patients with a brainstem or cerebellar stroke have a significantly shorter duration of depression than patients with left frontal or left basal ganglia strokes. Therefore, seemingly analogous evidence needs to be treated with much caution.

In his most recent writings, Woodward rightly considers a finer identification of variables as relevant for a proper reconstruction of causal connections:

> C will influence E to the extent that by varying the state of *C and its time and place of occurrence*, we can modulate the state of *E* in a fine-grained way (Woodward 2010, p. 305, italics added).

A correct temporal sequence and spatial location are essential not just to obtain a more or less abstract, or more or less fine-grained description, but for the very purpose of gaining a correct understanding of how causes act.[19]

Different factors do not act independently from each other, but can cooperate or compete, jointly affect risk and jointly bring about the disease, with high-level factors – at some point – "translating" their action into embodied effects. How is the *joint* behaviour of heterogeneous variables to be understood within an interventionist perspective? Dealing with mental disorders, we sometimes know the triggering causes, but not the mechanistic working of the disease; at other times, we have considerable knowledge of the pathogenesis, while the aetiology remains unknown. In any case, we are far from understanding any mental disorder as a *full* causal network. Building bridges linking different perspectives is a necessary step in the construction of some more integrated picture.

On the one hand, emphasis is often put on single, specific levels, for pragmatic purposes; on the other, deep interconnections among, e. g., genetic material, proteins, the environment, personal life events, must be entertained as part of the progress of scientific knowledge on mental disorders. A "divide [holds] between mindless biological psychiatry and brainless psychoanalysis/psychotherapy" (Garner and Hardcastle 2004, p. 372), which could be bridged by examining *how* the actions of genes, neurons and chemicals might in the end result in a given subjective experience and related behaviour. The rift between biological and psychosocial approaches makes different levels of variables often hardly mixed in causal accounts, but as research progresses theories integrating various aspects are gaining ground.[20] For some reductive neuroscientific story to be in-

---

[19] Some *biological gradient* can be relevant too. E.g., a correlation has been demonstrated to hold between the numbers of serotonin S2 receptors and the severity of depression in patients with stroke.

[20] For instance, roughly a decade ago, functional neuroimaging investigations revealed accelerated grey matter loss in very early-onset schizophrenia, starting from occipital areas toward temporal and parietal ones, up to frontal areas. More recently, some "rethinking of schizophre-

tegrated with psychosocial approaches, not only do different variables need to be acknowledged as playing a causal role, but their working and interactions have to be made explicit.

The interventionist account can be accorded the merit of encouraging – by making it in principle unproblematic – the presence of different levels of variables as causal relata. However, the challenge is uncovering how different levels interact in bringing about the behavioural symptoms. Even if we admit that "causal pathways exist in both directions between the mind and the brain," "the nature of such causal paths has remained frustratingly obscure" (Kendler and Campbell 2009, p. 881). What occurs that makes different variables be somehow "embodied" in the same symptoms? How do causes of psychiatric illness best understood as mental processes interrelate with those best understood as biological ones? This issue falls outside the interventionist's goals, but is definitely among the aims of much research on mental disorders, and also among the purposes underlying suggestions such as Kendler's to employ different explanatory accounts in the framework of an explanatory integrative pluralism.[21] The interventionist theory tells us that borders between different aetiological frameworks shall be crossed, but we are not helped to understand how levels are actually bridged, although the latest suggestions in Woodward (2011 and 2013), giving room to some fine-grained information, seem to point in the right direction.

2.3 Which Explanations? What Causes Disorders, and *How*

What about explanations? Disciplinary fields stressing the organic components of the disorder tend to look for *general* models of the disease, and hence to consider patients as belonging to large reference classes of individuals basically

---

nia" (see Insel 2010) as a neurodevelopmental disorder has yielded new hopes for prevention and treatment, since the detection of prodromal neurodevelopmental changes could permit early intervention. Furthermore, genetic and epigenetic factors (multiple genetic susceptibility; acetylation and methylation of the histones due to the cellular conditions related to environmental factors) and psycho-social elements (e.g., neglect and traumas; an overcrowded and impoverished urban context; belonging to an ethnic minority) have been shown to co-cause the disorder (see e.g., van Os, Kenis, and Rutten 2010; Feder, Nestler, and Charney 2009).
[21] "Recent examples of integrative pluralism in psychiatric research would include the incorporation by Gutman and Nemeroff of early traumatic events into neurobiological models for depression and the efforts of Caspi and colleagues to include specific genotypes in an epidemiological study examining the development of antisocial behaviour and depression after exposure to environmental adversity" (Kendler 2005b, p. 437).

sharing the same features. Part of the use of biological and neural models in psychiatry is their alleged universality, namely their representing something that runs through all living human bodies. A focus, instead, on reports by the patient and on affective or emotional features is usually associated with the belief that first-person experiences of the mental disorder are *unique* to *each patient*. And while, for instance, psychiatric epidemiology looks for difference-making *risk factors* to build up causal accounts concerning *populations* for preventive reasons, clinical psychiatry and psychotherapy look for the *actual causes* that brought about the disorder in the *single* patient under examination, to elaborate causal explanations ex post.

We cannot do without general models. Relationships are hence drawn between a single patient's distress and some more general phenomenon whose features are re-tailored on the patient to explain her specific condition. An issue worth stressing for all theories of causation – and extremely relevant for the health sciences – is the relation between type and token causation. Woodward holds his approach can grasp both. He believes that to state "C is causally relevant to E" is to make, in the first place, a type causal claim. However, he stresses that such claim also indicates that changing the value of C instantiated in particular spatiotemporally located individuals changes the value of E instantiated in other particular individuals. Type-causal relationships are maintained to play an essential role in elucidating actual, token causal relationships; both are believed to embody a counterfactual-manipulationist notion of causation. In a medical context, enquiries cannot but start from many single occurrences from which invariant generalizations are extracted to create exemplars of diseases; exemplars are then called into play to account for the individual features of the single patient under consideration. No patient is likely to exhibit *all* the symptoms and signs that are regarded as "standard" of a given disorder, but a general model is fundamental to frame and explain what occurs in the individual.

Once difference-making causal variables are identified, it is possible to construct a what-if-things-had-been-different explanation. However, an adequate explanatory account can require, in addition, to provide clues on what occurs *in between* causes and effects. A causal picture might need have to identify both *what* brings about the disorder, and specify *how* causal factors have done so. Productive activities might be spelt out from a mechanistic perspective, which, while not incompatible with the interventionist view, embraces a different standpoint on explanation. Woodward recently stated:

> In some cases the relevant difference-making factors may be very concrete and specific. [...] In other cases, the difference-making factors may be "higher-level" and less specific. [...] [It]

is these latter cases that often strike us as comparatively "non-mechanistic" (2013, pp. 47–48).

I believe some clarification is warranted. It is definitely true that variables can be more or less concrete, more or less specific, and belong to higher or lower levels. In principle, high and low levels can be equally dealt with both within an interventionist and a mechanistic perspective, properly devised. The difference between mechanistic and non-mechanistic explanatory accounts does not have to do only with fine-grainess, but with the conception of explanation itself, which, according to mechanistic views, implies some opening-up of "the black box" underlying the phenomenon at stake. At the same time, in contexts in which a mechanistic description of the disorder's functioning is (still) hard to obtain, interventionist explanations might be both the most likely to be elaborated and the most useful.

How many levels are considered, how fine-grained their description is, and to what extent their actual interactions are elucidated are problematic issues. Interestingly, in the last few years interventionist and mechanistic approaches have partially come closer together: as recalled in section one, mechanistic approaches have increasingly acknowledged the heuristic role of interventions, while the interventionist approach has recently admitted mechanistic descriptions as finer descriptions of difference-making variables. Mechanisms are more often than not incomplete, and hence count as "mechanism sketches;" the causally relevant variables composing them are identified by means of interventions. Shall we then wonder how "sketchy" an account can be before it stops being genuinely mechanistic, and tell exclusively which variables are causally connected and what invariant under intervention generalizations hold, thus shifting towards a thoroughly interventionist picture?

Woodward considered few years ago that

> whether we should think of the mechanical/non-mechanical contrast as a sharp dichotomy, or instead more in the nature of a graded (perhaps multi-dimensional) continuum according to which some explanations are more 'mechanical' than others (in various respects) (2013, p. 41).

This prospect is very promising, although it might not capture the specific interest mechanistic accounts have for what happens *in between* cause-effect variables and for *the way* in which they carry out their activities. The mechanistic account per se, though, does not suffice either. For instance, at a physiological level, a panic attack during a near-fatal climbing accident in a psychiatrically healthy individual or a in a crowded shopping mall in a patient with agoraphobia are probably the same (Kendler 2005b, p. 437).

But only the latter phenomenon is related to a mental disorder. A mechanistic account at the physiological level here will not do. Reasoning in terms of hypothetical interventions on the individual's specific situation can easily and straightforwardly tell the difference.

> What is at issue is *the optimal level* in the causal processes underlying psychiatric illness at which *intervention* can be best focused *and understanding* most easily achieved (Kendler 2005b, p. 436, italics added).

In this sense, a "continuum" of explanatory options might provide both researchers and clinicians with a broad set of – potentially complementary – tools.

3 Concluding Remarks

Biological psychiatry, genetic psychiatry, psychiatric epidemiology, neurobiology, behavioural neurology, pharmacology, pharmacopsychology, neuropsychology, cognitive psychology, clinical psychology, and other disciplines are currently striving to describe and explain disorders from different – although not necessarily diverging – standpoints. The challenge is to construct a multi-faceted and coherent picture of mental disorders through some integration of the extraordinary advances in biomedical research and the methodological peculiarities of clinical practice. Various efforts have this end in view. A paper co-authored by Drozdstoj Stoyanov, Peter Machamer, and Kenneth Schaffner (2012) discusses the notion of evidence in clinical psychology, and points out some methodological deficiencies in the field. An exemplary case (the Minnesota Multiphasic Personality Inventory) is examined to stress the subjective character permeating both the investigation methods and the emerging data, with the cognitive content of clinical judgment being deemed as subjective as the narrative of the patient. This is seen as a serious shortcoming of clinical psychology, to be overcome to construct a theoretically sound and genuinely scientific model of the discipline.

However, methodological rigour shall not be construed to de-personalize and objectify psychic activity. Very interestingly, around the same time (2011) one of the authors of the paper, Schaffner, together with Tim Thornton, discussing perspectives on the mental health sciences, has considered "psychiatry for the person", which calls for a more comprehensive approach to psychiatry in which conventional elements are combined with a specifically person-centred extra ingredient [...], and aims to balance a growing emphasis on the natural scientific underpinnings of psychiatry with an increased focus on the importance and role of the person (Thornton and Schaffner 2011, p. 128).

The proposal to balance natural science with the role of the so-called personal elements mirrors the need to entrench efforts from different perspectives. A growing plea for the introduction of different elements is being made: strict methodological rules, experimental activity, RCTs and imaging techniques are required – as the paradigmatic scientific tools – to acknowledge also the relevance of individual and subjective features, increasingly highlighted by patient-centred care and personalized medicine.

These issues can be seen to somehow converge with further concerns about the traditional distinction between explanation and understanding. A few years after wishing to move past the "Cartesian" mind-brain dualism (Kendler 2005b), Kendler and Campbell suggest a rethinking of the very framework of explanation and understanding. Their (2013) paper addresses progress in neuroscience and neuropsychology, and describes two explanatory models of psychotic symptoms, which both start off describing pathological brain processes at a biological level in neuroscience language and then adopt neuropsychology language to move on from brain dysfunctions to the mental level. Neuropsychology provides hypotheses about the functional and physiological correlates of subjective experiences, and is seen as helpful in reframing the relation between explanation and understanding: it can expand the boundaries of what can be understood through a process Kendler and Campbell label "explanation-aided understanding,"[22] by providing some – more scientific? – grounding for empathic understanding.

What place can be occupied by an interventionist theory in such a scenario? Woodward states that

interventionists about causation think that the acquisition of information relevant to manipulation and control is among the goals centrally associated with causal thinking, but of course there are other candidates for such goals – for example, information compression and simplification or unification of patterns of correlation (2012, p. 963).

---

22 Kendler and Campbell specifically discuss the impact of advances in neuroscience and neuropsychology for the construction of models of schizophrenia and ADHD. On neuropsychology as a bridging field between psychology and neuroscience, in a non-reductionist perspective, see Wright and Bechtel (2007).

Undoubtedly further research must focus on the achievement of more detailed accounts concerning patterns of correlations and the workings of the variables involved. Different standpoints might fit different needs.

> A representation of the brain in terms of coarse-grained psychological variables like "cognitive judgment" and "emotion" might be highly non-modular, a representation at the level of individual neurons more modular (Woodward 2013, p. 52).

An explanation appealing to "cognitive judgment" and "emotions" might also be regarded as more suitably framed in interventionist rather than mechanistic terms at this stage.

However, I am by no means claiming that interventionist causal accounts are to be seen as just partial or provisional explanations. Quite the contrary, given the issues emerging from mental disorders and the recent proposal to insert the interventionist account in the context of an "explanatory continuum," it must be there to stay and help bridge the gap between differently oriented approaches. As I have argued, to do so plausibly and convincingly, the interventionist account needs to pay adequate attention to such elements as the actual modes of interactions among variables, their spatial and temporal dimensions, the role of observational evidence, and the background assumptions in the constructions of causal models of disorders. Only by accounting for these aspects too can a proper understanding of mental disorder be pursued, and the rapprochement of different conceptions of causation and causal explanation be seen in the prospect of conciliating different disciplinary approaches to mental disorders.

If a proper integration of organic, biomedical-oriented approaches and psychosocial strategies is to be pursued, then the framework to be promoted could also be that of an "understanding-aided explanation," with genuine scientific explanations including subjective, mental aspects together with information on brain processes. The neurosciences increasingly provide hypotheses on structures underlying subjective experiences,

> even though we do not yet understand how those subjective correlates are generated. Neuropsychology does not of itself allow us to understand the mechanisms by which those brain states realize a subjective life in the first place. In fact, at the moment, we do not understand at the most basic level how the mechanisms might work through which particular patterns of brain activity generate particular patterns of experience. Neuropsychology nonetheless does put us in a position to clarify *which patterns* of brain activity are generating *which patterns* of experience (Kendler and Campbell 2013, p. 5).

This looks like a scenario that can be perfectly captured in interventionist terms: we have a causal chain whose middle is currently blank, with the tracking of intermediate causal pathways and their specific functions being the object of further research. The ongoing evolution of the interventionist account and its burgeoning relation with the neo-mechanist view offer a promising approach to capture disciplinary integrations and trends in investigations of mental disorders.

Acknowledgments: I would like to thank Angelo Fioritti, Roberta Passione and Francisco Rodriguez Valls for suggestions and comments on a draft version of this paper.

References

Adam, M. (2011): "Multi-level Complexities in Technological Development: Competing Strategies for Drug Discovery." In: Carrier, M. and Nordmann, A. (eds.): *Science in the Context of Application*, pp. 67–83. Dordrecht: Springer.

American Psychiatric Association (2013): *Diagnostic and Statistical Manual of Mental Disorders*. Washington, DC: American Psychiatric Association.

Baedke, J. (2012): "Causal Explanation beyond the Gene: Manipulation and Causality in Epigenetics." *Theoria*, v. 74, pp. 153–174.

Bonawitz, E. B., Ferranti, D., Saxe, R., Gopnik, A., Meltzoff, A. N., Woodward, J., and Schulz, L. E. (2010): "Just Do it? Investigating the Gap between Prediction and Action in Toddlers' Causal Inferences." *Cognition*, v. 115, pp. 104–117.

Campaner, R. (2014): "Explanatory Pluralism in Psychiatry: What Are We Pluralists about, and Why?" In: Galavotti, M. C., Dieks, D., Gonzalez, W. J., Hartmann, S., Uebel, T., and Weber, M. (eds.): *New Directions in the Philosophy of Science*, pp. 87–103. Dordrecht: Springer.

Campbell, J. (2007): "An Interventionist Approach to Causation in Psychology." In: Gopnik, A. and Schulz, L. (eds.): *Causal Learning: Psychology, Philosophy and Computation*, pp. 258–266. New York: Oxford University Press.

Caspi, A., McClay, J., E. Moffitt, T., Mill, J., Martin, J., Craig, I. W., Taylor, A., and Poulton, R. (2002): "Role of Genotype in the Cycle of Violence in Maltreated Children." *Science*, v. 297, pp. 851–854.

Cavanna, A. (ed.) (2013): "Researching Tourette Syndrome in Europe." *Behavioural Neurology*, Special Issue 27, n. 1.

Civita, A. (1996): *Introduzione alla storia e all'epistemologia della psichiatria*. Milan: Guerini Studio.

Craver, C. (2007): *Explaining the Brain*. Oxford: Oxford University Press.

Debes, N. M. (2013): "Co-morbid Disorders in Tourette Syndrome." *Behavioural Neurology*, v. 27, pp. 7–14.

DSM 5 (2013) *Diagnostic and Statistical Manual of Mental Disorders*, 5th edition, Washington, DC: American Psychiatric Association.

Feder, A., Nestler, E. J., and Charney, D. S. (2009): "Psychobiology and Molecular Genetics of Resilience." *Nature Review Neuroscience*, v. 10, pp. 446–457.

Garner, A. and Hardcastle, V. G. (2004): "Neurobiological Models: An Unnecessary Divide – Neural Models in Psychiatry." In: Radden, J. (ed.): *The Philosophy of Psychiatry. A Companion*, pp. 364–380. Oxford: Oxford University Press.

Gert, B. and Culver, C. M. (2004): "Defining metal disorder." In: Radden, J. (ed.): *The Philosophy of Psychiatry. A Companion*, pp. 415–425. Oxford: Oxford University Press.

Glennan, S. (2010): "Mechanisms, Causes, and the Layered Model of the World." *Philosophy and Phenomenological Research*, v. 81, pp. 362–381.

Gorman, D. A., Thompson, N., Plessen, K. J., Robertson, M. M., Leckman, J. F., and Peterson, B. S. (2010): "Psychosocial Outcome and Psychiatric Comorbidity in Older Adolescents with Tourette Syndrome: Controlled Study." *British Journal of Psychiatry*, v. 197, pp. 36–44.

Gutman, D. A. and Nemeroff C. B. (2003): "Persistent Central Nervous System Effects of an Adverse Early Environment: Clinical and Preclinical Studies." *Physiology and Behaviour*, v. 79, pp. 471–478.

Henderson, D. (2005): "Norms, Invariance and Explanatory Relevance." *Philosophy of the Social Sciences*, v. 35, pp. 324–338.

Insel, T. R. (2010): "Rethinking Schizophrenia." *Nature*, v. 468, pp. 187–193.

Kano, Y., Ohta, M. Nagai, Y., and Scahill, L. (2010): "Association between Tourette Syndrome and Comorbidities in Japan." *Brain Development*, v. 32, pp. 201–207.

Kendler, K. (2005a): "Psychiatric Genetics: A Methodological Critique." *American Journal of Psychiatry*, v. 162, pp. 3–11.

Kendler, K. (2005b): "Toward a Philosophical Structure for Psychiatry." *American Journal of Psychiatry*, v. 162, pp. 433–440.

Kendler, K. (2008): "Explanatory Models for Psychiatric Illness." *American Journal of Psychiatry*, v. 165, pp. 695–702.

Kendler K. (2012): "Levels of Explanation in Psychiatric and Substance Use Disorders: Implications for the Development of an Etiologically Based Nosology." *Molecular Psychiatry*, v. 17, pp. 1–18.

Kendler, K. (2013): "What Psychiatric Genetics has Taught Us about the Nature of Psychiatric Illness and What Is Left to Learn." *Molecular Psychiatry*, v. 18, pp. 1058–1066.

Kendler, K. and Campbell, J. (2009): "Interventionist Causal Models in Psychiatry: Repositioning the Mind-body Problem." *Psychological Medicine*, v. 39, pp. 881–887.

Kendler, K. and Campbell J. (2013): "Expanding the Domain of the Understandable in Psychiatric Illness: An Updating of the Jasperian Framework of Explanation and Understanding." *Psychological Medicine*, v. 43, pp. 1–7.

Machamer P., Darden L., and Craver C. (2000): "Thinking about Mechanisms." *Philosophy of Science*, v. 67, pp. 1–25.

Miller, D. W. and Miller, C. G. (2005): "On Evidence, Medical and Legal." *Journal of American Physicians and Surgeons*, v. 10, pp. 70–75.

Radden, J. (ed.) (2004): *The Philosophy of Psychiatry. A Companion*. Oxford: Oxford University Press.

Sadler, J. Z. (2004): "Diagnosis and Antidiagnosis." In: Radden, J. (ed.): *The Philosophy of Psychiatry. A Companion*, pp. 163–179. Oxford: Oxford University Press.

Saver J. L and Kalafut, M. (2001): "Combination Therapies and the Theoretical Limits of Evidence-based Medicine." *Neuroepidemiology*, v. 20, pp. 57–64.

Schaffner, K. (2013): "Reduction and Reductionism in Psychiatry." In: Fuldord, K. W. M. et al (eds.): *The Oxford Handbook of Philosophy and Psychiatry*, pp. 1003–1022. New York: Oxford University Press.

Stoyanov, D. S. (2009): "The Cross-validation in the Dialogue of Mental and Neuroscience." *Dialogues in Philosophy, Mental and Neuro Sciences*, v. 2, pp. 24–28.

Stoyanov, D. S., Machamer, P., and Schaffner, K. (2012): "Rendering Clinical Psychology an Evidence-based Scientific Discipline: A Case Study." *Journal of Evaluation in Clinical Practice*, v. 18, pp. 149–154.

Tabery, J. (2009): "Difference Mechanisms: Explaining Variation with Mechanisms." *Biology and Philosophy*, v. 24, pp. 645–664.

Thagard, P. and Findlay, S. (2011): "Conceptual Change in Medicine: Explaining Mental Illness." In: Gonzalez, W. J. (ed.): *Conceptual Revolutions: From Cognitive Science to Medicine*, pp. 157–177. A Coruña: Netbiblo.

Thornton T. and Schaffner, K. (2011): "Philosophy of Science Perspectives on Psychiatry for the Person." *The International Journal of Person Centered Medicine*, v. 1, pp. 128–130.

Van Os, J., Kenis, G., and Rutten, B. P. (2010): "The Environment and Schizophrenia." *Nature*, v. 468, pp. 203–212.

Van Reekum, R., Streiner D. L., Conn, D. K. (2001): "Applying Bradiford Hill's Criteria for Causation to Neuropsychiatry: Challenges and Opportunities." *Journal of Neuropsychiatry and Clinical Neuroscience*, v. 13, pp. 318–325.

Waters, K. (2007): "Causes that Make a Difference." *Journal of Philosophy*, v. 104, pp. 551–579.

Woodward, J. (2000): "Explanation and Invariance in the Special Sciences." *The British Journal for the Philosophy of Science*, v. 51, pp. 197–254.

Woodward, J. (2002): "What Is a Mechanism? A Counterfactual Account." *Philosophy of Science*, v. 69, n. 3, pp. S366–S377.

Woodward, J. (2003): *Making Things Happen*. Oxford: Oxford University Press.

Woodward, J. (2004): "Counterfactuals and Causal Explanation." *International Studies in the Philosophy of Science*, v. 18, pp. 41–72.

Woodward, J. (2007): "Interventionist Theories of Causation in Pychological Perspective." In: Gopnik, A. and Schulz, L. (eds.): *Causal Learning: Psychology, Philosophy, and Computation*, pp. 19–36. New York: Oxford University Press.

Woodward, J. (2008): "Cause and Explanation in Psychiatry." In: Kendler, K. S. and Parnas, J. (eds.): *Philosophical Issues in Psychiatry. Explanation, Phenomenology, and Nosology*, pp. 132–184. Baltimore, MD: The Johns Hopkins University Press.

Woodward, J. (2010): "Causation in Biology: Stability, Specificity, and the Choice of Levels of Explanation." *Biology and Philosophy*, v. 25, pp. 287–318.

Woodward, J. (2011): "Mechanisms Revisited." *Synthese*, v. 183, pp. 409–427.

Woodward, J. (2012): "Causation: Integration between Philosophical Theories and Psychological Research." *Philosophy of Science*, v. 79, pp. 961–972.

Woodward, J. (2013): "Mechanistic Explanation: Its Scope and Limits." *Proceedings of the Aristotelian Society, Supplementary Volume*, v. 87, pp. 39–65.

Woodward, J. (2014): "Causal Reasoning: Philosophy and Experiment." In: Knobe, J., Lombrozo, T., and Nichols, S. (eds.): *Oxford Studies in Experimental Philosophy*, pp. 294–324. Oxford: Oxford University Press.
Wright, C. and Bechtel, W. (2007): "Mechanisms and Psychological Explanation." In: Thagard, P. (ed.): *Philosophy of Psychology and Cognitive Science*, pp. 31–80. New York: Elsevier.

Index of Names

Acero, J. J. 241
Adam, M. 253, 265
Adams, C. M., 153, 156
Adams, F. 67
Adolphs, R. 66
Ahn, W. 6, 15, 45, 77, 99, 105, 112, 129–136
Aitken, M. R. F., 151f., 155f.
Albantakis, L. 165, 176
Alcock, J. 60
Alcolea, J. 16, 54, 199
Allaire, E. 52
Allegri, R. F. 154
Allman, J. 28, 59, 61
Andersen, H. 55
Anderson, S. W. 150, 155
Angrist, J. 85, 99
Anscombe, G. E. M. 49, 53, 57
Antoun, N. 151, 156
Anzulewicz, A. 166, 171, 174
Apel, J. 67
Aquinas, Th. 208, 217
Arana, J. 203
Arbuckle, R. 153, 156
Ardila, R. 140, 155, 195, 198
Arminger, G. 57
Armstrong, D. M. 165f., 174
Aru, J. 172–174
Asanowicz, D. 160f., 166, 174, 177
Atas, A. 165, 177
Aue, M. A. E. 57f.
Aue, T. 145, 154
Ausubel, D. 184

Baars, B. J. 164, 174
Bachmann, T. 172, 174
Baedke, J. 243, 265
Baillargeon, R. 76, 99
Baillet, S. 164, 174
Banich, M. T. 151, 157
Barrett, A. 160f., 175
Barry, B. 66
Baumgartner, M. 67
Bechara, A. 147–150, 152, 155f., 182, 198

Bechtel, W. 263, 268
Beck, S. R. 58, 64
Beebee, H. 58, 64f., 67
Behrens, T. E. J. 152, 157
Bennett, S. M. 153, 156
Bergholt, B. 170, 176
Bermpohl, F. 153, 156
Berstein, J. 184
Bickhard, M. H. 234, 242
Bigge, W. 160, 175
Black, S. E. 151, 155
Blackmore, J. C. 67
Blake, R. 163, 174, 176
Blanco, A. 241
Blanke, O. 171f., 174
Block, N. 67, 160, 162f., 165, 174, 232f., 241f.
Boeker, H. 153, 156
Bogen, J. 23, 53, 60, 66f.
Bolla, K. I. 153, 155
Bonawitz, E. B. 27, 53, 61, 84, 99, 244, 265
Botterill, G. 67, 241
Boumans, M. 67
Bovens, L. 63
Braun, R. A. 198
Bravo, E. 168, 175
Breedlove, S. M. 140, 157
Breinlinger, K. 100
Brentano, F. 162, 168, 174
Brett, M. 142, 155
Brewer, W. F. 68
Broncano, F. 241
Bruin, L. 68
Bruner, J. 184, 234, 241
Brzechczyn, K. 55
Bunge, M. 140, 155, 160, 174

Cacioppo, J. T. 145, 154
Cadet, J. L. 153, 155
Calvo, P. 67
Camerer, C. F. 140, 155
Campaner, R. vi, 12–15, 243, 246, 265
Campbell, J. 247f., 256, 259, 263–266
Carnap, R. 9, 15, 37, 196, 198

Carrier, M. 265
Carruthers, P. 67, 166, 174, 241f.
Cartwright, N. 66–68, 186, 200
Caspi, A. 259, 265
Castellanos, F. X. 153, 156
Cavanna, A. 249, 265
Chacón, P. vi, 12f., 15, 221
Chalmers, D. 160, 164, 174
Changeux, J.-P. 160, 164, 174, 182, 198
Charney, D. S. 259, 266
Cheng, P. 96, 100, 123, 125–129, 131, 137
Chinn, C. A. 68
Chisholm, M. R. 67
Chomsky, N. 12, 221f., 229, 241
Christensen, S. 60
Churchland, P. M. 181f., 198
Churchland, P. S. 182, 198
Civita, A. 252, 265
Clark, A. 239, 241
Clark, L. 151f., 155f.
Claus, E. 151, 157
Cleeremans, A. 160f., 165–168, 170, 172–174, 176f.
Clogg, C. C. 57
Cohen, M. A. 160, 165, 168, 174
Coli, E. 91
Collingwood, R. G. 27, 53, 62
Collins, J. 68, 100, 136
Conn, D. K. 267
Contoreggi, C. 153, 155
Corry, R. 58, 63, 69
Costantini, D. 68
Couch, M. 64
Cowie, F. 63
Craig, A. D. 182, 198
Craig, I. W. 265
Craver, C. 246, 265f.
Crick, F. 160, 163, 165, 174, 182, 185, 199, 201
Critchley, H. D. 160, 175
Crumley, J. 60
Culver, C. M. 248, 266
Curd, M. 63

Dalwani, M. 151, 157
Damasio, A. 147–150, 152, 155, 182, 185, 199, 204, 217
Damasio, H. R. 148–150, 155

Daniusis, D. 100
Danks, D. 68f., 122, 136–137
Darden, L. 246, 266
Darwin, Ch. 212, 217
Dascal, M. 223, 241
Dasgupta, S. 47, 53
Davis, L. 85, 100
De Gardelle, V. 165, 175
de Regt, H. W. 37, 53
De Vreese, L. 31, 53, 68
Debes, N. M. 253, 265
Dehaene, S. 160, 164f., 168, 174f., 177
Del Cul, A. 164, 168, 174f.
Dennett, D. C. 160f., 164f., 168, 174f., 223, 241
Dieks, D. 55, 265
Dienes, Z. 160, 166, 171, 175–177
Diosdado, C. 203
Dolan, R. J. 152, 155
Dowe, Ph. 37, 54, 68, 74, 100, 113f., 116
Dummett, M. A. E. 38, 54
Dupoux, E. 165, 175

Eberhardt, F. 68, 136
Eccles, J. C. 187, 199f.
Edelman, G. M. 182, 186, 199
Eilen, N. 1, 16, 64, 67
Eldreth, D. A. 153, 155
Ellacuría, I. 218
Elliott, R. 152, 155
Ernst, M. 153, 155
Evans, J. 214, 217
Ezquerro, J. 240f.

Feder, A. 259, 266
Fehl, K. 170, 176
Fei-Fei, L. 163, 175
Ferranti, D. 53, 61, 99, 265
Fetzer, J. 65
Findlay, S. 245, 267
Fioritti, A. 265
Fisher, R. 28
Fleming, L. 44, 54
Fodor, J. A. 1, 12f., 15, 184f., 199, 221–242
Fong, G. W. 153, 156
Ford, K. M. 57
Frankish, K. 214, 217

Freeman, A. W., 175
Frege, G. 183
Froese, T. 160 f., 175
Froeyman, A. 69
Fujiwara, E. 151, 155
Fukui, H. 152, 155
Fukuyama, H. 152, 155
Fuldord, K. W. M. 267

Gadamer, H. G. 193, 199
Gage, Ph. 185
Galavotti, M. C. 54, 63, 68, 265
Gao, F. 151, 155
García-Albea, J. E. 227, 231, 239 f., 242
García Sedeño, M. A. vi, 9 f., 15, 181
García Vega, L. 183, 199
Garfinkel, S. N. 160, 175
Garner, A. 255, 258, 266
Gazzaniga, M. S. 182, 199
Gelman, S. 6, 15, 99, 136
Gendler, T. S., 88 f., 100, 175
Gert, B. 248, 266
Giere, R. N. 10, 190 f., 199
Gijsbers, V. 68
Gillies, D. 43, 53
Gleichgerrcht, E. 182, 199
Glennan, S. 246, 266
Glymour, B. 68, 136
Glymour, C. N. 28, 37, 57, 61, 72, 86, 100, 110-f., 136
Glynn, L. 68
Goldman, A. 192, 196, 199
Goleman, D. 204, 217
Gonzalez, W. J. v, 1, 3 f., 7, 10, 12, 15 f., 21, 23–28, 30–32, 34–36, 39 f., 42–45, 49, 51, 54–57, 68, 156, 190, 193, 198–200, 203, 242, 265, 267
González-García, C. 145, 155
González-Marqués, J. 142, 157
Goodin, R. 66
Goodstein, D. 60
Goodwin, W. 68
Gopnik, A. 27, 53, 58, 61, 63, 68, 70, 76, 99–101, 131, 265, 267
Gorman, D. A. 253, 266
Goshwami, U. 99
Gould, C. 161, 175

Granger, C. 29, 39, 55
Gray, J. A. 205, 217
Greeno, J. G. 56
Greenwood, J. 60
Griffiths, T. 72, 100
Grimm, S. 153, 156
Grünbaum, A. 48, 55
Guillan, A. 15
Gutman, D. A. 259, 266

Hahn, L. E. 54
Hajek, P. 63
Hall, N. 68, 97 f., 100, 121, 135 f.
Halpern, J. 68, 108, 136
Hanakawa, T. 152, 155
Hansell, N. K. 163, 176
Hanzel, I. 69
Hardcastle, V. G. 255, 258, 266
Hare, B. 195, 199
Harris, P. 154
Harris, T. 69
Harsay, H. A. 169, 177
Hartmann, S. 63, 265
Hausman, D. M. 60 f., 67
Hawking, S. 186, 200
Hayashi, T. 152, 155
Hayes, P. J. 57
Heavey, C. L. 161, 175
Heidegger, M. 208–210, 217
Hell, D. 153, 156
Hempel, C. G. 25, 32 f., 50, 52, 55
Henderson, D. 266
Henderson, L. 62, 243
Henkin, L. 57
Herfeld, W. E. 56
Hiddleston, E. 69
Hintikka, J. 54
Hitchcock, Ch. 58, 61, 63–65, 67, 69, 107 f., 111, 137
Hoefer, C. 63
Hoerl, C. 58, 64
Hogarth, R. M. 56
Hohwy, J. 63, 137
Hommer, D. 153, 156
Horgan, T. 48, 55, 60
Humphreys, P. 64, 69
Hubner, A. 67

Index of Names

Hurlburt, R. T. 161, 175
Husserl, E. 161, 175
Hutcherson, C. A. 62
Hutchison, K. 151, 157
Hyafil, A. 151, 154, 156

Ibanez, A. 182, 199
Illary, M. 67
Imbert, C. 69
Insel, T. R. 252, 259, 266
Iwasaki, Y. 37, 55

Jackendoff, R. 242
Jacobson, K. 100
Janis, A. 63
Jansson, L. 69
Jantzen, B. 69
Janzig, D. 72, 78
Jeffrey, R. C. 56
Jessell, Th. 181, 200
Jessor, R. 57
Jódar-Vicente, M. 155
Johnsrude, I. S. 142, 155
Joja, A. 57
Jollant, F. 152, 156
Jones, M. 66

Kahneman, D. 45, 55f.
Kalafut, M. 251, 267
Kalish, C. 6, 15, 99, 136
Kallestrup, J. 63, 137
Kandel, E. 181, 200
Kano, Y. 253, 266
Kaplan, D. 59, 65
Karbasizadeh, A. E. 69
Karnath, H.-O. 145, 157
Kendler, K. S. 64, 244–248, 251, 256, 259, 262–264, 266f.
Kenis, G. 259, 267
Kenny, A. 47, 56
Keuzenkamp, H. A. 57
Kiani, R. 169, 176
Kierkegaard, S. 208f., 212, 217
Kincaid, H. 64
Kistler, M. 69
Kitcher, Ph. 10, 50, 56, 62, 190f., 196, 200
Knobe, J. 58, 64, 111, 137, 268

Knowles, D. 62
Knutson, B. 153, 156
Koch, C. 160, 162f., 165, 174–176, 199
Koechlin, E. 151, 154, 156
Koepfli, J. 52
Kolb, B. 142, 156
Kouider, S. 165, 175
Krain, A. L. 153, 156
Krajewski, W. 56
Kreiman, G. 162f., 176
Kuokkanen, M. 56
Kurian, V. 153, 155

Lack, L. C. 163, 173, 175
Lakatos, I. 52
Lamme, V. A. F. 160, 163, 165, 175
Lau, H. C. 161f., 165–168, 175f.
Laudan, L. 10, 191f., 200
Lavelle, L. A. 145, 154
Lawrence, N. S. 152, 156
Lazarus, R. 204, 217
Leahey, T. H. 185, 200
LeDoux, J. 205, 215, 217
Lee, S. W. 148, 155
Lemeire, J. 100
Leonelli, S. 69
Lerman, H. 1, 16, 64, 67
Leuridan, B. 69
Levine, A. 234, 242
Levine, S. 151, 155
Lewis, D. 37, 50, 73f., 90, 93, 96, 99f., 128
Liao, M. 64
Lien, Y. 96, 100, 123, 125–129, 131, 137
Ling, S. 163, 176
Little, D. 58, 63
Liu, G. B. 163, 176
Llinás, R. 186, 200
Loewer, B. 223, 241f.
Logothetis, N. K. 144, 156, 163, 174
Lombrozo, T. 58, 64, 95f., 98, 100, 268
Luckhardt, C. G. 57f.
Lycan, W. G. 60
Lynch, T. E., 156
Lynch, Z. 181, 200

Machamer, P. 55, 63, 262, 266f.
Machery, E. 122, 137

Macomber, J. 100
Maestú Unturbe, F. 142, 157
Malaterre, Ch. 69
Manes, F. 151, 156, 182, 199
Maniscalco, B. 168, 176
Mantzavinos, C. 64
Marcel, A. 175
Marek, J. C. 67
Margolis, J. 67
Martin, J. 265
Martin, N. G. 163, 176
Martinez-Freire, P. 192, 200, 242
Martínez Selva, J. M. v, 7 f., 16, 139 – 141, 144, 147, 156
Martínez-Solano, J. F. 15, 66
Mason, K. 67
Massey, G. 63
Massimi, M. 69
Matochik, J. A. 153, 155
Mayer, J. D. 204
McAleer, M. 57
McCabe, C. 7, 16, 140, 156
McCabe, K. A. 148, 156
McCormack, T. 58, 64
McCulloch, W. S. 183, 185, 200
McDermott, M. 111, 137
McDonnell, J. S. 52, 99
McGann, M. 160, 175
McKim, V. 63
McLaughlin, B. 242
McNaughton, N. 205, 217
Mealor, A. D. 160, 176
Medin, D. 6, 15, 99, 136
Melloni, L. 172, 174
Meltzoff, A. N., 53, 61, 99, 265
Menzies, P. 27, 37, 58, 64, 67, 69
Metzinger, T. 171 f., 174
Middleton, H. C. 152, 156
Milham, M. P. 153, 156
Miller, C. G. 251 f., 255, 266
Miller, D. W. 251 f., 255, 266
Miller, G. 159, 176
Miller, K. 54
Miller, S. M. 163, 176
Mitchell, S. 61, 69
Moisil, G. C. 57
Montaser-Kouhsari, L. 62

Monserrat, J. 200
Mooij, J. 100
Morgado, I. 217
Morgan, G. 64
Mountcastle, V. 182, 200
Mouratidis, M. 153, 155
Mouridsen, K. 170 f., 176
Moya Santoyo, J. 183, 199
Munevar, G. 54
Murai, T. 152, 155

Naccache, L. 160, 164, 174
Nagel, E. 32 – 35, 50 f., 216
Nagel, Th. 56, 216 f.
Nemeroff, C. B. 259, 266
Nestler, E. J. 259, 266
Ngo, T. T. 163, 176
Nguyen, V. A. 173, 175
Nichols, S. 58, 64, 268
Niiniluoto, I. 4, 16, 44 f., 56
Nordmann, A. 265
Northoff, G. 153, 156
Nussbaum, M. 204, 217
Nyman, H. 57 f.

O'Daly, O. 152, 156
Oizumi, M. 165, 176
Ortega y Gasset, J. 211, 217
Overgaard, M. 161 f., 166, 170 f., 176 f.
Owen, A. M. 142, 152, 155 f.

Paprzycka, K. 55
Parnas, J. 64, 267
Paslaru, V. 69
Passingham, R. E. 168, 176
Passione, R. 265
Paul, L. A. 68, 100, 135 f.
Paulewicz, B. 160 f., 166, 174, 177
Pearl, J. 28 f., 37, 47, 56, 68, 72, 100, 108, 136
Penrose, R. 186, 200
Perona, P. 163, 175
Persson, J. 56, 70
Pessoa, L. 166, 177
Pettigrew, J. D. 163, 176
Pexton, M. 70
Pfeifer, J. 64

Phillips, M. L. 152, 156
Piaget, J. 184
Piatelli-Palmarini, M. 242
Picard, R. W. 204, 217
Pickard, J. D. 152, 156
Pinker, S. 235f., 242
Pischke, J.-S. 85, 99
Pitts, W. 183
Plotkin, H. 235, 242
Poldrack, A. R. 145, 156
Popper, K. R. 187, 189, 200
Pozo, J. I. 242
Price, H. 27, 37, 58, 63, 65, 67, 69
Priest, G. 69
Psillos, S. 32, 43, 49f., 56, 63, 67, 69f.
Puhl, J. 54
Pujadas, L. M. 233, 242
Putnam, H. 12, 221f., 237
Pylyshyn, Z. 242

Quine, W. v. O. 37, 189f., 200

Radden, J. 266
Radder, H. 58, 63
Ramachandran, V. S. 182, 200
Ramón y Cajal, S. 188
Ramsey, J. L. 68, 70, 136
Ramsøy, T. Z. 161, 171, 176
Rangel, A. 62
Redoute, J. 148, 156
Rees, G. 152, 155, 162f., 176
Reiss, J. 70
Rescher, N. 37, 40, 56f., 63
Resulaj, A. 169, 176
Rey, G., 223, 241f.
Rey, J. 15, 66
Reyes, P. 168, 175
Ridderinkhof, K. R. 169, 177
Ríos-Lago, M. 142, 157
Risjord, M. K. 63
Rivière, A. 240, 242
Robbins, T. W. 152, 155
Rodriguez Valls, F. vi, 9–11, 203, 217, 265
Roessler, J. 1, 16, 64, 67
Rogers, R. D. 151f., 156
Rolls, E. T. 148, 156
Román, F. 147, 156

Rorden, C. 145, 157
Rose, D. 122, 137
Rosenberg, A. 70
Rosenthal, D. M. 161f., 165–168, 172, 175f.
Rosenzweig, M. R. 140, 157
Ross, D. 64
Rote, J. 171, 176
Roth, G. 181, 200
Rothwell, J. C. 168, 176
Rounis, E. 168, 170, 176
Ruben, D. H. 32, 56, 59
Rubin, D. 85, 100
Ruinov, M. 145, 157
Ruiz, M. J. 142, 157
Rushworth, M. F. S. 152, 157
Russell, B. 183
Russo, Ph. 67
Rutten, B. P. 259, 267
Ruz, M. 145, 155

Saatsi, J. 70
Sackur, J. 164f., 174f.
Sadler, J. Z. 253, 266
Sahakian, B. J. 151f., 155f.
Salmon, M. H. 24, 37, 56
Salmon, W. C. 35, 37, 42, 50, 56f., 62, 113f., 116, 137
Salovey, P. 204
Sanchez Navarro, J. P. 147, 156
Sandberg, K. 161f., 166, 170f., 176
Sartre, J. P. 208, 217
Savage, C. W. 241
Saxe, R. 53, 61, 99, 265
Scazzieri, R. 54
Schaffer, J. 74, 100
Schaffner, K. 255, 262f., 267
Scheines, R. 28, 57, 68, 72, 100, 136
Scheler, M. 213, 217
Schindler, S. 70
Schmidt, C. 153, 156
Schollkopf, B. 72
Schulz, L. E. 53, 58, 61, 63, 68, 99–101, 265, 267
Schwartz, J. 181, 200
Schwartz, M. L. 151, 155
Searle, J. R. 160, 176, 188, 200
Segal, G. 223, 242

Sergent, C. 164, 174, 177
Seth, A. K. 160, 166, 171, 175, 177
Shadlen, M. N. 169, 176
Shannon, C. E. 184
Sherman, P. 60
Shimony, A. 186, 200
Silberstein, M. 63
Simon, H. A. 7, 16, 24, 26, 28, 36 f., 47, 55, 57, 183
Singer, W. 172, 174, 181, 200
Sintonen, M. 54
Skinner, F. B. 203, 217
Sklar, L. 64
Slachevsky, A. 168, 175
Sloman, S. 98, 100, 113, 137
Smith, P. K. 242
Sobel, D. M. 70
Sobel, M. E. 39, 57
Sorenson, O. 44, 54
Sosa, E. 57
Spelke, E. 76, 100
Spiers, A. 160, 175
Spirtes, P. 28, 57, 68, 72, 100, 136
Sporns, O. 145, 157
Sripada, Ch. S. 67
Steel, D. 70
Steudel, B. 100
Stich, S. 67
Stoyanov, D. S. 249, 262, 267
Strawson, P. 23, 43 57
Streiner, D. L. 267
Strevens, M. 70
Suppes, P. 37, 54, 57, 63, 68, 74, 100
Suzuki, K. 160, 175
Symons, J. 67

Tabery, J. 246, 267
Tal, E. 70
Tanabe, J. 151, 157
Tenenbaum, J. B. 62, 70, 72, 100
Teng, C. 68, 136
Tetlock, P. 88, 100
Thagard, P. 1, 16, 48, 57, 67, 192, 200, 238, 245, 267 f.
Thompson, L. 151, 157
Thompson, N. 266
Thomte, R. 217

Thornton, T. 262 f., 267
Timmermans, B. 161, 166, 176 f.
Tirapu-Ustáriz, J. 142, 157
Tononi, G. 160, 165, 176 f., 182, 199
Tooley, M. 57, 60
Tranel, D. 149 f., 155
Tsakiris, M. 171, 177
Tudela, P. 145, 155
Tuomela, R. 34
Turing, A. 183, 236
Turner, D. R. 60
Turner, S., 63
Tversky, A. 45, 56

Uebel, Th. 55, 265
Ullsperger, M. 169, 177

Valdes-Villanueva, L. 63
Van der Linden, M. 150, 155
Van Os, J. 259, 267
Van Reekum, R. 250 f., 257, 267
Vermeiren, A. 165, 177
von Neumann, J. 183
von Wright, G. H. 25, 27, 34, 37, 49, 57 f.
Votsis, I. 70

Walsh, C. 98, 100, 113, 137
Waskan, J. 70
Waters, C. K. 65, 70, 243, 267
Watson, J. B. 203, 218
Watson, J. D. 185, 201
Watson, N. V. 140, 157
Weber, M. 70, 265
Weisberg, J. 162, 166 f., 176
Weiskopf, D. 67
Weslake, B. 70
Wessel, J. R. 169, 177
Westerstahl, D. 63
Wheeler, G. 55
Whishaw, I. Q. 142, 156
Whitehead, A. N. 183
Wiener, N. 184
Wierzchoń, M. v, 8 f., 16, 159–161, 166, 171, 174, 177
Williams, E. J. 152, 156
Williamson, J. 67
Wilson, A. M. 153, 156

Wilson, R. A. 223, 238, 242
Windey, B. 165f., 174, 177
Wittgenstein, L. 48f., 57f., 224
Wojcicki, R. 56
Wolfson, P. 59
Wolpert, D. M. 169, 176
Wolters, G. 55
Woodward, J. F. v, 1–7, 13–17, 21–67, 71, 73, 75, 77–80, 83–85, 90f., 95f., 98–101, 105–108, 112, 115, 117, 119, 121, 123f., 127, 129, 135, 137, 205, 218, 243f., 246–249, 253f., 258–261, 263–265, 267f.
Wright, C. 263, 268
Wright, M. J. 163, 176
Wundt, W. 48

Yablo, S. 6, 17, 70, 105, 123–127, 137
Ylikoski, P. 54, 56, 70

Zahavi, D. 161, 177
Zalta, E. 61
Zamora Bonilla, J. P. 191, 201
Zelaya, F. 152, 156
Zellner, A. 57
Zhang, J. 68, 136
Zhang, K. 100
Zscheischler, J. 100
Zubiri, X. 207, 218
Zwier, K. R. 70

Subject Index

abductive reasoning 236
actual
– cause attributions 134
– cause judgments 105–113, 115, 119, 129–131, 134
– or token cause 108
actual, token causal relationships 260
adaptationist Darwinism 223
aetiology of mental disorders 244
agency theory of causation 37
alcohol dependence 256
Alzheimer's disease (AD) 251, 257
ambiguity 141, 146, 151
analogical reasoning 230
angst 9–11, 203, 205, 207–217
animal(s) 11, 47, 49, 74, 76, 83, 189, 203–209, 212–214, 216, 239
– experimentation 25, 205f., 216
– learning 47, 74
anterior cingulate cortex (ACC) 147
anthropology 47, 74, 214
anti-Darwinism 222
anti-naturalist methodology 30
anxiety 9–11, 203, 205–207, 211–217, 252, 255
application of science 4, 21, 30, 36, 41f., 44, 46, 51
applied science 4, 21, 36, 41f., 44f., 51
artificial intelligence (AI) 1, 26, 53, 67, 71, 183f., 204, 230, 238
attention deficit hyperactivity disorder (ADHD) 253, 255
attribution of blame, responsibility, and/or fault 110
awareness
– access 8f., 74, 159–169, 172, 184
– hierarchical models of 159, 161, 165–168
– interoceptive 8, 160
– introspective 166
– metacognitive 162, 166–169, 171
– neural correlates of 162–164, 170
– neurobiological mechanisms of 162
– of learning 8, 45, 88, 160, 167

– of tactile information 8, 160
– perceptual 8, 161, 169f.
– phenomenal 163, 165, 229f.
awareness 8f., 159–173
axiology 192

background conditions 5, 90, 92f., 96f., 120
backward causation 38
basic science 4, 30, 36, 41, 44f., 51
Bayesian treatments of causal inference 47, 72
behavioral
– and neurological reductionism 223
– flexibility 148, 150, 154, 195
– indeterminacy 207
– neurology 13, 243, 248, 262
– sciences 93
behaviorism 11, 48, 203
behavio[u]r 5, 7f., 45f., 48, 83, 111, 131, 133, 139–146, 181–183, 195–198, 203f., 206–208, 212, 223–225, 230f., 233, 238f., 243, 245, 252f., 255, 258f.
– biopsychosocial model of 251
– causes of 182
– disorders 183
– intelligent 204, 207, 230
– neurological determination in 182
– objective 2, 23, 36, 51, 181, 189, 193, 203, 211, 226, 250
biological
– explanations for behavior 7, 139f.
– psychiatry 245, 248, 258, 262
– reductionism 244
– sciences 91
– variables 141, 247
biology 23, 31f., 39, 44, 93, 140, 182, 239, 243, 255
biology of decision making 7f., 140
body-mind problem 226, 233
bounded rationality 45
brain 7f., 95, 123, 139–147, 149f., 152–154, 163–165, 168, 170, 181f., 184–188,

https://doi.org/10.1515/9783110576054-012

Subject Index

191, 205 f., 214 f., 244 f., 247, 249–251, 254–257, 259, 263 f.
- activity 139–141, 144–146, 264
- based psychiatry 255
- functions 8, 142–144, 250
- nonhuman 248
- structure 7, 139

Cartesian mind-brain dualism 244, 263
causal
- asymmetry 74
- attributions 77, 112, 130 f., 133 f.
- cognition 1 f., 4–7, 34, 71, 75–78, 82–84, 105, 108, 125
- concepts 72 f., 79, 84, 136
- conclusions 47, 71, 74, 81
- connections 29, 133, 247, 254, 258
- content 38
- description(s) 6, 123 f., 127–129
- history 34, 110
- inference 39 f., 47, 71–73, 76, 80 f., 83, 133 f.
- information 34, 108 f., 112, 245
- interaction 113, 115, 228
- judgment(s) 5–7, 23, 47, 71 f., 74, 76–78, 81, 88 f., 91, 97, 105, 107, 109 f., 112–116, 118, 122–124, 129, 131, 133–136
- knowledge 76, 135, 249
- learning 47, 71, 76–79, 81–84, 88, 244
- mechanisms 105, 246, 254, 256
- models 14, 71, 196 f., 251, 255 f., 264
- monism 41
- notions 33 f., 43, 106, 135
- pluralism 41 f.
- processes 34, 49, 105, 113, 115 f., 119, 262
- process theories 113, 116
- reasoning 2–4, 6 f., 33 f., 47, 71 f., 76–78, 81 f., 88 f., 105, 108–113, 118, 130, 135
- relata 88, 106, 244, 259
- relevance 38 f.
- specificity 5, 10, 71, 81, 125, 128, 143, 145, 151
- techniques 143–148
- thinking 34, 78, 81, 91 f., 119, 136, 183, 253, 263
- understanding 92, 255, 257
- variables 247, 256 f., 260

causal explanation(s) 1–4, 6, 14–15, 21–28, 30–35, 41–45, 49–50, 52, 91, 123, 128–129, 227, 239, 243, 260, 264
- interventionist 3–6, 13, 21, 23 f., 26, 29, 31, 33, 41 f., 45, 49 f., 71, 73, 76–81, 83, 85, 87, 89 f., 106, 108, 113, 117 f., 127, 129, 134, 243 f., 246–249, 253, 256, 258–261, 263–265
- logical and epistemological configuration of 25
- naturalist conception 23, 29
causality 1–4, 13, 15, 21–30, 34–52, 59, 66 f., 75, 152, 215, 243, 247
- and explanation 30–32
- and prediction 4, 36, 38–41, 44, 51, 95, 119 f.
- and teleology 34
- conceptions of 10, 14, 22, 26, 28, 41, 47, 49
- in application of science 4, 21, 44–46
- in applied science 36, 42, 44 f.
- in basic science 44 f.
- in criminal law 22
- in descriptive models 35
- in ordinary life 25, 28, 136
- in psychology and human affairs 1, 21, 24, 46
- in science 4, 22, 24
- in scientific practices 25, 27
- within prescriptive models 35
causal relationship(s) 2–4, 22 f., 25 f., 28–30, 35 f., 39 f., 45–47, 49–51, 71 f., 74, 76, 79–84, 91 f., 95–98, 107, 109, 112, 114, 116, 118, 121, 123, 125, 133–136, 153, 191, 197, 226, 233 f., 244, 247, 249, 253, 256, 260
- counterfactual interpretations 23
- descriptions of 25, 47, 123, 125, 128 f.
- over-determination 116
- prescriptions on 47
- token-causal 23
causation/causality 1–6, 12–14, 21–52, 59, 66–67, 71–78, 80, 82–85, 90–93, 97 f., 105 f., 108–110, 113–118, 120, 122, 129 f., 132–136, 152, 181, 205, 215, 221, 243–247, 250, 260, 263 f.
- by omission 114

Subject Index

- counterfactual-manipulationist notion of 260
- functional approach to 29, 34, 78
- interventionist conception of 13, 23f., 26, 45, 246, 263
- manipulationist approach to 23, 29, 42
- mechanistic accounts of 246
- metaphysics of 72, 85, 110, 135
- physical 252
- probabilistic theories of 74
- psychological 93
- regularly theory of 37
- semantics of 85
- theories of 37, 51, 71, 74f., 80, 97, 108, 134, 243, 260
- token 6, 41, 49, 108–115, 260
- traditional conceptions on 26

cause(s)
- and explanation 24, 29–32, 40, 67, 92
- and motive 224
- dynamic approach 31
- of mental disorders 248
- pluralism in 31, 41, 246
- structural perspective on 24, 31

chemistry 24, 39
choices of variables 35, 82
circumstance 35f., 39, 44, 46, 80, 89, 91, 94f., 106, 119–122, 124, 128, 134f., 143, 211
clinical psychiatry 252, 260
clinical psychology 13, 243, 248–250, 252, 262
cognition 1f., 4–7, 9, 13, 34, 47, 71, 74–78, 82–84, 105, 108, 125, 181, 183f., 196, 235–237, 243, 245, 252

cognitive
- alterations 143
- capacity(ies) 222, 230
- judgment 264
- neuroscience 7, 140, 184
- processes 149, 171, 194, 225, 230, 237f.
- psychology 12, 48, 188, 192, 221f., 227f., 230, 232f., 238–240, 262
- science 123, 183, 192f., 226, 230f., 235–238, 240
- strategies 75f.
- system 165, 167f., 188, 214, 249

cognitivism 11, 183, 185, 191f., 196, 203
cognitivist turn 192
common cause 133, 253
comparative animal cognition 47, 74
complexity 8, 11, 42, 53, 140f.
- dynamic 42
- structural 42
computation 185, 226, 236
- languages 183
- of internal representations 227
computational 2, 12, 75, 162, 165, 184, 219f., 223–226, 228–238
- functionalism 233, 235
- intelligence 184
- mechanisms 230
- model 12, 221f., 227f., 231, 233, 236f., 239
- processes 225f., 232f., 240
- theory 12f., 75, 222, 225, 231, 233–236
computational psychology 2, 12f., 221, 231f., 235–237, 240
computer sciences 37, 75
concepts 29, 48, 194, 207
conditional probabilities 127
connecting process between cause and effect 72, 74, 112–117
conscious
- access 8f., 159–169
- and unconscious information processing 8, 159, 162, 171
- content 159–162, 166–169, 172
- experience 8, 159–173
consciousness 8–12, 28, 159–168, 170–173, 182, 185–188, 197f., 203, 214–216, 221, 228f., 233f., 236f.
- approaches to 161
- classical neurobiological theory of 163
- empirical theories of 162
- hierarchical models of 159, 161, 165–168, 171
- models of 8, 159–161, 163, 165
- neurobiological and cognitive mechanisms of 8, 159
- phenomenal 160, 165
- philosophical theories of 162
- physicalist theories of 186
- subjective measures of 170

constraint-based approach to causal inference 72
constructivism 184, 193
continuity between science and philosophy 26, 28
contributing cause 35
control 5, 29, 42, 78f., 81, 117, 126, 263
- observations 32, 48
- variables 247
conventional causal modeling techniques 71
convergent validation 146f.
correlational technique(s) 153
correlation(s) 32, 39, 46, 72, 76, 84, 133, 247
counterfactual 6, 23, 26, 39, 43, 50, 73, 82, 85, 88, 106, 127, 243
- approach 26
- dependence 5, 23, 74, 80f., 89f., 93, 97–99, 106f., 112, 116–122, 246
- dependence without physical connection 107, 118
- theory(ies) of causation 37, 73, 97, 106, 116
covariational information 77, 125, 130–134
cybernetics 185
cybernetic theory 184

danger 11, 203, 206f., 211
Darwinism 235
Darwinist adaptationism 235
decision-making 7f., 10, 36–38, 45, 47, 139–154, 224, 249
decision-making models 141
deductive model of scientific explanation 34

deductive nomological model of scientific explanation 34
demography 39
direct cause 25, 35
distributed brain system(s) 142–144, 152
dorsolateral prefrontal cortex (DLPFC) 147
double prevention 72, 78, 97–99, 107, 115, 120, 129
dualist approaches 187
dual systems theory 88
dynamic level interaction hypothesis 8f., 159f., 167f., 171–173

econometrics 24, 28f., 37, 39, 85
economics 7f., 32, 36f., 40–42, 45, 93f., 140
- application of 36, 41, 44
- applied 36, 41, 44
economic theory 41
eidetic reduction 161f.
electroencephalography (EEG) 139, 141
electrophysiological techniques 145
eliminativism 9, 181, 183
eliminativist
- approach to psychology 183
- models 186
emergent properties 188
emotional
- computers 204
- subjects 10, 204
emotion(s) 11, 150, 182, 186, 194, 196, 203–217, 249, 264
- contemporary theory of 11, 204
- self-reflexive 212
- unconscious 204
empirical
- methods 183
- sciences 24, 27
empiricism 33, 96, 189
environmentalism 223
epigenetics 243, 245
epiphenomena 128, 247
epistemic
- boundedness 13, 230, 235
- engineering 4, 34
- value of controversies 223
epistemology 185, 189f., 192, 205
Erklären and *Verstehen* 24, 49
ethical values 28, 216
ethics 53, 208, 213
etiology of sensations 227
evolution 50f., 184, 186, 233, 263
evolution of science 191
experimental
- biology 243
- design 28, 96
- epigenetics 243, 245
- interventions 249
experimentation 35, 53, 107, 205–207, 213, 216, 249

experiment(s) 3, 8, 21, 23, 25, 27, 30, 35, 46, 49 f., 75, 77 f., 80, 85–89, 96–98, 112 f., 125 f., 130–134, 140–142, 151, 205 f., 216, 249, 251 f.
explanandum 33
explanation(s)
– about "type causation" 35
– and description 32, 36
– and understanding 49
– biological 7 f., 139–141, 255
– etiological 248
– functionalist 232, 234
– functional or teleological 3, 33, 35, 49
– genetic 4, 33–35, 50 f.
– inductive-probabilistic 3, 33, 35, 50
– in logic and mathematics 25
– in ordinary contexts 27
– in science 4, 27, 32, 52
– level of 6, 32, 105
– mechanistic 91 f.
– mentalist 224, 231
– non-causal 31, 35, 80 f., 84, 86, 88, 98, 116
– probabilistic 3, 28, 33, 35, 41, 50, 74, 80, 122
– psychological 1 f., 6, 12, 45, 222–224, 226 f., 229, 231–235, 238
– regarding cases 35
– scientific 1, 3 f., 21, 24 f., 30, 32–35, 49–51, 182, 185, 196, 264
– singular causal 35, 49
– specific to the social sciences 50
– theories of 21, 29, 49
– type 41
explanations of
– mental disorders 247
– mental phenomena 195, 228
– singular cases 23
– social behavior 48
explanatory
– integrative pluralism 246, 259
– pluralism 244, 246
externalist conception of meaning 221, 223

fear 11, 203, 205–207, 209, 215, 252
finitist approaches 25
first- and second-person methods 161

first order representation 171
Fodor's First Law of the Nonexistence of Cognitive Science 230, 240
folk psychology 22, 46, 48, 181 f., 197
formal sciences 24, 45
freedom 11, 95, 203, 208–210, 212 f.
functional 4, 7 f., 29, 33–35, 50, 78, 98, 118, 136, 139 f., 144, 147, 152 f., 182, 184, 220, 226 f., 229 f., 232, 235, 237, 254, 256, 261
– account of causation and explanation 33, 50, 92
– equivalence 222, 231
– magnetic resonance imaging (fMRI) 8, 140, 153
– neuroimaging investigations 147, 152, 258
– neuroimaging techniques 144
– states identity theory (FSIT) 232
functionalism 196, 221, 225, 232–234, 239
functionalist theories 12, 221, 231, 234

genetic psychiatry 13, 243, 248, 262
Gestaltpsychologie 48
gist perception 163
global workspace 164–166
gradations in causal judgment 116

health care ethics 250
health sciences 250, 260, 262
hermeneutics 181, 193 f., 197
historical turn 10, 189, 193
historicity 4, 21, 31, 34, 50 f.
– external 34
– internal 34
history 34, 51 f., 85, 110, 167, 169, 192 f., 195
– of philosophy 207
– of science 50, 192, 240
homo psychologicus 47
humanism 216
humanistic psychology 214–216
hypothesis of a language of thought 12, 222, 225, 234
hypothetical
– deductive method 190
– deductive methodology 197 f.
– experiments 21, 25, 50, 78, 80, 85–89, 251

- explanations 3, 21, 30
- interventions 25, 43, 262

iconic memory 163, 165
ideal
- experimental manipulation 23, 25 f., 29 f., 43, 85, 108, 172
- interventions 3, 21, 24 f., 30, 254
identity theory 182, 232 f.
inductive-statistical model of scientific explanation 33
inference procedures 76, 81, 238
inferential psychological processes 227
information 6 f., 34, 36, 41 f., 74, 76 – 78, 81, 84, 88 f., 92, 94 f., 97, 105, 107 – 114, 120, 124 – 134, 140 f., 147 – 149, 151, 153 f., 159, 163 – 170, 172, 183 – 188, 192, 194 – 196, 215, 229 – 231, 238 f., 245 – 247, 252, 257, 259, 263 f.
- about covariation 132 – 134
- at the token level 109, 111 – 113
- at the type level 108 – 110, 112
- cognitive 147, 154
- emotional 147, 154
informational dependence and independence 78
innatism 12, 221 f., 235
innatist Cartesian mentalism 229
inner corporal states 182
instrumental
- rationality 36, 45 f.
- success 29
intentionality 12, 38, 48, 221
intention(s) 48
interdisciplinarity 205, 213
interpersonal behavior 141
intervening and conditioning 83
interventionism 71, 76, 79, 83, 105, 133, 245 f.
interventionism as a normative theory 79
interventionist
- conception of causality 13, 23 f., 26, 29, 31, 37, 45
- condition for causation 106
- counterfactuals 50, 106, 127
- theory 12, 13, 31, 42, 66, 243, 246, 259, 263

intervention(s) 1 – 6, 13 f., 21 – 27, 29 – 32, 40, 42 f., 49, 50, 76, 78 – 80, 83 – 87, 89, 106, 134, 146 f., 243, 246 f., 249, 251, 253 – 256, 259, 261 f.
introspection 161 f., 166
intuitions 37, 74, 110, 129, 135, 252
invariance 4 – 6, 31 f., 34, 39, 43, 50, 71, 78, 80, 82, 89 f., 92 – 97, 99, 117 f., 123, 243, 249
invariance under intervention(s) 31 f., 43, 50, 243, 249
inverted spectrum argument 232 f.
Iowa gambling task (IGT) 139, 146 f.

law 22, 37, 140
lawhood 32, 50
law of nature 32
learning theory 12, 224, 239
lesion technique 142 f., 153
levels of causal explanation 123
logical
- asymmetry between explanation and prediction 40
- positivism 184, 189
logical empiricism 33

machine learning 47, 71 f.
magnetoencephalography 144
manipulation 1, 5, 23, 25 – 27, 30, 41 f., 43, 77, 79, 84 f., 87, 89, 95, 108, 119 f., 169 – 173, 196, 253
manipulation and control 5, 29, 42, 78 f., 81, 117, 263
manipulative or interventionist conception 24, 26
materialism 195, 222, 233, 245
materialist monism 187
mathematical
- logic 183
- proofs 24
mathematics 25, 45, 52
mechanisms 8, 28, 48, 77, 88, 91, 105, 130, 132 – 134, 140, 147, 153 f., 159 f., 163, 167 f., 171 – 173, 191, 194, 196, 198, 212, 216, 229 f., 245 f., 252, 255 f., 261, 264
mechanistic
- description 91 f., 261

Subject Index — **283**

- information 77, 92, 133, 246
medicine 32, 36, 45f., 53, 140, 186f., 244, 252, 263
memory cues manipulation 173
mental
- activity 140, 228
- acts 9, 48
- causation 12, 115, 221
- disorder(s) 2, 12–14, 243–248, 250–254, 256, 258–260, 262, 264f.
- health sciences 262
- illnesses 13, 243–246, 255
- processes 8, 12, 140f., 145, 149, 182, 187–189, 222, 225–227, 229, 231, 234, 236, 238, 240, 245, 256, 259
- representations 192, 225f., 231, 233f., 237, 240, 256
- states 28, 162, 166, 182, 188, 191, 226–228, 231f., 234, 236, 238
mentalism 224, 226
meta-analysis 146, 153
metacognition 159, 162, 166, 168
metacognitive
- judgment(s) 162, 169
- representations 171
meta-methodology 192
metaphysics 72, 85, 110, 135, 189
metarepresentation 165
methodological
- anti-naturalism 3, 21, 23, 30
- universalism 30, 42
methodology 14f., 30, 49, 53, 66, 130, 162, 171, 188, 192, 197f., 203, 246
mind 8, 12f., 22, 26, 28, 47, 67, 160, 181–187, 189, 192–197, 221–226, 228–231, 233–240, 244f., 249, 254f., 259, 263
- and brain 181, 189, 244f.
- as a subproduct of the brain 185
- brain dualism 244, 263
- brain system 254
- computational and representational theory of (CRTM) 221, 223, 225f., 228, 234
- computational theory of (CTM) 12f., 222, 225, 231, 233–235
- human 13, 26, 182f., 187, 189, 193, 195, 221–223, 229, 231, 235f., 239f.
- modularity of 13, 221, 229, 236, 238, 253

- multiplicity of 239
- representational theory of (RTM) 223, 225f., 233
- self-conscious 187
- to-brain causality 245
- *versus* machine 184
models of representation 191
modularity 13, 184, 230, 253
molecular biology 255
multi-level causal claims 73
multi-level representation system 169

natural
- experiments 49
- history 195
- methods 183
- sciences 10, 15, 22–28, 31f., 34f., 37, 39f., 42, 48, 50f., 183, 189f., 195, 197, 263
naturalism 1, 3, 10, 14, 21, 23f., 27–31, 48, 190–192, 195–197, 216
- axiological 3, 28, 198
- contemporary 192, 196
- epistemological 3, 10, 21–24, 28, 48
- methodological 3, 10, 21, 28, 43, 192, 197
- normative 192
- ontological 3, 9f., 21, 28, 30, 192, 194, 198
- semantic 3, 27
- varieties of 3, 14, 21, 24, 27
naturalization of epistemology 189
naturalness 209
necessary conditions for successful explanation 33
neo-Darwinian model 212
neo-Darwinism 206
nervous system 139–141, 182, 185f., 188
neural
- global workspace theory 164, 166
- mechanisms 28, 48, 163–165, 230
- models in psychiatry 255, 260
- networks structure 182
neurobiology 27, 255, 262
neuroeconomics 7, 139f.
neuroimage techniques 185
neurology 10, 13, 182f., 188f., 197, 243, 248, 262

284 — Subject Index

neuronal
- networks 8, 140, 142, 182, 188, 234
- processes 9, 163, 181, 187
- system 7f., 140, 249, 256

neuropharmacology 250, 255
neurophysiology 185, 254
neuropsychiatry 250, 254
neuropsychology 181, 184f., 187f., 197, 203, 248f., 262–264
neuroscience(s) 7, 10, 23, 48f., 140, 184f., 188, 238f., 245, 263f.
nomic expectability 33
non-causal learning 75
nonreductive materialism 245
normative
- causal learning theories 71
- theories of causation 75, 97

nosology 248

observations and experiments in science 3, 27, 35
obsessive compulsive disorder (OCD) 253
ontological commitment 31, 245f., 256

passions 11, 207f., 211, 213
passive observations 79, 84, 249
patterns 41, 186
- of correlation 263f.
- of covariation 76f., 125, 127, 130

penal law 22
perception 12f., 67, 159, 163, 166, 194, 196, 224, 226, 228f., 238, 245
perceptual awareness scale 161, 170
perspectivism 190
pharmacology 13, 32, 39, 243, 262
pharmacopsychology 262
phenomenological approach 162
phenomenology 162, 181
philosophy 2, 21, 26, 28, 32, 41, 47, 66, 71, 136, 187, 195, 205, 207, 213, 216f., 221, 224f.
- analytic 50, 129, 224
- of language 12, 38, 222f.
- of mind 38, 47, 221, 223f., 234
- of psychology 1, 3f., 9f., 14, 21f., 27, 48f., 52, 59, 66f., 203–205, 207, 214, 216, 221, 223–226, 237

philosophy of science 14, 22, 24, 30, 47, 52, 59, 66, 123, 192, 216, 244
- contemporary 1, 14, 21, 24, 53
- general 30
- special 30

physical connection 5f., 78, 99, 105, 107, 112–115, 117–122
physics 23f., 37, 39, 44, 93, 135
pluralism on scientific explanation 31, 50, 244, 246, 259
positron emission tomography (PET) 144, 252
pragmatics of explanation 35
pragmatism 3, 21, 27, 29f., 190
prediction(s) 4, 21, 36, 38–42, 44f., 96
- and causation 4, 31f., 39–41, 51
- and climate change 39, 45
- and control 126
- and manipulation 95, 119f.
- psychological 45
- rational 36
- scientific 4, 39–41, 45, 49

predictive accuracy 39
prescription(s) 4, 30, 36, 42, 44–47
probabilities and causes 33
problem solving 230f.
process 6f., 26, 34, 42, 44, 49f., 72, 74, 98, 105, 111–117, 119, 193, 214f., 225f., 231f.
process theory 26, 37
production 98
proportionality 5f., 71, 73, 78, 80, 82, 96, 105, 116, 123–125, 127–129
propositional attitudes 227, 231–234, 237, 239
psyche 195
psychiatric
- disorders 245
- epidemiology 243, 248, 250, 260, 262
- explanations 13, 243
- genetics 245, 251, 255
- illness 259, 262

psychiatry 1f., 12f., 206f., 243–246, 248, 252, 255, 258, 260, 262f.
psychoanalysis 48, 243, 249f., 258
psychobiological explantions 7, 139
psychobiology 7, 10, 26, 42, 51, 140f., 228
psychodiagnostic tests 252

psychofunctionalism 234
psychological
- intervention 6, 247
- knowledge 13, 237, 239
- mechanisms 88, 229
- metatheory 224, 238
- philosophy 47
- process 10, 88, 142f., 145, 147, 225, 227, 229f., 232
- states 223, 232
- subject 1f., 9-12, 14f., 59, 74, 204, 206, 211
- therapy 46, 207, 245, 256
- variables 247, 264
psychology 1-7, 9f., 12-15, 21-28, 31f., 42, 45-49, 51f., 59, 66f., 71, 74, 79f., 82f., 98, 140, 181-185, 188-192, 194-197, 203-208, 212-216, 221f., 224-233, 235-240, 243f., 248-250, 252, 255, 262f.
- animal and human 11, 49, 74, 76, 83, 203-205, 216
- a reductionist vision of 188
- as a dual science 10, 26
- as a natural science 48
- as an independent science 10, 12, 189, 222
- as a science 1, 9, 22, 49, 181, 196f., 229
- as a social science 48
- as basic science 45
- as independent from neurology 189
- as one of the special sciences 23, 25
- contemporary 185
- descriptive 2-6, 23, 25f., 28, 35, 47, 71f., 74-83, 85, 89, 92, 98, 113, 116, 124f., 128, 135f., 188, 227
- developmental 12, 76, 224, 239
- empirical basis for 184
- empirical 5f., 47, 52, 74, 80, 83, 105, 129, 234
- experimental 48, 196, 204-206, 216
- naturalistic 28, 181, 191f., 205f., 214-216
- non-reductionist 214, 263
- physicalization of 9f., 181, 183
- rational 47
- scientific 10, 22, 46, 48, 183, 189, 196f., 221, 225, 238
- unified 238

psychoneurological models 187
psychopathology 249, 255
psycho-pedagogy 26, 51
psychophysiology 26, 228
psychotherapy 250, 252, 258, 260

qualia 8, 12, 160, 167, 171, 185, 188, 221, 228, 231-233
quantum mechanics 186

radical plasticity thesis 167, 173
rationality 36, 45-47, 191f., 227
realism 3, 30f., 53, 193
- instrumental 30
- modest 3, 30f.
- scientific 31, 193
reasoning and learning in functional terms 78-79
reductionism 189, 214, 223, 244, 255
regularities 82, 224, 239
reinforcement learning 249
representations with semantic content 233
risk 139, 141, 146, 151, 260
robustness 5, 89

schizophrenia 249, 252, 258f., 263
sciences of the artificial 24, 26, 32, 34f., 39, 50f.
science, technology, and society 44
scientific
- creativity 44
- values 30
semantic holism 223, 234
sensitivity 90, 168, 173
sensory evidence manipulation 172
singular causal explanations 35, 41
social
- dimension of science 191
- sciences 10, 15, 22-29, 31f., 34f., 37, 39f., 42, 45, 48, 50f., 85, 190, 244
- turn 193
social psychology 10, 12, 26, 42, 224, 239
somatic changes 147-150
somatic marker hypothesis 147, 149
special sciences 22f., 25, 136, 243
specificity 5, 10, 71, 81, 125, 128, 143, 145, 151, 216, 256

stability 5f., 39, 73, 89, 116–118, 121–123, 243
statistical
– analysis 145f.
– relationships 82
statistics 37, 47, 71, 85
structural equations modeling 47, 71f.
subject and object 185
subjective
– emotions 182
– experience 9, 159, 168–171, 173, 232, 245, 258, 263f.

technological innovation(s) 37, 44
technology 4, 14, 34, 36, 44, 52f., 193
testable implications 40
theories
– of causal learning and inference 47, 71
– of dual processes 214f.
theory of evolution 212
thought experiments 88
three worlds 187, 189
token causal relations 23, 109, 114, 260
total cause 35
Tourette syndrome 249, 253
transitivity principle 162, 166–168

type-causal relationships 112, 260
type-cause 111, 132
type-cause judgments 107f.
type-explanation(s) 41
type-level causal judgments 6, 105, 109, 114f.
types of scientific explanation 3, 21, 32, 35, 50
typicality 93, 96

uncertainty 139, 141, 146, 151, 211
unified psychology 238
universal rationality 47
usefulness 29, 34

ventromedial prefontal cortex (VMPFC) 8, 139, 147–154
Vienna Circle 189
visual
– awareness 159, 163, 165, 170f., 173
– mechanisms of conscious experience 8, 160, 172
– perceptual awareness 8, 160
– system 76, 165, 168, 215

working memory 145, 147, 151, 154, 165, 212

www.ingramcontent.com/pod-product-compliance
Lightning Source LLC
Chambersburg PA
CBHW032056230426
43662CB00035B/482